MULTICULTURALISM ON CAMPUS

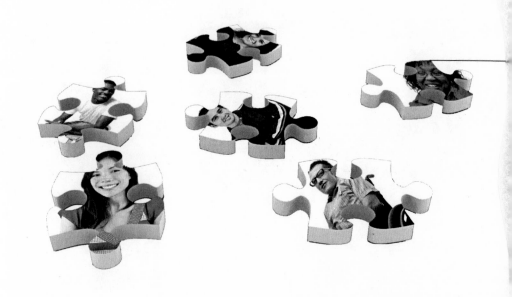

MULTICULTURALISM ON CAMPUS

Theory, Models, and Practices for Understanding
Diversity and Creating Inclusion

Edited by
Michael J. Cuyjet,
Mary F. Howard-Hamilton,
and Diane L. Cooper

1996–2011 15TH ANNIVERSARY

Stylus
PUBLISHING, LLC.

COPYRIGHT © 2011 BY STYLUS PUBLISHING, LLC.

Published by Stylus Publishing, LLC
22883 Quicksilver Drive
Sterling, Virginia 20166-2102

Library of Congress Cataloging-in-Publication Data
Multiculturalism on campus : theory, models, and practices
for understanding diversity and creating inclusion / edited
by Michael J. Cuyjet, Mary F. Howard-Hamilton, and
Diane L. Cooper.—1st ed.
    p.   cm.
  Includes bibliographical references and index.
  ISBN 978-1-57922-463-9 (cloth : alk. paper)
  ISBN 978-1-57922-464-6 (pbk. : alk. paper)
    1. Multicultural education—United States.   2. Cultural
pluralism—United States.   3. Minorities—
Education (Higher)—United States.   4. Educational
equalization—United States.   I. Cuyjet, Michael
J.   II. Howard-Hamilton, Mary F.   III. Cooper, Diane L.
LC1099.3.M87   2011
378'.017—dc22   2010026521

13-digit ISBN: 978-1-57922-463-9 (cloth)
13-digit ISBN: 978-1-57922-464-6 (paper)

Printed in the United States of America

All first editions printed on acid free paper
that meets the American National Standards Institute
Z39-48 Standard.

First Edition, 2011

10   9   8   7   6   5   4   3   2

DEDICATIONS

To my Mom and Dad for introducing me to the concept and responsibilities of privilege at a very early age and with gratitude to my friends and colleagues at the University of Georgia for your support during the development and publication of this book.

—Diane L. Cooper

To my parents and grandparents who taught me to value the "otherness" of those different from me; to my wife, Carol, who has been a consistent supporter of my research and writing; and to my daughters, Allison, Leslie, and Ashley, for whom I do this work, hoping to make the members of our society more tolerant and understanding of each other.

—Michael J. Cuyjet

To God be the glory for giving me the strength and endurance to run this race. I also dedicate my passion for "educating my people and uplifting the race" to Barbara Sizemore (1927–2004), an unsung *s/hero* in multicultural education.

—Mary F. Howard-Hamilton

CONTENTS

vii

INTRODUCTION

*Michael J. Cuyjet, Mary F. Howard-Hamilton,
and Diane L. Cooper*

This book constitutes a comprehensive resource for students, faculty, and higher education administrators about multiculturalism and diverse populations on college campuses. This is the first text to gather in a single volume the related theories, assessment methods, and environmental and application issues pertinent to the study and practice of multiculturalism.

The topic of multiculturalism on campus has been more openly discussed during the last quarter of the 20th century and the early 21st century than in previous decades, prompted by demographic projections indicating that African Americans and Latinos and Latinas will be the predominant racial and ethnic groups in the country by 2015, only a few years away (Spring, 2007). Even though there have been numerous projections about the changing complexion of the college student population, a "how-to-prepare-for . . ." text for students and practitioners has not yet been written. This book reviews the theories and models that have been the primary guides to understanding the development of college students, and it attempts to rectify past interpretations that were made through a monocultural lens of the voices of students who are not part of the dominant culture. In addressing the inclusion of the ethnic groups on campus, this book considers students in the ethnic majority while providing new frameworks as well as best practices for creating an inclusive environment for marginalized groups. Each chapter addressing one of these campus populations includes either a case study, list of questions, suggested interventions, or a set of exercises to enhance understanding of the group's behaviors and characteristics.

I

While aiming for completeness, the editors recognize that some cultural subpopulations are not included among the groups whose characteristics and issues are addressed in this book. For example, student athletes form a distinct subculture on some campuses that have large athletic programs. Similarly, fraternity and sorority members can be a significant subgroup on campuses where their numbers constitute a large plurality or even a majority of the students. Neither of these is covered. Nonetheless, this book is designed to fill a void in the current student development literature by presenting an in-depth review of the issues multicultural students bring to our campuses. One's cultural identity is more than ethnicity or race, which is the general focus of most other texts on this subject. Gender, age, religion, geographic identity, and sexual orientation are equally part of the cultural makeup of a multicultural individual—all factors this book takes into account. Furthermore, with this book the contributors provide student affairs professionals, students, and faculty an opportunity to assess their own levels of multicultural sensitivity, awareness, and competence.

To assist readers to understand more fully the problems they will encounter with increasing diversity on college campuses and enable them to frame appropriate policies, this book approaches multiculturalism from three perspectives, each of which is a section of this book: Awareness, Information on Cultural Populations, and Components of Culturally Competent Practice.

Section One: Awareness

This section begins with a chapter that introduces multiculturalism and multicultural competence and provides the background information, definition of terms, and key concepts to understanding multicultural issues in higher education settings. It also highlights changes in the way multiculturalism is perceived and manifested in the demographic college student trends and issues that have occurred in the first decade of the 21st century. This section also includes a competency assessment to help readers gain some insight into their own level of understanding of multiculturalism and racial identity awareness. This section stresses the importance of observing environmental influences (physical, organizational, structural, and human) that may impede the successful matriculation of multicultural students, as well as outlining methods to create support systems within the campus community.

In chapter 1, Mary Howard-Hamilton, Michael Cuyjet, and Diane Cooper set the context with definitions of multiculturalism and multicultural competence as a foundation for understanding how these central concepts connect with each diverse group presented in subsequent chapters. This chapter proceeds to explain why multiculturalism is important and necessary and why the competencies (awareness, knowledge, ability) are significant to multicultural development. The chapter also explores how commonalities among cultural groups tie multiculturalism together (rather than focusing on the differences) and finally suggests how faculty, administrators, students, and related constituents and stakeholders might use this book and apply its insights across campus.

In chapter 2, "Oppression and Its Effect on College Student Identity Development," Mary Howard-Hamilton and Kandace Hinton provide an overview of privilege, power, oppression, and identity development from a 21st-century perspective that takes into account the varying complex identities students internalize and bring to campus as part of their persona. The chapter includes a case study that presents readers with a set of hypothetical student problems and connects them with theories related to racial identity, oppression, and critical race ideology. In chapter 3, Michael Cuyjet explores the environmental influences on culture and offers some perspectives on campus ecological systems using a multicultural lens. This perspective also presents an overview of environmental influences on nonmajority students that includes issues of campus size, type, location, and mission.

Rounding out this first section of the book, Jane Fried in chapter 4 shares a philosophical interpretation of how our multicultural identities should be carefully connected with new paradigms that acknowledge that traditional theories have not kept pace with the dynamic and shifting demographics of our society. Fried provides a series of perspectives that illuminate the new order of consciousness among individuals who are multidimensional in their identity development.

Section Two: Information on Cultural Populations

This section focuses on the problems, concerns, issues, and perspectives of various racial/ethnic cultural groups on college campuses. Each chapter examines demographic trends, issues, and practices that can promote the academic success of specific different groups, and successful programs that promote student growth and development. The chapters in this section include case studies, discussion questions, recommended interventions, or learning activities that student affairs professionals can implement on their own campuses. They also consider the characteristics that each specific ethnic or cultural population has in common with other groups. This echoes the emphasis in the book's first chapter on commonalties rather than differences among cultural groups.

In chapter 5, Anna Ortiz and Susana Hernandez look at the history of Latinos in the United States, mainly focusing on the Mexican, Puerto Rican, and Cuban experience, and explore their current conditions in a sociological context—income levels, generational factors, and the impact of discrimination. The chapter also examines student experiences that can inform student affairs professionals, especially the role of family and campus climate issues, particularly at community colleges.

Chapter 6 examines the demographics of the Asian American and Pacific Islander (AAPI) collegiate population in general, as well as several of the largest Asian ethnic groups. Anneliese Singh, Michael Cuyjet, and Diane Cooper also explore the ramifications of the Asian *model minority* stereotype and describe some of the differences among the dozens of individual ethnic groups and their levels of acculturation to the American majority culture and their interaction with the American college environment. The chapter authors also look at some developmental models pertinent to AAPI groups.

In chapter 7, Lamont Flowers and Bettina Shuford provide a thorough review of the 2000 census data on African Americans in the United States in higher education. Their description of this population includes an overview of the historical struggles African American students have faced while attending colleges and universities across the nation. The authors also connect Cross's (1971) Nigrescence theory to the issues presented and conclude with effective practices for university faculty and administrators.

In chapter 8, Vasti Torres and LeManuel Bitsói explore issues of self-identification with tribal culture and community, tribal sovereignty, and government oppression, and offer an overview of the history of American Indians to help the reader understand Native American college students. They present a model of America Indian identity development and define important issues for higher education practitioners to consider while working with this student population.

Chapter 9 explores some of the experiences particular to biracial and multiracial college students: the quest for self-identification, the impact of their physical appearance (and others' reactions to it), and the establishment of a multiracial peer culture. Kristen Renn's chapter also includes a description of several identity development models that can apply to this population, and offers corresponding suggestions for student affairs professionals to help these students find a place in the campus community.

In chapter 10, B. Afeni McNeely Cobham provides a historical and sociological perspective of White Americans who attend colleges and universities. Addressing race, privilege, and identity is not an easy process for White students and student affairs administrators, yet it is vital to the overall development of a social justice environment for our campuses. This chapter concludes with best practices to assist professionals working with White American college students.

International students face challenges on college campuses ranging from language barriers to visa issues and xenophobic behavior by Eurocentric Americans. In chapter 11 Sevan Terzian and Leigh Ann Osborne discuss the multicultural competencies necessary for student affairs professionals to become more aware and knowledgeable about the issues these students face, and the need to acquire the skills to be effective communicators and empathetic advisers for this population.

The history of women and men in higher education is in many ways the history of the education of White men, and initially only those of substantial means. For many, the term *gender issues* translates to *women's issues*. A more honest and complete exploration requires the inclusion of men. To do less provides a picture of only part of our world and ignores the important understandings gained from studying the interplay between women and men. Chapter 12 by Merrily Dunn provides us with an examination of sex and gender roles and offers examples of methods we can use in practice to help students developmentally, socially, and cognitively.

Tony Cawthon and Vicki Guthrie address the collegiate experiences of lesbian, gay, bisexual, and transgender students in chapter 13, including the impact of heterosexism and homophobia on identity development and campus community involvement. They also present different developmental models for gays, lesbians, bisexuals, and transgender students and describe some characteristics of students with multiple sexual identities. Examples of best practices from a number of campuses conclude this chapter.

As we get further into the 21st century, the number of students over the traditional age range of 18–21 entering colleges and universities continues to increase. In chapter 14, Fiona MacKinnon and Rosiline Floyd share information on the challenges facing college campuses to enable faculty and administrators to better serve the adult population on campus. Fiona MacKinnon provides a conceptual cognitive and psychosocial map called the Adult Persistence in Learning Model to give student affairs professionals an overview of how this population has become a central demographic on many college campuses today.

In chapter 15, Martha Wisbey and Karen Kalivoda explore issues faced by students with disabilities on today's college campuses. With the passage of the Americans With Disabilities Act in 1990, students with disabilities were given the same rights and legal protections from discrimination as those mandated for all citizens based on race, color, sex, national origin, religion, or age. As a result, while the number of students with disabilities on college campuses has grown, remaining visible and hidden barriers need to be addressed to create an environment of full inclusion.

Chapter 16 considers the issues of religious affiliation among college students and provides an overview of issues of spirituality that affect students. To clarify the role of religion in the modern system of higher education, Laura Dean and Edward Grandpré review the history of religion at colleges, including religious diversity and religious conflict, and its impact on students and the student affairs practitioners who serve them.

Section Three: Components of Cultural Competence In Practice

In the comprehensive concluding chapter, the editors stress the need for student affairs professionals, students, and faculty to apply the material in this volume to become more culturally competent in their personal and professional approach to their work on college campuses. They also share examples of current best practices and suggest how they might be implemented to enhance the collegiate experience for all students. Sections of this chapter specifically address issues for administrators, faculty, and students related to the application of the material presented. Successfully applying the knowledge presented and personally incorporating the concepts, models, theories, and practices outlined can bring about systemic change in the college environment.

The editors and chapter authors of this volume identify the areas where we need to hone our cultural awareness, describe the defining characteristics of a broad array of identifiable cultural groups among our student population, and discuss frankly the skills we need to develop to bring us to cultural competency. It is our hope that the cumulative effect of this collection of information, data, and recommended practices will encourage and motivate students, faculty, academic administrators, student affairs professionals, and others who care about the state of higher education to foster greater understanding, acceptance, interaction, and common appreciation among all the members in the collegiate community. To strive for anything less will be a failure to live up to the ideals of American higher education in the 21st century.

References

Cross, W. E., Jr. (1971). The Negro-to-Black conversion experience: Toward a psychology of Black liberation. *Black World, 20*(9), 13–27.

Spring, J. (2007). *Deculturalization and the struggle for equality: A brief history of the education of dominated cultures in the United States* (5th ed.). Boston: McGraw Hill.

SECTION ONE

AWARENESS

I

UNDERSTANDING MULTICULTURALISM AND MULTICULTURAL COMPETENCE AMONG COLLEGE STUDENTS

*Mary F. Howard-Hamilton, Michael J. Cuyjet,
and Diane L. Cooper*

Delgado and Stefancic (2001) defined multiculturalism as a perspective through which "social institutions should reflect many cultures" (p. 151). Historically, the colonists from England who began creating a new community in this country "rejected the idea of a multicultural society and advocated the creation of a unified American culture" (Spring, 2007, p. 10). The unified culture or melting pot became difficult to maintain, given the influx of immigrants from all around the world coming to the land of opportunity. The primary insight, which is a message of recognizing differences and understanding biases that could impede the process of an individual, is that multiculturalism is embedded in the social and systemic structure of our society. However, there are personal, political, educational, and legal methods of blocking the multicultural movement and perpetuating a sense of fear and mistrust among those who have not been part of the dominant group in our society. This type of hegemony has persisted in predominantly White campuses because of a failure to require multicultural courses, the paucity of multicultural faculty and administrators, and finally the small representation of multicultural students, thus enabling the dominant culture to maintain an attitude of intellectual and cultural superiority. Spring (2007) used the term *deculturalization* to describe the "educational process of destroying a people's culture (cultural genocide) and replacing it with a new culture" (p. 7).

The issue of multiculturalism and insensitivity toward groups marginalized by race, ethnicity, gender, sexual orientation, religion, and/or other cultural characteristics has become a prominent issue on college campuses because students are no longer willing to allow their college careers to be impeded by a hostile or uncaring environment. Indeed, many colleges and universities wishing to maintain or create supportive climates for all students have implemented hate crime policies because they recognize the need to change the perception and behaviors of those who are insensitive to diverse individuals. Additionally, these policies give victims a voice and the power to expose discriminatory acts. Overall, more administrators are attempting to find ways to support the need for multicultural programming and maintain funding for diversity issues on their campuses.

The increasing diversity among the U.S. population in general and on college campuses in particular (Justiz, 1994; Spring, 2007), has led many administrators of student affairs and higher education administration graduate preparation programs to attempt to better prepare their students to work with diverse populations of college students, in short, to become *multiculturally competent*. Administrators of student affairs units on some campuses are undertaking similar efforts in their professional development programs to help working professionals become better able to serve diverse student populations.

What cultural competencies should student affairs staff members be able to demonstrate? Pope, Reynolds, and Mueller (2004) developed a list of 33 such competencies, organized into three sections: awareness, knowledge, and skills. The following are examples of competencies in the awareness component (p. 271):

- "a belief that differences are valuable and learning about difference is necessary and rewarding"
- "openness to change and belief that change is necessary and positive"
- "awareness of self and the impact it has on others"

In the knowledge component, examples include:

- knowledge of "diverse cultures and oppressed groups"
- "information about how change occurs for individual values and behaviors"
- "knowledge about within-group differences and understanding of multiple identities and multiple oppressions"

The ability to work with people from diverse cultures is reflected in skills such as the

- "ability to identify and openly discuss cultural differences and issues"
- "capability to empathize and genuinely connect with individuals who are culturally different from themselves"
- "ability to gain the trust and respect of individuals who are culturally different from themselves"

Multicultural competence extends beyond the student affairs staff, and it is the responsibility of the whole institution to challenge faculty to learn how to apply this cultural competence in the classroom and to engage students in shifting their views about themselves and others.

A similar set of multicultural attributes for students (see Table 1.1) was developed by Howard-Hamilton, Richardson, and Shuford (1998) who included the following characteristics: "knowledge of self as it relates to one's cultural identity," "ability to identify similarities and differences across cultures and the ability to articulate that with others," and "pride within one's own cultural group" (p. 11). Creating a culturally inclusive environment takes a considerable amount of time. The entire community should become involved in creating an environment that has diversity initiatives as its central mission. Furthermore, as Delgado and Stefancic (2001) noted, the entire institution should have a multicultural frame of reference embedded in its overall mission and structure, such as cultural artifacts, curricular offerings, and extracurricular activities that reflect the various demographic groups on campus. After identifying and endorsing the competencies and attributes associated with the diversity reflected in the enrollment at their colleges and universities, students, faculty, and administrators can then use these to guide student learning initiatives and classes, as well as programs in the curricular and cocurricular arenas.

A paradigm that may be able to explain the difficulties students have when attempting to connect cognitively with the diversity literature, course work, and other programmatic initiatives on campus is the Howard-Hamilton and Hinton Behavioral Model of Multicultural Competence (Torres, Howard-Hamilton, & Cooper, 2001). The behavioral model (see Figure 1.1) is a cyclical behavioral response to the challenging material presented to college students. The authors created the model after teaching master's-level graduate students in student affairs programs at three different institutions. After analyzing 5 years of journals written by students who took one multicultural course for a 16-week period (one semester), evident patterns of

TABLE 1.1
Attributes of a Culturally Competent Student

	Knowledge	*Skills*	*Attitudes*
Awareness	Knowledge of self as it relates to one's cultural identity	Self-reflection	Pride within one's own cultural group
	Knowledge of other cultures and how they are similar or different from one's own cultural group	Ability to identify similarities and differences across cultures and the ability to articulate that with others	No one group is better than another
Understanding	Knowledgeable about issues of oppression and the effect it has on different cultural groups	Ability to see things from multiple perspectives	Discrimination due to one's cultural status is unjust
	Knowledge about interactions between multiple oppressions such as race, gender, class, lifestyle, & religion	Understands difference in multiple contexts	Assumptions about an individual cannot be based solely on one's group membership
Appreciation/Valuing	Knowledge about elements involved in social change	Able to challenge acts of discrimination	One must take risks in life
	Knows the effect cultural differences can have in communication patterns	Ability to communicate cross-culturally	Cross-cultural interactions enhance the quality of one's life

Note. From "Promoting Multicultural Education: A Holistic Approach," by M. F. Howard-Hamilton, B. J. Richardson, and B. Shuford, 1998, *College Student Affairs Journal, 18*(1), pp. 5–17. Copyright 1998 by Dennis E. Gregory. Reprinted with permission of the author.

behaviors emerged from which the authors formed the labels on the behavioral model cycle. A circular model is used because students were required to revisit one or more behaviors when presented with diversity materials that were challenging, thought provoking, or even discomforting.

The exhibited behaviors began with a sense of anxiety about engaging in intense discussions about diversity, reflecting students' fear they would be blamed or ridiculed for being racist or supporting the continuation of racism in our society. However, some students were excited about enrolling in

FIGURE 1.1
The Behavioral Model of Multicultural Competence

Multicultural Competence Is a Lifelong Process

Anticipatory Anxiousness/ Anxiety

Comfort With Yourself and Others

Curious With the Acquisition of Knowledge

Epiphany/Acceptance With Privileged Status

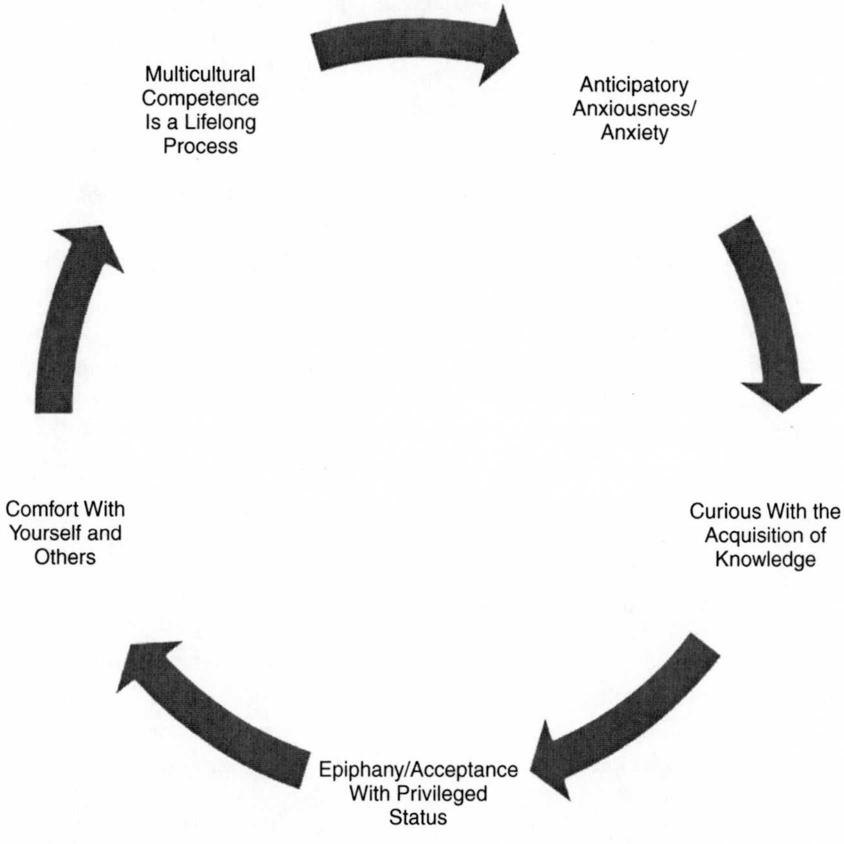

multicultural course work because they wanted to learn more about themselves and others. The authors found that most students became curious about the literature and experiences they were asked to participate in, which characterized the second phase of the cycle.

Students who read and consciously internalized the literature pertaining to privilege, oppression, and racial identity development moved into the third phase of the cycle and accepted the notion that there is a dominant group in our society. The epiphany that occurs at this phase allows the students to enter into difficult dialogues about race because they are comfortable with themselves and others. Concomitantly, they recognized there was no need to be afraid or ashamed about their culture or racial ethic identity because challenging prejudice is a lifelong process. The last phase of the cycle allows everyone to recognize the differences and commonalities that make us unique, embrace multiculturalism, and move to multicultural competence.

Differences and Commonalities

At the beginning of the chapter we mentioned the systemic pressure the early colonists were under to unify the cultures in America. Our intention in this book is not to be divisive but to help the readers understand that it is important to value, respect, and embrace our cultural differences. In addition, we must also understand that intersections of our lives create a framework of commonalities. This means that an intentional effort to deconstruct one's racial ethnic identity should be made first before attempting to understand the complexity of another person's cultural background. An in-depth discussion of this process is explained in chapter 2 in which theories/models of privilege, identity development, and oppression are presented.

Recommended Use of This Book

This book is a guide to gaining a deeper understanding of the various multicultural groups on college campuses and is intended to be useful to faculty and students in the classroom as well as to professional staff who desire to increase their understanding of the complexity of the students they serve. Freire (2005) said that teachers should always be learning, and he firmly believed that previously learned knowledge may need to be reassessed and reevaluated to understand how one's political and ethical obligation affects the other. Specifically, learning is a dynamic process particularly for people in a constantly changing and evolving environment. Traditional methods that up to now may have worked well for administrators and faculty may no longer be appropriate techniques or interventions for students entering college the next semester or academic year.

This book also presents a number of relevant theoretical frameworks and connects them to professional practice. Our purpose is to encourage the use of new concepts, not by dichotomizing theory and practice but by inclusively using both to make informed decisions about teaching and learning in a universal fashion (Freire, 2005). The universal perspective gives the individual an opportunity to step into the shoes of another person and react to a situation differently than if a traditional lens had been used. When a 360 degree universal perspective is used, everyone is empowered because it gives the marginalized person a chance to have a voice and gives the listeners a chance to gain an appreciation for diversity.

A third feature of this book makes it uniquely useful to the campus community in understanding the application of multicultural principles on campus. In addition to identifying the general characteristics that define and differentiate each of the various cultural groups included in this book, each chapter addresses the multiple identities and cultural intersections of diverse groups. Moreover, when coupled with an appreciation for these differences, personal growth, a practical understanding of inclusiveness, and the resolve to dismantle privilege could lead to the moral forthrightness to bring about civility and a higher sense of moral reasoning among the students, faculty, and staff on our campuses.

Furthermore, by including a chapter on the cultural characteristics of White students, the book provides an opportunity for members of the majority culture to perceive themselves in a cultural sense. As Spring (2007) explained, members of the majority culture who perceive their cultural characteristics to be the the norm often cannot see that their customs and characteristics are, in fact, artifacts of their culture. They see divergent cultural characteristics as "deficient" and often have difficulty seeing other cultures as valid. Helping such individuals to recognize and appreciate their own culture is a first step in allowing them to recognize and appreciate other cultures.

The Town and Gown: How the External Community Can Use the Book

We can all gain a deeper understanding of the millennial cohort that is entering graduate school and the workforce, as well as of our next generation of young adults and how their perspectives on diversity and social justice are beginning to make a significant impact on society. An example of their openness to change was their overwhelming support of Barack Obama from candidacy to nomination to election as the 44th president of the United States. The impact of college students in the election process was felt in every community across the country. The 2008 election process made it virtually impossible for the majority of Americans to remain isolated from the influence college students had by knocking on doors and canvassing neighborhoods to solicit support for a biracial African American. The material provided in the book may help those outside the campus environment, including the private sector, gain awareness of various cultural groups from a safe distance and, with encouragement from the authors, to move closer and not "let the fear of what is difficult paralyze you" (Freire, 2005, p. 49).

A new era has clearly begun with college campuses creating administrative positions—such as chief diversity officer—that assist with the promotion, creation, development, and assessment of diversity initiatives on campus. The establishment of this high-ranking position on more and more campuses clearly signals that conversations about race, racism, and multiculturalism will not be left to a few disconnected individuals, but that we are all being held accountable collectively for the successful inclusion of diverse students, faculty, and staff because everyone is affected when discrimination exists on campus. Given the changing demographic landscape from the leadership in our nation's capital to our own hometown communities, the promotion of social justice and the development of marginalized groups is a cause that should be everyone's passion, because as Martin Luther King Jr. so eloquently stated, "What impacts one directly, impacts us all indirectly," thus calling each of us to invest in the promotion of every one of our fellow citizens, particularly those who have been historically underrepresented.

References

Delgado, R., & Stefancic, J. (2001). *Critical race theory: An introduction.* New York: New York University Press.

Freire, P. (2005). *Teachers as cultural workers: Letters to those who dare to teach* (D. Macedo, D. Koike, & A. Olivei, Trans.). Boulder, CO: Westview Press.

Howard-Hamilton, M. F., Richardson, B. J., & Shuford, B. (1998). Promoting multicultural education: A holistic approach. *College Student Affairs Journal, 18*(1), 5–17.

Justiz, M. J. (1994). Demographic trends and the challenges to American higher education. In M. J. Justiz, R. Wilson, & L. G. Bjork (Eds.), *Minorities in higher education* (pp. 1–21). Phoenix: Oryx Press.

Pope, R. L., Reynolds, A. L., & Mueller, J. A. (2004). *Multicultural competence in student affairs.* San Francisco: Jossey-Bass.

Spring, J. (2007). *Deculturalization and the struggle for equality: A brief history of the education of dominated cultures in the United States (5th ed.).* Boston: McGraw-Hill.

Torres, V., Howard-Hamilton, M. F., & Cooper, D. L. (2003). *Identity development of diverse populations: Implications for teaching and administration in higher education.* San Francisco: Jossey-Bass.

2

OPPRESSION AND ITS EFFECT ON COLLEGE STUDENT IDENTITY DEVELOPMENT

Mary F. Howard-Hamilton and Kandace G. Hinton

This work deals with a very obvious truth: just as the oppressor, in order to oppress, needs a theory of oppressive action, so the oppressed, in order to become free, also need a theory of action. The theory of oppression is learned, transmitted, and replicated.

—Freire, 1968/1987, p. 185

Systematic oppression is a central part of the foundation of our national identity, and its eradication requires the uprooting and changing of the existing hierarchy of power (Spring, 2009; Takaki, 1993). For change to occur in the majority culture, a significant loss of privilege and power will result. Thus the recognition of the notions of privilege and power are critical to understanding the development of individuals from marginalized groups. A difficult, yet important, aspect of being nonmajority is the potential of experiencing oppression.

Before addressing issues related to identity development of diverse populations and designing practices to empower these groups, a connecting theory of oppression to understand how behavior is shaped by outside influences is required. A theoretical framework is necessary for several reasons. First, as Bell (1997) stated, theory allows us to reason and think clearly about our intentions and how we implement our actions in various settings (classroom, residence hall, meetings, etc.). It allows us time to think and mobilize our energy, then move in a direction of certainty. Theory can also mobilize social energy; a group of people can work toward a common goal grounded in theory. Without such a base, personal dominance may become the focal point. Second, old approaches to interacting with individuals can be queried as well as challenged, and new paradigms can be created when we infuse oppression theory with our actions. In other words, theory protects us against our own unconsciousness. "Ideally we keep coming back to and refining our theory as we read and reflect upon the emerging literature on oppression, and as we continually learn through practice the myriad ways oppression can seduce our minds and hearts or inspire us to further learning and activism" (Bell, p. 4). Last, oppression theory reminds us that people are historical subjects, and this influences the way we think, act, and behave toward others. It is important that we "learn from the past as we try to meet current conditions in more effective and imaginative ways" (Bell, p. 4).

Theory of Oppression

According to Paulo Freire (1968/1987), oppression is overwhelming control, and "an act is oppressive only when it prevents men [*sic*] from being more fully human" (p. 42). Furthermore, Freire stated that the oppressors see only themselves as "human beings" and other people as "things." "For the oppressors, there exists only one right: their right to live in peace, over against the right, not always even recognized, but simply conceded, of the oppressed to survival. And they make this concession only because the existence of the oppressed is necessary to their own existence" (Freire, p. 43). Those who are oppressed live in a culture of silence or have no voice when determining their destiny, thus they are politically and economically powerless (Spring, 1998, 2007). The oppressed develop a mental construct called "the wheels in the head" syndrome (Spring) when internalized ideas are not their own but thoughts prescribed by others to subjugate them. Oppressed people are not independent thinkers controlling their own destiny: their future is determined by the oppressor.

The method most commonly used to dictate prescribed thoughts and minimize creative power to oppressed groups is called *banking education* (Freire, 1968/1987). Teachers dictate to learners information from an oppressive historical ideology. The learners become passive by not talking about, sharing, or discussing the information they receive; conversely, they simply receive, memorize, and repeat what has been dictated. Where banking education exists, the oppressed groups become the objects of history rather than its subjects. "A subject of history is a conscious maker of history. . . . As objects of history, their actions are determined by history, but they do not make history" (Spring, 1998, p. 148). This is a form of deculturalization, or the educational process of destroying a people's culture and replacing it with a new culture (Spring, 2009).

When people accept oppression in their lives they become dehumanized and lack any will, consciousness, or motivation to make societal or systemic changes (Freire, 1968/1987). Without the critical consciousness to become self-determining rather than self-deprecating, the oppressed will continue to allow the oppressor to make choices for them that limit their freedom. Even when a collaborative breakthrough occurs between the oppressors and the oppressed, praxis still needs to occur. Praxis is when dialogue, reflection, and action take place between the oppressors and oppressed in order to transform the world (Freire).

Spring (1998, 2007) separates attributes of the oppressor and the oppressed into two categories: a revolution from the right and a revolution from the left, respectively. When defining a revolution from the perspective of the oppressor, or right, it means creating a dominant overt and covert environment and systemic structures in which there is very little freedom or flexibility for the oppressed to attain success, become empowered, and move comfortably through life without doubts about one's abilities and future aspirations. The maintenance of the dominant environment is a generational inhibitor as well, leaving the future bleak for prodigy of the oppressed.

The revolution for the oppressed, or the left, is grounded in a framework that knowledge is the key to changing one's perception that being different from the majority is dysfunctional. The revolution to the left empowers the oppressed so that they begin to name their own identity rather than having the oppressor define their personalities and cultural background. The revolution is a gathering of people who create a base of power to change societal misconceptions about who they are and their contributions to the world.

The oppressor exhibits behaviors from a revolutionary right perspective by fearing freedom for others and perceiving them as lifeless individuals. Domination is exhibited by the desire to keep the oppressed muted, dependent, and domesticated. The oppressed operate from a revolution from the left, which is a liberating experience. Freire (1968/1987) describes the domestication process as *banking education*, in which knowledge is created and disseminated in a manner that does not allow for dialogue and differing opinions to be shared. Those who are the subjects of the information may find that their culture, history, and attributes are misrepresented because the stories of the oppressed are not part of the information created by the dominant group. The information has been banked and deposited into the minds of the oppressed and the oppressors. Withdrawal of that information is manifested in the form of stereotypes, language, and policies that subjugate the oppressed and uplift the oppressors. The revolution to the left engages people to become part of a utopian vision that is liberating because there is empowerment, dialogue, and a stream of information or education that engages people to be nonconformists and create their own destiny. The basic premise is that unconditional support, liberation, and dialogue move the group to a point of reflection and transformation. The oppressed begin to create their own history by organizing and finding solutions to problems by continuously operating from a revolutionary frame of mind to the left that is dichotomous to the perspectives of the oppressors' revolution to the right. Specifically, even though both are using revolutions to garner support from large groups of constituents, one group subjugates and dominates (i.e., the oppressor from the right) and the other group is collaborative and empowering (i.e., the oppressed from the left). Therefore, when the oppressed begin to adopt a social change perspective from the left, the "revolution will result in the transformation of consciousness and personality of all people" (Spring, 1998, p. 149).

To define the dialogue between the oppressor and oppressed, Alschuler (1986) created a three-stage developmental response to oppression: magical conforming, naive reforming, and critical transforming. The magical conformist does not see any problems in society and passively colludes with the oppressor, believing the problems that exist among the oppressed are unchangeable and hopeless. The naive reformist blames others for problems that exist because the others have deviated from the rules and expectations of society. Critical transformation of these beliefs occurs with a critical analysis of the system and one self, and when people name the ways they have oppressed others and "victimized themselves by their active collusion in supporting the conflict-producing rules and roles" (Alschuler, p. 493).

Overall, oppression exhibits six significant characteristics according to Bell (1997), which are

1. Pervasiveness: Oppression is the pervasive nature of social inequality woven throughout social institutions as well as embedded within individual consciousness.
2. Restricting: Oppression represents structural and material constraints that significantly shape a person's life chances and sense of possibility.

3. Hierarchical: Oppression signifies a hierarchical relationship in which dominant or privileged groups benefit, often in unconscious ways, from the disempowerment of subordinated or targeted groups.
4. Complex, multiple, cross-cutting relationships: Power and privilege are relative since individuals hold multiple and cross-cutting social group memberships.
5. Internalized: Oppressive beliefs are internalized by victims as well as benefactors.
6. "Isms": Shared and Distinctive Characteristics: Oppression is manifested through racism, sexism, classism, anti-Semitism, ableism, and heterosexism, and the dimensions of experience that connect "isms" in an overarching system of domination. (pp. 4–5)

It is important to understand how these theories intersect with the day-to-day issues at higher education institutions. When faculty members do not teach students how to view their own work and personal space from a multicultural lens they create a covert bias that limits students' growth and development. The classroom becomes a place in which specific material from the dominant culture is presented, giving a subtle message that this model fits everyone, thus marginalized groups must accept the norm. This type of acclimation process occurs frequently on campuses. Examples include invited speakers who are only male; programs for marginalized groups that are limited to one specific period of the year, such as women's or Latino/Latina history month; and committees that are made up of one demographic group. Alschuler (1986) would view such an institution as magical conformist because the system has always operated in this manner and is part of the pervasive oppression in institutions. Moving into a transformation state requires that student affairs staff and faculty teach students how to analyze and assess the organizational structure that is covertly and overtly oppressive. This may take the form of challenging units to evaluate their organization from a multicultural frame of reference and providing the appropriate incentives and support to help them become more inclusive. This often means training student affairs administrators in how to become continuous and not occasional diversity advocates.

Faculty and administrators who are transformational leaders from Alschuler's (1986) perspective will find methods to create an environment that is not oppressive. Implementing diversity workshops, creating committees to assess the campus and departmental climates, advocating workshops that support underrepresented groups, diversifying membership on key university committees that are part of retention efforts, and hiring staff members who are compatible with the demographic makeup of the institution all help to dismantle the hierarchical form of oppression that manifests itself on many college campuses. Furthermore, these methods recognize that complex, multiple, and cross-cutting relationships must be recognized and changed before diversity initiatives can become a routine part of the campus environment.

The Social Oppression Matrix

According to Hardiman and Jackson (1997) "oppression is not simply an ideology or set of beliefs that assert one group's superiority over another, nor is it random violence, harassment, or discrimination toward members of target groups" (p. 17). These researchers identified a social oppression model that is pervasive when one social group, consciously or subconsciously, devalues another social group for its own gain (Hardiman & Jackson). Four key elements are associated with social oppression:

1. The agent group has the power to define and name reality and determine what is "normal," and "real," or "correct."
2. Harassment, discrimination, exploitation, marginalization, and other forms of differential and unequal treatment are institutionalized and systematic. These acts often do not require the conscious thought or effort of individual members of the agent group but are rather part of business as usual that become embedded in social structures over time.
3. Psychological colonization of the target group occurs through socializing the oppressed to internalize their oppressed condition and collude with the oppressor's ideology and social system.
4. The target group's culture, language, and history are misrepresented, discounted, or eradicated and the dominant group's culture is imposed. (Bell, 2007, pp. 3–5)

Social oppression exists when one group is the beneficiary of privileges because of its social group membership. An example of privileged social group membership is when there is an organization that is composed of administrators or leaders who are from one racial/ethnic group and gender, allowing them to create all the hiring practices, policies, as well as pay structure for the organization without consultation from those who are different from the leaders (Hardiman & Jackson, 1997). These privileges are supported by the institutions and structures of society as well as by individuals who assist in the operation, support, maintenance, and perpetuation of these benefits. The social oppression matrix comprises individual, institutional, and cultural/societal levels. These levels work in a dynamic fashion along three dimensions "that operate to support and reinforce each other: the context, the psychosocial processes, and the application" (Hardiman & Jackson, p. 18).

The context dimension intersects with the individual, institutional, and cultural/societal levels. The boundaries are not rigid but fluid, allowing for interaction and thus making all three levels mutually supportive. The individual level emphasizes the beliefs, views, values, and practices of the person rather than an entire social or institutional system. The impact of social oppression on an individual and the institution is reciprocal. Individuals are affected by the institution when they abide by, maintain, and sustain oppressive rules, regulations, and structures. Conversely, individuals have an impact on the institution when they internalize and value dominant societal values, codes, and mores.

Institutions, such as corporations, schools/colleges/universities, religious groups, local/state/federal government, as well as the family, construct and are affected by two levels: individual and cultural/societal. "The application of institutional policies and procedures in an oppressive society run by individuals or groups who advocate or collude with social oppression produces oppressive consequences" (Hardiman & Jackson, 1997, p. 19). Policies barring people of color from country club golf courses or women who are excluded from assuming primary roles of power in religious organizations are examples.

The psychosocial processes may be conscious or unconscious when individuals decide to support, collude, or actively participate in a system of social oppression (Hardiman & Jackson, 1997). People act as conscious participants in social oppression when they engage in activities that support and maintain a system that denigrates others; for example, providing funds for a White supremacist group or voting against human rights legislation. Individuals may unconsciously support social norms that are culturally demeaning, such as people of color turning to plastic surgery to mirror White facial features.

The application dimension recognizes that social oppression is evident at the behavioral and attitudinal levels of the individual and system interface (Hardiman & Jackson, 1997). "The attitudinal level describes the individual and systemic values, beliefs, philosophies, and stereotypes that feed the other dimensions" (Hardiman & Jackson, p. 19), like the stereotypes that the Irish are drunks, Italians belong to the Mafia, White people have no rhythm, and White men cannot jump. When zoning laws are designed to keep poor children in dilapidated schools or people of color are systematically overlooked for promotion and relegated to low-paying positions, individuals are behaviorally taking actions that sustain and preserve social oppression.

Social Identity Development Theory

Social identity development theory (Hardiman & Jackson, 1997) details the characteristics that are common to the identity development of oppressed and dominant groups. The theory should not be used to label people, because they may be in one or more stages simultaneously coping with differing emotional and cognitive struggles with oppression. The theory is helpful in understanding the perspectives of students, and in developing training or teaching modules.

The first stage of the theory, naive/no social consciousness, is when individuals from oppressed and dominant groups "are unaware of the complex codes of appropriate behavior for members of their social group" (Hardiman & Jackson, 1997, p. 23). They may experiment and push the boundaries or norms, but the social structure provides information and cues about what it is like to be part of a particular social category. They begin to accept the roles prescribed by teachers, parents, clergy, or the media and note differences between and among individuals.

In the second stage, acceptance, these roles are internalized, and the oppressed and dominant groups conform to the characteristics society has deemed for them whether consciously or unconsciously. Members of the dominant group who are in the passive acceptance stage have "to some degree internalized codes of appropriate behavior, [so] conscious effort is no longer required to remind them of what to do and how to think" (Hardiman & Jackson, 1997, p. 24). If the dominant group is in the active acceptance stage, its members receive messages in a very overt and direct method that people from oppressed groups are inferior, deviant, and weak. Privileges are evident for dominant members of the active acceptance stage, although they are oblivious to these societal perks. Oppressed people in the acceptance stage have learned to internalize and accept messages about the inferiority of their culture and themselves and overtly or consciously connect with the views, beliefs, and ideology of the dominant group. The passive acceptance individuals are oblivious to how they emulate the oppressor and reflect the oppressor's views.

Increased awareness occurs in the resistance stage. In this third stage, members of the dominant group have experienced a challenging life event that provides some impetus for creating a new worldview and rejecting their old frame of reference. In the resistance stage, those who are oppressed begin to acknowledge and question the collective experiences of oppression and their damaging effects.

Stage four, redefinition, requires that a new identity be created "that is independent of an oppressive system based on hierarchical superiority and inferiority" (Hardiman & Jackson, 1997, p. 27). Dominant group members start to reframe and create new definitions for their social group identity that is independent of social oppression and the projection of prejudicial views toward oppressed groups. Members of the oppressed group find themselves independently defining who they are and developing a new personal identity in the redefinition stage. This is a significant stage for the oppressed because "it is at this juncture that they shift their attention away from a concern for their interactions with agents of oppression towards a concern for primary contact with members of their own social group who are at the same stage of consciousness" (Hardiman & Jackson, 1997, p. 27).

The final stage, internalization, is geared toward infusing the identity developed in the redefinition stage into every phase of one's life. The dominant groups work toward creating a more inclusive and egalitarian society. The oppressed groups are engrossed in embracing and accommodating their new level of critical consciousness and group dignity.

Critical Race Theory

There are similarities between Freire's (1968/1987) pedagogy of working with oppressed populations and critical race theory. Both theories believe in raising the consciousness of individuals who have been silenced and eliminating every form of oppression (race, class, gender, religion, sexual orientation, etc.; Delgado & Stefancic, 2001; Freire). Critical race theorists believe in the role of storytelling to give the oppressed an opportunity to be empowered and heard (Delgado & Stefancic). The stories also allow people to interpret their own experiences and validate them with individuals who are in similar situations. Counterspaces according to Delgado and Stefancic (2001) are physical locations within an existing environment that are affirming as well as comfortable niches for interactions that can be verbal or nonverbal, for marginalized or oppressed groups. Cultural centers, for example, are considered counterspaces on predominantly White campuses. Students of color often create counterspaces by sitting together in conspicuous locations in a student center, cafeteria or lounge area. Counterspaces are where these stories are often told, and they provide a safe space for marginalized groups to dissect how their lives have been affected by oppression. Critical race theorists also view racism as endemic and an integral part of our society, a reality that is normal and natural "because it is so enmeshed in the fabric of our social order" (Taylor, Gillborn, & Ladson-Billings, 2009, p. 23). It is also understood that attempting to create a color-blind society and embrace a neutral stance about race is detrimental to marginalized groups. Color blindness leads to an unconscious racism by oppressors that allows them to be oblivious to the needs of the oppressed; everyone is treated the same because they are blind to differences.

Critical race theory was developed by law scholars who believe this scholarship is transferable to other disciplines (Litowitz, 2009). It respects previous diverse perspectives including "political activism of the 1960's, nationalism, postmodernism, Marxism, and pragmatism (Litowitz, p. 293). The subjective experiences of marginalized groups are valued because they have had actual encounters with oppressive acts. Last, critical race theorists recognize the role of history in oppressed groups because it frames a context for the events that occur in the lives of the oppressed.

The generation of students attending college today have a different perspective about diversity. Many of the students matriculating at our colleges and universities have encountered individuals from racial/ethnic or cultural groups different from their own. They have also been exposed to media that have provided a lens into the worlds of populations outside their respective environments. Students today have also been exposed to phenomena such as the increasing diversity within our federal political system, transitions in careers that have traditionally been deemed gender-specific domains, and the expanding opportunities to participate actively in community service. One would assume that this generation has already embraced the critical race perspective of understanding privilege through personal engagement and assessment. However, we need to be cautious about such assumptions because exposure to diverse groups is often experienced vicariously through the media, for example, rather than through direct and sustained personal encounters.

College students may view their comfort with diverse populations as being nondiscriminatory and color blind to differences. This perspective relieves members of the dominant group from the guilt associated with seeing people as being from distinctly different cultures from their own.

The color-blind philosophy often allows the dominant group to make the assumption that our society provides equal access to everyone regardless of race, creed, or religious affiliation. Students should be exposed to cultural experiences throughout their college career, in the classroom as well as extra-curricular activities, to dispel this notion of color blindness.

The classroom experience is a key component in challenging the comfort level of students in college today. Denson and Chang (2009) found that "there are appreciable educational benefits associated with racial diversity" (p. 344). The authors continue, stating that "campuses where students are more engaged with racial diversity through related knowledge acquisition or cross-cultural interaction have measurable positive effects on all students irrespective of a student's own frequency of engagement with diversity" (p. 344). The institution's role in providing a diverse experience for students, in and out of the classroom, creates the perfect space for them to be purposeful in their cultural journey. The manner in which students are exposed to diversity experiences will challenge their sense of whether they have internalized their own racial identity and their understanding that society still views marginalized groups in a mostly stereotypical manner. The students need to be challenged to see diversity and differences in others, and they need to learn that to do so does not mean they are prejudiced, racist, sexist, or homophobic. It means they are comfortable with the discourse that leads to hearing the stories of oppressed individuals. Moreover, they will appreciate the need for counterspaces so that marginalized groups can share their experiences with those who are willing to listen and learn.

How Oppression Affects Privileged Groups

Oppression has a tremendous impact on the identity development of dominant or privileged groups. McIntosh (1998) metaphorically describes White privilege "as an invisible package of unearned assets that I could count on cashing in each day but about which I was meant to remain oblivious. White privilege is like an invisible knapsack of special provisions, maps, passports, codebooks, visas, clothes, tools, and blank checks" (p. 207). Based upon McIntosh's insights, it is important that the impact of oppression and privilege on dominant groups be explored from multiple aspects, specifically, psychological, social, moral and spiritual, intellectual, as well as material and physical (Goodman, 2001; Wise, 2007).

When social systems of oppression constrain people and keep them from becoming fully human, the psychological cost is a loss of mental health and an authentic sense of self (Goodman, 2001). The ways the psychological costs manifest themselves are as follows:

- Socialization into roles and patterns of behaviors—People in dominant groups are socialized to conform to certain rigid standards of behavior.
- Denial of emotions and empathy—Personal growth is further limited when people attempt to deal with the contradiction between what they are often taught (equality, love, and kindness) and what they are expected to do (treat people inequitably).
- Limited self-knowledge and distorted view of self—People from privileged groups are routinely denied information and opportunities to understand their role in an unjust social system as well as honest feedback from people in oppressed groups.
- Discrepancy between external perceptions and internal realities—Individuals do not feel like the powerful, privileged people they are presumed to be. Even though there may be material success, there can be emotional and spiritual emptiness.
- Fears and pain—There are fears of losing entitlement and power, the fear of losing respect within the dominant culture if there is collusion with the oppressed. There is pain when privileged groups that support justice are witness to a hostile or violent incident towards the oppressed group.
- Diminished mental health—People from dominant groups tend to develop unhealthy psychological mechanisms (such as denial, false justification, projection, disassociation, and transference of blame) to deal with their fears of minorities or people from oppressed groups. (pp. 106–107)

In the category of social costs, diminishment and loss of relationships happens when the dominant group lacks trust among the other groups, thus creating a climate that does not support boundary breaking and forging friendships (Goodman, 2001). These societal costs occur through isolation from people who are different, raised barriers to deeper and more authentic relationships, and the development of disconnection, distance, and ostracism within one's group.

In the case of nonrecognition of privilege (Goodman, 2001), critical moral and spiritual costs, specifically the loss of integrity and a spiritual center, can result. Feelings that surface when privilege becomes recognized are guilt and shame when people have more material goods than others, moral ambivalence when they begin to face family and societal disapproval for questioning the status quo, and spiritual emptiness or pain when the actions of the privileged are not part of the spiritual philosophies one lives by.

The intellectual cost of oppression to people from dominant groups is the loss of developing a full range of knowledge (Goodman, 2001). Those in the dominant groups remain miseducated, uninformed, and ignorant of their culture and history as well as that of the oppressed groups. Finally, the material and physical costs of oppression are loss of safety, resources, and quality of life (Goodman). When people are oppressed, they may inflict harm and violence upon the oppressor in the form of social unrest or create tension that leads people to fear for their safety. When oppressed people become desperate for food, shelter, and other necessities, they may turn to stealing or causing physical harm to those in power or to those who seem to have material wealth. This leads to higher costs for people who wish to live in safe and comfortable neighborhoods and to a waste of resources as tax dollars and other resources are spent incarcerating people who were denied the opportunity to live a life similar to that of the privileged. Most importantly there are negative health implications for the privileged people because they may "experience high degrees of stress and stress related illnesses as they feel increasingly fearful and disconnected from other human beings. Pressures to achieve and maintain status in a hierarchical and competitive social and economic system further undermine health" (Goodman, p. 119).

Conclusion

This chapter provides an overview of Freire's (1968/1987) pedagogy of the oppressed, a social oppression matrix, the social identity development theory, critical race theory, as well as the impact of privilege on dominant groups. This provides a context for understanding why identity development is difficult and why those who are oppressed often express different views about their experiences. This context is a critical foundation to understanding identity development among diverse populations. This overview may enable students, teachers, and administrators to find creative and collaborative methods for reducing oppressive behaviors in the classroom and on campus. Additionally, personal reflection on the issue of social oppression may bring about a change in individual identity.

Freire (1968/1987) cogently stated that we should not let the fear of what is difficult paralyze us and that there is no teaching without learning. One of the authors learned about the difficulty of peeling back layers of privilege, guilt, magical conforming, naive reforming, and critical transforming from a White male doctoral student who took a seminar course on critical race theory. The student agonized over the eye-opening yet hurtful experience of having been part of political, educational, professional, as well as societal systems that oppressed people who have dreams similar to his. The student used the following counterstory in poetry form that was written as a personal identity awareness class assignment to describe his transformational process and his realization that unpacking the invisible knapsack is a lifelong process.

TO SAVE ONE'S SOUL . . .

I see the colors I want to see
For the others I can look by obliviously.
To the left and to the right,
It is only the important that catches my sight.

Privilege is a word saved for the king,
For he is the person who owns everything.
To come and go and never have a care,
Are signified by royal robes that others can't wear.

In this modern world the king is deposed
But where is the power he bestowed?
To the white man whose ancestors conquered the world,
Unabated came power and privilege. Behold!

Today the world is in such a mess,
But those who created it have long since passed.
Forward to us hate comes to our space,
Our inheritance makes this an imperfect place.

Really, what does it mean to oppress?
To see injustice and choose to suppress.
The right to act on an un-equals behalf,
For most it is seen as a major gaffe.

Do I find joy to stand with my black friend at his wedding?
To celebrate his love in this life never ending.
Or am I proud I am the only male whitey,
To join in this sacred and holy party.

To stand with my friend as his good man,
When a sinner and hater has been my plan.
How did I deserve to be honored this way?
A bigot and racist I am today.

If I choose to be different from what I have known
I am afraid in *my* world I will stand alone.
Standing alone against the trespass
Of the woman, the ethnic, and all other outcasts.

The unwanted and lessors may have had their plan
But their lot in life was controlled by the Man
Straining against the waves of oppression
The outcome is judgment and calls of aggression

Four steps forward and three steps back,
For some that is the only attack.
To break free of the pain and the misery,
Who will bring the hope of delivery?

To hear the screams, the calls of oppression,
To hear not and see not and speak not can't be my expression.
Choosing to act will come at a cost.
All that I have known and felt will be lost.

Where I work and what I do is not important,
How I live will prove to be the most potent.
With them I will stand in the shame and the pain
Of another day of turmoil with little or no gain.

To side with the oppressed is to give up control.
To risk one's place, but to save one's soul.

Robert Dean Branson
Reprinted with permission of the author

Regardless of whether your profession is teaching, mentoring, counseling, advising, or administration, everyone is an educator and has a responsibility to encourage individuals to become the creators of their own destiny. The educational process should include modeling and teaching others how we can transform oppressive systems that subjugate marginalized groups and liberate them from the mechanized "wheels in the head" (Spring, 2007, p. ix) controlling behavior that has traditionally been utilized by media, books, technology, and schools. The student poem gives us insight into the dissonance-provoking process of developing a critical consciousness and becoming motivated to transform systemic oppression.

Case Studies

Translating theory to practice can be a daunting task for students and student affairs professionals. Understanding how the theories and models presented in this chapter can assist in helping individuals navigate the challenges of negotiating different environments and understanding marginalized cultures could assist in transforming the campus community or institutional environment. The mini cases presented are examples of how culture, race, ethnicity, and traditions can be misread and misinterpreted by others. Using a reflective lens, dialogue, and collaboration (i.e., Freire, critical race, or social justice models) can lead to an outcome that empowers everyone.

Corey is a master's student in the student affairs program at Midwest East Southern University. He was born in rural Mississippi and has an extended family (aunts, uncles, cousins, and grandparents) living within a few miles of his home. Corey attended school with a cohort of children from kindergarten through high, school and upon graduation many of them stayed in the community to continue farming or learning about their family business. Corey attended a small college near his hometown and was encouraged to continue studying at Midwest East Southern University, a large public institution two states away from home. Corey was stumped by the required Diversity in Higher Education course, because as a White male he did not think that the content would be applicable to his future experiences. Corey confidently stated, "I will be heading back to Mississippi and my goal is to work at one of the small colleges. There isn't a large multicultural population at our colleges so why do I need to learn this material? I need to know more about administration and how to manage an office."

Remy is an undergraduate at North Sensitive University and is preparing to become an accountant. She received stellar grades as a freshman with the help of her sorority sisters and is looking forward to becoming more active on campus during her sophomore year. Remy has stated on numerous occasions that her diverse high school always kept the students involved in local service projects because the city had a large indigent community. She worked with her organizations to gather food during the holiday seasons and tutor children who struggled with math and science. This exposure was enlightening for her because she was raised in an affluent suburb of the largest city in

Indiana. Remy's goal was to find organizations that would give her experiences similar to those in high school. One afternoon Remy's classmate Lilia encouraged her to attend a meeting at LaCasita, the campus Latino/Latina cultural center. Remy quickly stated that she was afraid because there would not be anyone there who looked like her and the center was for students of color. Lilia tried to be supportive yet encouraging because they needed as many hands as possible to help with the upcoming holiday gift basket giveaway. Remy said she would think about it but admitted that she would be more comfortable if the members of her sorority attended the meeting as well so they could make this an organizational effort.

Case Questions

1. What are Corey's and Remy's developmental responses to oppression according to the social oppression matrix and the social identity development theory (Bell, 2007; Hardiman & Jackson, 1997) as well as Alschuler's (1986) three-stage developmental response to oppression?
2. What can the institutions' responses be to the developmental challenges Corey and Remy internalize with regard to diversity issues?
3. How can Corey's cohort be supportive yet challenging when communicating and working with him?
4. How can Remy's classmate Lilia encourage her to become less fearful of being a minority among marginalized students?
5. What are some of the privileges Corey and Remy were unaware of as they were growing up and that are available to them while in college?
6. Even though Corey and Remy are part of a generation that has been exposed to the Internet and other technological conveniences, why do you think there is still some reluctance to step into another person's culture?

References

Alschuler, A. S. (1986). Creating a world where it is easier to love: Counseling applications of Paulo Freire's theory. *Journal of Counseling and Development, 64,* 492–496.

Bell, L. A. (1997). Theoretical foundations for social justice education. In M. Adams, L. A. Bell, & P. Griffin (Eds.), *Teaching for diversity and social justice: A sourcebook* (2nd ed., pp. 1–14). New York: Routledge.

Delgado, R., & Stefancic, J. (2001). *Critical race theory: An introduction.* New York: New York University Press.

Denson, N., & Chang, M. J. (2009). Racial diversity matters: The impact of diversity-related student engagement and institutional context. *American Educational Research Journal, 46*(2), 322–353.

Freire, P. (1987). *Pedagogy of the oppressed.* New York: Continuum. (Original work published 1968)

Goodman, D. J. (2001). *Promoting diversity and social justice: Educating people from privileged groups.* Thousand Oaks, CA: Sage.

Hardiman, R., & Jackson, B. W. (1997). Conceptual foundation for social justice courses. In M. Adams, L. A. Bell, & P. Griffin (Eds.), *Teaching for diversity and social justice: A sourcebook* (pp. 16–29). New York: Routledge.

Litowitz, D. E. (2009). Some critical thoughts on critical race theory. In E. Taylor, D. Gillborn, & G. Ladson-Billings (Eds.), *Foundations of critical race theory in education* (pp. 291–310). New York: Routledge.

McIntosh, P. (1998). White privilege, color, and crime: A personal account. In C. R. Mann & M. S. Zatz (Eds.), *Images of color and images of crime: Readings* (pp. 207–216). Los Angeles: Roxbury.

Spring, J. (1998). *Wheels in the head: Educational philosophy of authority, freedom, and culture from Socrates to human rights* (2nd ed.). New York: McGraw-Hill.

Spring, J. (2007). *Wheels in the head: Educational philosophies of authority, freedom, and culture from Confucianism to human rights (3rd ed.).* New York: McGraw-Hill.

Spring, J. (2009). *Deculturalization and the struggle for equality: A brief history of the education of dominated cultures in the United States* (6th ed.). New York: McGraw-Hill.

Takaki, R. (1993). *A different mirror: A history of multicultural America.* Boston: Little, Brown.

Taylor, E., Gillborn, D., & Ladson-Billings, G. (Eds.). (2009). *Foundations of critical race theory in education.* New York: Routledge.

Wise, T. J. (2007). *White like me: Reflections on race from a privileged son.* Brooklyn, NY: Soft Skull Press.

3

ENVIRONMENTAL INFLUENCES ON COLLEGE CULTURE

Michael J. Cuyjet

From the early days of the student affairs profession, theorists have recognized the impact of environment on the lives of the individuals who populate our campuses. Kurt Lewin (1936) proposed the formula $B = f(P \times E)$ to explain that behavior (B) is a function (f) of the interaction between person (P) and environment (E). Kaiser (1975) applied Lewin's concept to the college setting and identified this interaction as a "transactional relationship" in which "the students shape the environment and are shaped by it" (p. 38). Unfortunately, when we consider concepts such as these in the general sense, we tend to focus on the impact environment has on all the members of the community as a single entity. Typically, this means we look at the interaction of environment with the elements of culture as reflected in the dominant American culture. While this may help us gauge the impact of environment on the cultural and social lives of a majority of our students, it does not accommodate the differences that exist among people who do not embrace the dominant culture. According to Strange and Banning (2001), a 1991 report by the Council of Ontario Universities concluded that "the environment is experienced differently according to a person's ethnicity, race, class, age, ability, and sexuality" (p. 10). Thus, it becomes necessary to examine the impact of environment in smaller, more focused, less-general terms to observe how the same element of the environment can have different—sometimes minutely, sometimes drastically—effects on the inhabitants of the community who constitute the particular environment under examination.

This chapter presents a representative model of person-environment interaction and examines its components from a different viewpoint: their relative inclusiveness of divergent cultural perspectives. In conducting such an examination, we will be able to explore ways to better use the concepts represented in these models to make college and university environments more accommodating and welcoming to students who embrace cultural perspectives other than dominant American cultural norms.

Environmental Models

A number of useful models exist that help conceptualize the influence that environment has on participants in a college community. Huebner and Lawson (1990) offer six constructs that affect students' development and performance in the college setting, the first five of which are considered environmental dimensions: heterogeneity/homogeneity, support-challenge balance, social support, social climate, and the physical environment. The sixth construct, person-environment congruence, is explicitly interactional. Strange (1996) organized the elements of campus environments into a framework with four dimensions: physical environments, the designated features of the campus physical plant; human aggregates, the collective characteristics of the campus human population; organized environments, the dynamics of the interaction among campus members and groups; and constructed environments, the meanings that campus members put on these interactions. The material in this chapter is organized to follow Strange's model and address these constructs using the four dimensions he has outlined, with reference to one of Huebner and Lawson's constructs (person-environment congruence) added appropriately for emphasis.

Physical Environments

The first of Strange's (1996) environmental dimensions, physical environments, examines the influence of physical structures on the behavior of individuals within a community. Strange and Banning (2001) described three distinct positions of the physical environment: architectural determinism, architectural possibilism, and architectural probabilism. In architectural determinism there is "a rather direct link between the built environment and the behavior within it" (p. 13). People behave in a certain way because the physical structure and design allow few other options. Fences and gates that limit access to areas of the campus and buildings that have few entrances are examples of deterministic architecture. Architectural possibilism describes a physical environment as a source of opportunities that may set limits on, but does not restrict, behavior. According to Wissler, the environment serves as an influence of "passive limiting agency" (as cited in Strange & Banning). An attractively designed campus restaurant in a very visible location is an example of possibilism; it is more than just another place to eat, it is an attraction that draws patrons. Architectural probabilism assumes that certain behaviors have "probabilistic links to the built environment" (Strange & Banning, p. 14). The layout, location, and arrangement of space and facilities render some behaviors much more probable than others. For example, the location of a multicultural center in a remote building on the periphery of the campus rather than in the student union in the center of campus affects the probability of its use by students.

The physical environment of the campus "communicates messages that influence students' feelings of well-being, belonging, and identity" (Kuh, Kinzie, Schuh, Whitt, & Associates, 2005, p. 106). Yet, architecture affects different students differently based on cultural conditioning. The dominant American culture tends to be individualistic, concentrated on internally focused individual characteristics and self-aggrandizement. Those individuals from collectivist cultures, which tend to focus more on benefiting the entire social group even at the expense of the individual, who have a greater desire to congregate and interact socially would be inhibited by an architectural arrangement that provided few spaces for such congregation to occur. The lack of outdoor seating, few open plazas, small lounges in classroom buildings, even narrow hallways does not facilitate impromptu, collective social interactions that may be more characteristic of some cultures than of the dominant American culture.

Strange and Banning (2001) contend that the probable influence of architecture is functional and symbolic. What they do not mention is that symbolism is often culturally interpreted. While it is important to observe the symbolic influence of the campus architecture, it is also very important to try, to the best of one's ability, to imagine how that symbolism is perceived by members of the campus subpopulations through their differing cultural lenses. A mural on the wall of a lecture hall at Indiana University provides a stark example. Painted in 1933 to depict the history of the region at that time, the mural includes images of robed Ku Klux Klansmen burning a cross. Students have occasionally objected over the years, but a serious protest occurred during the spring 2002 semester when several African American students who were attending a class in that lecture hall found the images offensive and requested that they be painted over. The perspective of the "pro-mural" people was that this was a valuable piece of art that accurately (although not politically correctly) depicted a chapter in Indiana's history. The perspective of the protesting students was that the mural reminded them of a particularly offensive series of events perpetrated on their ancestors and that the images were stressful for them to have to see on a regular basis. The dilemma in such situations is that both perspectives have merit, and administrators must be sensitive to the differences in viewpoints, the people, and the cultures that spawn such feelings.

By emphasizing that environments provide symbolic nonverbal cues for behavior, Strange and Banning (2001) seem to agree with Rapaport (1982) who suggested that the significant link between function and symbol in the physical environment is nonverbal communication. Various aspects of the physical environment evoke nonverbal interpretations in the members of the community. These interpretations can be positive or negative; they can be aligned with the intention of the campus administrators or they can be the opposite of what was intended. The prominent, central location on campus of an imposing student center that houses the offices of the various student service agencies sends a clear nonverbal message about the importance of student services and cocurricular activities in the life of the campus. The location of the women's center in the basement of an older building on the periphery of the campus sends a message to some that the program lacks significance in the eyes of the leaders of the campus community even if those leaders themselves do not intend to project that view. Nonverbal messages (covert) are often seen as more truthful than verbal or written messages (overt; Mehrabian, 1981). Double messages have a strong impact, and when a person on campus perceives an inconsistency between the language and the nonlanguage message, the nonverbal often becomes the most believable (Eckman, 1985). Imagine the perceptions of a first-generation Latino student and his parents sitting in a freshman orientation session in which an all-White, all-Anglo team of orientation advisers reads the nondiscrimination statement from the college catalog. Which message—verbal or nonverbal—is most likely to be believed?

The physical environment is more than bricks and mortar. Strange and Banning (2001) referred to the *behavior setting* as part of the physical environment. As a behavior setting, the college environment is composed of two parts: the physical, or nonhuman, aspects and the social, or human, aspects. Humans interact on campus among nonhuman components (buildings, pathways, parking lots) and "it is the transactional (or mutually influential) relationship between the human and nonhuman elements in the behavior setting that shapes behavior" (p. 19). As with any human interaction, this aspect of the physical environment is influenced by culture. According to Strange and Banning, two of the ways nonverbal influence is manifested are through proxemics, or spatial zones, and through artifacts.

Proxemics is the study of the social implications of use of physical space. Thus, the implication of a classroom with rows of seats bolted to the floor and an instructor's lectern on a podium 20 feet away from the first row of seats offers a very distinct message about the formality of student-teacher relations in the classroom. The arrangement of outdoor benches in groups facing each other rather than isolated benches in remote spots across the campus gives an indication of the ease with which impromptu casual conversations among groups of students and faculty might take place. As with other aspects of the campus, we must also examine these physical characteristics for their differing implications toward people of different cultural backgrounds. Individuals from cultures with greater tendencies for animated verbal and tactile expressions of communication would be more greatly affected by physical spaces that inhibit such contacts. Spatial zones describe the distances people tend to establish between themselves and others when they engage in social interaction. Strange and Banning (2001) indicated that the literature on proxemics traditionally identifies four distinct social zones of interaction: intimate (0 to 1.5 feet), personal (1.5 to 4 feet), social (4 to 12 feet), and public (more than 12 feet). Yet, there is a cultural dimension to this as well. The Children's Museum of Indianapolis has an exhibit consisting of a life-size silhouette of a human figure on a wall and five sets of footprints painted on the floor. The first set of footprints is about 12 inches from the wall, and each of the ensuing sets of footprints is a bit farther from the wall with the fifth set being about five feet away. The signage accompanying this exhibit explains that each set of footprints represents the distance at which people from various cultures feel comfortable engaging in face-to-face conversation. Realizing this, when we consider spatial zones, we must understand that the placement of physical items all across campus—from the desks in the classrooms to the chairs in the cafeteria—can send different messages to different people. A campus whose staff is sensitive to this matter and that allows flexibility and variety in such arrangements conveys a message of welcome and comfort to a wider spectrum of members in the community.

Physical artifacts include "synthetic objects made and often placed on a campus for intended purposes, for example, to give directions, to inspire, to warn, or to accommodate" (Stage & Banning, 2001, p. 21). Artifacts include signs and symbols, artwork or posters, graffiti, and specific physical structures (Banning & Bartels, 1993). All of these can convey significant nonverbal messages. Signage can give confusing signals. Signs that are placed midway up a wall instead of nearer the ceiling or signs placed on the side of a door instead of above it convey a welcoming message to individuals using wheelchairs. Signs that have a Braille translation or that are written in English and another language offer a message of inclusive welcome. Campus symbols can have important cultural messages too. A current example of how symbols can be interpreted very differently by individuals with different cultural perspectives is the controversy that has erupted in past years over college mascots that depict American Indians. Although the circumstances may vary from school to school, generally those who favor keeping such mascots unaltered argue for maintaining a time-honored tradition that fits the majority culture's perspective of American Indians, while those who advocate changing the mascots usually see them as a distortion or an insult to American Indian culture and American Indian people (Longwell-Grice & Longwell-Grice, 2003).

Artwork can often convey nonverbal social messages. Are the paintings, sculpture, photographs, posters, and even flyers for upcoming events around the campus representative of one culture or several? The photographed individuals in the recruitment brochures of the institution and what they are doing in relation to other people in the photos can be more important in conveying the character of the institution than the text in that pamphlet. Graffiti is another form of art that can present a problem. While it can be argued that the content of graffiti is the message of its author only, Strange and Banning (2001) contend that the total of campus graffiti begins to communicate campus culture. Any delay in removing graffiti, particularly graffiti that is clearly offensive to any particular group, conveys the complicity of the entire campus in the offensive message.

In regard to physical structures, curb cuts, ramps and handrails, easily accessible elevators, or other accommodations send a clear welcome message to those with disabilities as well as a symbolic message of openness to the nondisabled.

Among several other elements of the physical campus environment discussed by Strange and Banning (2001) is the use of a concept called *display of self* proposed by Zeisel (1981) that explores the use of the physical environment by individuals or groups to convey messages of presence or ownership. A banner hanging from the second floor of a College of Business building declaring its ranking in a national magazine or the huge signs in the windows of some residence hall announcing the residents' pride in their living community are familiar examples. Strange and Banning (2001) said that "such displays become important to the process of individualizing and personalizing spaces" (p. 25). What is very important in these displays is that a representative balance be maintained among various cultural groups on campus in displaying their personalization of space. So, just as the predominantly White fraternities and sororities that own large houses in the Greek Row section of campus display their letters on the front of those buildings, the smaller, traditionally Black or Latino/Latina fraternities and sororities that do not have houses should be encouraged to create brightly painted personalized areas on the campus quad, such as those typically seen on many historically black colleges and universities (HBCUs). Campus administrators must make it clear to the campus community that if one group is allowed to contribute to the campus physical environment with a display of self, any group can do so, as long as their expression is not harmful to others. The right of the lesbian/gay/bisexual/transgendered student organization to hang a gay pride banner on the door of its assigned campus office must be as easily accommodated as the freedom of the Baptist Student Union to place a welcome sign in the window of its office.

Human Aggregates

The second of Strange's (1996) environmental dimensions examines the characteristics of the human population within the campus community and the effect the various components of that population have on the campus as a whole as well as on each other. Moos reminds us that the character of an environment is dependent on the typical characteristics of its members (as cited in Strange & Banning, 2001). This raises two important issues that affect the ability of members of any particular campus community to grasp the impact that the human element has on their environment. The first issue relates to who is represented among the human aggregate and the proportion of that representation among various identifiable groups of members. The second issue concerns the relative strength or weakness of the impact any or all of these groups have on the environment. Strange and Banning described these two elements as *differentiation* and *consistency,* and they claimed that these two influence "the pattern, strength, and character of any human aggregate" (p. 49). Differentiation is the degree of homogeneity of type among inhabitants of an environment. Consistency is the similarity of type among those community inhabitants. A particular campus is said to be highly differentiated if there is a single type of student who tends to be dominant in the environment, while an environment that is characterized by a relatively broad distribution of types is said to be undifferentiated or *diffused*. A good example of the effect of environmental differentiation can be seen in the description of environments by Holland (1973). In his model of Vocational-Interest Personality Types, Holland describes six different types of individual personalities and the environments they inhabit: Realistic, Investigative, Artistic, Social, Enterprising, and Conventional. In Holland's model, the six social environments corresponding to these six personality types tend to be dominated by individuals who reflect the typical characteristics of the dominant type. In turn, because a particular type tends to dominate a particular social environment, a certain set of behaviors, attitudes, and skills tend to be reinforced (e.g., artistic environments reinforce artistic characteristics). Thus, Holland's environments are said to be highly differentiated.

From a multicultural perspective, there are three concerns with differentiation. The first is the relative strength of the dominant group or type in a highly differentiated environment and the effect that strength has on the ability of nondominant groups to function freely. It might be acceptable, even desirable, under Holland's (1973) model to have an Investigative vocational environment dominated by Investigative types with their preferred interest in systematic physical investigation. The fact that such an environment is not particularly conducive for the highly interpersonal or persuasive competencies of Enterprising individuals may actually create a productive work situation. However, a small college campus environment that is overwhelmingly Greek, and as such, has an extracurricular cultural milieu that diminishes or excludes the participation of non-Greeks should be unacceptable to student affairs administrators committed to cultural diversity.

The second concern is the differentiation of subenvironments within the larger campus environment. While an assessment of the total campus population may reveal a relatively even representation of a number of different cultural groups, the impact of any high concentration of a certain type leading to high differentiation in a part of the campus community should also be of concern to student affairs professionals if it might prove stifling to any nondominant group. Thus, the high differentiation of the College of Engineering with White males with backgrounds in the natural sciences could be problematic for Black females interested in the social applications of civil engineering. To take the Greek example one step further, it would be similarly unacceptable if among a campus dominating type (in this case, Greeks) a majority of predominantly White Greek organizations were allowed to diminish the open pursuit of "atypical" activities by a minority of historically Black or Latino/Latina Greek groups.

The third concern that may affect the human aggregate on campus is the matter of *false differentiation*. Strange and Banning (2001) pointed out that "highly differentiated environments are readily distinguishable to those within them, as well as to those outside them, precisely because the dominance of a single type consistently encourages certain behaviors, values, attitudes, and expectations while discouraging those that are dissimilar" (p. 50). False differentiation occurs when observers of the campus environment— whether campus administrators, faculty, students, or external constituencies—look at some of the more apparent behaviors, values, and attitudes and infer the dominance of a particular group that is not really represented in numbers equal to that status to the exclusion of the impact or influence of other groups that merit higher status. In one all-too-common example, because traditional-age, full-time residential students are more visible and active in most out-of-classroom activities, they are allowed considerable influence in the form and function of campus activities, even though such students may actually be in the minority and do not represent the characteristics, attitudes, and interests of the nontraditional-age, part-time commuter students who tend to constitute the numerical majority on many campuses. Under such conditions, for example, budgeting for homecoming activities may get more support from student government participants and advisers than subsidizing the campus child care center to allow part-time students' children to use it during evening classes.

Consistency, the similarity of type among the inhabitants of an environment, has a significant effect on the human aggregate of a campus community. Consistency differs from differentiation in that a campus can be somewhat diverse (or undifferentiated), yet these heterogeneous groups may exhibit very similar characteristics, providing consistency to the environmental milieu. This can sometimes be a positive thing, since high consistency in a particular environment tends to make social interaction easier among the inhabitants because they already have similar characteristics to build relationships. On the other hand, in environments in which a message is sent, overtly or covertly, that consistency in human characteristics among all community members is highly desirable, those whose cultural characteristics are in any way dissimilar to the consistent norm will be marginalized. This is the pattern that plays itself out for such groups as African American students and international students on campuses across the country. As an example of this condition, consider two international graduate students in the College of Engineering. One is a Chinese student from a middle-class background with a strong record of achievement in a highly rated technical institution in his home country. The other is a Guatemalan student who demonstrates a potential to do well in the engineering field but comes from an economically depressed region and was trained in an institution that does not have access to the latest and most sophisticated technology. The Guatemalan student is quite capable of succeeding in the graduate program but may need a little extra help to do so. Both students add to the heterogeneity and diversity (i.e., undifferentiation) of the college's student body; but the Chinese student exhibits consistency with those middle-class American students who have been trained at highly rated U.S. institutions. The danger here is that the success of the former student's background and training may set a potentially false expectation that all international students will have this level of consistency and those who do not are personally deficient, without giving appropriate consideration to the environmental factors that contribute to their differences. Moreover, if all international students are expected to have consistency with the American students, those who do not are unfairly perceived (by others as well as themselves) as deficient and marginal. One other insidious aspect of consistency is that those whose behaviors make them consistent with the majority can seldom see the negative effect that forced consistency can have on others whose cultural characteristics are not consistent with the dominant norm.

The last of Huebner and Lawson's (1990) environmental constructs, person-environment congruence, helps explain the impact of this concept of consistency on the college campus. Defined as the "fit" between an individual's characteristics and the environments in which he or she finds comfort, person-environment congruence measures one's similarity or dissimilarity with the dominant normal characteristics exhibited in a particular campus community. Strange and Banning (2001) claimed that a person is congruent with an environment "if his or her type is the same or nearly the same as the dominant type within that environment" (p. 52). If this is so, it can be difficult for individuals whose characteristics, behaviors, and values may be considerably different from those of the dominant group to feel connected to that particular environment. The first task of administrators in such a community is to recognize and call to the attention of others around them the presence of groups of students who do not have consistency with the dominant group. The second task is to ensure that what qualifies members of the community to receive acceptance and achievement is not dominated by the characteristics of the predominant type. Helping community members who appear different to identify similarities and commonalties is an effective way of beginning to build consistency where it may not be readily apparent. For example, it is not enough to merely be concerned about bringing a viable population of Latino/Latina students to the campus without making an even greater effort to develop a cultural environment in which they can feel comfortable. If these students believe they are expected to assimilate into the Anglo culture to find success on the campus, many of them may consider this too high a personal price to pay.

If "nonconsistent" groups are struggling to find a person-environment fit on the campus, it is the role of student affairs administrators to help them accomplish this objective. "Lack of congruence must lead to dissatisfaction and instability, a condition that is likely to be resolved in one of three ways: by seeking a new and congruent environment, by remaking the present environment, or by adapting behavior to the dominant characteristics of the present environment." (Strange & Banning, 2001, p. 53). Too often, predominantly White institution (PWI) administrators assume that the third option will naturally occur if nondominant groups such as African Americans, Latinos/Latinas, or American Indians are to adjust to the campus environment. While that is true for some members of these populations who find assimilation relatively easy, some find it very difficult, and even those who do adapt expend considerable emotional and psychological energy that might have better been directed at other positive pursuits such as academic studies. Perhaps the second option, remaking the environment, is a more viable choice for some students. Student affairs professionals often talk about changing the environment to fit students rather than changing students to fit the environment. We must be willing to walk the walk and actually accommodate new cultural behaviors in the rhythms and activities of campus life and to help all members of the community understand the benefits of allowing this to happen.

This may not be easy. Strange and Banning (2001) stated that "a highly differentiated and consisted environment is thought to be resistant to change in that its strongest tendency is to reinforce itself" (p. 53). Nonetheless, by analyzing any resistance in this manner—in terms of differentiation and consistency—we can begin to see what characteristics are dominant, which of these dominant characteristics are problematic for diverse and nonconsistent groups, how to accommodate the characteristics of other groups in the community, and how to react to the natural resistance of the dominant group. One final challenge for student affairs professionals is not only simply to accommodate different elements of the campus human aggregate and make them feel included but also to bring together the various components of the aggregate and help them to learn to interact positively. Spitzberg and Thorndike (1992) observed,

> The architecture of racial and ethnic difference, especially, is one of informal and formal subgroupings, significantly isolated from each other, ignorant of each other, and, for the most part, unconcerned about the disconnections. It is as much this ignorance and lack of interest as the more visible clash of different factions that detracts from the potential for community on campus. Grouping by special interest or need is natural and inevitable. (p. 28)

Recognizing that the divergent subgroups of the campus populations are not likely to facilitate interaction much (if at all) on their own, we must create mechanisms to entice them to interact so they can not only appreciate and honor each others' differences but, more importantly, find and celebrate their cultural commonalties.

Organized Environments

Simply stated, the organizational dimension of an environment is measured by the interactions among people and groups within that environment and by what they are able to achieve when they interact. Each of the four components of the Strange (1996) environmental model builds on the components that precede it. Thus, in the same way that the human aggregate of an environment brings life to the physical component, the organizational component is the manifestation of the various human aggregate elements interacting with each other to achieve common goals. Strange and Banning (2001) tell us that varying degrees of "organized patterns of structure and process" (p. 59) are found in all environments. These patterns exist for people to achieve specific goals. Each college or university generally has a set of common goals, including the collection and dissemination of knowledge and imparting that knowledge to students in some systematic way. However, it is the patterns of structure and process that give each institution its distinct characteristics and is also what determines its relative success or failure in meeting those goals. For example, many universities are organized into academic colleges, each of which consists of a series of academic departments, each of which may contain several different academic programs of study.

Yet, each of those programs is probably different, the number of programs and the organizational structure in the departments probably differ, and consequently, the structures of the various colleges are not quite the same. So, while there may be a common structural pattern, the actual components themselves may be different (slightly or significantly). For example, some institutions may define *college* completely differently. Schools such as Rice University in Houston are organized into residential colleges; each student upon enrollment becomes a member of a residential college whether or not he or she actually lives in that residence hall. The student remains identified as a member of that college through matriculation and even after graduation, regardless of academic major. As stated at the beginning of this section, the interaction of individuals forms the organizational dimension of an environment. Thus, the major factors contributing to the unique characteristics of a particular institution's organizational environment are its people and the ways they interact as they move toward a common goal. Strange and Banning describe organizations as "environments with a purpose" (p. 61). The purpose or goal of an organization is not insignificant to its structure. The Carnegie Classification of Institutions of Higher Education (http://classifi cations.carnegiefoundation.org/) speaks to this purposeful difference among institutions. Some institutions are focused on granting bachelor's degrees in a limited number of subject areas. Other institutions are meant to provide a setting for substantial empirical research in a wide range of physical and social science disciplines. The key to the success of all such institutions is the appropriate fit of the personnel in each; in other words, the organizational patterns must match the population, and vice versa.

One noticeable phenomenon of matching patterns with people is that homogeneity will often contribute to the success of the institution's ability to attain its goals. So, an institution whose mission focuses on science and technology with lesser emphasis on the social sciences will likely be more easily able to achieve many of the typical measures of success for such an academic institution—prominent faculty, high-quality students, numerous science and technology research grants from federal and industry resources, substantial graduation rates—although the students may get significantly less exposure to the study of the humanities and social sciences than at other institutions. Not all such characteristics are academic. Cultural characteristics can shape the organizational environment of a campus. A clear example is that of HBCUs whose characteristics, notably different from those at PWIs, include the infusion throughout the curricula of Black history and examples of Black culture that are missing from PWI curricula; a more prominent use of in loco parentis attitudes by administrators and faculty in attending to the personal behavior of students, particularly at smaller, private HBCUs; and strong ties to the surrounding community, particularly the local Black community. Technical institutions and the HBCUs are examples of highly homogeneous aggregates that influence the organizational structure of their environments. These examples reflect Strange and Banning's (2001) contention that homogenous aggregates "attract, satisfy, and sustain individuals who already share those same interests" (p. 165). While the positive benefits of this homogeneity are apparent in the strength of curricula and culture and the stability of the organizational structure, in the context of this book it is important to examine the patterns of structure in an organizational environment not only as they might affect the predominant characteristics of the majority of the population, but also as they relate to various cultural subpopulations within that community. For example, large urban institutions with high numbers of commuter students (many of them nontraditionally aged) and no, or relatively few, residential students should be very concerned about the ways organizational structures affect the different types of students on the campus. Institutions that employ a typical administrative structure developed in years past when the majority of students were traditional 18-to-22-year-old full-time, residential students may find their operational methods failing to serve the needs of large numbers of the student population (Kilgore & Rice, 2003).

At the beginning of this section, we stated that the organizational dimension of an environment is measured by the interactions among people and groups within that environment. Thus, from a multicultural perspective, it is imperative that mechanisms be developed that facilitate interactions among various subpopulations within the campus community, particularly those that are nondominant or that are prone to marginalization. Kuh et al. (2005) emphasize this point by advising campus administrators to make certain they demonstrate their commitment to interactions among diverse people and groups early by overtly socializing all newcomers to this value. However, just attending to the particular needs of various subpopulations within the campus community may not be the proper solution to making the environment comfortable for all. Balancing organizational structure to accommodate various components of the campus community is often quite difficult to achieve because invariably the needs of one group conflict with the needs of some other group. Thus, providing one subpopulation with resources that strengthen the status of its members on campus will often diminish the status of another subpopulation. As an example of this, consider the ongoing debate over whether it is prudent to have separate Greek councils for the predominantly White and predominantly Black fraternities and sororities. Proponents of a unified all-Greek governance body protest that separate councils weaken efforts to benefit the entire Greek community, while proponents of different councils claim that the needs of divergent groups can better be served separately. Strange and Banning (2001) reflected on this dilemma of whether focusing on the environmental needs of subpopulations can weaken the entire campus environmental structure when they remarked, "That which contributes to strong subcommunities usually detracts from the community of the whole, and that which sustains the whole community often does so at the expense of various subcommunities" (p. 169).

Strange and Banning (2001) suggested that the campus environment comprises seven organizational structures: complexity, centralization, formalization, stratification, production, efficiency, and morale (p. 62). By examining the environmental structure using these organizational structures we can explore how each can be used to make the environment comfortable for different subpopulations in the campus community while still providing an overall organizational environment that is multicultural and welcoming of diverse components of the campus community. At least we should be able to heighten our sensitivities to cultural concerns so that these structures are not employed in a way that is offensive to any of the subpopulations in the campus environment.

Complexity. The fundamental concern of organizational complexity is the question of how many units and subunits serve the purposes of the organization and how they should be arranged. Organizational complexity is also affected by the intensity and extensity of the knowledge and expertise required in these subunits. Cultural diversity affects complexity in two ways. First, as more distinct subunits are required to meet the needs of distinct subpopulations, the campus becomes more complex. So adding a separate agency to attend to the concerns of lesbian, gay, bisexual, and transgendered students or establishing an office to serve returning veterans and military students may have clear advantages to those distinct populations. But if additional funding and personnel are not available, these services will have to compete with other agencies for existing resources. Second, units that are responsible for providing a service to the entire campus will need to decide if they are capable of adequately meeting the needs of a complex organizational environment. For example, administrators of a counseling center on a homogenous campus need not be as concerned about the diversity of their staff as their counterparts at a counseling center on a campus with broad cultural diversity. The latter agency would require greater organizational complexity and cultural competence to ensure having a staff with the knowledge and expertise to address the needs of a diverse clientele.

Centralization. Organizational centralization refers to the way power is distributed in a setting. Power is the "capacity of one social position to set the conditions under which other social positions must perform, that is, the capacity of one social position to determine the actions of other social positions" (Hage & Aiken, 1970, p. 19). This structure is also affected by cultural diversity in two ways. First, care must be taken to decentralize the structure enough that no single agency or small group of agencies (such as a small, powerful student government executive committee composed of individuals with homogeneous social characteristics) has such power that it can dictate to other agencies without sufficient input from all quarters. Second, since it is inevitable in any organizational structure that some centralization must exist—someone has to make decisions for the entire community—the people in those centrally powerful roles must have the knowledge of and sensitivity to the needs of diverse elements of the campus community, particularly those that may be more easily marginalized.

Formalization. Formalization refers to the importance of rules and regulations (whether formally written or customarily understood) in an organization (Hage & Aiken, 1970). Certainly, rules and regulations are necessary in any organization regardless of its diversity. However, three culturally related concerns apply to the discussion of formalization. The first issue is the degree of formality different groups place on rules and regulations they are expected to abide by. For uniform effectiveness, the cultural interpretations of these rules and the relative importance of enforcing them must not be significantly different among various groups governed by them. Second, rules need to be equitably enforced so no group has, or appears to have, an unfair disadvantage or advantage by the application or formality of the rules and regulations. Third, rules need to take into account cultural sensitivities. Strange and Banning (2001) tell us that "high degrees of formalization are associated with organizational rigidity and inflexibility. Low degrees of formalization lend themselves to organizational fluidity and flexibility" (p. 66). So too can cultural characteristics be described as more rigid or more fluid (e.g., the more rigid concept of time in European individuals versus a much more relaxed perception of time among American Indians). Rules developed by one group without considering the different perceptions of formality of another culture are likely to require some modification when cultural clashes arise.

Stratification. Stratification in an organization is manifested in the differential distribution of its rewards. Generally speaking, culturally sensitive organizations should have less stratification in the way rewards and resources are distributed for a number of reasons. Not only does high stratification tend to be divisive because "reward structures are often cast into a competitive environment" (Strange & Banning, 2001, p. 67), but this very competitive environment itself is not reflective of the various cultures to which members of the campus community may belong. Individuals who manifest characteristics of some collectivistic Asian or American Indian cultures, for example, rather than the individualistic dominant U.S. Eurocentric culture may find a competitive process of reward allocation difficult to embrace. Another detrimental effect of high levels of stratification is that those who may receive a disproportionate amount of accrued rewards "have a vested interest in maintaining the status quo" (p. 67). Thus, if one subpopulation on a highly stratified campus tends traditionally to have acquired a disproportionate amount of the rewards, that group is likely to be resistant to efforts to enhance cultural diversity and cross-cultural sharing of resources. Administrative stratification is an additional concern. Members of various subpopulations should be able to see individuals who reflect their cultural characteristics among the decision makers at all levels of the organizational structure, particularly near and at the top. For example, the absence in a particular institution of any vice presidents or deans who are female or Latino/Latina or openly gay sends a signal to the women or Chicanos/Chicanas or gay/lesbian staff and students that the institution's stratification is not welcoming to them.

Production. Strange and Banning (2001) state that "the value of any organization is often assessed by what it does, most frequently in terms of what it produces" (p. 67), and that "all organizations need to produce, for reasons of justifying their existence, for maintaining current resources or attracting additional ones, and for creating a sense of accomplishment among members who contribute to the organization's goals" (p. 68). When evaluating the success or failure of an institution's production (e.g., the number of students matriculating, the number of graduates, the amount of grant money won by faculty) administrators of the culturally sensitive campus should monitor the assessment not just in the aggregate but broken down by subpopulations to see if the effects are being equally felt. So an overall undergraduate graduation rate of 50% is a less-than-adequate gauge of success if the rate for African American men within that group is only 25%. Strange and Banning also point out that "how much to produce, though, is often a trade-off with the quality of production" (p. 69). So simply measuring the number of Latino/Latina graduates, for example, is not a true assessment of production if large numbers of these students leave the institution having felt alienated or disconnected during their matriculation.

Efficiency. Organizational efficiency involves the assessment of the relative cost of the products and/or services produced by an organization. Efficiency generally implies an emphasis on the efficient use of resources and on cost reduction (Strange & Banning, 2001). A cultural perspective in measuring efficiency calls for institutional administrators to give ample consideration to the development and maintenance of cultural diversity in personnel and programs as they make determinations about the efficient use of resources and search for ways to keep costs to a minimum. Accordingly, for example, an Asian studies department might be supported even if it maintains a relatively lower number of majors, or the Student Life Office may hire an adviser for the nine traditionally Black fraternities and sororities even though their chapter memberships are measurably lower than the average for their traditionally White counterparts. Strange and Banning also suggest that "colleges and universities are in the business of creating new ideas and programs responsive to changing conditions and needs" (p. 70). Thus, a culturally responsive perspective on efficiency is sensitive to the needs and situational conditions of smaller cultural subpopulations, such as those with physical or learning disabilities, as well as more traditional campus units, such as academic departments, or the general student body as a whole.

Morale. Strange and Banning's (2001) last structure of organizational environment, morale, examines the satisfaction of the members and participants in an organization. They call particular attention to the relationship between morale and turnover—higher morale usually results in lower turnover in students and staff, and higher turnover is often indicative of lower morale. Once again, as has been emphasized throughout this chapter, the need to assess cultural subpopulations of the campus community is necessary to determine a full picture of the campus community's morale. Moreover, it is not sufficient simply to measure the morale of various identifiable groups on campus. Hage and Aiken (1970) suggested that human organizations must "maintain a minimal level of morale" (p. 27) among their members. Institutional administrators must determine what those minimum levels for different campus subpopulations will be and work diligently to keep morale above those minimums. So, for example, the amount of faculty/student interaction needed to keep morale at sufficient levels among a group of majority-culture graduate students might not be adequate to maintain appropriate morale among a small group of African American graduate students in the same department who may perceive the academic environment as somewhat hostile. Even if that perception is viewed as incorrect by some department faculty, the task of addressing the matter is critical to maintaining good morale among all the members of the entire department.

Constructed Environments

Constructed models of the environment "focus on the subjective views and experiences of participant observers, assuming that environments are understood best through the collective perceptions of the individuals within them" (Strange & Banning, 2001, p. 86). Critical to this perception of human environment is the notion that "examining collective personal perspectives of an environment (from inside participants as well as from outside observers) is critical for understanding how people are likely to react to those environments" (p. 86). In other words, each person's perceptions are the reality of that environment for him or her.

Thus, of the four sets of environmental dimensions in the Strange and Banning (2001) model, the constructed model might seem to reflect most accurately a multicultural perspective because the collective identity of the environment is composed of the collective viewpoints of the various individuals who inhabit that environment. Or, as Strange and Banning described it, the constructed dimension espouses "a phenomenological orientation to human environments that seeks what participants see in the environment as a basis for understanding and predicting their behavior" (p. 87). However, a closer examination of the way this environmental dimension is used in most situations reveals that, like the physical, human aggregate, and organizational dimensions, the typical application does not necessarily employ a fully multicultural perspective without some additional considerations and adaptations to accommodate the needs and worldviews different from the dominant American cultural viewpoint.

Three perspectives employing the work of other theorists—environmental press, social climate, and campus culture—are offered by Strange and Banning (2001) to demonstrate the interaction of elements in a constructed environment.

Environmental press. Stern (1970) said that environmental press is inferred from consensual self-reporting of activities by either participants in or observers of an environment. However, the examples used describe how the actions of the majority are often used to define an environment. For example, if 75% of the undergraduate students at a particular college are members of fraternities and sororities, the environment is inferred to have a press toward Greek involvement. In such an environment it might then be appropriate for student affairs professionals to respond with behaviors that reflect the Greek constructed environment. For example, several staff members in the student activities office might be assigned to advise Greek organizations and assist in the programming of events focused on the fraternity and sorority chapters' activities. The housing office might construct and operate fraternity houses that are leased by the institution to the housing corporations of these fraternities and sororities, or residence life staff may designate sections of the residence halls for the exclusive occupancy and use of separate Greek chapters. Such allocation of resources would probably be beneficial to the overall development of the students who are members of the Greek organizations. However, a comprehensive, inclusive, multicultural perspective goes beyond serving the majority and provides for the needs of recognizable minorities within the environment. So at such a highly Greek college, appropriate attention must be paid to that minority of students who elect not to affiliate with fraternities and sororities or to those students who might not be accepted readily into the Greek organizations through their normal intake procedures. Moreover, these efforts need to guarantee that the support of non-Greek students is not marginalized and that the efforts to address their needs are not subsumed by the efforts being devoted to the Greek students.

Stern's (1970) explanation of environmental press mentioned above includes the observation that "the perceived environment is both personal and consensual" (p. 12). Stern goes on to explain that "the collectively perceived significes of various press are an entirely adequate source from which to infer the environmental situation to which individuals are responding" (p. 12). However, the concept of consensus can fail to accommodate the needs of minorities; for even when consensus is apparently achieved, it can result because some of the members of an environment feel compelled to select one single status to represent the entire group. Thus, it is not simply enough to find a course of action that seems to elicit a consensus of perception among the members of that population, be it a particular group of students or the entire student body or the entire college community. The absence of dissent does not imply total agreement or even full acceptance of the consensus position. Marginalized groups (such as the non-Greek students) may believe that expressing any opposition to the status quo is futile and simply may choose to accept a less-than-desirable situation as inevitable. Student affairs professionals need first to identify the particular constructed environmental press in various aspects of the campus community and determine whether that press truly represents characteristics and inclinations of all the students (and faculty and staff) in the environment. Then, if necessary, they need to seek out any members of the community whose cultural characteristics and consequential needs are not being fully addressed in that environment.

Social climate. Strange and Banning referred to "the nature and effects of various 'environmental personalities' as perceived by participants" (2001, p. 94) as the social climate dimension of the environment as described by Moos (1979, 1986). They tell us that according to Moos's model, social climate, is composed of three socioenvironmental domains, each with a respective set of dimensions: relationship dimensions, personal growth dimensions, and system maintenance and change dimensions. Relationship dimensions indicate how people are directly involved in the setting and how they support each other. Personal growth dimensions assess the extent to which personal development and self-enhancement occur. System maintenance and change dimensions measure how the environment maintains control and responds to change and how orderly it functions. As with other aspects of the environment examined in this chapter, student service professionals are advised to hone their sensitivities and establish measures to determine that all members of the campus community, particularly any individuals or groups that are traditionally marginalized, are given equal opportunity to experience these dimensions of the social climate of the campus. Thus, by recognizing the impact that the campus social climate has on all students and the reciprocal impact that all students have on the collective social fabric of the campus community, campus administrators provide an environment where relationships can cross typical cultural lines. Also, personal growth can be fostered even for those with divergent lifestyles, and the environment maintains the orderly functioning of its system while accommodating widely differing aspects of social interaction.

As professionals overseeing these social climate environments, we routinely conduct assessments to determine the state of the environments we monitor. Even with standardized assessment instruments, we need to exercise caution to determine that the results of such evaluations truly measure the perceptions and needs of all the participants and not simply the majority.

As an example, let us look at the University Residence Environment Scale (Moos & Gerst, 1988). Using this assessment tool, six characteristic environments can be identified in various living groups (Moos, 1979). Results of such an assessment may indicate that a particular environment (e.g., a certain residence hall complex) may represent one of Moos's (1979) six particular environments. However, the culturally sensitive professional takes this assessment one step further to protect against the consensus phenomenon in which the perspective from the dominant culture may give a false analysis of social climate among individuals who do not exhibit all the typical characteristics of that dominant culture. For example, two of the personalities Moos (1979) identified are a *traditionally socially oriented living environment* and an *independence-oriented living environment.* In describing traditionally socially oriented living units, Moos indicated that they "give priority to dating, going to parties, and other traditional heterosexual interactions as well as to aspects of formal structure and organization, such as rules, schedules, established procedures and neatness" (p. 55). Let us now imagine a not-yet-out-of-the-closet homosexual man who would function best in this structured social environment but chooses not to engage in these "traditional heterosexual interactions." What he truly needs is a socially oriented living environment with "formal structure and organization" that best suits his climatic needs but also with the possibility of engaging in nonheterosexual interactions. An alternate response (and a less culturally responsive one) to this situation might be to perceive that this hypothetical student, possibly because in the course of this assessment process he indicates a tolerance for gay and lesbian lifestyles, is determined to best fit into Moos's (1979) independence-oriented environment, which he describes as encouraging "a wide diversity of student behaviors without specific social sanction and do not value socially proper or conformist behavior" (p. 57). We can see this could be a totally wrong social climate for this hypothetical student. But we are also able to see how easy the use of a single assessment could result in a significant mismatch of climate and the placement of a student in a nonsupportive, and possibly hostile, residential environment. Having the sensitivity to detect the nonconforming individual who may be marginalized or even hurt in a particular social setting by being made to conform to the construct of the environment is what makes us better student affairs professionals.

Campus culture. Kuh and Hall (1993) defined campus culture as the "confluence of institutional history, campus traditions, and the values and assumptions that shape the character of a given college or university" (pp. 1–2). To give substance to this definition, Kuh and Hall described four levels of culture: artifacts, perspectives, values, and assumptions. Artifacts refer to tangible features and, as such, are very similar to the environmental features discussed in the section on physical environments (see pp. 41–42). However, artifacts can be verbal or behavioral as well as physical. Verbal artifacts can include language or phrases that are connected to the institution's culture, and behavioral artifacts are certain activities, rituals, or events that tend to connect members of the community to the institution. Sometimes these nonphysical forms of artifacts should be examined or reexamined to assess their cultural significance to the changing populations of the campus (Kuh & Whitt, 1988).

An example of a verbal artifact is the former name of the street where a number of the fraternity and sorority houses are located at the University of Louisville. Named for a 19th-century monument located in an adjacent plot of land, the street was named Confederate Place after the nearby statue commemorating the members of the Louisville community who served in the Confederate army. While that name may not have been of any consequence many years ago, the location of university-owned facilities on such a street running through a section of campus was deemed offensive to an increasing number of students, faculty, and administrators. University administrators judged the discomfort caused by this verbal artifact from the past to be significant enough to take action and in 2003 the name of the street was changed to Unity Place. An example of a behavioral artifact that has significant implications for a discussion of cultural sensitivity is one that used to take place at home football and basketball game half-time activities at the University of Illinois. Near the end of half-time activities, Chief Illiniwek emerged and performed a dance routine that was part of these festivities for many decades. However, his performance was being met by boos from those in the crowd who deemed it inauthentic, stereotypical, and offensive to American Indians. After years of debate between those who were offended by the performance and those who saw it as a cherished artifact of the university's culture, Chief Illiniwek performed his last dance at a basketball game in February 2007.

Perspective. Kuh and Hall (1993) describe cultural perspectives as "the socially shared rules and norms applicable to a given context" that allow members of the community to "determine what is 'acceptable behavior' for students, faculty, staff, and others in various institutional settings" (p. 6). Strange and Banning (2001) point out that "students quickly become aware of appropriate campus customs, attire, and ideologies" (p. 101). Yet being aware is not the same as acceptance and comfortable conformity. While it is certainly a reasonable expectation that all students accept certain customs and norms for the good of the whole community, it is important to ensure that all those community members have an equal opportunity to express their own perspective on what are preferred norms and to try to influence the decisions that help establish or maintain those customs. As an example, consider the policies of a certain public university in a small rural community where dances in the student union ended at midnight because the students who were prohibited by university policies from drinking at those events would go to the local bars that stayed open until 2:00 a.m. to continue their partying. When this custom originated, there were almost no minority students and, in fact, most students were very monocultural in economic status and hometown background as well as race. Later, representatives of the African Americans who represented almost 15% of the student body petitioned for permission for the dances to continue until 2:00 a.m. The African American students not only tended to drink less than their White counterparts, but they indicated that they felt unwelcome at the bars whose clientele included not only the students but the small population of nonuniversity White townspeople as well. What is the student perspective—the socially shared rules and norms—here? Should the African American students be expected to honor the long-standing traditions of the institution's social activities, or is the institution guilty of not accommodating divergent perspectives in the determination of the students' cultural norms? If the institution does not at least acknowledge the variance in viewpoints about the social norms and take steps to resolve such a matter, those students for whom these norms are not culturally familiar can quickly assume that their own cultural perspectives are unappreciated in the campus community.

Kuh and Hall (1993) are quick to state that values are much more abstract than perspectives or artifacts, yet some common values are needed for members of the university culture to be able to judge situations on their appropriateness to the group or to subpopulations of the group. In determining the cultural values of an institution, administrators have a responsibility to articulate clearly those values all members of the community are expected to adhere to, such as the importance of attaining and disseminating knowledge or certain religious principles at sectarian institutions affiliated with a particular sect. On the other hand, culturally sensitive administrators are careful to recognize how different cultural values may influence the ways some members of the institutional community may react differently to certain values held by the majority of members. The fact that most of the values in the dominant American culture have a Judeo-Christian and heterosexual foundation does not mean we should not respect value-driven perspectives of people of other theological beliefs (or the absence of such beliefs) or of individuals with a homosexual orientation.

It is important to mention that cultural sensitivity is not cultural anarchy. While it is understood that different people bring different values to the campus community, for that community to function, certain commonly held values are necessary (i.e., adherence to basic civil laws). Being sensitive to others' values does not mean an abdication of the responsibility to establish some common values for the good of the society and to hold all members accountable to them, even if for some they are newly learned as part of an acculturation process.

Assumptions are described as the "tacit beliefs that members use to define their role, their relationship to others, and the nature of the organization in which they live" (Kuh & Hall, 1993, p. 7). In the context of the discussion in this chapter, this aspect of campus culture is a call for continuous assessment of the student culture by continual contact by student affairs professionals with students in all facets of student life. Strange and Banning reminded us that participant perceptions and understandings of campus organizational culture are an important source of information for designing responsive educational environments, and educational administrators must be particularly sensitive to any discrepancies between their views of the institution and those of students. Moreover, these relationships must be developed and nurtured so that students are willing to share openly their own tacit beliefs with student affairs professionals, regardless if these assumptions fit with those of the majority population. As an example of the importance of uncovering the tacit assumptions of minority groups on campus, consider the implications if a small group of American Indian students assume they have no valuable role on the campus, which leads them to the conclusion that they are not welcome or that they are destined to be permanently marginalized in the campus social culture. Making the tacit understandable is seldom an easy task, but student affairs administrators are expected to develop mechanisms to provide the divergent elements of the campus population with a means of expressing themselves to test their tacit assumptions against the realities of the community's other values in an attempt to find a harmonious fit for all the community's participants.

Summary

College and university environments and the individuals who populate them have significant reciprocal impacts on each other—what Kuh (2009) calls "the mutual shaping of cultural properties . . . the physical attributes, of a campus, established practices, celebratory events, symbols and symbolic actions, and subcultures" (p. 72). If the environment is affected by the members of the community, that environment will be as diverse as the characteristics of all the individuals in it. Likewise, the collective effects of the environment will touch each member in a way as individualistic as each person's own cultural identity. A number of good models are available to help us assess and understand the influence of environments on their participants. This chapter has used one such model, Strange and Banning's (2001) dimension design, to look at the composition of a typical collegiate environment and how that environment may have an impact on the campus populations. However, the most significant message of this chapter has been that even the best model can probably use some tweaking to make it more sensitive to the nuances of the cultural characteristics of the individuals (and subgroups) that populate the environment. We must pay particular attention to identifying and understanding the cultural differences of the nonmajority people and groups on our campuses to give them the same opportunities as majority member individuals have to gain the benefits of environmental impact.

References

Banning, J. H., & Bartels, S. (1993). A taxonomy for physical artifacts: Understanding campus multiculturalism. *Campus Ecologist, 11*(3), 2–3.

Council of Ontario Universities. (1991). *Women's campus safety audit guide* (Report No. HE 024–970). Toronto, Canada: Ontario Ministry of Colleges and Universities. (ERIC Document Reproduction Service No. ED338129)

Eckman, P. (1985). *Telling lies: Clues to deceit in marketplace, politics, and marriage.* New York: Norton.

Hage, J., & Aiken, M. (1970). *Social change in complex organizations.* New York: Random House.

Holland, J. L. (1973). *Making vocational choices: A theory of careers.* Englewood Cliffs, NJ: Prentice Hall.

Huebner, L. A., & Lawson, J. M. (1990). Understanding and assessing college environments. In D. G. Creamer & Associates (Eds.), *College student development: Theory and practice for the 1990s* (pp. 127–151). Alexandria, VA: American College Personnel Association.

Kaiser, L. R. (1975). Designing campus environments. *NASPA Journal, 13*, 33–39.

Kilgore, D., & Rice, P. J. (2003). *Meeting the special needs of adult students.* San Francisco: Jossey-Bass.

Kuh, G. D. (2009). Understanding campus environments. In G. S. McClellan Stringer & Associates (Eds.), *The handbook of student affairs administration* (3rd ed., pp. 59–80). San Francisco: Jossey-Bass.

Kuh, G. D., & Hall, J. E. (1993). Using cultural perspectives in student affairs. In G. D. Kuh (Ed.), *Cultural perspectives in student affairs work* (pp. 1–20). Lanham, MD: American College Personnel Association.

Kuh, G. D., Kinzie, J., Schuh, J. H., Whitt, E. J., & Associates (2005). *Student success in college: Creating conditions that matter.* San Francisco: Jossey-Bass.

Kuh, G. D., & Whitt, E. J. (1988). *The invisible tapestry: Culture in American colleges and universities.* College Station, TX: Association for the Study of Higher Education.

Lewin, K. (1936). *Principles of topological psychology.* New York: McGraw-Hill.

Longwell-Grice, R., & Longwell-Grice, H. (2003). Chiefs, braves and tomahawks: The use of American Indians as university mascots. *NASPA Journal, 40*(3), 1–12.

Mehrabian, A. (1981). *Silent messages* (2nd ed.). Belmont, CA: Wadsworth.

Moos, R. H. (1979). *Evaluating educational environments.* San Francisco: Jossey-Bass.

Moos, R. H. (1986). *The human context: Environmental determinants of behavior.* Malabar, FL: Krieger.

Moos, R. H., & Gerst, M. (1988). *The university residence environment scale manual* (2nd ed.). Palo Alto, CA: Consulting Psychologists Press.

Rapaport, A. (1982). *The meaning of the built environment.* Thousand Oaks, CA: Sage.

Spitzberg, I. J., Jr., & Thorndike, V. V. (1992). *Creating community on college campuses.* Albany, NY: SUNY Press.

Stern, G. G. (1970). *People in context: Measuring person-environment congruence in education and industry.* New York: Wiley.

Strange, C. C. (1996). Dynamics of campus environments. In S. R. Komives, D. B. Woodard, & Associates (Eds.), *Student services: A handbook for the profession* (3rd ed., pp. 244–268). San Francisco: Jossey-Bass.

Strange, C. C., & Banning, J. H. (2001). *Educating by design: Creating campus learning environments that work.* San Francisco: Jossey-Bass.

Zeisel, J. (1981). *Inquiry by design.* Monterey, CA: Brooks/Cole.

4

MULTICULTURAL IDENTITIES AND SHIFTING SELVES AMONG COLLEGE STUDENTS

Jane Fried

On April 4, 2007, radio broadcaster Don Imus stated that the women on the Rutgers University basketball team who played in the NCAA women's basketball championship looked rough, had tattoos, and described them as "nappy-headed ho's," which led to a national furor. Imus later said he was surprised at the reaction and that too much was read into "some idiot comment meant to be amusing" (Carr, 2007). His statements seemed "to impugn both the physical and moral characteristics of a team composed mostly of Black players" (Carr) and led to career-changing consequences for him. More significantly, his remarks appear to have reflected a profoundly uninformed understanding of the world. Although very few of us will have the opportunity to use the media to denigrate and humiliate a group of individuals, most of us share Imus's apparent belief that we are generally in charge of our own lives, and making disparaging comments about others does not have a direct impact on us. Many of us consider that the context of our lives is less significant than our own individual perceptions. Much more cultural introspection on this topic is necessary before we as a society truly understand how profoundly our sense of self is shaped by culture and context.

Identity: Single, Plural, or Contextual?

American culture has inherited a 19th-century belief in a coherent, consistent sense of self, which is typically referred to as one's identity. Erikson (1968) popularized the notion of identity as "a sense of personal coherence through time and changing role requirements, a sense of one's value and consistent contributions to one's social world" (as cited in Okun, Fried, & Okun, 1999, p. 137–138). Traditional studies of identity formation adopt a unidimensional focus (Croteau, Talbot, Lance, & Evans, 2002) emphasizing ethnic identity formation (Helms, 1994; LaFramboise, Berman, & Sohi, 1994; Vasquez, 1994), homosexual identity (D'Augelli, 1994), or gender identity (Enns, 1991; Josselson, 1987). These models often fail to address either the life experiences of people with multiple sources of identity or the interaction among those sources for a specific person. A great deal of theory has fallen behind because of the complexity of postmodern experience.

The unidimensional paradigm for self or identity is quite unusual when considered from a multicultural perspective and is increasingly out of date from a postmodernist perspective.

> The Western concept of the person as a bounded, unique, more or less integrated motivational and cognitive universe, a dynamic center of awareness, emotion, judgment and action organized into a distinctive whole is . . . a rather peculiar idea within the context of the world's cultures. (Geertz, 1983, p. 126)

Geertz pointed out that every culture has some concept of personality or self, but that most of them construct people as integrated with and responsive to context, including family, role, and work expectations and occasionally gods, goddesses, and the spirits of the departed. Robinson and Howard-Hamilton (2000) described this way of being as the extended self. The Western notion of consistency regardless of context is quite unusual. In short, most other cultures frame the notion of self or identity as a relationship between the person and his or her community, rather than as the existence of the bounded whole Geertz refers to.

The notion of a coherent identity is challenged from another direction—postmodern psychology. Erikson's (1968) original definition of identity as those elements of personality that remain stable and coherent was based in a context that assumes stability of surroundings including parent figures, other adults, peers, and social institutions such as one's school and religious community. The stable environment produces constant, consistent feedback to a child that reinforces the community's ideas about who that child is expected to be, what the child is expected to believe, and how the child is expected to behave. The postmodern critique challenges these assumptions and questions the existence of these processes (Anderson, 1997; Gergen, 1991). Anderson identified four reasons why our world and our sense of self have been challenged in this fashion: population mobility—migration as the norm rather than the exception, people tend not to live near the same people for long periods of time; symbol mobility—symbols are transported from place to place via electronic communications, transforming interpretations across context; cultural pluralism resulting from reasons 1 and 2; cultural change, which is largely a function of the interaction among all the other forms of change that sweep through the modern world.

The consequence of these and other conditions in the United States is the emergence of the saturated self (Gergen, 1991), which is a person who has little to no experience of a coherent center. The person can occupy past and present simultaneously by using an answering machine, a VCR, or viewing movies or television; maintaining friendships widely separated by context because of personal mobility, job mobility, or Internet communication; and maintaining numerous relationships in a single location (home/work/community) that require dramatically different personae. These personae might include the hard-driving business person, the person who moves slowly and tentatively to understand cultural differences in his or her child's day care center without hurting feelings, the father who is the primary caretaker of a small child, the volunteer coordinator who leads by creating consensus, the demanding person whose car hasn't been repaired on time, the patient person who transports cancer patients to medical appointments, and the spouse/parent who becomes efficient and skilled in maintaining relationships in the family because she or he spends so little time there. One person could get psychological whiplash moving from role to role in this fragmented world. It might be asserted that life in the postmodern world has forced westerners into a more global experience of self because context changes so often in our daily lives that we have no choice but to become more responsive to it. Unfortunately, we do not experience our expanded sense of self as a greater unity. Instead, we experience ourselves as increasingly fragmented.

This decentering of the Western ideas about self has been profoundly disorienting. Gergen (1991) coined the term *multiphrenia* to describe the phenomenon. Multiphrenia involves developing an ability to function in multiple contexts that may have mutually exclusive expectations. It also involves feeling off balance when it comes to personal values, frequently feeling inadequate because of one's inability to keep up with a constant flood of new information, and often being unable to articulate the reasons one has for taking a particular action. Anderson (1997) has also identified the *protean self,* quite useful in marriage/divorce counseling, characterized by its willingness to change, going "through many metamorphoses in the course of a life" (p. 41), and the *decentered self,* characterized by its "elusiveness of . . . subjective consciousness" (p. 44). Another way to describe the decentered self is that the person is unable to identify strong values or good reasons for doing something or even to express a personal preference or commitment. "Whatever" is one of the favored words in the decentered vocabulary.

Identity Development: Linear, Circular, or Chaotic Pattern?

Student development literature is filled with theories written from a linear, unidimensional perspective that, when applying the monolithic stages as part of these theories, assume an integrated, single self. Stage theories, which are generally descriptive of cognitive and intellectual development, are characterized by their invariant sequential nature (Evans, Forney, Guido, Patton, & Renn, 2010). These theories focus on the ways people think, not on the subjects they think about (Evans et al.), and emphasize the progress people make toward increasingly complex ways of understanding the world. The Epistemological Reflection Model (Baxter Magolda, 2009) describes the ways college students think about a range of issues in their lives with a specific emphasis on gender differences where they exist. The Reflective Judgment Model (King & Kitchener, 1994) emphasizes the patterns students use to organize and evaluate information and to justify decisions they make. The focus of students' thought processes is intentionally wide ranging so that the patterns of thought can be inferred and described. The generic description of process supersedes the idiosyncratic content. This approach is generally positivist (Lincoln & Guba, 1985) and similar in method and epistemology to most empirical research. The goal of this research is to describe a process that can subsequently be used to understand the development of other individuals across time and context. The greater complexity a person exhibits in managing information, developing constructs, and making judgments the higher the level of development. Higher is privileged over lower in this situation. Organizing principles and deeply held beliefs become clearer to each person as he or she moves up the hierarchy.

Theories of ethnic identity formation have generally followed the pattern used in theories of cognitive development. Once again, these theories use the content of a person's thought, whether it is the nature of ethnic identity, sexual orientation, or gender, to describe a stage model of development. Because all these sources of identity formation are, to a certain degree, the product of a particular context, the development process is far more complex than the theories imply. One can only develop into an African American or an Asian American in the United States. The history of these ethnic groups, and others, must be understood in the context of U.S. history as well as the current status of race/power relations in the culture (Takaki, 1993).

The Minority Identity Development Model (Atkinson, Morten, & Sue, 1998) is perhaps the most abstract ethnic identity formation model because it presumes a certain amount of uniformity among nondominant, or minority, groups in the ways members of each group react to their minority status in the dominant culture of the United States (see Table 4.1). Although the details of each group's historical experience, frame of reference, and salient characteristics are discussed, the major focus is generic. The reader is presumed to be a counselor from the dominant culture who is trying to help a client from one of the nondominant cultures progress through the stages described in the theory. Progress is more or less linear, and the process is more or less uniform, although timing may vary. Although context shapes the experience of ethnic or minority identity within U.S. culture, positivist assumptions of linearity and uniformity shape the theory. Levels of acculturation, interaction of gender and ethnicity, class, and individual phenomenology are not discussed. Used as a single framework for understanding minority identity formation without considering these mitigating factors that can affect the way an individual's identity development unfolds, this model can become harmful rather than helpful in a counseling context where the empowerment of a particular individual is the focus.

At least two models bring more complexity to understanding the interaction between individual phenomenology and group context. Ho (1995) developed a concept that mitigates potential harm by using a unidimensional model of development with specific individuals. He suggested examining the external culture the person operates in as well as the culture the person has internalized. He defined *internalized culture* as "the cultural influences operating within the individual that shape (not determine) the personality formation and various aspects of psychological functioning" (p. 5). Ho suggests the use of at least two lenses when attempting to understand and assist a person who identifies with a culture that is different from the one the counselor is identified with. In a comparable model, Leong (1996) used three lenses to explore cross-cultural interaction more completely. He identified the individual perspective, the group perspective, and the universal perspective as three components of any counseling relationship. At any given time,

TABLE 4.1
Summary of Minority Identity Development Model

Stages of Minority Development Model	Attitude Toward Self	Attitude Toward Others of the Same Minority	Attitude Toward Others of Different Minority	Attitude Toward Dominant Group
Stage 1 Conformity	Self-depreciating	Group depreciating	Discriminatory	Group appreciating
Stage 2 Dissonance	Conflict between self-depreciating and appreciating	Conflict between group depreciating and group appreciating	Conflict between dominant-held views of minority hierarchy and feelings of shared experience	Conflict between group appreciating and group depreciating
Stage 3 Resistance and Immersion	Self-appreciating	Group appreciating	Conflict between feelings of empathy for other minority experiences and feelings of culturocentrism	Group depreciating
Stage 4 Introspection	Concern with basis of self-appreciation	Concern with nature of unequivocal appreciation	Concern with ethnocentric basis for judging others	Concern with basis of group depreciation
Stage 5 Synergetic Articulation and Awareness	Self-appreciating	Group appreciating	Group appreciating	Selective appreciation

Note. From *Counseling American Minorities* (5th ed.), by D. R. Atkinson, G. Morten, and D. W. Sue, 1998, p. 35. Boston: McGraw Hill. Copyright by McGraw-Hill Companies, Inc. Adapted with permission of the author.

he believed that each member of the dyad is interpreting the conversation through one of these lenses. It is the counselor's role to identify his or her perspective in use and the perspective the client is using at the time. Understanding each of these perspectives enables the counselor to respond from a perspective that the client will find helpful and will simultaneously help the client untangle the multiple ways the person sees the world. This approach is particularly helpful when dealing with issues of acculturation or multiple sources of identity, as in the case of biracial or bisexual people or people whose parents come from different ethnic groups.

The next iteration of identity theories becomes more complex. In addition to personal characteristics and group behaviors and values, a person's status as privileged or oppressed in a particular context is taken into account. Referring to "taken-for-granted dimensions of identity," Susan Jones asks how privilege and oppression mediate one's sense of identity in specific settings (S. Jones, personal communication, March 14, 2007).

Abes, Jones, and McEwen (2007) described a model of identity that is fluid and tripartite. The inner core is composed of personal attributes, characteristics, and a sense of identity. Moving around the core are the various identity groups that shape a person's perspective, somewhat similar to Ho's (1995) description of internalized culture. Surrounding the moving middle section is the chaotic context of a person's life in all its complexity, including "family background, sociocultural conditions, current experiences and career decisions and life planning." All three levels interact in a highly fluid manner, although one might assume that the inner core changes the slowest. Issues of privilege and oppression emerge at the boundary between context and identity group, depending on the salience of the particular group in a specific context. In Jones's terms, each context evokes particular taken-for-granted dimensions of identity, those which grant the person privilege (Abes, Jones, & McEwen). As context changes, the dimensions of identity taken for granted also change. Because of the complexity of these interactions, patterns are difficult to discern in the short term.

For example, the most generically taken-for-granted identity in the United States is the White male heterosexual Christian able-bodied person. A person who possesses all those attributes in American culture represents the norm. Following closely behind is a female with similar characteristics. Our male will often not think of himself as being ethnic or possessing ethnic status. He doesn't think of American culture as ethnic. He thinks of it as the norm, the standard by which all ethnic groups are judged. He may be prone to asserting that everything he has, he has earned by his own efforts. He seems largely unaware that the entire culture is set up with his particular set of characteristics as the norm and that others who deviate have to find ways to compensate for their differences in this culture. Some differences are more significant than others. Seeing flesh-toned Band-Aids in the store that are a closer match to White skin than brown skin may be aggravating to people of color, but Band-Aids are not a particularly significant source of oppression. Being profiled as a potential threat if you drive in a White neighborhood and are a person of color or being harassed by department store security officers and followed around when you shop is quite oppressive. Most White people are not aware that these practices exist. Most people of color have no choice but to be aware. Their lives literally might depend on their awareness. When a White male (assuming he is not dressed as a member of a targeted group, wearing multiple piercings and tattoos for example) goes shopping, that is all he's doing, shopping. When an African American male goes shopping, he's watching his back, his hands, and his family if they are with him. Is one of these situations more oppressive than the other? When a White male has a job interview, his job skills and personal demeanor are the major items under consideration. When a Puerto Rican or Mexican female goes for a job interview, she is scrutinized for her childbearing practices, her family relationships, her language competence and accent, and her nonverbal behavior as well as her job-related skills. An unmentioned factor in her interview is the comfort level of the person conducting the interview who may or may not realize that the interviewer's discomfort is a personal reaction, not a legitimate judgment about the skills of the applicant. In the context of the dominant American culture, the taken-for-granted status is White, and others have to work harder to prove themselves competent.

If we change context, salience changes as well. If our White job applicant applies for a job with the Boys' Choir of Harlem, he will probably be scrutinized for his racial attitudes and his comfort in an all-Black environment as well as his management skills. If our Puerto Rican female applies to be a manager in a company that does a lot of business in Latin America or with the Puerto Rican population in her city, her bilingual skills will become far more important and her childbearing practices far less so. Gender matters less in a balanced male/female environment than it does if the new hire is the first woman, or the first man, to be placed in the situation. This author applied for a position as the first dean of women at an engineering college that had decided to go co-ed in the late 1960s. The major topic of conversation during the interview was bathroom facilities, not a core issue that a dean of anything normally spends a lot of time on. I still wonder if every applicant had the same conversation or if the interviewers couldn't think of anything else to discuss with females. When all the toilets are urinals, it's not hard to figure out what the taken-for-granted identity is in that context. What condition is more oppressive than not being able to find a bathroom? Ask any African American who lived in the segregated South. Which job applicant is going to be more secure in self-presentation during the interview—the one with taken-for-granted identity or the one who has to prove that his or her identity is just as good?

The New Science and Identity/Context Interaction

A foolish consistency is the hobgoblin of small minds.

—Attributed to Ralph Waldo Emerson

We have reviewed unidimensional, sequential stage theories of development and multidimensional theories of identity presentation. Each set of theories has its strengths and its limitations. It may be that we can no longer separate our theories of identity from our theories of cognition because the interaction between the ways we think about self and the content of the self we think about are inseparable. Distinctions made for the purpose of conducting research generally cannot be found in the real world of application. In our current global context, we need to move to a new "order of consciousness" (Kegan, 1994) in which we think about our multiple sources of identity and the systems that govern interaction among those sources in any given context. It is no accident that Kegan presented his theory in a book titled *In Over Our Heads*. This is an incredibly complex undertaking.

The next level of insight into multicultural, multidimensional identity may come from the concept of self-organizing systems. All living systems are self-organizing, which means that living systems are open to the environments where they exist. When confronted with new and disruptive information in their environment, they reorganize themselves adaptively and do not remain rigid (Wheatley, 1999). Through a process of self-reference, each system simultaneously changes in response to new information and remains true to its internally consistent self-concept. "A living system changes in order to preserve itself" (Wheatley, p. 85) but remains stable over time. The hypothetical issues that a person is always addressing are, Who am I here and now? What is happening in this environment? and How do I want to engage with these events in order to be simultaneously responsive and stable? Wheatley posed a paradox that the self is stable and fluid simultaneously. The system retains a sense of identity or integrity while fully engaged in dialogue with the environment so that self and environment coevolve "toward better fitness for each other" (p. 88). In North American culture in ages past, this process might be considered as not knowing who you are. In postmodern culture this is the protean self on steroids with whiplash.

Kegan's (1994) notion of orders of consciousness provided insight into the way this process functions. People who use the fourth order, "cross-categorical constructing" (Love & Guthrie, 1999, p. 68), experience themselves, subjectively, as playing multiple roles in life and constructing, or authoring, a sense of self that integrates multiple perspectives and roles. "Individuals who think in the fourth order develop the capacity to stand outside their values and form a deeper internal set of convictions that form a context for and regulate their behavior" (Love & Guthrie, 1999, p. 72). This internal set of convictions can be considered to form a fluid identity that is able to reflect on new information and evolve as a self-referencing system. Fourth order thinking enables people to construct, reflect on, and compare values and determine which values are most appropriate to rely on in a particular context. The person believes his or her internal process for judging provides the compass or gyroscope of identity. Identity becomes an ability to respond with some sense of consistency via process rather than consistency via content. These process structures are used by self-organizing systems as they determine what best supports their ability to thrive in a particular environment. Once again, we see the paradox of stability and fluidity coexisting as self and environment interact. "Stability comes from a deepening center, a clarity about who it is, what it needs, what is required to survive in its environment" (Wheatley, 1999, p. 83). Fluidity comes from constant evaluation of new information flowing through the system.

From Psychology to Philosophy to Physics: The Wave/Particle/Poetic Self?

Now we must ask ourselves about the capacity for self-reflection and self-authorship. Wheatley (1999) asserts that the stability of the self comes from a clarity about who it is. We must begin to ask who is watching and who is being watched? This subject/object dichotomy is one of the oldest problems in Western philosophy, which has been profoundly shaped by an either/or approach. This thought process appears in the culture as dualism, the law of the excluded middle that shapes scientific research and, in its earliest form, Aristotle's principle that something cannot be both A and not A simultaneously. So pervasive is our dualistic thought process that we do not think about it as a constructed way of interpreting our world. We think of this approach to understanding as normal, just as we consider our White male person normal. The new science is telling us that if we want to have a sense of identity based on an accurate understanding of the ways living systems thrive and evolve, we need new data, new thought processes, and a new sense of the mutuality that exists between people and their environment. We need to move toward Kegan's fifth order of consciousness in which individuals hold suspect their sense of their own and each other's wholeness; they reject false assumptions of distinctness or completeness. The self-as-system is seen as incomplete—only a partial construction of all that the self is. It is the process of creating self through relationships that is imperative. (Love & Guthrie, 1999, p. 73)

We have now moved away from psychology and back toward its parent discipline, philosophy.

One way to describe this new way of thinking about the evolution of self is through a process known as *transformative teleology* (Stacey, 2001), which is "movement toward a future that is under perpetual construction by the movement itself. There is no mature or final state, only perpetual iteration of identity and difference, continuity and transformation, the known and the unknown at the same time. The future is unknowable but yet recognizable, the known-unknown" (p. 60). In transformative teleology either/or thinking is ineffective. A is both A and not A simultaneously. Self evolves through time and space, which become dimensions of life experience. Further, the split between the individual and the communal also disappears in an iterative rhythm of evolution. "Human subjects and social institutions are jointly constituted through recurrent practices. The properties of the individual mind and of social practices do not exist outside action, but are constituted in it" (p. 61). If a tree falls in the forest and no one is there to hear it, does it make a sound? Can a sound occur without an instrument that registers vibration, such as an ear drum? There is no noise in a vacuum because there is no medium to carry sound waves. Is there a process of being, often known as an individual, outside context, in the absence of a knower? If you were born into a different family, in a different time, place, and culture, would you be a different person?

In considering these questions about how we think about the self or identity we are suddenly in a realm that has been deeply explored by Buddhists, using notions of "interbeing" and "mutual co-arising" (Hanh, 1987). In considering these concepts, logic diminishes in importance and storytelling and metaphor that leads to intuitive understanding become far more important. Thich Nhat Hanh asks his students to find a cloud in a piece of paper. He then tells the whole story of how paper is created, beginning with the clouds that yield the rain that waters the tree that is turned into pulp that becomes paper. With deep seeing, we can find the cloud. Can we find the top of our hand without also finding the bottom? Holding a stick in front of us, can we experience the left end of the stick without the right end?

If we want to have a stick with only a left end, and we break off the right end, what do we have? The point is that left and right require each other in order to have any meaning. Top requires bottom. Good requires evil. Individual requires group. Each without the other is incomprehensible and meaningless. Life acquires meaning in comparison and contrast moving in rhythmic relationship to each other.

A closer-to-home experience for Western readers might be to remember what a propeller on an airplane looks like as it is starting up. First the unmoving individual blades are perceived. Then they begin to revolve slowly and can still be perceived as the speed accelerates. Finally the blades appear to become a transparent circle as acceleration continues, and ultimately the propeller becomes almost invisible and the plane takes off. If we could still perceive single blades, the plane would not fly. Form has not changed, but perception and function have. Things are the same and different simultaneously. A propeller at rest is not the same as a propeller functioning to pull a plane through the air. Yet it is—but not exactly. Dimensions of its functioning have changed. Its context has certainly changed. This perception is simultaneously a unified experience and a mental paradox. If we try to take the experience apart, it becomes quite confusing. If we simply experience it, things work as they should. Teleologically, our expectation is that the plane will fly. That is its purpose. Conceptually, we do not generally think about solid objects changing form before our eyes.

The interpenetration of subject and object, person and context, observer and observed has been discussed in many disciplines. Using the framework of physics, David Bohm (1998) described the activity of the mind in comparing what is known to what is experienced and looking for a deeper order in which experience relates harmoniously to previous knowledge. This is Bohm's definition of learning. He stated that "self-sustaining confusion occurs when the mind is trying to escape the awareness of conflict. . . . in which one's deep intention is really to avoid perceiving the fact" (p. x). The result of such avoidance is increasing fragmentation in personal and cultural belief systems. A great deal of our difficulty in understanding and appreciating cultural differences in worldview, values, and behavior patterns reflects the efforts of those of us who are trained in either/or thinking to avoid perceiving the disturbing facts of cultural/personal interpenetration and evolution over time. Our categories are not broad enough to explain, and bring coherence to, the complexity of cultural evolution that we are experiencing. Bohm suggested that we create new structures of ideas in order to increase our understanding of complexity. We get into trouble as individuals and as a culture when new data are perceived but not integrated because integration of the new into the previously held belief system would be disruptive to our beliefs. He observed, "As new knowledge and institutional structures accumulate, they tend to become ever more rigidly fixed. Eventually it seems as if the whole of our society and the security of each individual would be endangered if these structures were to be seriously questioned or changed" (Bohm & Peat, 1987, p. 208).

Freire (1968/1990) framed the issue somewhat differently but is fundamentally describing the same process. He talks about the need for encounter, dialogue, and *naming the world*. "Men [*sic*] are not built in silence, but in word, in work, in action-reflection" (p. 76). Freire's term for creating structures of thought, naming the world, means the world is named in dialogue among people who are making meaning in their world, establishing categories of thought that enable them to engage as full human beings, equal in value and different in perspective. The purpose of Freirean dialogue is to establish respectful relationships among committed people to enhance freedom for all. People learn from each other, and in learning together they create a world of freedom, respect, and possibility. They establish meaning and a sense of self together for all to be included in the evolution of a just society. Freire is describing the active practice of transformative teleology by another name. His emphasis on freedom implied disorder to some, but from another perspective (Wheatley, 1999), the greater the freedom, the greater the order. This phenomenon constitutes another paradox in which A is both A and not A simultaneously.

> This is, for some, the most illuminating paradox of all. The two forces that we have placed in opposition to one another—freedom and order—turn out to be partners in generating healthy, well-ordered systems. Effective self-organization is supported by two critical elements: a clear sense of identity and freedom. (Wheatley, p. 87)

That clear sense of identity must be further explored so that we understand how identity works with community rather than against it in a changing world.

This chapter points out that Buddhist scholars have offered a great deal of insight into this person/context interaction that can be so confusing for Westerners. From a Buddhist frame of reference, the entire universe is an integrated process. Change is the only constant. Stability is considered an illusion, and clinging is a cause of suffering. Individuals are aspects of this system and have individual perspectives, but they are not separate from it. Individuals emerge from the cosmos and return to it, carrying with them an evolving perspective over lifetimes. Alan Watts (1972) described this relationship of individual to universe poetically when he wrote, "As the ocean waves, the universe peoples" (p. 8). This metaphor makes intuitive sense. The ocean is simultaneously constant and changing. It is always water. The water contains multitudes of substances, many of which we consider living. Waves are not separate, but they emerge from the surface and return to it. Waves are visible, can be described in height, length, direction, and duration. Nevertheless, they never lose their embeddedness, their oceanic essence. From a Buddhist perspective, this metaphor describes life.

The closest that a Western scientist has come to describing the Buddhist idea of self is the quantum self, articulated and developed by Danah Zohar (1990). She discussed a wave/particle phenomenon in which self has content sometimes (comparable to particles) and is process at other times (comparable to waves), Self is in constant fluctuation in response to context over time. Self consists of what she calls "overlapping wave functions" (p. 120) that evoke ripples on some fundamental integrity or energy that is metaphorically similar to the ocean. "Thus each self that I was, moment by moment, is taken up into the next moment and wedded to all that is to come—wedded both to old memories . . . as these are fed back into the condensate (i.e., energy) and to new experiences" (p. 120). The self can be considered a process that is "composed over time from all the lived states which get etched on character" (p. 121) where the etching is constantly responsive to new information. Self can be considered a vibration of memories on the templates of time, space, and character.

In Buddhism, the closest experience to a constant is memory, but memory is problematic because it interferes with accurate perception. Bohm (1998) noted that memory can constitute imposing a tacit, and inaccurate, structure of ideas on an experience, interfering with accurate perception and destroying freshness. The Buddhist belief in living in the moment can be considered comparable to not imposing preconceived ideas on experience. If Buddhism offers its adherents any sense of security or stability it is to be found in the consciousness of eternal change, the ebb and flow, and the belief in allness—the totality of experience, which makes us all connected, from which we emerge and to which we return.

A New Paradigm for Multicultural Understanding

With this insight, let us return to the issue of identity/self and multiculturalism. As long as a person thinks that the self, or identity, is a constant, there will be boundaries that must be negotiated and value judgments about separate selves and cultural differences. As long as we think of ourselves as separate from each other, we will be competing for advantage in a shrinking world. One need go no further than the conflicts over affirmative action in admissions and hiring to find this phenomenon. When the number of slots in an entering class is finite, and each potential student is in competition with all other qualified students, fairness and equality of opportunity become a contested boundary. If getting in is the paramount goal, the people who set the standards for evaluating applicants are the power brokers. Power to shape the categories of evaluation becomes the elephant in the living room, the unquestioned set of criteria by which opportunity is allocated. Categories that give an advantage to one group and not to another in a finite universe become contested issues. If an unexamined concept of "normal" governs the conversation, affirmative action in any context will continue to be a problem. Another way to conduct this process would be to bring the assumptions about qualifications to the table and to conduct a dialogue about the purposes of the particular college. Who does this institution want to be at this time in history? How do our admissions criteria reflect our purpose? Is the purpose we have lived with for so many years still relevant? In the words of the *Servant Leadership* (Greenleaf, 1977) literature, what are we trying to do here? Does our old paradigm still work? There may still be a limited number of spaces in the entering class, but the criteria for selection will be open, relevant to the mission of the institution and the people who made the decision will be visible. Furthermore, is the institution being a good steward to the students, faculty, administrators, staff, and those in the community who rely on the ingenuity of scholars maintaining the integrity of the mission yet capturing the progressive movement of change in our society?

A new paradigm develops while the old paradigm is still working (Burkan, 1990). The new paradigm is experienced as disruptive of the normal ways of doing things, unnecessary, and confusing. Our old ways of thinking about culture, delivering services to students and so forth are still working, with greater or lesser adequacy depending on the institution and the student body. If we were to change our ideas about how to think about people, their sense of self, their ethnicity, sexual orientation, gender, and so forth, it would be quite confusing and would challenge all our methods of working. Nevertheless, we need to change our way of thinking in order to get out of some insoluble problems that are a product of the old paradigm of separate categories and rigidly defined groups. When people refuse to check one box for ethnic status on the federal census, as a nation we need to develop some new ways of keeping track of things that are important to us, using new categories that accurately reflect current experience.

Current experience tells us that this generation of students is the most multicultural in history. The boomer parents married or had children with people who were different from themselves in many ways including race. People migrate, marry each other, and have children who refuse to choose between one side of the family and the other. The significance of race has diminished somewhat in understanding differences between people and their life experience. Class has become more important to some observers (Cose, 1993; Wilson, 1996), although there does not seem to be a clear consensus about this issue. The relative oppressions of race and class may well vary from place to place within American society. We eat fusion cuisine, dishes that represent the integration of cultures. We listen to fusion music. We have become fusion people whether we belong to the elite who travel or the less privileged who watch television and stay in one place. What has apparently not fused is the difference in power reflected in class. The gap between the haves and the have-nots is getting wider. Yet, in the American culture, identifying class differences of opportunity seems to be the last great taboo.

Paradigms are not invented from the whole cloth. They evolve when people reflect on lived experience and find new patterns of explanation emerging that explain more than the old explanations could account for. The new paradigm for multicultural understanding will be a vision that reflects the wave/particle paradox, person/environment interaction, the spaces between the blades of a propeller, the time when the space is "there" and when it is not. An understanding of culture as concept and lived experience provides us with a very useful way to understand new people when they appear in our world. But culture, like self, is a process, constantly changing. People, especially students, move between cultures constantly, and the cultures themselves evolve self-referentially over time. People eat rice all over the world, but they prepare it differently, use different sauces, and eat it differently in different settings, on the floor or around a table, from one bowl or many. In Montana, people eat pastrami on white bread with mayonnaise, a phenomenon a New York Jew may find absolutely astonishing. Nevertheless, if the New Yorker could actually taste it, he or she might find this approach to pastrami not distasteful, as long as he or she did not compare it to what it was expected to taste like. Once at a Buddhist retreat, the author drank tea with salt prepared by the teachers to help us get over our preconceived ideas. Drinking tea with salt was a new experience. Try as she might to compare it to something familiar, she could not find anything and was forced into the unnamed place where sense data had to be experienced directly without mediating language. All of our categories are constructed in language. There was a time before these categories existed and probably will be a time after which they will not. Categories and descriptions should not be reified, made into rigid things. They need to be held lightly, as hypotheses about relationships that might be helpful in meeting an unfamiliar person. But our ideas about culture must also be fluid—or they will get in the way of understanding. If the world is composed of relationships, as Wheatley (1999) has suggested, then we need to envision a new paradigm that flows between people and events, connecting them, identifying them, and reconnecting them in a context that is broader than any of us can currently imagine. We can no longer put people in boxes or trap cultures in time and space. We need to learn to experience the flow of content and process as people move, symbols change meaning, and people evolve self-referentially in our connected worlds.

Chaos theory tells us that new paradigms evolve slowly and only become apparent over long periods of time. In this age of instant communication, we expect these processes to become visible immediately and a new website that explains everything to appear a week after the change was noticed. We need to strive in our work and personal lives to look at cultural identity from multiple lenses, and when we talk about shifting paradigms in culture, we need to wait, to think, to observe, and to watch the flow of people and events.

References

Abes, E. S., Jones, S. R., & McEwen, M. K. (2007). Reconceptualizing the model of multiple dimensions of identity: The role of meaning-making capacity in the construction of multiple identities. *Journal of College Student Development, 48*(1), 1–22.

Anderson, W. (1997). *The future of the self.* New York: Tarcher/Putnam.

Atkinson, D., Morten, G., & Sue, D. (1998). *Counseling American minorities* (5th ed.). Madison, WI: McGraw-Hill.

Baxter Magolda, M. B. (2009). *Authoring your life: Developing an internal voice to navigate life's challenges.* Sterling, VA: Stylus.

Bohm, D. (1998). *On creativity.* New York: Routledge.

Bohm, D., & Peat, D. (1987). *Science, order and creativity.* New York: Bantam.

Burkan, W. (1990). *Paradigm summary notes.* Farmington Hills, MI: Alternative Visions.

Carr, D. (2007, April 7). Networks condemn remarks by Imus. *The New York Times.* Retrieved from http://www.nytimes.com/2007/04/07/arts/television/07imus.html?_r=1&hp

Cose, E. (1993). *The rage of a privileged class.* New York: HarperCollins.

Croteau, J., Talbot, D., Lance, T., & Evans, N. (2002). A qualitative study of the interplay between privilege and oppression. *Journal of Multicultural Counseling and Development, 30*(4), 239–258.

D'Augelli, A. (1994). Identity development and sexual orientation: Toward a model of lesbian, gay and bisexual development. In E. J. Trickett, R. Watts, & D. Birman (Eds.), *Human diversity: Perspectives on people in context* (pp. 312–333). San Francisco: Jossey-Bass.

Enns, C. (1991). The new relationship models of women's identity: A review and critique for counselors. *Journal of Counseling and Development, 69,* 209–217.

Erikson, E. (1968). *Identity: Youth and crisis.* New York : Norton.

Evans, N., Forney, D., Guido, F., Patton, L., & Renn, K. (2010). *Student development in college: Theory, research, and practice* (2nd ed.). San Francisco: Jossey-Bass.

Freire, P. (1990). *Pedagogy of the oppressed* (M. B. Ramos, Trans.). New York: Continuum. (Original work published 1968)

Geertz, C. (1983). *Local knowledge: Further essays in interpretive anthropology.* New York: Basic.

Gergen, K. (1991). *The saturated self.* New York: Basic.

Greenleaf, R. (1977). *Servant leadership.* New York: Paulist Press.

Hanh, T. (1987). *Interbeing.* Berkeley, CA: Parallax.

Helms, J. (1994). The conceptualization of racial identity and other "racial" constructs. In J. Trickett, R. Watts, & D. Birman (Eds.), *Human diversity: Perspectives on people in context* (pp. 285–311). San Francisco: Jossey-Bass.

Ho, D. (1995). Internalized culture, culturocentrism and transcendence. *The Counseling Psychologist, 23*(1), 4–24.

Josselson, R. (1987). *Finding herself: Pathways to identity development in women.* San Francisco: Jossey-Bass.

Kegan, R. (1994). *In over our heads: The mental demands of modern life.* Cambridge, MA: Harvard University Press.

King, P., & Kitchener, K. (1994). *Developing reflective judgment: Understanding and promoting intellectual growth and critical thinking in adolescents and adults.* San Francisco: Jossey-Bass.

LaFramboise, T., Berman, J., & Sohi, B. (1994). American Indian women. In L. Comas Días & B. Greene (Eds.), *Women of color* (pp. 30–71). New York: Guilford Press.

Leong, F. (1996). Toward an integrative model for cross-cultural counseling and psychotherapy. *Applied and Preventative Psychology, 5*(4), 189–209.

Lincoln, Y., & Guba, E. (1985). *Naturalistic inquiry.* Newbury Park, CA: Sage.

Love, P., & Guthrie, V. (1999). *Understanding and applying cognitive development theory*. San Francisco: Jossey-Bass.

Okun, B., Fried, J., & Okun, M. (1999). *Understanding diversity*. Pacific Grove, CA: Brooks/Cole/ITP.

Robinson, T., & Howard-Hamilton, M. (2000). *The convergence of race, ethnicity and gender*. Upper Saddle River, NJ: Prentice Hall.

Stacey, R. (2001). *Complex responsive processes in organizations: Learning and knowledge creation*. New York: Routledge.

Takaki, R. (1993). *A different mirror: A history of multicultural America*. Boston: Little, Brown.

Vasquez, M. (1994). Latinas. In L. Comas Días & B. Greene (Eds.), *Women of color* (pp. 114–138). New York: Guilford Press.

Watts, A. (1972). *The book: On the taboo against knowing who you are*. New York: Random House.

Wheatley, M. (1999). *Leadership and the new science* (2nd ed.) San Francisco: Berrett-Koehler.

Wilson, J. (1996). *When work disappears*. New York: Knopf.

Zohar, D. (1990). *The quantum self*. New York: Quill/William Morrow.

SECTION TWO

INFORMATION ON CULTURAL POPULATIONS

5

LATINO/LATINA COLLEGE STUDENTS

Anna M. Ortiz and Susana Hernandez

Colleges and universities in many settings are already experiencing an influx of Latinos/Latinas in their student populations. The impact of the Latino/Latina infusion into higher education will only grow and become more widespread. By 2050 Latinos/Latinas will be responsible for 60% of the nation's population growth. Latinos will move from being 14% of the population today to 29% in 2050 making them the largest minority group in the United States (Passel & Cohn, 2008). Depending on a number of individual characteristics (e.g., time of immigration, precollege educational environments, extended family units, family history with higher education) these students may require paradigm shifts in the way higher education professionals have structured campus programs, written educational policy, and executed individual work with students in and out of the classroom. This chapter explores the experiences of Latinos/Latinas in higher education and seeks to shape a picture of their participation that is most representative of the diversity of the group and of the higher education institutions they inhabit. After a review of Latinos/Latinas in the United States, the chapter considers the sociological context that Latinos/Latinas inhabit and then moves into a discussion of student experiences in higher education. Particular attention is paid to the role of the family in higher education, the experience of Latinos/Latinas in community colleges, and campus climate issues that impede and promote the success of Latino/Latina students. The chapter concludes with an overview of select programs and interventions that have proven successful for Latino/Latina students.

The panethnic term Latino/Latina is used throughout this chapter to refer to men and women whose ethnic origins are found in Central American, Caribbean, and South American countries (Spring, 2010). More discrete terms may be used, when appropriate to refer to specific groups, such as Chicano/a or Mexican American, Cuban, Puerto Rican, and so on. Individuals from these groups often use several labels to identify themselves depending on the immediate context. A person can be comfortable using a specific label, such as Dominican, and the panethnic Latino/Latina. Mexican Americans who take a more politicized view of their ethnicity would likely use Chicano/Chicana as their ethnic label. While most Latinos/Latinas reject the term *Hispanic* as a word constructed by government bureaucrats, some embrace that term especially if they see themselves as genealogically closer to Spain. In the 2000 census, 7% of all people of Hispanic or Latino descent used Hispanic as their ethnic label. Interestingly, in New Mexico one third of all Latinos/Latinas used this label.

Brief History of Latinos/Latinas in the United States

Each Latino ethnic group has a unique history in the United States. Mexican Americans, the largest of the ethnic groups (58.5% of all Latinos/Latinas; Guzman, 2001), were first incorporated into the United States when northern Mexico was annexed by the United States through the Treaty of Guadalupe Hidalgo in 1848 (Spring, 2010). While the treaty transferred governance of the southwest to the U.S. government, it allowed Mexican citizens to retain their land and choose whether to become U.S. citizens. However, shortly after annexation, laws were established to block U.S. and dual citizenship. A series of laws and common practices served to dispossess Mexicans of their lands, transferring large parcels in Texas, New Mexico, Arizona, and California to pioneer hands. The history of Mexicans in the United States during the 20th century was one of welcome immigration when a ready, inexpensive labor force was necessary and then deported once the labor was no longer needed. For example, prior to the Depression of the 1930s, trains of Mexicans were brought into the United States to fill the demand for labor after immigration laws restricted entry of Asian groups that had been a primary source of labor. However, the shortage of jobs during the Depression, resulted in the expatriation of thousands of Mexicans. Less than 10 years later, the labor needs of World War II again required the mass migration of Mexican laborers who were allowed to work legally through the

Bracero Program (Portes & Bach, 1985), which facilitated the importation of Mexican immigrant workers to the United States as temporary contract laborers. Labor needs and inconsistent immigration policies created a pattern of cyclical migration where many Mexicans come north to work and return to Mexico in the off season. This sojourn pattern is of course a generalization because so many Mexicans have taken up residence they are now a substantial presence in the Southwest. Mexican Americans make up 76% of the total Latino/Latina population in Texas, 77% in California, 82% in Arizona, and 43% in New Mexico (Guzman, 2001). The numbers in Texas and New Mexico are actually higher as many Latinos/Latinas of Mexican origin prefer the term Hispanic rather than Mexican American or Latino/Latinas in these states. Thus, the total of Latino/Latinas of Mexican origin may be as high as 75% in New Mexico and 88% in Texas.

The second most populous Latino/Latina group in the United States are Puerto Ricans (9.9% of all Latinos/Latinas; Guzman, 2001). Of course, Puerto Ricans cannot be considered immigrants since they are U.S. citizens. Puerto Rico became a U.S. territory after the Spanish-American War of 1898. Unlike the Philippines, which also became a U.S. territory at the time, Puerto Rico has not achieved independent status as a nation or state. The migration of Puerto Ricans to the mainland has primarily been attributed to the industrialization of the agricultural economy in Puerto Rico in the early part of the 20th century. Large agribusiness firms acquired sugar plantations and mechanized much of the production, eliminating many of the jobs that had been held by whole towns of rural people. No longer able to make a living through agriculture many Puerto Ricans migrated to cities in the American Northeast to work in the industrial and service sectors. In New York State, 39.5% of all Latinos/Latinas are of Puerto Rican origin (Guzman, 2001).

Cubans are the third largest Latino/Latina ethnic group, making up 3.5% of all Latinos/Latinas (Guzman, 2001). Nearly one third of all Latinos/Latinas in Florida are Cuban. The history of Cubans in the United States is long and complex. Contrary to popular belief, they did not begin their migration to the United States as a result of Fidel Castro's takeover of Cuba in the late 1950s. Rather, patterns of sojourning from Cuba to the United States and back began at the time of the Spanish-American War. It was quite common for Cuban politicians to regroup in Florida after a change in leadership. Cuba's elite and middle class also saw Florida as a vacation destination; these segments of the Cuban population were quite comfortable in the Miami area. After Castro took control in 1958 many of the Cuban political and economic elite traveled north for what would eventually become a permanent stay, although many Cubans maintain the belief that they will return to their homeland after the Castro government is no longer in power (Portes & Stepick, 1993). Cubans from other socioeconomic classes followed the upper-class refugees, culminating in the highly controversial Mariel emigration of the 1980s. This last mass migration was made up of Cubans from the working class (and lower) who were more racially mixed than previous immigrants. Unlike refugees from other Latin countries, Cubans have consistently received political asylum in the United States. Despite government programs seeking to relocate Cuban refugees, Miami remains home to the largest Cuban population outside the island itself (Portes & Stepick).

Other significant groups of Latin immigrants have come to the United States in the past 25 years because of political unrest in their home countries. Nicaraguans, political refugees from the Contra-backed war of the Reagan administration, have primarily settled in Miami. Guatemalans and Salvadorians have mainly settled in California. Colombians are the third largest Latino ethnic group in Florida. Dominicans are the second largest Latino ethnic group in New York. Most have come to the United States as political refugees, all experiencing the same economic, cultural, and language barriers faced by the immigrants before them. However, for these later Spanish-speaking immigrant groups, the established ethnic enclaves in the Southwest, New York, and Miami have served as a sociocultural welcome wagon to ease their transition to the United States.

Sociological Context

Given the diversity of the Latino/Latina group, generalizations about its sociological context can be precarious. Nonetheless, a number of common factors influence the context in which Latinos/Latinas find themselves. A primary factor, as with other non-White ethnic groups, is income, with 23.2% of all Latino/Latina families living below the poverty line (DeNavas-Walt, Proctor, & Smith, 2009). While this number is nearly 10% more than the national rate, it does reflect the lowest poverty rates for Latinos since 1973. For many Latino families poverty is related to the immigrant experience, with successive generations achieving higher socioeconomic levels. Therefore, generational status influences other sociological factors related to Latinos, such as educational attainment, familial influence and structure, and Spanish language use.

Generational status, a key construct in understanding the progress and experiences of Latinos/Latinas as a group, refers to the number of generations a family has been in the United States. Conventionally, the first generation is the immigrant generation, with the second generation being the first of the family to be born as U.S. citizens. The closer to the immigrant generation, the more likely the family is at risk for the socioeconomic conditions that impede occupational, financial, and educational attainment. As individuals spend time in the United States, an acculturation process may result in a blending of two cultures where individuals take on characteristics dominant in mainstream culture. For Latinos/Latinas, an effect of acculturation has been that students who are at a higher level of acculturation demonstrate a greater desire to attend and actually enroll in college than those with lower levels of acculturation (Hurtado & Gauvain, 1997). Therefore, students in families farther from the immigrant experience have a higher probability of college attainment.

With Latino/Latina families, generational status also has an effect on language use and the primacy of Spanish as the language spoken in the home. For many children who speak Spanish in the home, entry to the educational system may be their first significant exposure to English. Learning English while simultaneously learning the lessons of primary education can cause many children to fall behind in achievement levels. This is complicated by the variety of policies and practices in bilingual education in K–12 school districts. Several states eliminated bilingual education (where students are taught their native language while also learning to speak English) beginning in California in 1998. In states where bilingual education has been eliminated, students learn all subjects in English and receive supplemental English language instruction for a short amount of time. Results have been mixed; some states show small improvement in standardized test scores using English immersion (Martineau, 2000), while others show continuous declines (Tracy, 2008). While the effects of bilingual education on English-language proficiency remains in question, the effect of English-only education on Spanish-language use and literacy is clear: A lack of bilingual education results in a progressive loss (use and fluency) of the native language (Hasson, 2006). This is important as language use is an important marker of cultural identity and a source of pride for students (Phinney, 1995; Santiago-Rivera, Arredondo, & Gallardo-Cooper, 2002). Therefore, a loss of language has the potential for a negative impact on a student's identity and sense of self as he or she encounters other Latinos/Latinas who expect them to speak

Spanish (Bernal, 2001). Students who have maintained their language experience a sense of comfort and even anticipate economic rewards for being bilingual in today's multicultural world (Bernal). Maintenance of language is also important to the family as a societal unit. Children of immigrants often serve as language brokers, translating and interpreting for their parents and other individuals they encounter in schools and other public facilities (Morales & Hanson, 2005). Not only do these children play important roles in the lives, survival, and success of immigrant families, but at times place themselves in adult situations that may have complex implications for personal development. Thus, language acquisition, maintenance, and fluency remain significantly challenging sociological issues for Latinos/Latinas.

Generational status also helps to determine the type of family systems students experience. More often than not, especially in families closer to the time of immigration, the family is a collectivist entity (Ramirez, Castaneda, & Herold, 1974; Santiago-Rivera et al., 2002). These early-generation families tend to be more traditional in relationships with authority and in gender roles (Falicov, 1998; Halgunseth, Ispa, & Rudy, 2006). Students from traditional families may be less likely to question or challenge teachers or offer their opinions readily in class, primarily because of cultural values that emphasize obedience and deference to elders (Marin & Marin, 1991). Often this is perceived as disinterest in academics or a lack of critical thinking. Stricter adherence to gender roles also poses a problem for girls as they make college and career decisions (Aguilar, 1996; Ethier & Deaux, 1990). In traditional families there is significant pressure for young people to remain close to or in the home until marriage, and the clash of cultures more often affects girls as they may feel forced to conform to more traditional familial expectations (Padilla, 2006). The tension that may arise between parent and child can lead to risk for psychological distress, especially in the case of Latinas who may already experience greater acculturative and college stressors (Rodriguez, Mira, Myers, Morris, & Cardoza, 2003).

Of course, like other non-White ethnic and racial groups, Latinos/Latinas experience exclusion, discrimination, and racism that impede their ability to fulfill their desired destiny in this country. The degree of overt discrimination they experience is related to factors similar to those experienced by African Americans. Educational attainment, income, and occupational levels can mediate overt discrimination. However, broken or accented English and phenotype often serve to prompt discrimination regardless of the factors that may mediate discrimination (such as educational level, English-language fluency). The general public's lack of understanding of Latino culture, in concert with periodic episodes of political anti-immigration sentiment, may also lead to readily accepting stereotypes of Latinos/Latinas as illegal immigrants and undereducated manual laborers. Like African Americans, Latinos/Latinas also suffer discrimination in the workplace (such as a lack of advancement opportunities or overscrutiny) and the negative effects of experiencing a frequent barrage of microaggressions related to racism and stereotypes. Solorzano (1997) has characterized microaggressions as comments and opinions that may be meant as innocuous or even complimentary but are hurtful to Latino/Latina students. These include statements such as "You speak English so clearly" or "You aren't like most Mexicans." Many educators also assume that family structures and cultural values actually keep students from excelling in academics, that Latino families prefer their children to work rather than go to college. Students reported that high school teachers had low expectations of them, and they felt they had to constantly prove themselves academically to their teachers (Aguilar, 1996).

Latino/Latina Participation in Higher Education

Latino/Latina students compose 11.3% of the national student population, which is below parity for the group's proportion of the national population (*Chronicle of Higher Education*, 2009a). This gap in parity and participation is the highest for all non-White ethnic groups. African American and Native American students participate at parity, and Asian Americans participate at 50% higher than their proportion of the general population (*Chronicle of Higher Education*, 2009a). Complicating this parity gap is the fact that Latino/Latina students are overrepresented in public 2-year community colleges. Nearly 50% of all Latino/Latina students in higher education are in community colleges, making them 15.5% of the total 2-year college population. Only 8.4% of the student population in 4-year colleges and universities are Latino/Latina (*Chronicle of Higher Education*, 2009a). As one would expect, given these numbers, the proportion of degrees conferred on Latino/Latina students also falls below parity. Latino/Latina students earned 11.3% of associate's degrees, 7.2% of bachelor's degrees, 5.5% of master's degrees, 3.4% of doctoral degrees, and 5.1% of the professional degrees conferred in the 2005–2006 academic year (*Chronicle of Higher Education*, 2009b).

Half of all Latinos/Latinas attend a Hispanic-serving institution (HSI), which are private or public colleges and universities where Latinos/Latinas make up at least 25% of the student population of which 50% of all students must be low income. Of the more than 210 HSIs (in 2010), 53% are 2-year institutions (http://www.fastweb.com/college-search/articles/851-hispanic-serving-institutions). California accounts for the largest HSI student enrollment with almost one third of all HSI students, followed by Texas and Puerto Rico, which enroll about 20% each of the total HSI student population. Although HSIs account for only 5% of all institutions of higher education in the United States, almost half of all Latino students attend a designated HSI institution.

Many Latinos/Latinas are the first in their families to participate in higher education, with only 13.2% of all Latinos/Latinas holding a bachelor's degree or higher, compared to 29.5% of the total population (*Chronicle of Higher Education*, 2010b). More telling is the fact that 22.8% of all Latinos/Latinas have an eighth-grade education or less. This number is 17% higher than every other ethnic group in the United States (*Chronicle of Higher Education*, 2010b). Lack of experience in U.S. educational systems—higher education or K–12—leaves many Latino families at a disadvantage in conferring knowledge about the college-going process. A lack of preparation for and knowledge of higher education may be a primary reason so many Latino/Latina students attend community colleges. Fry (2004) reported that Latino/Latina students said that the cost of tuition, the need to work to earn money, receiving a poor high school education, and feeling that success did not require a college degree were the major reasons students did not go to college or left college before graduation. Another factor that impedes the success of Latinos/Latinas in higher education is that Latinos/Latinas are more likely to be enrolled in the least selective institutions. In Fry's analysis he found that over two thirds of Latinos/Latinas enroll in "open-door" institutions, a rate that is over 20% higher than that of White students. These types of institutions have the lowest bachelor's degree completion rates. He found that institutional selection mattered because the highest-achieving Latinos/Latinas who enroll at the most selective institutions not only enroll at the same rate as White students but graduate at the same rate as well.

Current Research, Trends, and Issues

The research literature on postsecondary Latino/Latina students primarily revolves around their getting to college, persisting once there, and the quality of their experiences in the college environment. In addition, ethnic identity overlaps many of these factors but primarily focuses on how students come to define themselves as they interact in the college environment and balance issues of salience, acculturation, assimilation, or biculturalism.

Precollege Experiences

The importance of early college aspirations to the success of Latinos/Latinas as a group cannot be overstated. In the beginning of the 21st century, efforts to develop outreach programs to Latinos/Latinas in middle school and high school have increased dramatically. This outreach is especially pertinent since affirmative action in college admissions has been eliminated in several states where there are high numbers of Latinos. For example, in the first year after the elimination of affirmative action when race could not be considered a factor in admissions, the number of Latinos in the entering class of 1998 at the University of California, Berkeley, decreased by 7.6% (Garcia, Jorgensen, & Ormsby, 1999). There is speculation that Latinos do not necessarily have lower grade point averages and standardized test scores than their peers from other ethnic groups but rather that admission standards have risen dramatically, which actually prevents qualified students from applying to prestigious institutions (Garcia et al., 1999; McDonough, Antonio, Walpole, & Perez, 1998). Hernandez (2002) found that students in his study were enrolled in high school honors and advanced placement courses yet still perceived themselves as less prepared academically than their White counterparts.

Given the funding structure for education in the United States it is expected that groups with high levels of poverty would also experience disparity in the quality of the education they receive. Coupled with continuing residential segregation in the United States (Charles, 2000), it is likely that many Latino/Latina youth have had poor experiences in primary and secondary schools. The achievement gap between Whites and Latinos is now larger than ever, with little conclusive evidence of the cause (Lee, 2002). In addition, high schools with high proportions of minority students and those in urban areas have nearly half as many college counselors as those in predominantly White and suburban schools (McDonough, 2005). Insensitive policies that neglect the needs of migrant or working students and discouragement of extra-curricular activities by school personnel also impede Latino/Latina educational attainment (Aviles, Guerrero, Howarth, & Thomas, 1999). Factors like these result in only a quarter of Latinos/Latinas as being college ready at high school graduation, thus producing leaks in the educational pipeline for these students.

Solorzano, Villalpando, and Oseguera's (2005) classic article on the educational inequities of Latino/Latina students reported that out of every 100 elementary school students only 52 will graduate from high school and only 31 will enroll in college. The two pathways to college—the 4-year university and the community college—result in differential attainment because of the 31 who go to college only 11 will go to a 4-year college directly from high school, and of the 20 who attend community colleges, only two will transfer to a 4-year college. Of those 13 who make it to a 4-year college, 10 will graduate with a bachelor's degree, 4 of those students will complete a graduate or professional degree, and, at best, 1 will complete a doctorate. Thus, the institution with the highest persistence rate for Latinos is the 4-year college, making their enrollment in such schools critical.

When Latinos/Latinas have the opportunity to engage in challenging academic programs the results are often quite favorable. Nyberg, McMillin, and O'Neill-Rood (1997) found that when students were retracked out of occupational curricula into more rigorous college preparatory courses they did not have lower grade point averages. Crawley (1998) reported that a Saturday science academy for Latino/Latina students provided an academic environment that countered the negative socialization that often occurs in students' peer groups. He wrote, "participants often report that being bright and academically motivated makes them feel like outsiders at their home school, so they enjoy the company and encouragement of the other bright students at the academy" (p. 37). Nearly all the students who completed classes at the academy eventually enrolled in the university of their choice, many of them on full scholarships. Participation in rigorous college prep programs not only helps students succeed academically but also gives them opportunities to gain confidence in their own academic abilities regardless of the grades they earned in the courses. The resulting academic self-concept is important because of the link between high achievement expectancies and persistence in 4-year institutions (House, 1999).

Cultural bias inherent in the American College Testing Assessment (ACT) and Scholastic Aptitude Test (SAT) is a well-documented controversy in the higher education literature (Jencks & Phillips, 1998; Perez, 2002; Zwick, 2004). While creators of the standardized tests work to make the exams more reflective of students' diverse backgrounds, epistemologies, and content knowledge, boards of trustees are reconsidering their use in college admissions because of growing evidence that standardized test scores are not the best predictors of college success. The lack of a relationship between test scores and college achievement has also been demonstrated for Latino/Latina students (Rodriguez, 1996). Pearson (1993) found that although Latino SAT scores were significantly lower than those of Whites, their college grades were equivalent. Gandara and Lopez (1998) found no relationship between SAT scores and retention or time to degree. Students with lower SAT scores did experience a low academic self-concept in their freshman year but rebounded in subsequent years. Gandara and Lopez also found that Latinos/Latinas with high SAT scores were no more likely to go to graduate school than those with lower scores. Indeed, the most serious consequence of low test scores was students' perceptions that low scores would prevent them from availing themselves of all educational opportunities.

High-achieving students also experience isolation and alienation from coethnics in their home communities who do not have aspirations for higher education. Crawley's (1998) description of the affiliation students found in the Saturday science academy is evidence of the struggle many students go through as they move away from the norms and expectations of their friends. Students with a high degree of loyalty to their ethnic group are more likely to perceive a social cost (alienation) in pursuing higher education. Niemann, Romero, and Arbona (2000) found that Latina high school students thought that by pursuing higher education they were educating themselves out of finding Latino marriage partners. Additionally, girls and boys felt they needed to support the family and community by working after high school rather than going to college. The students from this study also felt that college-educated Mexican Americans were perceived as elitists. Latinas in Aguilar's study (1996) also experienced expectations from within and outside their cultural group that questioned their desire to pursue higher education. They too felt pressure to prepare for marriage and family life. However, coethnics were not consistently a barrier for students in reaching college. Hurtado and Gauvain (1997) found that Spanish language preference and identification with one's ethnic group did not predict low levels of college attendance among Latinos/Latinas. In fact in a national study, Latinos/Latinas reported that coethnics and parents were sources of support in their success in college (Hurtado, Carter, & Spuler, 1996). Rendon's (1994) work on validation shows that family and friends outside the college environment are important agents in retention.

Also problematic is that many Latinos/Latinas have perceptions of financial aid and college access that are incorrect and serve to build self-imposed barriers to higher education. Many Latinos/Latinas begin their college careers in community colleges, not because of poor academic records but because they perceive 4-year colleges as an unviable choice in view of the repeal of affirmative action policies and a lack of financial aid. To compound this misunderstanding, a study by Zarate and Pachon (2006), found that Latino/Latina students and their families had misunderstandings about the cost of college and financial aid policies. Specifically, 80% of students overestimated the cost of attending in-state public universities and had misperceptions regarding financial policy, the criteria needed to obtain government grants, citizenship status for federal and state financial aid, and availability of guaranteed student loans (e.g., 30% of students said they would go to a commercial bank to get a loan for college). Most troubling was the finding that almost 40% of the respondents said they felt the cost of college outweighed the benefits of a college education.

The Latino/Latina Family

Latino/Latina families also serve as a source of support in helping a student develop college aspirations and in aiding retention in college. Aguilar's (1996) study showed that students relied on family values to help them achieve their goals. They received support and respect from their parents, which helped them to survive under adverse conditions. Supportive families contribute to the resiliency necessary for Latino/Latina students to overcome barriers in higher education, especially for students from low-income backgrounds or those whose first language is Spanish. Many have found the academic achievement of Latino/Latina students was linked to individual and familial influences (Hassinger & Plourde, 2005; Ong, Phinney, & Dennis, 2006; Sy, 2006).

Many parents use their own truncated formal education and manual labor experiences as motivators for their children to finish college. Sanchez, Reyes, and Singh (2006) found that despite a lack of college knowledge, parents were able to "provide cognitive guidance (asking questions, giving advice) regarding students' classes" (p. 61). They also found that of the key supporters students named, 42% were family members. This was also true in Ceja's (2004) study of Chicanos/Chicanas and their college aspirations: "It was not so much what the parents said through their direct messages but what these Chicana students perceived to be important, as a consequence of being keenly aware of the conditions and struggles of their parents" (p. 345). In addition to parents' being sources of support and expectation, parents and families also play more customary college-going roles for their children. For example, when Mexican mothers had educational achievement of high school completion or beyond, their children were more likely to complete high school and go to college (Hurtado & Gauvain, 1997). Older siblings who attended college were also a resource and source of support by serving as role models or by offering guidance in the application process or by tutoring in higher-level courses (Hurtado-Ortiz & Gauvain, 2007; Sanchez et al., 2006).

Using family experiences as motivation for college aspiration and educational success can be considered a cultural resource, a "set of cultural practices, beliefs, norms and values that, among other things, may nurture and empower individuals who associate with the group" (Villalpando, 2003, p. 621). This position is taken in Latino Critical Race Theory (LatCrit), which has become an important development in the research on Latino/Latina students. Through this theoretical framework, the intersection of such forces as ethnicity, race, immigration, class, sexual orientation, language, and gender allows for critical analysis of the oppressive nature of societal institutions and the opportunity to view cultural resources, experiential knowledge, and resistance as important tools for social justice and equity. Scholars such as Daniel Solorzano, Delores Delgado Bernal, Miguel Ceja, Octavio Villalpando, and Tara Yosso have been leaders in the development of this scholarship. As an example of the application of LatCrit, Chicana feminist pedagogy more formally acknowledges cultural resources present in the home as valuable sources of strength for students. "The teaching and learning of the home allows Chicanas to draw upon their own cultures and sense of self to resist domination along the axes of race, class, gender, and sexual orientation" (Bernal, 2001, p. 624). An accompanying *mestiza* (mixture of native and colonized histories) consciousness "includes how a student balances, negotiates, and draws from her bilingualism, biculturalism, commitment to communities and spiritualities" (p. 628) to resist discriminatory and racist practices and ideologies. An example Bernal offers is that by continuing to speak Spanish, Chicanas draw personal strength and pride through their ethnic identity and can convert a practice many perceive as interfering with educational success to an asset in the educational and work environments.

Latinos/Latinas in Community Colleges and College Choice

Because of many of the factors already discussed (poor academic preparation, misinformation about access and financial aid), community colleges serve as the primary entry point for Latinos/Latinas pursuing higher education.

Despite the high number of Latino community college students who aspire to transfer to 4-year institutions, the research suggests that few Latino students are transferring. A study by Rivas, Perez, Alvarez, and Solorzano (2007) draws attention to this. In California 75 of 100 first-time Latino college students enrolled in a community college. Of these 75 students only 7 transferred to a 4-year university. Six of these students enrolled at a Californian State University institution while only 1 enrolled at a more selective University of California school.

In Person and Rosenbaum's (2006) study of college choice among midwestern community college students, they found that despite academic eligibility to attend 4-year colleges, students primarily chose to attend community colleges because of existing networks at those colleges. Their analysis likens this trend to that of ethnic enclaves where much like new immigrants to the United States, college students choose colleges based on knowledge and encouragement provided by peers and older family members already attending or working at the community college. Existing networks make it easier for these students to make the transition from high school to college.

Leading community college scholars note that "the actual transfer rate is debatable and mysterious because there is little agreement as to how it should be measured" (Hagedorn & Lester, 2006, p. 833). The multiple missions of community colleges make transfer rates irrelevant for many students who have no intention of transferring or who enroll simply to establish or update workplace skills or engage in lifelong learning. Dual (or multiple) enrollment and reverse transfer (from a 4-year to a 2-year college) further complicate determining accurate transfer rates. Hagedorn and Lester found that remedial and prerequisite transfer-level courses become barriers to transfer, that women were more likely to complete transfer-ready courses, and there were no differences in transfer readiness between native Spanish or English speakers.

Retention of Latinos/Latinas

A research study drawn from the National Center for Education Statistics' National Longitudinal Study of the 1988 class of U.S. eighth graders found that by 2000, eight years after scheduled high school graduation, only 23.2% of Latinos/Latinas received a bachelor's degree, and 12.8% obtained a certificate or associate's degree (Swail, Cabrera, & Lee, 2004). This rate is extremely low and signals that in higher education we know very little about how to achieve higher retention among Latino/Latina students. According to Swail, Redd, and Perna (2003), a more holistic model of student persistence explains that the student experience is shaped by three sets of factors: cognitive (i.e., quality of learning, study skills, and time management) social, (i.e., financial issues, social coping skills, cultural values, and parental and peer support) and institutional (i.e., how institutions react to students and the ability of the institution to provide support). Students attain equilibrium when the cognitive, social, and institutional forces combine in a manner that supports student persistence and achievement. The geometric model suggests that a student must find a balance between all three factors to reach equilibrium. Balance does not require all three factors to be equal. A Latino/Latina student may have strong social support, such as a family and friend network, to compensate for a shortage of college survival skills like time management and knowledge of institutional resources. Thus students' family and social networks prior to college can assist in persistence rather than impede integration as Tinto (1993) argues in his classic work on student retention.

There is a cyclical relationship between campus racial climate, college adjustment, and persistence. Students' ability to find membership or a sense of belonging on campus has long been connected with persistence (Hurtado & Carter, 1997; Tinto, 1993). Experiences with discrimination or racism on campus serve to block that sense of belonging and then become barriers to achieving a degree. Students have reported that discrimination from campus administrators, advisers, and support staff has a negative effect on their ability to succeed (Lopez, 1995). However, social support systems and cultural connections have been shown to mediate the effects of a negative campus racial climate. Social support, coupled with high self-efficacy, is significantly responsible for success in college adjustment and a decrease in psychological and physical distress (Solberg, Valdez, & Villareal, 1994; Solberg & Villarreal, 1997). Ethier and Deaux's (1990) study of Latinos/Latinas at Ivy League institutions found that "cultural background seems to act in a protective fashion, at least in the early months of the Ivy League experience" (p. 428). In fact, the ability for Latino students to create, negotiate, and sustain social networks can positively influence their college experience and persistence (Saunders & Serna, 2004).

Campus Climate and Community Affiliations

Race relations on campus affect Latinos/Latinas in many of the ways they affect members of other ethnic minority groups. In the classroom, students experience disregard from faculty and other students and seldom see Latino/Latina scholars or researchers teaching their courses or represented in course material. Since these students often come to college with varying levels of preparation because of uneven precollege educational experiences, any disconnect they experience in the academic environment at college is exacerbated. In the cocurricular environment Latino/Latina students may experience the same chilly climate they experience in the classroom. Affiliation needs for these students are great since they frequently come from close-knit communities where there is mutual responsibility for community members through extended family networks. This often gives Latinos/Latinas an expectation that communities they join in the college environment reflect similar values and behaviors.

Ethnic student organizations and Chicano or Latino studies programs provide opportunities for Latino/Latina students to build community with other students, faculty, and staff. Belonging to these organizations helps students maintain their cultural identity or become more familiar with a cultural identity that may have been de-emphasized prior to college (Ortiz & Santos, 2009). However, membership in these communities often plays a contradictory role in students' acclimation to college. Hurtado and Carter (1997) found that involvement in student organizations led to a sense of belonging for Latino students but simultaneously was associated with a greater awareness of racial and ethnic tensions on campus. Conversely, Latinos/Latinas who did not belong to these clubs experienced a lower sense of belonging despite reporting lower levels of racial and ethnic tension on campus. However, other important outcomes are associated with these clubs and organizations. The opportunity for Latinos/Latinas to affiliate with each other has been shown to have positive outcomes, such as commitment to the community and altruistic career choices. Further, this affiliation, which some may consider to be a form of self-segregation, is often considered to be an act of self-preservation in predominantly White institutions (Villalpando, 2003).

Students of lower-generational status (first- or second-generation in the United States) are more likely to be raised in environments where maintenance of cultural attributes is higher than Latinos/Latinas who have had more time in the United States to become acculturated. The level of acculturation students have experienced often determines the extent to which they need communities of coethnic peers to fulfill their affiliation needs. This is an important distinction because researchers and student affairs professionals often overgeneralize the specific needs of Latino/Latina students without acknowledging differences in acculturation. Students who identify more with being an American are least likely to be comfortable with speaking Spanish, to prefer the company of coethnics, or to be politically active on behalf of the ethnic group (Felix-Ortiz, Newcomb, & Myers, 1994).

Ethnic Identity and Biculturalism

Ethnic identity as a psychological construct and as a contributor to characteristics that positively affect the educational experience of students continues to be a vibrant line of research on Latinos/Latinas. Classic dispositions associated with ethnic identity include increased self-efficacy and self-esteem, which have an influence on students' academic performance (for a review see Phinney, 1995; Phinney, Cantu, & Kurtz, 1997). Torres (2003) suggested that for Latino college students, a strong ethnic identity may be associated positively with educational engagement.

While the connection among ethnic identity, self-esteem, and academic achievement has been established in the psychological literature, additional research has found that ethnic identity sometimes interferes with positive perceptions of and experiences in the campus environment. When students have a strong ethnic identity, they perceive a more negative university environment and feel less committed to finishing college (Castillo et al., 2006). Further, biculturalism, which enables Latinos/Latinas to relate to two different cultural groups, making them stronger people, also makes them prone to stress in racist environments (Bernal, 2001). This contradiction arises because students have a strong ethnic identity but also the skills and knowledge to interact with the dominant culture on campus, making them more adept at perceiving covert acts of racism and having greater insight to the potential for individuals to change racist views. Helping students to set realistic expectations for themselves and others as well as providing forums for dialogue can be important in helping students manage this stress.

Best Practices for Latino/Latina Students

Programs that have been successful are those that seek to integrate home, schools, communities, and universities in ways that promote seamless educational environments for Latino/Latina students. Programs and practices need to be highly intentional, even invasive at times, with staff and counselors moving beyond traditional service delivery models that rely on students' initiating contact with service providers. Students and parents often believe that college is too expensive to consider, that admission policies intentionally exclude Latinos/Latinas, and that one's immigration status may be revealed through the college application process. These myths are true for some segments of the community but are largely overexaggerated for the typical student and his or her family. The programs highlighted in the next section represent partnerships and collaboration among communities, high schools, community colleges, and 4-year universities that work together to prepare Latino/Latina students for higher education, build college aspirations, and bring families into the college-going process.

Innovative Programs and Partnerships

Engaging Latino Communities for Education (ENLACE). One of the most ambitious collaborative efforts to address the needs of Latino/Latina students nationwide is the ENLACE initiative funded by the W. K. Kellogg Foundation and Houston Endowment, Inc. ENLACE funds 13 collaborations among HSIs, K–12 schools, and community organizations with the primary purpose of strengthening the educational pipeline for Latino/Latina students. These initiatives include elementary and middle school college awareness programs, summer bridge programs for incoming high school and college freshmen, peer mentoring at all educational levels, and leadership development for high school students. Some students who may lack some eligibility requirements are dually enrolled in the 4-year college and the local community college with a detailed set of requirements for transfer. When those requirements are satisfied, the student does not have to submit a separate application to the 4-year institution. Other partnerships make explicit efforts to include family and community members in the educational process, not only through college awareness programs but through literacy and reading programs intended to enhance the education of the adults in the communities. Several partnerships also include teacher recruitment and training initiatives. As might be expected, the paucity of Latino/Latina college graduates has created a shortage of Latino/Latina teachers in the nation's schools. Programs funded through ENLACE give prospective teachers practical experience in schools and provide financial support for Latino/Latina aides who are working in schools to become teachers. Each of the 13 initiatives is unique and designed to meet specific needs of the local community, therefore all program features are not found in each initiative. The ENLACE sites, funded until 2010, are in California, Arizona, New Mexico, Texas, Florida, New York, and Illinois.

High school and university partnerships. With or without external funding many campuses have constructed programs that reach across educational sectors. For example, the College Assistance Migrant Program identifies talented high school students from migrant families and works with them to prepare academically for college and apply to college. Each cohort of students participating in the program attends a summer institute prior to entering college. The cohort then enters a three-tiered mentoring program that matches its members with an upper-division graduate student and faculty member. The mentoring program guides the student through the 1st year of college with regular academic support programs, cultural activities, and opportunities to network with Latino/Latina faculty and professionals in the community. Program administrators work closely with personnel from the more centralized academic support services, such as the advising, career, or tutoring centers, and with faculty from Chicano/Chicana studies programs. This seamless experience has helped students more quickly integrate academically and socially into the university environment.

An example of a partnership among higher education institutions, high schools, and local corporations is the Lancaster Partnership Program, which identifies Latino and African American high school students who show promise for college (Gregoire & Redmond, 1997). These students must attend a comprehensive precollege program, and those who successfully complete the program are guaranteed admission to a private university in the area. The corporate partners give scholarships to the students for their educational costs not covered by financial aid. Students are also able to work during the summer at the local corporations and are also guaranteed employment at one of the companies after graduation.

Comprehensive services. Programs limited to a single campus are the most common design for supporting Latino/Latina students in college. At many institutions these services, such as educational opportunity programs, minority student services, and the like, which are often labeled ALANA (African American, Latino, Asian, and Native American) offices, are housed in a common office for all targeted minority groups. Institutions with larger enrollments of students from specific ethnic groups may have programs directed at each group. Still other institutions may have academic support systems for minority students housed by functional area rather than by specific ethnic group support services. The physical location of these services is often significant in the staff's ability to reach out to Latinos/Latinas on campus. Multiple services housed in a central location enable students to make needed connections without having to go to several offices. This also promotes building relationships between the students and staff members they are likely to need throughout their college career. Common elements of support programs include tutoring services, counseling and advising, faculty mentor programs, student organizations, computer assistance and access, study skills sessions, summer orientation programs, and first-year experience courses. However, in states where affirmative action policies have been repealed, housing student services by ethnic group demarcations has also been prohibited, and programs like those described in this paragraph have been integrated into more general service areas.

Community college programs. Many community colleges centrally house programs collectively in the offices of educational opportunity programs and services. In California these offices provide specially trained academic counselors for students with program structures, such as mandatory advising tied to financial support, that work to enhance student success. Programs that service community college students also feature linkages among high schools, community colleges, and 4-year institutions.

The Puente program is being implemented at 33 high school and 59 community college sites across the state of California as a joint effort by the University of California and the California Community College system. The Puente community college program trains a team of faculty, staff, and counselors to implement rigorous instruction, focused academic counseling, and mentoring. For example, English instructors incorporate culturally relevant reading and writing assignments enabling students to develop their critical reading, thinking, and writing skills with information that is culturally relevant to their experience. Puente community college counselors provide sustained and in-depth academic and career counseling. In addition to advising services in admission, financial aid, and academics, students participate in workshops on test-taking strategies and ways to balance work and school. Counselors are trained to incorporate the family in the counseling process. Students are also paired with a member of the local community who serves as a role model for academic and professional support. The program structure includes opportunities to attend civic and cultural events in the community. During its 29-year history, the Puente program has improved the college-going rates of thousands of underrepresented students and has positively facilitated their educational success.

Recommendations, Implications, and Future Trends

Whenever Latino/Latina students express their aspirations for a college education and their dreams for the future, faculty and administrators should be energized to do everything possible to work on their behalf—to look for the institutional barriers that need to be removed; to network across campus to find them excellent mentoring, work, and involvement opportunities; to connect them with other Latino/Latina students; and to run interference in the classroom to help protect them from insensitive or ignorant classmates and professors. However, this may not be enough. Latino/Latina student advocates also must work to change structures, policies, and programs in the university that impede the success of Latinos/Latinas. Student affairs professionals, researchers, academic administrators, as well as graduate students studying to enter the student affairs field, should all become familiar with the topics summarized below.

Integrated Outreach

The literature explicitly shows how critical it is to design outreach programs that connect 4-year colleges and universities with K–12 school systems and community colleges. New programs indicate that college awareness programs are most successful when they are directed at students in middle school. The idea of going to college must be introduced to students early enough to provide motivation for their academic success. Because many Latino/Latina students come from families with little experience in higher education, this introduction to college awareness must also include the nuclear and extended family. Families and parents often communicate to students that college is a dream for other people not for them. They do not do this to discourage their children but to try to give them a realistic sense of their available opportunities. Our legislative and legal environment has reinforced messages about those opportunities. Many families believe that by filing financial aid forms, their immigration status will be questioned. The anti-immigration laws enacted at the federal level and in numerous states across the country tell families this is a very real possibility. The repeal of affirmative action policies in three of the most populous states for Latinos/Latinas (California's Proposition 209 in 1997, *Hopwood v. Texas* in 1996, and Florida's One Florida Initiative in 2000) tells families their children are not welcome in public higher education, and many families might even believe they are actually prohibited from admission. Therefore, education efforts to dispel these myths among families must be aggressive and consistent.

Outreach to community colleges and their students is also vital. More than half of all Latinos/Latinas in higher education are in community colleges. Because these institutions have open admission policies that do not require standardized tests, minimum grade point averages, or expensive application fees, they are ideally suited to serve as the intake institutions for many Latinos/Latinas. However, these features of convenience can allow students to put their education behind the other roles they play. This makes progress to attaining the degree slow and tenuous. Four-year colleges and universities either need to work harder at making themselves points of entry for the majority of Latino/Latina students or work more closely with the community colleges to transfer students who intend to complete a baccalaureate degree. It is the responsibility of the 4-year institution to help to design programs that actively help students and community college advisers navigate articulation agreements and course eligibility.

Career Preparation

Interesting trends regarding career preparation of Latinos/Latinas have implications for ensuring their presence in higher education. Latinos/Latinas tend to take a highly pragmatic view of their career preparation and higher education's role in that preparation. Students and families expect that college will prepare them for a job and career that offers opportunities for income and advancement beyond what would be possible without a college education. One study reported that Latinos/Latinas are more likely than any other ethnic group to major in business (Leppel, 2001). This pragmatic view of the college experience has several implications. First, it inhibits students from exploring alternative career and academic opportunities in college. Students who choose careers and majors that are perceived to be less tied to employment after graduation face criticism and resistance from families that expect a college graduate to be well employed. Career and counseling centers need to be prepared to assist students who experience this difficulty. Second, it raises the issue of the cultural disconnect that students experience when they leave home communities that have few college-attending youths in the environment. Students who do go to college and then pursue pragmatic degrees, like business, are often thought to be sellouts by their ethnic group. This tension is common for members of socioeconomic groups where a college education is less valued. However, Latino/Latina students who major in business-related fields face this opposition from their friends from home and from their more activist-oriented Latino/Latina peers in the college environment (Gross, 2001). Pressure like this from external actors makes it even more important that support structures exist in the university, such as academically based Latino/Latina student organizations, community mentoring programs, and ongoing communication with family.

The third implication of the tendency to view a college education pragmatically is the realization that we may not be able to attract Latino/Latina students to careers in higher education. This affects higher education in a number of significant ways. Latino/Latina faculty represent only about 3.6% of the national full-time faculty (*Chronicle of Higher Education*, 2010a). Often, students who may consider doctoral-level work are encouraged by family expectations to enter the workforce after completing the undergraduate degree. This problem perpetuates the lack of Latino/Latina role models in higher education. Programs like the Doctoral Scholars Program of the Southern Regional Education Board to increase the numbers of underrepresented minorities in the nation's professoriate are slowly making a change in the number of Latinos/Latinas who teach in U.S. colleges and universities. Change could be accelerated by being more candid with undergraduates about faculty work, academic salaries, and consulting opportunities so they understand that a life in academia can have pragmatic benefits.

Seamless Partnerships in Student Services

Just as partnerships between 4- and 2-year institutions need to be strengthened to improve transfer and persistence, partnerships in student service areas are critical for student success. These partnerships should not be limited to innovative support programs that reach across student and academic affairs but should also include utilitarian partnerships that educate university personnel about Latino/Latina student issues from a holistic perspective. Personnel who work in academic support need to be updated constantly about changes in financial aid policies and procedures so that continuing students get current information before their registration status is threatened. Navigating financial aid policies is not only a task for the high school senior or community college transfer but for all student service personnel. Issues that may complicate financial aid eligibility include confusion over dependency status, continued reporting of parental income and tax information, satisfactory course load if remedial courses are taken, and minimum grade point average standards.

Student supportive services also need to be in regular communication about the progress of Latino/Latina students. On larger campuses this type of communication is often a significant barrier because of discrete organizational structure reporting lines, overlap of job responsibilities, and the sheer number of students served. Because early support programs, such as summer bridge programs and other precollege programs are often housed in targeted support service units, other student service units need to be prepared to work closely with students and these early programs so that students receive the help they need throughout their matriculation. This also applies to partnerships and communication between faculty and staff. Often classroom and academic issues are viewed in isolation from other student issues, which leads to a poor diagnosis of student problems and incomplete plans to address the problems. Early-alert programs include communication channels between classroom faculty for 1st- and 2nd-year students and student support personnel so intervention takes place before education problems become insurmountable.

Policy-Oriented Research

The higher education research community also has a responsibility in the success of Latino/Latina students. A solid foundation of research (Fry, 2004; Hagedorn & Lester, 2006; Hernandez, 2000; Hurtado & Carter, 1997; Longerbeam, Sedlacek, & Alatorre, 2004; Rivas et al., 2007) exists on the persistence of Latino/Latina students and identified variables that are key to persistence. However, questions remain. One key area for further development is the college choice process for Latino/Latina students. What times in a K–12 education are best for changing the mythology about higher education? How are parents, families, and communities best employed to guide students to college? What kinds of programs have been most effective in helping students get to college? There is also room for higher education researchers to conduct empirical research on existing Latino/Latina college students and to broaden the research agenda of student achievement to include Latinos/Latinas in their precollege years. The research reviewed earlier in the chapter (Person & Rosenbaum, 2006; Sy, 2006), which identifies the high school experiences that are positive contributors to matriculation and persistence, are examples of how research on student achievement affects topics such as high-stakes testing.

We have a special opportunity to do the right thing at the right time for Latino/Latina students. The numbers of Latinos/Latinas in higher education will increase faster than our ability to design programs, conduct the needed research, or transform policies and institutions. Understanding their unique precollegiate experiences is an important way to begin to assist these students once they arrive on campus. Latinos/Latinas' history as a people and as individuals in a complex sociocultural context challenges many basic assumptions in higher education. Practitioners, researchers, and students should examine policies and practices to see how our hidden assumptions and misunderstandings of Latino/Latina students may affect their academic progress and satisfaction with college. We might incorrectly assume that all our students, having made it to college, have similar K–12 experiences, have similar family and community models, and have equal beliefs that all opportunities are open to them. Latino/Latina students will come to believe that they have infinite possibilities for the future, but getting to that point often requires closer guidance and support than necessary for the typical White student. It is hard work for a staff or faculty member to do this on a regular basis, but the benefits are well worth the investment.

Discussion Questions

1. Discuss the similarities and differences among the variety of nationalities and cultures described as Latino/Latina. How will you as a student affairs professional endeavor to attend to their collective and specific needs?
2. Identify the major impacts resulting from Latino Critical Race Theory and discuss how student affairs practitioners may use these impacts to provide best practices with Latino/Latina students.
3. Discuss how to use the strong connections with family of most Latino/Latina students to enhance their positive experiences while enrolled in college and to improve the likelihood of their retention and completion.

References

Aguilar, M. A. (1996). Promoting the educational achievement of Mexican American young women. *Social Work Education, 18*, 145–156.

Aviles, R. M., Guerrero, M. P., Howarth, H. B., & Thomas, G. (1999). Perceptions of Chicano/Latino students who have dropped out of school. *Journal of Counseling and Development, 77*, 465–473.

Bernal, D. D. (2001). Learning and living pedagogies of the home: The *mestiza* consciousness of Chicana students. *Qualitative Studies in Education, 14*, 623–639.

Castillo, L. G., Conoley, C. W., Choi-Pearson, C., Archuleta, D. J., Phoummarath, M. J., & Van Landingham, A. V. (2006). University environment as a mediator of Latino ethnic identity and persistence attitudes. *Journal of Counseling Psychology, 53*, 276–271.

Ceja, M. (2004). Chicana college aspirations and the role of parents: Developing educational resiliency. *Journal of Hispanic Higher Education, 3,* 338–362.

Charles, C. Z. (2000). Residential segregation in Los Angeles. In B. Lawrence (Ed.), *Prismatic metropolis: Inequality in Los Angeles.* New York: Russell Sage Foundations.

Chronicle of Higher Education. (2009a). College enrollment by racial and ethnic group in selected years.

Chronicle of Higher Education. (2009b). Degrees conferred by racial and ethnic group, 2006–07.

Chronicle of Higher Education. (2010a, August 27). Percentage of faculty by sex, rank and racial and ethnic origin, 2009, p. 20.

Chronicle of Higher Education. (2010b, August 27). Educational attainment of the U.S. population by racial and ethnic group, 2009, p. 26.

Crawley, P. (1998). Extracurricular opportunities. *Science Teacher, 65*(3), 37–38.

DeNavas-Walt, C., Proctor, B. D., & Smith, J. C. (2009). *Income, poverty, and health insurance coverage in the United States: 2008* (U.S. Census Bureau, current population reports, P60–236). Washington, DC: U.S. Government Printing Office. Retrieved August 20, 2010, from http://www.census.gov/hhes/www/poverty/data/incpovhlth/2008/index.html

Ethier, K., & Deaux, K. (1990). Hispanics in ivy: Assessing identity and perceived threat. *A Journal of Research, 22,* 427–440.

Falicov, C. J. (1998). *Latino families in therapy: A guide to multicultural practice.* New York: Guilford Press.

Felix-Ortiz, M., Newcomb, M. D., & Myers, H. (1994). A multidimensional measure of cultural identity for Latino and Latina adolescents. *Hispanic Journal of Behavioral Sciences, 16,* 99–115.

Fry, R. (2004). *Latino youth finishing college: The role of selective pathways.* Washington DC: Pew Hispanic Center. Retrieved May 22, 2008, from http://pewhispanic.org/reports/report.php?ReportID = 30

Gandara, P., & Lopez, E. (1998). Latino students and college entrance exams: How much do they really matter? *Hispanic Journal of Behavioral Sciences, 20,* 17–38.

Garcia, E. E., Jorgensen, R. E., & Ormsby, C. (1999). How can public universities still admit a diverse freshmen class? The case of Latinos, the SAT, and the University of California. *Journal of College Admission, 164,* 5–11.

Gregoire, K. A., & Redmond, M. W. (1997). Corporate-academic partnerships: An expanded model. *College and University, 72,* 14–19.

Gross, L. S. (2001). *Intersections of cultural and career identity in Mexican American college students.* Unpublished doctoral dissertation, Michigan State University, East Lansing.

Guzman, B. (2001). *The Hispanic population: Census 2000 brief.* Retrieved on August 29, 2010, from http://www.census.gov/population/www/cen2000/briefs/index.html

Hagedorn, L. S., & Lester, J. (2006). Hispanic community college students and the transfer game: Strikes, misses, and grand slam experiences. *Community College Journal of Research and Practice, 30,* 827–853.

Halgunseth, L. C., Ispa, J. M., & Rudy, D. (2006). Parental control in Latino families: An integrated review of the literature. *Child Development, 77,* 1282–1297.

Hassinger, M., & Plourde, L. E. (2005). Beating the odds: How bilingual Hispanic youth work through adversity to become high achieving students. *Education, 126,* 316–327.

Hasson, D. J. (2006). Bilingual language use in Hispanic young adults: Did elementary bilingual programs help? *Bilingual Research Journal, 30,* 45–64.

Hernandez, J. C. (2000). Understanding the retention of Latino college students. *Journal of College Student Development, 41,* 575–588.

Hernandez, J. C. (2002). A qualitative exploration of the first year experience of Latino college students. *NASPA Journal, 40,* 69–84.

House, J. D. (1999). Self-beliefs and background variables as predictors of school withdrawal of adolescent students. *Child Study Journal, 29,* 247–268.

Hurtado, M. T., & Gauvain, M. (1997). Acculturation and planning for college among youth of Mexican descent. *Hispanic Journal of Behavioral Sciences, 19,* 506–516.

Hurtado-Ortiz, M. T., & Gauvain, M. (2007). Postsecondary education among Mexican youth: Contributions of parents, siblings, acculturation, and generational status. *Hispanic Journal of Behavioral Sciences, 29,* 181–191.

Hurtado, S., & Carter, D. F. (1997). Effects of college transition and perceptions of the campus racial climate on Latino college students' sense of belonging. *Sociology of Education, 70,* 324–345.

Hurtado, S., Carter, D. F., & Spuler, A. (1996). Latino student transition to college: Assessing difficulties and factors in successful college adjustment. *Research in Higher Education, 37,* 135–157.

Jencks, C., & Phillips, M. (1998). *The Black White test score gap.* Washington, DC: Brookings Institution.

Lee, J. (2002). Racial and ethnic achievement gap trends: Reversing the progress toward equity? *Educational Researcher, 31*(1), 3–12.

Leppel, K. (2001). The impact of major on college persistence among freshmen. *Higher Education, 41,* 327–342.

Longerbeam, S. D., Sedlacek, W. E., & Alatorre, H. M. (2004). In their own voices: Latino student retention. *NASPA Journal, 41,* 538–550.

Lopez, E. M. (1995). Challenges and resources of Mexican American students within the family, peer group, and university: Age and gender patterns. *Hispanic Journal of Behavioral Sciences, 17,* 499–508.

Marin, G., & Marin, B. V. (1991). *Research with Hispanic populations.* Thousand Oaks, CA: Sage.

Martineau, P. (2000, August). Testing report details gains: Data said to show "achievement gap." *Sacramento Bee,* Metro Section, p. 1.

McDonough, P. M. (2005). *Counseling and college counseling in America's high schools.* A white paper commissioned by the National Association for Admission Counseling. Retrieved August 27, 2010, from www.nacacnet.org/ . . . /Research/ . . . /WhitePaper_McDonough.pdf

McDonough, P. M., Antonio, A. L., Walpole, M., Perez, L. X. (1998). College rankings: Democratized knowledge for whom? *Research in Higher Education, 39*(5), 513–537.

Morales, A., & Hanson, W. E. (2005). Language brokering: An integrative review of the literature. *Hispanic Journal of Behavioral Sciences, 27,* 471–503.

Niemann, Y. F., Romero, A., & Arbona, C. (2000). Effects of cultural orientation on the perception of conflict between relationship and education goals for Mexican American college students. *Hispanic Journal of Behavioral Sciences, 22,* 46–63.

Nyberg, K. L., McMillin, D. J., & O'Neill-Rood, N. (1997). Ethnic differences in academic retracking: A four-year longitudinal study. *Journal of Educational Research, 91,* 33–41.

Ong, A. D., Phinney, J. S., & Dennis, J. (2006). Competence under challenge: Exploring the protective influence of parental support and ethnic identity in Latino college students. *Journal of Adolescents, 29,* 961–979.

Ortiz, A. M., & Santos, S. J. (2009). *Ethnicity in college: Advancing theory and improving diversity practices on campus.* Sterling, VA: Stylus.

Padilla, A. (2006). Bicultural social development. *Hispanic Journal of Behavioral Sciences, 28,* 467–497.

Passel, J. S., & Cohn, D. (2008). *U.S. Population Projections: 2005–2050.* Washington DC: Pew Hispanic Center. Retrieved May 22, 2008, from http://pewhispanic .org/reports/report.php?ReportID = 85

Pearson, B. Z. (1993). Predictive validity of the Scholastic Aptitude Test (SAT) for Hispanic bilingual students. *Journal of Behavioral Sciences, 15,* 342–356.

Perez, C. (2002). Different tests, same flaws: Examining the SAT I, SAT II, and ACT. *Journal of College Admission, 172,* 20–25.

Person, A. E., & Rosenbaum, J. E. (2006). Chain enrollment and college enclaves: Benefits and drawbacks of Latino college students' enrollment decisions. In C. L. Horn, S. M. Flores, & G. Orfield (Eds.), *Latino educational opportunity* (pp. 51–60). San Francisco: Jossey-Bass.

Phinney, J. (1995). Ethnic identity and self-esteem: A review and integration. In A. Padilla (Ed.), *Hispanic Psychology: Critical Issues in Theory and Research* (pp. 57–70). Thousand Oaks, CA: Sage.

Phinney, J., Cantu, C. L., & Kurtz, D. (1997). Ethnic and American identity as predictors of self-esteem among African American, Latinos, and White adolescents. *Journal of Youth and Adolescence, 26,* 165–185.

Portes, A., & Bach, R. L. (1985). *Latin journey: Cuban and Mexican immigrants in the United States.* Berkeley: University of California Press.

Portes, A., & Stepick, A. (1993). *City on the edge: The transformation of Miami.* Berkeley: University of California Press.

Ramirez, M., III, Castaneda, A., & Herold, P. L. (1974). The relationship of acculturation to cognitive style among Mexican Americans. *Journal of Cross-Cultural Psychology, 5*, 424–433.

Rendon, L. I. (1994). Validating culturally diverse students: Toward a new model of learning and student development. *Innovative Higher Education, 19*, 33–51.

Rivas, M. A., Perez, J., Alvarez, C. R., & Solorzano, D. G. *An examination of Latina/ o transfer students in California's postsecondary institutions* (Latino Policy and Issues Brief No. 16). Los Angeles: University of California, Los Angeles, Chicano Studies Research Center.

Rodriguez, N., Mira, C. B., Myers, H. F., Morris, J. K., & Cardoza, D. (2003). Family or friends: Who plays a greater supportive role for Latino college students? *Cultural Diversity and Ethnic Minority Psychology, 9*, 236–250.

Rodriguez, R. (1996). Life after Hopwood. *Black Issues in Higher Education, 13*(12), 8–10.

Sanchez, B., Reyes, O., & Singh, J. (2006). Makin' it in college: The value of significant individuals in the lives of Mexican American adolescents. *Journal of Hispanics in Higher Education, 5*, 48–67.

Santiago-Rivera, A. L., Arredondo, P., & Gallardo-Cooper, M. (2002). *Counseling Latinos and la familia: A practical guide*. Thousand Oaks, CA: Sage.

Saunders, M., & Serna, I. (2004). Making college happen: The college experiences of first-generation Latino students. *Journal of Hispanics in Higher Education, 3*, 146–163.

Solberg, V. S., Valdez, J., & Villareal, P. (1994). Social support, stress, and Hispanic college adjustment: Test of a diathesis-stress model. *Hispanic Journal of Behavioral Sciences, 16*, 230–239.

Solberg, V. S., & Villareal, P. (1997). Examination of self-efficacy, social support, and stress as predictors of psychological and physical distress among Hispanic college students. *Hispanic Journal of Behavioral Sciences, 19*, 182–201.

Solorzano, D. G. (1997). Images and words that wound: Critical race theory, racial stereotyping and teacher education. *Teacher Education Quarterly, 24*, 5–19.

Solorzano, D. G., Villalpando, O., & Oseguera, L. (2005). Educational inequities and Latina/o undergraduate students in the United States: A critical race analysis of their educational progress. *Journal of Hispanic Higher Education, 4*, 272–294.

Spring, J. (2010). *Deculturalization and the struggle for equality: A brief history of the education of dominated cultures in the United States* (6th ed.). New York: McGraw-Hill.

Swail, W. S., Cabrera, A. F., & Lee, C. (2004). *Latino youth and the pathway to college*. Washington DC: Pew Hispanic Center. Retrieved May 22, 2008, from http://pewhispanic.org/reports/report.php?ReportID = 31

Swail, W. S., Redd, K., & Perna, L. W. (2003). Retaining minority students in higher education: A framework for success. *ASHE-ERIC Higher Education Report Series, 30*(2). San Francisco: Jossey-Bass.

Sy, S. R. (2006). Family and work influences on the transition to college among Latina adolescents. *Hispanic Journal of Behavioral Sciences, 28,* 368–386.

Tinto, V. (1993). *Leaving college: Rethinking the causes and cures of student retention* (1st ed.). Chicago: University of Chicago Press.

Torres, V. (2003). Influences on ethnic identity development of Latino college students in the first two years of college. *Journal of College Student Development, 44,* 532–547.

Tracy, J. (2008). *Bilingual teachers wanted: Boston schools recruiting in Puerto Rico.* Retrieved June 9, 2008, from http://www.boston.com/news/local/articles/2008/03/18/bilingual_teachers_wanted/

Villalpando, O. (2003). Self-segregation or self-preservation? A critical race theory and Latina/o critical theory analysis of a study of Chicana/o college students. *Qualitative Studies in Education, 16,* 619–646.

Zarate, M. E., & Pachon, H. P. (2006). *Perceptions of college financial aid among California Latino youth.* Retrieved May 22, 2008, from http://www.trpi.org/PDFs/Financial_Aid_Surveyfinal6302006.pdf

Zwick, R. (2004). *Rethinking the SAT: The future of standardized testing in university admissions.* New York: Routledge.

6

ASIAN AMERICAN AND PACIFIC ISLANDER COLLEGE STUDENTS

Anneliese A. Singh, Michael J. Cuyjet, and Diane L. Cooper

I think growing up as an Asian American there has always been a label: they're quiet, they don't have a strong presence on campus, they don't stand up for themselves. I think we have a really strong presence on campus, and it's frustrating when people don't realize we're doing good things. I'm very proud of my culture, very proud of my heritage, so it's something I want to share with everyone.

—Lauren Talentino, Northeastern University student (www.thinkexist.com/quotes/laurentalentino)

Asian American and Pacific Islanders (AAPI) face unique challenges in college and university settings. While many families of AAPI students have been in the United States for several generations, AAPI students often experience being treated as a "perpetual foreigner" (Alvarez, 2009). For instance, it is all too common that AAPI students hear questions such as "Where were you born?" (implying that the United States could not be their country of origin) or comments like "Your English is so good!" At the same time, AAPI students may be stereotyped as the "model minority." This is a detrimental myth because it places AAPI people under immense pressure to succeed while simultaneously masking their struggles as college and university students (Singh, 2008).

AAPI students also have sources of resilience that student affairs professionals should recognize and support. Despite the immense diversity of subgroups under the AAPI umbrella, many of them share a common worldview of collectivism. Collectivism refers to the valuation of the group (e.g., family) as opposed to the individual as the most essential component of healthy functioning (Lowe, 2008). At the same time, the forces of acculturation, immigration status, educational attainment, and the intersections of race/ethnicity with other factors (e.g., sexual orientation, socioeconomic status, disability status, gender) for AAPI students further diversify what could be called the AAPI student experience. Adequately meeting the needs of AAPI students in college and university settings requires student affairs professionals to strike a balance between being aware of students' broad, shared AAPI cultural values and avoiding stereotyping *all* AAPI students because of the student affairs professionals' backgrounds. Best practices in working with AAPI students on college campuses require student affairs professionals to seek to see AAPI students holistically with all the complexity of their identities and cultural backgrounds while refraining from making stereotypical assumptions about what might be their ideal college experience. Diversity among AAPI students in terms of ethnic backgrounds, immigration patterns, and socioeconomic status continues to increase (U.S. Department of Education, 2007).

The purpose of this chapter is to assist student affairs professionals with this balancing act by first reviewing the landscape of the Asian American college student experience in the United States and then exploring the *myth of the model minority* regarding its impact on AAPI student learning, development, expectations, and performance. Next, a number of existing identity development models for AAPI students exploring some of their multiple identities are presented. The chapter also includes a review of important influences on the lives of AAPI students, such as family expectations, gender roles, and issues of racism and other oppressions. Examples highlighting common issues AAPI students face in college are included throughout the chapter. Some college resources important to the resilience and thriving of AAPI students are presented. The chapter ends with several discussion questions to facilitate student affairs professionals' work with AAPI student issues.

AAPI People in the United States

The U.S. Census Bureau (2000) defines AAPIs as individuals of Southeast Asian, Far Eastern, or the Indian subcontinent heritage. In the 2000 census, AAPIs constituted 4.6% of the total U.S. population. The relatively small size of the AAPI community belies its complexity in growth and ethnic diversity. There was a 21% increase of people of AAPI heritage between 2000 and 2005 in the United States, and the number of AAPIs is estimated to double by 2050 (U.S. Census Bureau, 2000), which means it is likely that student affairs professionals will increasingly work with an AAPI college student population.

The five largest AAPI subgroups in descending order are Chinese, Filipino, Asian Indian, Vietnamese, and Korean, with Chinese, Filipinos, and Asian Indians accounting for about 58% of the AAPIs in the United States. Of the foreign-born population in the United States, 28% were born in an Asian or Pacific Islander country, and foreign-born AAPIs make up 69% of all Asians in the U.S. (U.S. Census Bureau, 2000), and nearly fourth fifths of Asians in the United States speak a non-English language at home. Because there are more than 45 AAPI subgroups representing a vast array of values, behaviors, and worldviews (U.S. Census Bureau, 2000), student affairs professionals should not assume all students from these groups will respond to similar approaches of engagement (David & Okazaki, 2006).

The enrollment of AAPI students in college is rising at the fastest rate among racial/ethnic groups in the United States. AAPI students' representation in college more than doubles each decade, climbing from 0.8% AAPI students in 1971 to 8.8% in 2005 (Higher Education Research Institute, 2007). In 1978 the numbers of AAPI women students began to exceed the numbers of AAPI men enrolled in college (U.S. Department of Education, 2005). AAPI women's enrollment in higher education surpassed that of AAPI men in 1990, similar to national college enrollment trends for other racial/ethnic groups (U.S. Department of Education, 2005).

According to a research brief from the Higher Education Research Institute of the University of California, Los Angeles (2007), in 1995 Native English speakers in California represented 58.6% of AAPI college students, a jump from 48.1% in 1987. In this same research brief, the researchers documented an increase in the percentage of multilingual AAPI students from 53.4% in 1987 to 58.6% in 1995. Race/ethnicity and socioeconomic class intersect for many AAPI students, as college enrollment trends indicate there are high proportions of AAPI college students whose native language is not English, and they are from families with lower incomes (Kim, 2005).

The Myth of the Model Minority and College Life for AAPI Students

The model minority myth first emerged in a 1966 article in the *New York Times Magazine* titled "Success Story: Japanese-American Style" (as cited by

Inman & Alvarez, 2010). The authors of the article stressed the idea that AAPI families had somehow resolved the challenges of being an ethnic minority group in the United States (Inman & Alvarez). The implication that AAPI people could succeed in the United States despite significant barriers eventually became a tool of racism and has had detrimental impacts on AAPI students for three main reasons. First, the idea that AAPI students can somehow overcome racism places the focus on the individual and not on the institutional racism AAPI college students face (Osajima, 2007). Therefore, student affairs professionals, with all the best intentions, may mistakenly focus on individual issues AAPI students have while missing the opportunity to identify and address more systemic issues of racism. Second, this myth serves to separate AAPI people from other groups of color. In holding up AAPI students as the model minority, the myth fails to address the fact that AAPI families voluntarily migrated to the United States, as opposed to African Americans, many of whom have a history of forced immigration in the form of slavery (Singh, 2008). It is helpful to know this particular point, because student affairs professionals working with AAPI students can look for specific opportunities to ameliorate this divide and build bridges between AAPI students and other students of color. Finally, the myth can effectively mask various academic, financial, and familial challenges AAPI students may face throughout their college years (Museus, 2009).

In addition to these three major impacts, the model minority myth has also promoted the idea that AAPI students are "universally academically successful" (Suyemoto, Kim, Tanabe, Tawa, & Day, 2009, p. 41). Because the myth obscures the heterogeneity of AAPI students, it does not expose the low level of higher educational attainment among some Pacific Islanders (e.g., Hawaiians, Samoans, Filipinos) and Southeast Asians (e.g., Vietnamese, Laotian; Yeh & Chang, 2004). The model minority myth also promotes a stereotype of AAPI students as quiet and submissive individuals who are not like the "other minority" students on campus. Because they are supposed to be nonvocal, AAPI students, faculty, and staff are expected to quietly endure forms of racism, sexism, and heterosexism, as well as other forms of oppression. For this reason, some scholars have advocated that service providers view the model minority myth as a stigma rather than merely a myth (Singh & Chang, under review).

Student affairs professionals should recognize how the deleterious effects of the model minority myth may shape the college experience for AAPI students and develop specific strategies to ameliorate some of these harmful consequences. Despite the model minority myth that stereotypes AAPIs as having higher financial resources, in actuality, the household income of AAPI students was only slightly higher than that of other groups (U.S. Department of Education, 2007). For instance, the U.S. Department of Education calculated that 30.9% of AAPI students had a household income of $40,000 compared to the national percentage of 22.7%. However, these statistics do not reveal that the typical AAPI household is larger than the average national household and that AAPI families and communities are often concentrated in urban areas with extremely high costs of living (Kim, 2005). Adjusting for higher household size and costs of living, more AAPI families fall into the category of low income than the national population (47.4% compared to 39.5%; Higher Education Research Institute, 2007). Therefore, financial aid becomes an important component in AAPI students' decisions about applying to and enrolling in college.

Another myth is that the number of AAPI college students is greater than it actually is, resulting in a mistaken view that AAPI students are "taking over" (National Commission on Asian American and Pacific Islander Research in Education, 2008, p. 4). For instance, there is a large concentration of AAPI students at many U.S. colleges that are deemed "elite." However, this concentration belies the fact that two thirds of all AAPI college students attend only 200 colleges and universities in eight states, with almost half of AAPI students enrolled in schools in California, New York, and Texas. Despite this concentration, the fastest-growing rates of AAPI college enrollment are in the Southern and Midwestern regions of the United States (Higher Education Research Institute, 2007), where college administrators may not be prepared to attend to the needs of this increasing sector.

Although AAPI students are enrolled in U.S. graduate programs at higher rates than other racial/ethnic groups, and 32% of doctorates in 2003 were granted to Asians in science, technology, engineering, and mathematics programs, only 2% were awarded to AAPI students, with the rest being awarded to international students of Asian heritage (National Science Foundation, 2000). AAPI students are also more likely to attend 2-year and 4-year public colleges than private institutions, which is consistent with college enrollment trends of other racial/ethnic groups (National Commission on Asian American and Pacific Islander Research in Education, 2008). In California and Nevada, more than half of AAPI college students are enrolled in public community colleges. The rates of AAPI students selecting a public 2-year college are also increasing faster than enrollment in public 4-year colleges, which is largely attributed to issues of their socioeconomic status and English being their second language (Higher Education Research Institute,

2007). As a group, AAPI students increasingly begin their 1st year of college with high (top 10%) personal ratings in leadership abilities, public speaking, and self-confidence (Higher Education Research Institute, 2007).

As these statistics demonstrate, there is a wide variety of mistaken assumptions and misinformation about AAPI college students. In 2007 the U.S. Congress passed the College Cost Reduction and Access Act, which created the designation of an AAPI higher education serving institution.This designation was designed to identify and address the complexity of educational issues AAPI families and communities face with regard to college financial aid, admissions, selection of major, campus engagement, and other important campus life issues.

It is also important to note that proactively addressing the model minority myth in college and university settings may be challenging. As with any oppressive stereotype, this particular stigma of the model minority has been internalized by many students (Inman & Alvarez, 2010). Therefore, service providers must also be prepared to work with AAPI students who have internalized the mythical expectations and whose families may hold them to unrealistic standards as a result of this stigma. Internalized oppression is a challenging issue to identify and to address. AAPI students often exhibit stress in culturally bound ways (e.g., somatic symptoms; Lee, Su, & Yoshida, 2005). Indigenous healing methods relevant to their cultural background can be important to AAPI students (Yeh, Hunter, Madan-Bahel, Chiang, & Arora, 2004). Student affairs professionals can provide specific programming and outreach efforts designed to challenge the myth of the model minority while also inviting AAPI students to use potential indigenous methods of stress reduction that may be more culturally relevant for them (Yeh, 2004). In addition, student affairs professionals can also actively work with other service providers on campus who assist AAPI students individually, such as counseling center and health center staffs, to ensure they are aware of the ways AAPI students may have internalized this myth and that they are prepared to respond to this myth in a way that is helpful to AAPI students.

While it may be true that for some AAPIs the model minority myth represents a goal rather than a derogatory image (Cuyjet & Liu, 1999), ultimately, the main challenge for student affairs professionals working with AAPI students is to be aware that the characteristics that make up the model minority image may have negative consequences for those AAPIs who cannot live up to the high expectations that stem from the myth (Brydolf, 2009). Campuses that subscribe to the model minority image of AAPIs often do not see or believe there is a need to examine the issues of the AAPI community. As a result, AAPI students (including faculty and staff) are often overlooked and thus become invisible on campus (Cuyjet & Liu). This relative invisibility may affect how services are dispensed and may be especially problematic in the way services are provided to AAPI college students. Simultaneously, service providers should not view AAPI students as passive recipients of the model minority stigma, since some AAPI students will become active on this issue and will bring their activism to college campuses to confront and challenge this stereotype directly (Han, 2004).

AAPI Ethnic Identity Development

Ethnic identity development of AAPI students continues to be the subject of a growing body of literature. In her classic and groundbreaking text, *Asian Americans: Personality Patterns, Identity, and Mental Health,* Uba's (1994) description of the adhibition of ethnic identity (social support or understanding resulting from the invocation of one's AAPI ethnic identity) reminds us that a person is not only a member of an ethnic group but also a member of a sex, an age cohort, a nation, and a group with particular mental or physical abilities and interests. AAPI students' ethnic identity also intersects with their sexual orientation, ability status, socioeconomic status, generational marker, and other salient identities. It is also important to recognize that AAPI students are not just members of the campus community or members of their age cohort or a particular sex but are also members of an ethnic group with particular developmental issues different from those of other groups. In actuality, these developmental issues may be particularly different from those of similar students from the majority culture on campus. This acknowledgment of the importance of ethnic cultural identity is a major tenet of multicultural practice and service provision in the college environment.

This section presents a general ethnic identity development model useful for working with AAPI students on a more individual level. Because few general ethnic identity development models have been applied to AAPI students, caution is urged in using these models, and practitioners are encouraged to view them as a guiding framework for understanding AAPI ethnic student identity (West-Olatunji et al., 2007). Student affairs practitioners who work with college students should acquire at least a cursory knowledge of the particular developmental stages AAPI students may experience to avoid simply categorizing or labeling students and their respective behaviors.

Rather, a working knowledge of the elements of these stages provides professionals with a set of tools to accurately diagnose the student's current relationship with his or her surroundings and the influence—from the dominant culture and from the student's own identified culture—that affects her or his ability to function in that environment. Particularly for those AAPI students exhibiting some signs of distress in the college environment, knowledge of the student's stage or position in a particular applicable identity development model can not only give the counselor an explanation of the student's behaviors but also a strong suggestion of the direction (to the next stage in the model) the student's identity development ought to take to progress. After a description of general ethnic identity development models, this section also reviews identity development models relevant to specific subgroups under the AAPI heading, although there is a shortage of ethnic identity development models for specific subgroups (Perry, Vance, & Helms, 2009). This section concludes with an exploration of the multiple identity development (e.g., sexual orientation, socioeconomic status, generational status) that AAPI students may experience during college. While not intended to be a comprehensive list, these examples can offer the professional some assistance in identifying the status of ethnic identity development in students.

People of color racial identity development model. Helms's (1995) racial identity development model designates experiences of racist stereotypes, biases, and internalized racism as core components of the model, acknowledging the lived experiences people of color have as racialized beings. There are five ego statuses (previously termed *stages*) in the color racial identity model: *conformity, dissonance, immersion-emersion, internalization*, and *integrated awareness.* Helms (1996) later added that these stages should not be thought of as linear processes but rather as statuses that people of color may cycle into and out of based on their racialized experiences. It is important to note that Helms recognized the unique differences between racial and ethnic group experiences, asserting, however, that the majority of people of color shared their experiences of being treated as non-White individuals and therefore used similar coping strategies. To illustrate, a case example of AAPI students is woven through the model of each stage.

In the first stage, *conformity*, an AAPI student may be unaware of societal racism, having internalized dominant stereotypes about his or her cultural group while assimilating into the dominant values and belief systems of White culture. For instance, an AAPI first-year college student may have attended primarily White schools without much contact with other AAPIs other than family. In this example, it is possible the student may not even strongly identify as AAPI but rather sees himself or herself as White in some ways. In the second stage, *dissonance*, an experience (typically with racism) demonstrates to an AAPI student that he or she is not part of the dominant group. This experience is typically negative and shatters the belief an AAPI student may have that "everyone is the same" or that AAPI students are immune to acts of racism. At this stage, an AAPI student may feel disenfranchised and isolated in addition to having questions of belonging. For example, an AAPI student in this stage might wonder what groups he or she belongs to and where the student's place in the college campus actually is, and may isolate himself or herself from group activities as a result of these questions.

In the third stage, *immersion-emersion*, the same AAPI student may begin to see racial and ethnic groups in dichotomous manners, idealizing his or her own Asian/Pacific Islander heritage while distancing himself or herself from the dominant White culture. In this stage, an AAPI student might find refuge and support in AAPI student campus groups and activities while rejecting the dominant campus culture by not participating in more general campus activities. With emersion, the AAPI student continues to identify primarily with the cultural values of an AAPI background while also demonstrating a strong commitment to these cultural values. In this instance, a 1st-year AAPI student may prioritize his or her campus experiences according to the student's AAPI cultural values and beliefs, such as attending AAPI functions and selecting activities that offer the opportunity to delve more deeply into learning about or being connected to AAPI culture.

In the fourth stage, *internalization*, the AAPI student claims a more bicultural reality by internalizing a positive image and value of his or her racial group. For example, an AAPI student may infuse the experiences of living a bicultural reality into class discussions, selection of campus activities, and personal self-exploration. Finally, in the fifth stage, *integrated awareness*, the AAPI student acknowledges the salience of his or her racial identity while also demonstrating understanding and respect of the concerns and values of other racial/ethnic groups. In this stage, the AAPI student may feel confident in challenging the status quo when experiencing racial/ethnic discrimination, trusting that his or her experiences are valid while also being able to acknowledge the concerns and experiences of other groups.

Racial/cultural minority identity development model. Sue and Sue's (2008) model also has five statuses of identity development: conformity, dissonance, resistance/immersion, introspection, and integrative awareness. These statuses are similar to Helms's (1995) people of color model. However, whereas Helms centered experiences of racism and racial identity in her model, Sue and Sue's model addresses racial and cultural components of identity development. The contributions of Sue and Sue's model is that it brings attention to how ethnic minority people in the United States experience racism, which then in turn may influence the degree to which they subscribe to the values, belief systems, lifestyles, and pride of their cultural heritage (Chang & Kwan, 2009).

Revisiting the case example explored in the discussion of Helms's (1995) model, student affairs professionals would include an exploration of how each of the statuses influenced that student's endorsement of her AAPI cultural values and beliefs. In addition, it would also be important to support the cultural aspects of this student's pride and lifestyle. This support could come in the form of delivering programs centered on AAPI students' cultural pride and lifestyle as campuswide events, or it might simply consist of asking individual students questions that support growth of cultural values and beliefs as integral aspects of how satisfied they are with their college experience and environment.

Kim's Asian American identity stages. Although Kim's (1981) model is in need of revision and updating, we include the model to provide a sense of what AAPI students may have experienced in terms of ethnic identity development prior to college enrollment. In her research, Kim found that the process of Asian American identity development for her sample of Sansei (third-generation) Japanese women involves five conceptually distinct stages that are sequential and progressive: *ethnic awareness, White identification, awakening to social political consciousness, redirection to Asian American consciousness,* and *incorporation.*

The first stage, *ethnic awareness,* occurs in children about 3 or 4 years of age, prior to entering elementary school. Children's' attitudes toward being Japanese were either positive or neutral, depending on the extent of family involvement in ethnic activities (Ponterotto & Pedersen, 1993). In the second stage, *White identification,* Asian American children begin to develop a sense that they are different from Whites as they begin to have increased contact with them. These feelings of difference are primarily the result of negative encounters with other children's racial prejudices. Being treated as inferior leads to internalizing White societal values and becoming alienated from oneself and from other Asian Americans (Ponterotto & Pedersen). White identification can be "active," that is, considering oneself very similar to one's White peers and not acknowledging cultural differences, or "passive," in which one does not consider oneself as White but accepts White standards, values, and beliefs as a reference point (Ponterotto & Pedersen).

In the third stage, *awakening to social political consciousness*, one sees oneself as a minority in society and sheds previously held values identified as White and reassesses the merits of White standards. A person's self-concept becomes more positive and "centered around being a minority, being oppressed, not being inferior, and feeling connected to experiences of other minorities" (Kim, 1981). The fourth stage, *redirection to Asian American consciousness*, is when individuals begin to embrace their Asian American identity and demonstrate a desire to immerse themselves in Asian American culture (Ponterotto & Pedersen, 1993). During the immersion period they can feel anger or outrage at White society, but in time individuals work through the emotionally reactive phase and come to a reappraisal of themselves and other Asian Americans, feeling good about themselves and becoming proud to be Asian American. In the final stage, *incorporation*, individuals achieve a healthy, secure balance, feeling comfortable with their own identity and appreciative of other racial groups, including the White majority. One develops a realistic appraisal of all people and does not feel a need to identify either with or against White people.

A model for South Asian Americans. Ibrahim, Ohnishi, and Sandhu (1997) contended that other ethnic identity development models did not adequately attend to issues of immigration and colonization that affect the ethnic identity development of South Asians. Because South Asian immigrants are from countries with histories of colonization, Ibrahim et al. asserted that South Asian Americans could clearly see and accept the cultural differences between them and the host culture. Thus, for the immigrant generation, the authors argued there was no stage similar to the conformity stage where South Asian immigrants to the United States would want to be part of the dominant culture, as "the acceptance of cultural differences is a reality of life for this group" (p. 42). Additionally, because South Asian Americans may hold a belief that the "American dream [means] that hard work will overcome all differences" (p. 42), the dissonance stage for members of this generation occurs when they realize that hard work is not enough for them to succeed, cultural differences may not be overcome, and acceptance by White Americans or other U.S.-born people of color may not occur because this mainstream U.S. culture perceives them as "foreign."

In the resistance and immersion stage, the immigrant generation turns to its South Asian values and rejects all dominant culture and may seek out ways to align with other minority groups that have been oppressed in a like manner. In the introspection stage, South Asian Americans are sufficiently secure about their identity to begin to question previously held dogmatic beliefs. They also begin to seek their individuality within as members of a minority group and to recognize some positive elements in the dominant culture. In the synergistic stage, Asian Americans have a strong sense of self-worth and individuality and are able to accept or reject the cultural values of the dominant and the minority groups on an objective basis (Ibrahim et al., 1997).

Managing multiple identities. Although no model exists for how ethnic identity development of AAPIs intersects with other identity development, this remains an important topic for student affairs professionals to explore with AAPI students. The beginning of the college experience is a time when many traditional-aged students are exploring new aspects of themselves, and the same is also true for AAPI students who are nontraditional students.

College administrators should be aware of the various salient identities AAPI students may have and endeavor to construct college environments so they may explore these multiple identities. For instance, an AAPI student who identifies as lesbian, gay, bisexual, transgender, queer, or questioning (LGBTQQ) may feel very grounded in his or her ethnic/racial identity. However, this student may attend LGBTQQ-related campus events in primarily White LGBTQQ environments where his or her racial/ethnic identity becomes more salient. If this same student is taking courses or is involved with campus organizations with few LGBTQQ students, his or her sexual orientation or gender identity may become more salient to that student. In yet another situation, if this student has come out to friends and peers at college but not to family members, the student may be struggling to integrate his or her racial/ethnic and LGBTQQ identity. Although it is beyond the scope of this chapter to discuss the myriad ways AAPIs' multiple identities influence their college experience, student affairs professionals should strive to see the many layers of identities AAPI students have rather than seeing them only as racial/ethnic beings.

Environmental Influences on AAPI Students

The number of AAPIs in American higher education is growing (Suyemoto et al., 2009), yet AAPI students are often left out of the discourse on education and race (Osajima, 2007). As a means to provide culturally relevant and effective academic environments and services to AAPI college students, it is important to understand how they generally view higher education. Furthermore, it is important for college administrators and faculty to continually challenge their own assumptions about AAPI students to facilitate better academic experiences that match these students' actual needs in college and university environments.

Collectivism and interpersonal interactions. Many AAPI subgroups share a common value of collectivism, which is the valuation and priority of the group, in the form of family or community, as a central factor in relationships (Mau, de Ven, & McCormick, 2004). Although collectivism may seem like a worldview not common in the United States, it is important for student affairs professionals to be aware that collectivism is a value embraced across the globe, from indigenous American peoples and Latinos and Latinas to AAPIs and those of African heritage (Sue & Sue, 2008). Therefore, AAPI students may encounter culture clash in their college environments, as many of these environments are constructed from and grounded in individualistic paradigms that prioritize individuals over the group.

This conflict in cultural values can be immediately evident in the interpersonal interactions AAPI students have with their peers, instructors, and other campus personnel. For instance, a student whose family background is more collectivistic in nature may interact with authority figures on campus in a more deferential manner as a way of demonstrating respect (Brew & Cairns, 2004). However, those in authority positions may not view this deference from AAPI students as respectful or valued—in certain situations such as a class or workshop conducted in an egalitarian leadership style. At the same time, it is also critical for student affairs professionals not to fall prey to stereotypes, for example, such as thinking that this type of deferential respect translates to passivity, noninvolvement, or lack of investment on the part of the AAPI student. Also, because so many AAPI students are living bicultural realities—raised in a home with Asian/Pacific Islander values but socialized in Western learning environments—it is more likely that the AAPI students campus administrators interact with may have a mixture of individualistic and collectivistic components in their interpersonal style.

Faculty and staff should also be aware of the differences that may exist with *low context* and *high context* communication styles (Gudykunst, 2001), as they will influence interpersonal interactions with AAPI students. AAPI students from cultural backgrounds that use high context communication typically have conversational styles that are indirect yet imply meanings. Silence and the use of emotions may also be used to guide interpersonal relationships, including behaviors within these relationships. Low context communication is typically a more Western style of interpersonal interactions. For instance, low context communication is highly interactive, dramatic, and seeks to leave an impression. People who have a low context communication style tend to view silence as uncomfortable or a sign of discomfort in interpersonal relationships. Also important is that AAPI college students may change the degree of the context of their communication to "adapt to the university environment" (Park & Kim, 2008, p. 49). Therefore, faculty and staff should pay careful attention to the ways AAPI students communicate and be culturally responsive in interpersonal interactions. AAPI cultures are not alone in valuing high context communication; people in some Middle Eastern cultures and in countries such as Spain and Greece also value this style of interaction (Hall & Hall, 1990).

An additional cultural component to consider in working with AAPI students is the concept of *loss of face*, which refers to an AAPI student's deference to others within interpersonal relationships. For instance, AAPI students whose value systems are more traditional may refrain from pointing out flaws or faults and/or calling attention to someone's struggles for fear of causing that person loss of face (Zane & Yeh, 2002). An AAPI student might lose face if he or she made a mistake or hurt another person's feelings. This construct is important for student affairs professionals to know especially since loss of face combined with the stigma of being labeled a model minority can increase the pressure AAPI students feel to succeed academically at the risk of their own well-being.

Acculturation, and enculturation. Acculturation is the degree to which AAPI students are "participating in the cultural norms of the dominant group while maintaining the norms of their original culture" (Kim, 2009, p. 99). Acculturation has long been discussed as a salient factor in working with AAPI students. Originally conceptualized as a linear process (Suinn, Ahuna, & Khoo, 1992) describing the contact an immigrant culture has with the host culture (for instance, an immigrant Asian American/Pacific Islander's contact with people born in the United States), acculturation is now viewed as a more complex process (Chun & Akutsu, 2009). Based on the generational status of an AAPI student, there may be acculturation issues that need attention. For instance, an AAPI student who is newly acculturated to a U.S. college setting may need assistance with navigating an unfamiliar environment. A student who holds a more bicultural identity may wish to balance Asian/Pacific Islander and Westernized values. However, another AAPI student who is more acculturated to U.S. values, behaviors, and worldviews may not immediately be seen as a student with pressing needs but may also be exposed to substantial numbers of AAPI students and communities for the first time at college and may encounter his or her first experience with racism and stereotyping.

Although acculturation is a helpful framework in understanding the needs of AAPI students, Kim (2009) also urges a consideration of *enculturation*, "the process of socialization to and maintenance of the norms of one's indigenous culture, including the salient values, ideas, and concepts" (p. 99). Whereas the construct of acculturation presumes that AAPI students would have been socialized in Asian and Pacific Islander environments, enculturation does not make this presumption and is a more useful construct to use when considering how AAPI students who have not experienced acculturation may experience it as they become socialized into their Asian and Pacific Islander cultures. Acculturation and enculturation are important constructs for student affairs professionals, as levels of acculturation and enculturation have been found to influence vocational experiences, attitudes toward seeking help, and participation in counseling (Kim).

Family relationships. As AAPI students begin college, they may need to renegotiate family relationships. Families typically play a primary role in Asian and Pacific Islander communities, with extended family networks, multiple caregivers, and several generations of family members living in a home (Yee, DeBaryshe, Yuen, Kim, & McCubbin, 2007). While many college and student developmental theories address the importance of individuation as a student begins college and view family interdependence as impeding student development, service providers must be cautious in looking at AAPI students from this perspective. Often, the collectivistic values discussed in this chapter are a foundation for AAPI students' well-being and can positively contribute to their college experience. Because of values of familial pride and piety, student affairs professionals may seek to build ways family members may be involved in AAPI student experiences. Similar to many college students, AAPI students may view going to college as the first step in pursuing graduate and professional training or obtaining a job (Liu & Sedlacek, 1999). These functionalist (i.e., practical) views on college may reflect the perception of AAPI parents that their children's attending college should have a family-related pragmatic outcome (Cuyjet & Liu, 1999).

The literature has also suggested that balancing family and school obligations can become a liability for AAPI students (Hwang & Wood, 2008), especially when a student is laboring under the model minority myth (Garrod & Kilkenny, 2007). Findings have suggested acculturative family distancing has a significant psychological impact on AAPI college students when family distancing produces parent-child conflict, resulting in higher levels of psychological distress and greater risks for depression in the student (Hwang & Wood). Therefore, campus service providers should ensure that workshops and programming on college adjustment have a specific component on family concerns. Service providers can use these opportunities to engage AAPI students and their families in discussions about improving communication and navigating cultural conflicts within the family system. Often, AAPI students' success is viewed as a family issue. If an AAPI student is doing well, the AAPI community may regard his or her family in a positive manner, and if this same student is struggling academically or personally, these struggles may be viewed by the AAPI community as reflecting on the family (Singh, 2008). Combined with the model minority stigma, this may result in mounting pressure on AAPI students to succeed. In addition, many AAPI students may be caretakers in their families in some way, resulting in a role reversal (Yee, Su, Kim, & Yancura, 2009). For instance, if the student is the primary English speaker in the family, he or she may have continued commitments and obligations to the family that can prove especially difficult if the college is not located near the family's home. In this regard, AAPI students may have family obligations similar to those of Latinos and Latinas—juggling the role of student and being active, contributing members of the family (Saunders & Serna, 2004). Therefore, AAPI students may have large sources of resilience to manage college environments because of financial, legal, and other social service skills they may have developed. At the same time, these same students may feel stretched thin and worry about adequately serving their family's needs.

Gender roles. Although AAPI students may come from cultural backgrounds with strictly prescribed gender roles for women and men (Inman & Alvarez, 2010), it is important to not stereotype all AAPI students as ascribing to these roles. It is more helpful for faculty and administrators to be aware that patriarchal values are often an integral component of AAPI cultural values and that these patriarchal values may be no more or no less prescribed than the patriarchal values and gender roles in other cultures (Singh, 2008). Gender role conflicts can emerge as significant stressors in the lives of AAPI college students, especially if there are differing views within the family about roles for women and men (Garrod & Kilkenny, 2007). However, student affairs professionals should also seek to understand AAPI college students' potential sources of resilience in managing these types of gender role conflicts in their family and in the campus environment.

Best practices for student affairs professionals include conducting a self-assessment of the gender role stereotypes they assign to AAPI students. In conducting this self-assessment, stereotypes of women as "exotic" and men as "nonsexualized" and "emasculated" may emerge, as well as other gender role stereotypes such as "quiet" or "passive." These gender role stereotypes are inextricably linked to stereotypes of AAPI people that are rooted in misunderstanding and a lack of information. The danger of these gender role stereotypes is that they can preclude important attention to AAPI student concerns. Student affairs professionals should proactively seek to identify and address how these stereotypes interfere with proactive and effective attention to AAPI students' needs.

AAPIs seeking help on campus. Much literature has been written on the reluctance AAPI students have to access and engage such services as counseling (Kim, 2007; Liao, Rounds, & Klein, 2005). This is an increasing concern on college campuses, as recent studies have shown that AAPI college students—particularly AAPI women—are experiencing high rates of clinical depression and suicidal ideation and suicidal completion (Leong, Leach, & Gupta, 2008). Kim suggested that AAPI students' attitudes toward seeking counseling were associated with the loss of traditional AAPI norms of culture (acculturation), and were not associated with the acquirement of European American norms of culture (enculturation). This finding is particularly important for student affairs professionals because levels of acculturation and enculturation can be assessed when addressing the individual and campus community counseling needs of AAPI students. For instance, if an AAPI student is exhibiting psychological distress, asking questions that help assess levels of acculturation or enculturation may assist service providers in determining how likely the student is to follow through on a suggestion to seek counseling services. For those AAPI students who are less acculturated to U.S. norms, it may be helpful to explain thoroughly the purpose and nature of what counseling "looks like" and be proactive in helping the student access counseling resources (e.g., walking the student over to the counseling center and helping the student connect with a culturally responsive counselor).

Because the model minority myth does effectively mask many psychological challenges—such as substance abuse, dating or family violence, clinical depression and anxiety, or another more severe psychopathology—student affairs professionals should be active in ensuring that AAPI student needs are integrated into each outreach and advocacy effort involving campus mental health. Service providers should indeed ensure that images of

AAPIs are included on mental health outreach materials and that they are proactively involving AAPI faculty, staff, and student leaders in outreach and prevention efforts. It is just as important to ensure that staff at the counseling center and other campus units are prepared to actively respond to AAPI students in psychological distress and that they take these situations seriously to prevent further AAPI student distress.

AAPI College Students' Interaction With the Collegiate Environment

There are several opportunities for student affairs professionals to take steps in engaging and retaining AAPI students while being culturally responsive to their unique needs.

AAPI recruitment, retention, and research. Yeh (2002) argued that the model minority myth stigmatized AAPI college students as high achievers and therefore led campus service providers to assume AAPI students had the skill sets they needed to succeed in college environments. Yeh challenged this notion and encouraged service providers to focus on AAPI recruitment, retention, and research. In terms of AAPI recruitment, Yeh noted that service providers may likely be asked why they should focus on AAPI recruitment when AAPI percentages in college are already significant. Yeh responds by reminding student affairs professionals that AAPI students from first-generation, low-income families are still in need of recruitment as they are an under-privileged group. In addition to engaging in community outreach and recruitment efforts, student affairs professionals should also conduct AAPI student needs assessment so that college environments are culturally responsive when AAPI students arrive on campus.

Yeh (2002) also discussed AAPI student retention and suggests several ways to engage faculty and staff in supporting AAPI students who may be educationally at risk. In addition to educating faculty and staff about the presence of AAPI students who may struggle academically, Yeh also suggested creating summer orientation and advising programs geared toward at-risk AAPI students and their families. Yeh stresses the importance of hiring a diverse campus staff with multicultural and bilingual abilities to support the success of these efforts. Finally, with regard to research, Yeh discusses the relative invisibility of AAPI students in campus needs assessments and other developmental challenges AAPI students face in the college environment. Although Yeh does not provide as many specific strategies with regard to research, student affairs professionals can specifically include AAPI students in their general student needs assessment and also target their research on needs assessment through focus groups and individual qualitative interviews with AAPI students.

AAPI studies. Faculty and academic administrators should pay close attention to the curricula offered at college and university campuses to include AAPI history in course work and degree offerings. For those campuses with a formal AAPI department, service providers will have numerous opportunities to collaborate with this academic unit to provide culturally responsive programming geared toward AAPI student needs. The main benefit of this collaboration is that AAPI studies will be able to specifically draw on a rich and multidisciplinary AAPI literature to assist students in making meaning of the sociopolitical context of their campus learning experience. However, it is important to find ways that these collaborations do not occur merely once during the college year, but rather that student affairs professionals have an ongoing and "an integrative perspective involv[ing] a challenge to rethink service delivery as it relates to the educational and developmental needs of [AAPI] students" (Alvarez & Liu, 2002, p. 78). AAPI studies courses provide another place where AAPI students may gather (Chew & Ogi, 1987) and that may be good locations to market student support services and conduct assessments of campus services (Cuyjet & Liu, 1999).

For campuses without AAPI studies, service providers can support campus efforts to initiate such programs while seeking to connect with and involve AAPI faculty and staff in programming.

AAPI student organizations and student leaders. AAPI student clubs and organizations are another means of marketing and delivering services to students. Most of these clubs and organizations are organized along multiple dimensions (e.g., religion, acculturation status, language). However, gaining the trust of student leaders is important and may only come after extended involvement with them (Liu & Sedlacek, 1999). In essence, the notions of credibility (Sue & Sue, 2008) apply here in working with student leaders and groups. Dropping in from time to time to dispense advice or provide information typically is not enough to develop a rapport with student leaders. One may find that AAPI student leaders respond differently to AAPI counselors or student service providers than to non-AAPI personnel. This resonance with AAPI staff may reflect a reliance on ethnic/racial similarity in the absence of personal information about the staff. Thus, it may be necessary for non-AAPIs to work with student leaders to show their commitment to them and to their groups to develop trust and to help these students see that non-AAPIs may share a similar value system (Cuyjet & Liu, 1999).

Building a campus responsive to AAPI students. Suzuki (2002) provided eight specific actions student affairs professionals can take to create campus environments where AAPI students have a sense of belonging and are aware of administrators' responsiveness to their needs. First, he suggested student affairs staff take an active role in the ongoing education of campus units about the harmful effects of the model minority myth. Second, Suzuki argued for the establishment of a committee of people from across campus to track racial harassment of AAPI students while working with campus leaders to creative a more positive environment for them. Third, like Yeh (2002), Suzuki suggested active AAPI recruitment efforts, highlighting the importance of in-service training on AAPI student needs for student affairs staff. Fourth, Suzuki said that AAPI students who use English as a second language should be connected with college supports (e.g., tutoring) to foster their success. This support is especially important as English proficiency has been suggested to be a strong predictor of AAPI student success (Yeh). Fifth, Suzuki suggested developing leadership skills in AAPI student leaders to help increase their involvement with the campus. Sixth, he argued that AAPI student affairs professionals should pursue the enhancement of their leadership and administrative skills through professional development opportunities to support their promotion and advancement. Seventh, Suzuki recommended diversifying the staff of college and student affairs offices through recruitment of AAPI staff and student workers. Eighth, he described the importance of including the underrepresented AAPI subgroups (e.g., Hmong, Samoan) in admissions, outreach, and other recruitment efforts.

Conclusion

The college environment provides unique benefits and challenges for AAPI students. Student affairs professionals, including counselors, advisers, and other student service providers, as well as academic administrators and faculty who are concerned about providing meaningful, culturally-relevant services to AAPI college students have an obligation to educate themselves and their colleagues about the particular attributes of the AAPI student community. Because the term AAPI actually encompasses dozens of different ethnic groups—each with its own characteristic values, beliefs, customs, behaviors, social structures, and language—learning the nuances of each of the AAPI subgroups may seem overwhelming and untenable. Best practices in meeting the needs of AAPI students while also addressing systemic issues of racism and other oppressions in their lives demands that faculty, administrators, and student affairs professionals reframe this seemingly impossible task into an opportunity to learn and grow in awareness of the multicultural and social justice issues affecting this group. More important than simply learning about AAPI students, professionals should understand the effects the college environment and its various agencies and structures can have on AAPIs, particularly those that can aid or hinder successful matriculation and student resilience. Student affairs professionals should also continually assess their perceptions of AAPI students, the effectiveness of the services provided to AAPIs, and specific ways to improve communication and service delivery functions of the campus milieu that does not reinforce stereotypes or mistaken assumptions but rather creates a college environment where AAPI students can thrive.

Discussion Questions

1. Discuss the variety of subgroups in the term AAPI. How will you as a student affairs professional endeavor to refrain from stereotyping these groups while attending to their specific needs?
2. Identify the three major impacts resulting from the model minority myth and how college campuses may address these impacts to provide best practices with AAPI students.
3. Discuss the models of racial/ethnic identity development reviewed in this chapter. What are the similarities and differences? How might you work with AAPI students who have multiple salient identities?
4. What is the difference between acculturation and enculturation, and how would you apply these constructs to building culturally responsive campus environments for AAPI students?
5. How might you connect initial programming geared toward first-year AAPI college students to various campus entities and AAPI studies to foster ongoing collaboration throughout the year?
6. Apply Suzuki's (2002) eight suggestions for student affairs professionals' integration of AAPI student needs into campus environments to your current college environment.

References

Alvarez, A. (2009). Racism: "It's not fair." In A. Alvarez & N. Tewari (Eds.), *Asian American psychology: Current perspectives* (pp. 97–112). New York: Taylor & Francis.

Alvarez, A. N., & Liu, W. M. (2002). Student affairs and Asian American studies: An integrative perspective. In M. K. McEwen, C. M. Kodama, A. N. Alvarez, S. Lee, & C. T. H. Liang (Eds.), *Working with Asian American college students* (pp. 73–80). San Francisco: Jossey-Bass.

Brew, F. P., & Cairns, D. R. (2004). Do culture or situational constraints determine choices of direct or indirect styles in intercultural workplace conflicts. *International Journal of Intercultural Relations, 28*, 331–352.

Brydolf, C. (2009, January). Getting real about the "model minority": Asian Americans and Pacific Islanders fight their stereotypes. *Education Digest*, pp. 37–44.

Chang, T., & Kwan, K. L. K. (2009). Asian American racial and ethnic identity. In A. Alvarez & N. Tewari (Eds.), *Asian American psychology: Current perspectives* (pp. 113–134). New York: Taylor & Francis.

Chew, C. A ., & Ogi, A. Y. (1987). Asian American college student perspectives. In D. J. Wright (Ed.), *Responding to the needs of today's minority students* (pp. 39–48). San Francisco: Jossey-Bass.

Chun, K. M., & Akutsu, P. D. (2009). Assessing Asian American family acculturation in clinical settings: Guidelines and recommendations for mental health professionals. In N. Trinh, Y. C. Rho, F. G. Lu, & K. M. Sanders (Eds.), *Handbook of mental health and acculturation in Asian American families* (pp. 99–122). Totowa, NJ: Humana Press.

College Cost Reduction and Access Act of 2007, H.R. 2669, 110th Cong. (2007).

Cuyjet, M. J., & Liu, W. M. (1999). Counseling Asian and Pacific Islander Americans in the college/university environment. In D. S. Sandhu (Ed.), *Asian and Pacific Islander Americans: Issues and concerns for counseling and psychotherapy* (pp. 151–166). Commack, NY: Nova Science.

David, E. J. R., & Okazaki, S. (2006). Colonial mentality: A review and recommendation for Filipino American psychology. *Cultural Diversity and Ethnic Minority Psychology, 12*, 1–16.

Garrod, A., & Kilkenny, R. (Eds.) (2007). *Balancing two worlds: Asian American college students tell their life stories.* Ithaca, NY: Cornell University Press.

Gundykunst, W. B. (2001). *Asian American ethnicity and communication.* Thousand Oaks, CA: Sage.

Hall, E. T., & Hall, M. R. (1990). *Understanding cultural differences.* Yarmouth, ME: Intercultural Press.

Han, A. (2004). *Asian American X: An intersection of twenty-first-century Asian American voices.* Ann Arbor: University of Michigan Press.

Helms, J. E. (1995). An update on Helms' White and People of Color (POC) racial identity models. In J. G. Ponterotto, J. M. Casas, L. A. Suzuki, & C. M. Alexander (Eds.), *Handbook of multicultural counseling* (pp. 181–198). Thousand Oaks, CA: Sage.

Helms, J. E. (1996). Toward a methodology for measuring and assessing racial as distinguished from ethnic identity. In G. Roysircar-Sodowsky & J. C. Impara (Eds.), *Multicultural assessment in counseling and clinical psychology* (pp. 143–192). Lincoln, NE: Buros Institute of Measurement.

Higher Education Research Institute. (2007). *Beyond myths: The growth and diversity of Asian American college freshman: 1971–2005*. Retrieved August 15, 2009, from http://www.heri.ucla.edu/publicationstore.php

Hwang, W. C., & Wood, J. L. (2008). Acculturative family distancing: Links with self-reported symptomatology among Asian Americans and Latinos. *Child Psychology, 40*, 123–138.

Ibrahim, F., Ohnishi, H., & Sandhu, D. S. (1997). Asian American identity development: A culture-specific model for South Asian Americans. *Journal of Multicultural Counseling and Development, 25*, 34–50.

Inman, A., & Alvarez, A. (2010). Individuals and families of Asian descent. In D. G. Hays & B. T. Erford (Eds.), *Developing multicultural counseling competence: A systems approach* (pp. 246–276). New York: Pearson.

Kim, B. S. K. (2005, April). *The myth of the model minority: Classism*. Panel presentation at the American Counseling Association, Montreal, Quebec, Canada.

Kim, B. S. K. (2007). Adherence to Asian and European American cultural values and attitudes toward seeking professional psychological help among Asian American college students. *Journal of Counseling Psychology, 54*(4), 474–480.

Kim, B. S. K. (2009). Acculturation and enculturation of Asian Americans. In A. Alvarez & N. Tewari (Eds.), *Asian American psychology: Current perspectives* (pp. 97–112). New York: Taylor & Francis.

Kim, J. (1981). *Processes of Asian American identity development: A study of Japanese American women's perceptions of their struggle to achieve positive identities as Americans of Asian ancestry*. Unpublished doctoral dissertation, University of Massachusetts, Amherst.

Lee, R. M., Su, J., & Yoshida, E. (2005). Coping with intergenerational family conflict among Asian American college students. *Journal of Counseling Psychology, 52*(3), 389–399.

Leong, F. T. L., Leach, M. M., & Gupta, A. (2008). Suicide among Asian Americans: A critical review with research recommendations. In M. M. Leach & F. T. L. Leong (Eds.), *Suicide among racial and ethnic minority groups: Theory, research, and practice* (pp. 117–141). New York: Taylor & Francis.

Liao, H. Y., Rounds, J., & Klein, A. G. (2005). A test of Cramer's (1999) help-seeking model and acculturation effects with Asian and Asian American college students. *Journal of Counseling Psychology, 52*(3), 400–411.

Liu, W. M., & Sedlacek (1999). Differences in leadership and co-curricular perception among entering male and female Asian Pacific American college students. *Journal of the Freshman Year Experience, 11*(2), 93–114.

Lowe, S. M. (2008). A frank discussion on Asian Americans and their academic and career development. In N. Tewari & A. N. Alvarez (Eds.), *Asian American psychology: Current perspectives* (463–482). New York: Routledge.

Mau, L., de Ven, P. V., & McCormick, J. (2004). Individualism-collectivism, self-efficacy, and other factors associated with risk taking among gay Asian and Caucasian men. *AIDS Education and Prevention, 16*(1), 55–67.

Museus, S. D. (2009). A critical analysis of the exclusion of Asian Americans from higher education research and discourse. In L. Zhan (Ed.), *Asian American voices: Engaging, empowering, enabling* (pp. 59–76). New York: NLN Press.

National Commission on Asian American and Pacific Islander Research in Education. (2008). *Asian Americans and Pacific Islanders: Facts, not fiction—setting the record straight.* Retrieved August 15, 2009, from http://professionals.collegeboard-.com/profdownload/08–0608-AAPI.p df

Osajima, K. (2007). Replenishing the ranks: Raising critical consciousness among Asian Americans. *Journal of Asian American Studies, 10,* 59–83.

Park, Y. S., & Kim, B. S. K. (2008). Asian and European American cultural values and communication styles among Asian American and European American college students. *Cultural Diversity and Ethnic Minority Psychology, 14*(1), 47–56.

Perry, J. C., Vance, K. S., & Helms, J. E. (2009). Using the People of Color Racial Identity Attitude Scale Among Asian American college students: An exploratory factor analysis. *American Journal of Orthopsychiatry, 79*(2), 252–260.

Ponterotto, J. G., & Pedersen, P. B. (1993). *Preventing prejudice.* Beverly Hills: Sage.

Saunders, M., & Serna, I. (2004). Making college happen: The college experiences of first-generation Latino students. *Journal of Hispanic Higher Education, 3*(2), 146–163.

Singh, A. A. (2008). A social justice approach to counseling Asian American/Pacific Islanders. In C. Ellis & J. Carlson (Eds.), *Cross cultural awareness and social justice issues in counseling.* New York, NY: Routledge.

Singh, A. A., & Chang, P. L. (Under review). Current issues and trends in assessment with Asian American/Pacific Islanders. Manuscript submitted for publication.

Sue, D. W., & Sue, D. (2008). *Counseling the culturally different: Theory and practice* (5th ed.). New York: Wiley.

Suinn, R. M., Ahuna, C., & Khoo, G. (1992). The Suinn-Lew Asian Self-Identity Acculturation Scale: Concurrent and factorial validation. *Educational and Psychological Measurement, 52*(4), 1041–1046.

Suyemoto, K. L., Kim, G. S., Tanabe, M., Tawa, J., & Day, S. C. (2009). Research on Asian American college student experiences. *New Directions for Institutional Research, 142,* 41–55.

Suzuki, B. H. (2002). Revisiting the model minority stereotype: Implications for student affairs practice and higher education. *New Directions for Student Services, 97,* 21–32.

Uba, L. (1994). *Asian Americans: Personality patterns, identity, and mental health.* New York: Guilford Press.

U.S. Census Bureau. (2000). *General demographic characteristics for the Asian population* [PHC-T-15]. Retrieved August 20, 2009, from http://www.factfinder.censur s.gov/population/projection/nation/summary

U.S. Department of Education. (2005). *Gender differences in participation and completion of undergraduate education and how they have changed over time.* Retrieved on September 15, 2009, from http://www.nces.ed.gov/fastfacts/display.asp?id = 98

U.S. Department of Education. (2007). *Characteristics of minority-serving institutions and minority undergraduates enrolled in these institutions.* Retrieved on September 15, 2009, from http://www.nces.ed.gov/fastfacts/display.asp?id = 98

West-Olatunji, C. A., Frazier, K. N., Guy, T. L., Smith, A. J., Clay, L., & Breaux, W. (2007). The use of the racial/cultural identity development model to understand a Vietnamese American: A research case study. *Journal of Multicultural Counseling & Development, 35*(1), 40–50.

Yee, B., DeBaryshe, B., Yuen, S., Kim, S., & McCubbin, H. (2007). Asian American and Pacific Islander families: Resilience and life-span socialization in a cultural context. In F. Leong, A. G. Inman, A. Ebreo, L. Lang, L. Kinoshita, & M. Fu (Eds.), *Handbook of Asian American psychology* (2nd ed., pp. 69–86). Thousand Oaks, CA: Sage.

Yee, B., Su, J., Kim, Y. K., & Yancura, L. (2009). Asian American and Pacific Islander families. In A. Alvarez & N. Tewari (Eds.), *Asian American psychology: Current perspectives* (pp. 295–315). New York: Taylor & Francis.

Yeh, C. J., & Chang, T. (2004). Understanding the multidimensionality and heterogeneity of the Asian American experience. *PsychCRITIQUES, 49*(5), 583–586.

Yeh, C. J., Hunter, C. D., Madan-Bahel, A., Chiang, L., & Arora, A. K. (2004). Indigenous and interdependent perspectives of healing: Implications for counseling and research. *Journal of Counseling & Development, 83*(4), 410–419.

Yeh, T. L. (2002). Asian American college students who are educationally at risk. In M. K. McEwen, C. M. Kodama, A. N. Alvarez, S. Lee, & C. T. H. Liang (Eds.), *Working with Asian American college students* (pp. 61–71). San Francisco: Jossey-Bass.

Zane, N., & Yeh, M. (2002). The use of culturally-based variables in assessment: Studies on loss of face. In K. S. Kurasaki, S. Okazaki, & S. Sue (Eds.), *Asian American mental health: Assessment theories and methods* (pp. 123–138). New York: Kluwer Academic/Plenum.

7

AFRICAN AMERICAN COLLEGE STUDENTS

Lamont A. Flowers and Bettina C. Shuford

The experiences and concerns of African American college students have been the topic of considerable debate for many decades. In fact no other racial group in American history has been so misunderstood. The primary reason for this debate and resulting confusion can be traced to the period between slavery and the Jim Crow era of segregation, the effects of which continue to be felt to the present. The overt discrimination that existed during those times represented a clear impediment to democracy and educational opportunity. The fact that some African Americans were not permitted (by law, in some states) to exercise the basic human rights outlined in the Constitution is indicative of the negation of opportunities for African Americans. The overt signs of discrimination, including not being able to drink from certain water fountains and socialize in various establishments, had spillover effects on all other areas of human enterprise, especially education.

The fact that this level of discrimination was allowed to last for hundreds of years is the starting point for any real discussion on African American college students. It is important not to overlook the "peculiar institution" of slavery and the later Jim Crow era during which educational opportunities were limited for African Americans. Considering the African American college student in this context is important for uncovering the truth and for analyzing qualitative and quantitative data, historical documents, identity theories, and the latest research with a perspective that is rooted in reality and intellectual honesty. Intellectual honesty is defined here as an analytical process that considers the totality of the information in developing new viewpoints and reformulated practice. Keeping in mind four fundamental questions will better prepare the reader to work with and enhance the intellectual and social development of African American college students: What are my personal perspectives about African American people? What do I know about the history, circumstances, and lives of African American people? How can I learn more about African American people? and In what ways can I use my knowledge of African American history, culture, and research to better facilitate growth in African American students on campus?

Collectively, African American students represent a unique mixture of racial heritages that include African, Caribbean, Nigerian, and Haitian, just to name a few. However, for the purposes of this chapter, based on the definition used in the 2000 census (U.S. Census Bureau, 2001), the term *African American* refers to "people having origins in any of the Black race groups of Africa." Because African Americans represent a diverse mixture of individuals from a number of nationalities and countries, the answers to the preceding questions may differ depending on the Black or African American students one has encountered (the terms *Black* and *African American* are used interchangeably in this chapter).

The first section of this chapter is a discussion of the effects of historical discrimination on African Americans in general and African American college students in particular. The second section deals with student development theory and examines how African American students may develop in college. The four-stage model of African American identity development is defined along with behavioral examples in the third section of the chapter. The fourth section delineates selected characteristics, including demographic and precollege, of African American college students along with enrollment statistics. The fifth section offers a best practices list of programs that have been designed for the recruitment, retainment, and success of African American students on college campuses. The sixth section presents some relevant research findings and a brief discussion of needed future research.

History of African Americans in Higher Education

Access to higher education by African Americans has been greatly influenced by a social system that has perpetuated differential treatment of groups based on race and systematically affected the accessibility of higher education for African Americans. Because of past and enduring inequities in relation to educational opportunity, a multitier educational class has emerged, whose distinct levels remain hard to define. What is clear is that today's African American college students—many of whom are first-generation students—are the product of intense civil rights campaigns and significant legislation.

The dream of achieving a higher education for African Americans prior to the Civil War was suppressed by a social system that could only succeed if slaves were kept in ignorance and a state of submissiveness. A philosophical belief that African Americans were inferior and an elaborate legal system were used to deny them an education (Fleming, 1976). Despite the barriers, 28 African Americans obtained a baccalaureate degree by 1860 (Bowles & DeCosta, 1971). Alexander Lucius Twilight is documented as the first African American to receive a college degree in 1823 from Middlebury College (Fleming). Since formal preparation was not an option for the majority of African Americans and Whites, apprenticeships and self-study were acceptable means of training for professional and skilled laborers (Bowles & DeCosta, 1971; Fleming, 1976). A number of schools in the South were established during the pre–Civil War period for the sole purpose of educating African Americans. Cheyney University of Pennsylvania (created in 1842), Lincoln University (1854), and Wilberforce University (1856) were the first schools established for African Americans, and later became degree-granting institutions (Bowles & DeCosta, 1971; Thomas & Hill, 1987).

After the Civil War, many of the large church and missionary groups, along with the Freedmen's Bureau that was created by the War Department in 1865, established higher education institutions in the South for African Americans. Between 1865 and 1890, hundreds of private higher education institutions were founded with the words normal, college, or university in their names. Many of these institutions were established as elementary and secondary schools with the eventual goal of becoming degree-granting institutions. At one point in the early 1870s, the percentage of Black children enrolled in school was higher than that of Whites. However, by the 1900s the numbers had declined as discrimination laws began to proliferate (Spring, 2001). Despite the changing political climate, strides had been made toward the education of Blacks. According to DuBois and Dill (as cited in Bowles & DeCosta, 1971), over 1,000 individuals had graduated from historically Black institutions (HBIs) by 1895.

While the legal system was used to suppress African Americans' access to higher education in the 18th and 19th centuries, it began to open doors for African Americans in the late 19th century and into the 20th century. The second Morrill Act of 1890, which provided equitable funding for Black land grant institutions, and the 1896 Supreme Court ruling of *Plessey v. Ferguson*, which established the separate but equal doctrine, spurred significant growth among HBIs in the South (Bowles & DeCosta, 1971; Fleming, 1976; Pounds, 1987). However, the type of education Blacks should receive gave rise to philosophical debates within the Black community. The industrial education approach advocated by Booker T. Washington was influenced by the political climate in the South and focused on developing good work and moral habits. The industrial approach created a place for Blacks in the new industrial order in the South but maintained the social order of segregated schools. W. E. B. DuBois, on the other hand, believed in a traditional liberal arts education that would train future leaders within the Black community (Spring, 2001).

Opportunities for African Americans to attend predominantly White institutions (PWIs) were still very limited during this period. A turning point in the struggle for access to higher education was the 1954 Supreme Court ruling in *Brown v. Board of Education* (Bowles & DeCosta, 1971; Fleming, 1976; Pounds, 1987). Sparked by pressure from the NAACP, mounting tensions, and legal maneuverings of African Americans, the Supreme Court ruled that education could not remain disconnected and separate in America.

Brown v. Board of Education (1954) was revolutionary in its effects on education because of the inclusion of African Americans in the educational process. African Americans in the South were no longer limited to attendance at HBIs. Despite the ruling, some schools remained resistant to change. The Civil Rights Act of 1964 banning discrimination in federally funded programs further enhanced African American access to higher education (Fleming, 1976).

The period after the *Brown v. Board of Education* (1954) ruling was a great time of transition for HBIs and PWIs (Bowles & DeCosta, 1971). In addition to the factors already noted, other developments influenced college enrollment of African American students in the 1940s and 1950s. Prior to 1945, 90% of African Americans in college were enrolled in HBIs in the South (Garibaldi, 1991). The 1944 GI Bill of Rights and the Korean War significantly contributed to the increase in the number of African American males who enrolled in institutions of higher education (Garibaldi, 1991). The migration of African Americans to the North in the early 1940s positively affected enrollment of African American students in northern colleges (Bowles & DeCosta, 1971).

College enrollment for African American students continued to increase in the 1960s and 1970s as veterans from the Vietnam War used funding from the GI Bill to attend college (Garibaldi, 1991). Enrollment levels for African Americans increased significantly in the mid-1970s because of expansion of federal legislation and federal policies aimed at reducing barriers to minority and low-income students (Hill, 1983).

Over the years, the total college enrollment for African American students has steadily increased (Carter & Wilson, 1996; Nettles & Perna, 1997). These statistics show an upward trend for African Americans and reflect the continued desire of African Americans to pursue higher education in the United States. The interactions of various political, legislative, and governmental influences have been instrumental and indispensable in spurring and facilitating African Americans' pursuit for higher education. While significant progress has been made in the educational attainment of African Americans, their proportional representation in college continues to fall below the rate of White students. Improving access to higher education for African Americans continues to be a priority even in the 21st century.

Student Development Theory and African American College Students

The college experience enables African American students, like other students, to gain a variety of skills, values, and knowledge bases that promote academic and social development in college and beyond. To better assist student affairs professionals and to spur additional research on this topic, McEwen, Roper, Byrant, and Langa (1990) offered a list of developmental issues that need to be addressed by student affairs professionals and researchers who want to gain a better understanding of African American student development in college. Based on the literature and personal observations they articulated nine developmental tasks essential to academic and social growth for African American students in college. In this section we highlight their salient issues and suggest how student affairs professionals can assist African American students in achieving each task. To fully understand and promote the transitions and growth that African American students should make in each developmental area, we recommend that student affairs professionals explore the underlying theory more deeply.

Developmental Task 1: Developing Ethnic and Racial Identity

African Americans need to reflect on how the formal and informal structures of American society affect them and the extent to which their racial status influences their interactions with the larger society. This developmental task is extremely important because it speaks to African American students' perceptions of self-worth, self-confidence, and self-esteem in and out of the classroom. Since there is a proliferation of negative images, verbal and nonverbal, that can be found in various forms of the media (music lyrics, television, the Internet), it is important for African Americans to provide opportunities at critical junctures during the educational process to challenge problematic societal and personal interactions. Some suggestions to counteract these negative interactions are to connect African Americans with role models that exhibit positive attributes and communication tools to challenge the systemic challenges. Additionally support groups or counterspaces can be created so African American students can have an opportunity to engage in dialogue about issues they face on a daily basis. Other classroom and practice examples are noted in chapter 17 for teachers and administrators.

Developmental Task 2: Interacting With the Dominant Culture

This developmental task refers to the experiences and interactions that African American students have with other students on campus. It is important that campus administrators continually assess and improve the campus climate in ways that promote productive student-student and student-faculty interactions for all students on campus.

Developmental Task 3: Developing Cultural Aesthetics and Awareness

This task is a reminder that African American students may greatly value their racial heritage. This urges student affairs professionals to plan programs that support and celebrate African American culture and embrace African American history throughout the academic year, and faculty should incorporate culturally relevant material and perspectives in the curriculum.

Developmental Task 4: Developing Identity

This developmental task focuses on the extent to which African American students learn to understand themselves better and become comfortable with their personal identity. Faculty and staff must keep in mind that African American students' perceptions of their identity are constantly evolving and that their identity may influence their cognitive and affective growth in college.

Developmental Task 5: Developing Interdependence

Developing interdependence involves striking a balance between self-reliance, independence, and family identity. For maximum interdependence African American students must remain close to familial ties as well as engage in actions that promote personal development and individual growth. Connecting with family for encouragement and support can be accomplished with the use of technology, particularly, e-mail, text messages, and Internet social networking such as Facebook and MySpace. More families are using technology to share spiritual notes, updates on daily activities, and news about grades and classroom activities. Students are more transparent about their emotions when using technology, and they may be more receptive to online support, but it should not completely take the place of verbal contact.

Developmental Task 6: Fulfilling Affiliation Needs

This developmental task addresses a fundamental concern for all students: the sense of belonging. African American students who perceive the institution as hostile or alienating will be less likely to interact with the campus environment. Thus, campus administrators need to assess African American students' perceptions of the institutional environment and levels of engagement in and out of the classroom to ensure that these students perceive the campus environment as welcoming and friendly.

Developmental Task 7: Surviving Intellectually

Academic achievement is very important to African American students. Thus, they, like other students, are worried about their cognitive development and put forth the effort to study and earn good grades. Higher education professionals should consider the intellectual survival of African Americans as a top priority. They can promote African American students' academic success by including curricular and cocurricular content that is culturally relevant, incorporating pedagogies that are responsive to diverse needs, providing supportive mentors, and embracing the diverse perspectives African American students bring with them to campus (Quaye, Tambascia, & Talesh, 2009).

Developmental Task 8: Developing Spirituality

Spiritual development is also very important in the life of many African American students. Although higher education professionals may not have the knowledge to assist in the spiritual development of African American students, they should be aware of this important developmental task and put in place people and policies that can provide the necessary support.

Developmental Task 9: Developing Social Responsibility

This developmental task is intended to examine the reasons many African American students seek to help others and contribute their time engaging in community service. Student affairs professionals along with faculty who include service learning in the curriculum should keep in mind that some African American students will participate in service-oriented activities while others may need encouragement. This may be accomplished by establishing programs that seek to combine the needs of African American students to support the greater good while at the same time allowing them to realize the personal gains associated with helping others.

Although other tasks are important to African American student development, including developing vocational skills, developing meaningful interpersonal relationships, and navigating a hostile campus environment, these nine developmental tasks should be a primary charge for those who wish to enhance the educational experiences and outcomes for African American students. As McEwen, Roper, Byrant, and Langa (1990) state, "Student affairs professionals must develop out of the experiences of African Americans workable theories of student development" (p. 434). Although some research has explored these developmental tasks, the literature has not considered these issues in any great detail. Thus, while student development theorists have spent a great deal of time examining student developmental concerns for White college students, African American students have received less attention. In fact, most of the student development theories that shape our practice and research are based almost exclusively on studies conducted on White students at PWIs. While we do not advocate abandoning those theories, the situation calls for scholars and student affairs researchers to develop new theories that incorporate African American students' perspectives, concerns, and issues if we are truly to better assist and understand African American students on campus.

African American Identity Development

The sparse theoretical literature on African American students has overwhelmingly focused on how they develop a racial identity and the influence their identity has on academic achievement, student involvement, and perceptions of the institutional environment. In fact, most of the published research related to psychosocial development for African American students conducted over the past 30 years has addressed some aspect of their racial identity or the extent to which they have come to understand how their racial status affects their daily life on campus and society.

Until recently, Cross's (1971) racial identity development model represented the most detailed and most often used explanation of the transformative processes that African Americans go through as a result of personal and interpersonal experiences and interactions with different levels of American society. Cross's model includes five stages: pre-encounter, encounter, immersion-emersion, internalization, and internalization and commitment. Cross's theory of racial identity has been used by numerous researchers (Goodstein & Ponterotto, 1997; Helms, 1990; Helms & Carter, 1991; Mitchell & Dell, 1992; Parham & Helms, 1981, 1985a, 1985b; Parker & Flowers, 2003; Poindexter-Cameron & Robinson, 1997; Pope, 1998; Taylor & Howard-Hamilton, 1995). The cumulative findings of this research indicate that racial and ethnic identities are important predictors of self-esteem, student involvement, and academic achievement for African American college students. This section discusses the latest development in African American racial identity research and provides guidance for student affairs professionals to better serve African American students on campus.

Since 1971 Cross (1991) and other researchers (Cross & Vandiver, 2001; Vandiver, 2001; Vandiver, Fhagen-Smith, Cokley, Cross, & Worrell, 2001; Worrell, Cross, & Vandiver, 2001) have redefined and revised the original theory of racial identity in light of subsequent research and more than 20 years of reflection and refinement regarding conceptions of the importance of race in American society. The revised model incorporates four primary stages: pre-encounter, encounter, immersion-emersion, and internalization. The revised model presupposes that an individual may belong to a primary group and that his or her frame of reference or group affiliation is determined by his or her racial identity. Cross (1991) also suggests that the degree of significance race has in people's life plays an important role in their racial identity development. Vandiver (2001) stated, "Race salience refers to the importance or significance of race in a person's approach to life and is captured across two dimensions: degree of importance and the direction of the valence. Race salience can range from low to high in importance and from positive to negative in valence" (p. 168). Using this basic framework, one can begin to better understand the nature of African American racial identity and the possible outcomes of such developmental process stages in college settings. Stated differently, African American students may consider their racial identity positively or negatively, and at the same time race may or may not have a considerable amount of significance in their lives.

In the pre-encounter stage of the revised model, African Americans have not experienced a direct action (i.e., encounter) that has caused them to question their racial identity and move them into deeper self-reflection about the importance of race in their lives. Pre-encounter has three separate "identity clusters" (Vandiver et al., 2001) that typically characterize African American thought processes and actions: assimilation, miseducation, and self-hatred. A pre-encounter assimilation identity refers to people who do not attach a great deal of significance to their racial status and who most closely relate with the dominant perspective. A pre-encounter miseducation identity refers to people who accept the negative depiction of African American people in images and stereotypes that appear in the media (newspapers, television programs, etc.).

The pre-encounter self-hatred identity applies to individuals who have internalized a concept of African American inferiority and as a result may dislike themselves and other African American people.

The encounter stage refers to an experience that causes an African American to reflect on his or her racial identity. According to Vandiver (2001) "the Encounter stage represents a very fluid period in development and is not easily categorized as other stages" (p. 168). African Americans at the encounter stage may also show signs of depression or guilt in light of the encounter.

Following the encounter stage, immersion-emersion is characterized by an intense interest in and celebration of African American culture (referred to as intense Black involvement identity) and a disinterest in White culture and avoidance of White culture (anti-White identity). Based on the new conceptions of the model, both identities may be present in African American individuals and may even develop simultaneously.

The final stage, internalization, is based on the acceptance of and respect for African American culture. Internalization may develop into four separate identity clusters: Black nationalist, biculturalist, multiculturalist racial, and multiculturalist inclusive. A Black nationalist identity refers to "the positive internalization of being Black" (Vandiver, 2001, p. 169), characterized by an intense focus on African American history, culture, politics, and expression. People with the Black nationalist identity may hold a separatist view (e.g., African Americans should develop their own social, educational, and economic institutions) or an inclusive view (e.g., African Americans should work within the dominant social, educational, and economic institutions).

Those with biculturalist identities may support African American culture as well as the American cultural frame of reference (Vandiver et al.). African Americans who have strong connections to African American culture as well as other cultural groups represent the multiculturalist racial identity. The multiculturalist inclusive identity is characterized by African Americans who have cultural connections and belief systems that resonate with more than one ethnic group and more than one cultural group.

Higher education administrators and faculty at PWIs must recognize that African American students will have encounter experiences that may begin a process of identity exploration. This does not imply that all students will perceive every encounter in the same way or that all African American students will react or respond to acts of insensitivity and discrimination in the same way. Nor is it implied that all African American students will develop a racial identity or that African American racial identity will progress in the stages advanced by Cross (1991) and others (Cross & Vandiver, 2001; Vandiver, 2001; Vandiver et al., 2001; Worrell, Cross, & Vandiver, 2001). However, it is clear from additional research (Ancis, Sedlacek, & Mohr, 2000; Solórzano, Ceja, & Yosso, 2000) and the general observations of the authors that institutional environments on some PWI campuses provide African American students with multiple encounters of racism, discrimination, and intolerance, which may result in the development of a racial or ethnic identity.

Characteristics of African American College Students

In recent years the number of African American students on college campuses has increased. According to national estimates, in 1990 African American students made up about 10% of the total undergraduate enrollment; in 2000 African American students made up about 12% of the total undergraduate enrollment (National Center for Education Statistics [NCES], 1993, 2002). In 2008 African American college students were about 14% of the undergraduate student enrollment (Cominole, Riccobono, Siegel, Caves, & Rosen, 2008; Wei et al., 2009). The growth in the number of African American students has been accompanied by a change in their characteristics that student affairs professionals and others who are interested in facilitating growth for African American students need to understand. Toward that end, the following section presents descriptive data including demographic and precollege characteristics and enrollment statistics. All the data reported in this section are based on surveys from the National Postsecondary Student Aid Study, 2007–2008 (hereafter referred to as NPSAS:2008). The NPSAS:2008 student sample was statistically weighted to represent about 21 million undergraduate students attending 2-year and 4-year colleges during the 2007–2008 academic year. The results that follow are based entirely on NPSAS:2008 data collected during July 2007 through June 2008.

Demographic and Precollege Characteristics

The statistical results that follow were based on the percentage of African American students enrolled among the nation's 2-year and 4-year colleges in 2008. Based on data taken from the NPSAS:2008, African American females constituted about 63% of the total African American undergraduate enrollment, and about 37% percent were males. Most (47%) African American undergraduates were between the ages of 15 and 23. Nineteen percent were between the ages of 24 and 29, and 34% were 30 or above. Data showed that 23% of African American undergraduates had at least one parent who had attained a bachelor's degree or higher. Of all African American undergraduates, 16% were married and 84% were not married. Of all African American students, 10% reported having a disability.

Enrollment Statistics

Data also indicated that 66% of all African American undergraduates attended public colleges and universities, and 27% of all African American undergraduates attended private colleges and universities. Forty-one percent of all African American undergraduates attended 2-year institutions, and about 35% attended 4-year institutions. Forty-five percent of all African American students attended college exclusively full-time, and 38% attended college exclusively part-time. The remaining 17% attended college part-time and full-time. African American students pursued a wide array of academic subjects: humanities (12%), social/behavioral sciences (6%), life sciences (4%), physical sciences (less than 1%), math (less than 1%), computer/information science (4%), engineering (4%), education (5%), business/management (20%), health (21%), vocational/technical (2%), other technical/professional (13%). Seven percent were undeclared majors.

We recommend that individual campuses undertake their own data collection and that student affairs practitioners, academic administrators, and faculty consider the resulting data and compare them to other racial and ethnic groups on campus to determine whether African American students are just as likely as other groups to have interactions with faculty and staff, perceive a safe campus environment, and obtain adequate support in and out of class. This would be a preliminary step toward ensuring that African American students' needs are being met and that they are developing in meaningful and appropriate ways.

Sample Programs That Facilitate the Development of African American Students in College

A variety of programs and services have been identified as having an impact on the recruitment, retention, and success of underrepresented students. Smith (1997) found that programs that focus on students' transition to college, mentoring initiatives, and specialized services such as ethnic theme housing and support services contribute to the retention and satisfaction of students of color.

The following programs, under such categories as academic success, leadership, and mentoring, represent some of the best practices for serving African American students on college campuses. The list was compiled from a variety of sources, including a call for model programs addressing ethnic diversity from one of the Knowledge Communities of the Student Affairs Administrators in Higher Education (NASPA), the American Association of Colleges and Universities Diversity Web site, experts in the field, and from program presentations at national student affairs conferences.

Academic Success

Options Through Education at Boston College is a residential bridge program for a select group of diverse students who have demonstrated leadership for overcoming challenging educational and financial circumstances. Students receive course credits in English, math and oral communication and receive academic and financial support throughout their 4 years of college.

Contact Information: Office of AHANA Student Programs, Thea Bowman AHANA Center, 72 College Road, Boston College, Chestnut Hill, MA 02467, http://www.bc.edu/offices/ahana/pro grams/ote.html

NKUROCKS at Northern Kentucky University, designed to assist incoming African American freshman make the transition from high school to college, has four components: orientation, mentoring, Professional Mondays, and a credit-bearing transition course called UNV

100. Professional Mondays is a weekly convocation series on a wide range of topics that gives students the opportunity to apply knowledge and skills to real-world situations.

Contact Information: African American Student Affairs & Ethnic Services, University Center 209, Northern Kentucky University, Highland Heights, KY 41099, http://www.nku.edu/~aasa/

The Gateway Scholars Program at the University of Texas at Austin aims to maximize academic success and provide social connections for new first-generation and underrepresented students. The program offers smaller classes in math and science, course work in critical thinking and life skills, academic advising, individual counseling, peer advising, tutoring, and social, cultural, and recreational activities.

Contact Information: Longhorn Center for Academic Excellence, University of Texas at Austin, 100 West Dean Keeton Street, Student Services Building 4,400, Austin, Texas 78712, http://www.utexas.edu/diversity/ddce/lcae/gateway.php

Graduate Education Preparation

The Summer Research Opportunity Program at the University of Utah strives to increase the number of underrepresented students in PhD programs and encourage them to pursue careers in university teaching and research. Participants work with an individual faculty member on research and receive up to four semester hours of academic credit and a stipend.

Contact Information: University of Utah, Salt Lake City, Utah 84112, http://www.psych.utah.edu/srop/no.php

The Ronald E. McNair Postbaccalaureate Achievement Program, funded by the U.S. Department of Education, prepares students from disadvantaged backgrounds for doctoral studies by involving them in research and other scholarly activities. The ultimate goal is to increase the number of low-income, first-generation, or underrepresented students enrolling in graduate school.

Contact Information: http://www.ed.gov/programs/triomcnair/index.html

Leadership

The Minority Student Leadership Initiative at the University of Wyoming pairs first-year underrepresented students with a student mentor and a faculty/staff mentor, creating a triad mentoring relationship.

The student and the two mentors usually meet a few times each month to discuss transition issues and to explore leadership opportunities outside the classroom.

Contact Information: P.O. Box 3135, University of Wyoming, Laramie, WY 82071, http://www.uwyo.edu/MSLI/

Mentoring Programs

The African-American Faculty and Staff Association (AAFSA) Multicultural Mentor Project at California State University, Fullerton, pairs first-year students with members of the AAFSA and links them to existing campus support programs based on their individual needs. AAFSA members facilitate monthly dialogue sessions and activities with the students. The project is coordinated by the Multicultural Leadership Center, the African American Resource Center, the Dean of Students Office, and AAFSA.

Contact Information: Dean of Students Office, P.O. Box 34080, Cal State Fullerton, Fullerton, CA 92834, http://www.fullerton.edu/aafsa/

The Africana Mentoring Program at Duke University provides academic and social support for first- and second-year African American students and serves as a link between first-year students, upper-level students, faculty, and staff. Juniors and seniors serve as mentors to students in easing their transition to a PWI. Through academic support and guidance, the program aims to enhance the experience of African American students at Duke.

Contact Information: Mary Lou William Center for Black Culture, 201 West Union Bldg, Box 90880, Duke University, Durham, NC 27708, http://www.studentaffairs.duke.edu/mlw/programs-services/africana-mentoring-program

Recruitment

Multi-Ethnic Leadership Scholarship Program participants at Azusa Pacific University receive a $4,500 scholarship, must maintain a 3.0 GPA, get involved in student leadership, and promote diversity efforts on campus. Participants take courses in leadership studies and diversity and participate in meetings, retreats, workshops, and conferences throughout the academic year.

Contact Information: Multi-Ethnic Programs, Azusa Pacific University, Azusa, CA 91702, http://www.apu.edu/mep/scholarship/

Residential Programs

The Malcolm X House is one of several identity houses at Wesleyan University that provide a safe space for underrepresented student populations to live and learn, connect, and build social networks. The Malcolm X House allows students to live in an environment that explores and celebrates the cultural heritage of the African diaspora.

Contact Information: Residential Life, Wesleyan University, Middletown, CT 06459, http://www.wesleyan.edu/reslife/housing/program/malcolmx.htm

Retention Efforts

The Call Me MISTER Program, a multi-institution collaboration between Clemson University and other 2- and 4-year colleges in South Carolina (i.e., Anderson University, Benedict College, Claflin College, College of Charleston, Coastal Carolina University, Greenville Technical College, Midlands Technical College, Morris College, South Carolina State University, Tri-County Technical College, Trident Technical College, and the University of South Carolina-Beafort), aims to increase the pool of available teachers from diverse backgrounds in the state's lowest performing elementary schools. Participants in the program receive tuition assistance through a loan forgiveness program, academic support, and take part in a cohort system for social and cultural support.

Contact Information: Eugene T. Moore School of Education, 102 Tillman Hall, Clemson, SC 29634-0702; http://www.clemson.edu/hehd/departments/education/research-service/callmemister/

Student African American Brotherhood (SAAB), a student organization located on more than 100 campuses, embraces the principles of accountability, proactive leadership, self-discipline, and intellectual development for African American college males. SAAB provides structured opportunities for African American males by encouraging them to serve as role models to younger African American males, engage in service, and prepare to enter the workforce and make their place in society.

Contact Information: Tyrone Bledsoe, University of Toledo, Toledo, OH, http://www.2cusaab.org

Recommendations to Benefit African American Students

The presence of African American students in higher education has significantly changed since the first African American was awarded a baccalaureate degree in 1823. Although the number of African American students enrolled in college has increased to 13.5% (Demographics, 2007), African American students still face issues of marginality in PWIs (Cuyjet, 1998). As higher education administrators struggle with how to meet the needs of African American students on campus, they must first answer the question of whether a student's race or ethnicity should have an effect on the provision of services. Studies examining the racial identity of African American students at HBIs and PWIs have shown that race is an important part of African American students' identity in both institutional settings (Anglin & Wade, 2007; Cokley, 1999; Harper & Quaye, 2007). Since race is a salient factor for African American students, programs and services on campus should reflect African American life and culture (e.g., African American speakers, cultural events, performances, lectures, dialogues, African American studies).

Unfortunately, many of the programs and services for African American students function in isolation, and administrators make little effort to make connections across programs. Holmes, Ebbers, Robinson, and Mugenda (2000–2001) developed a conceptual model that takes a holistic approach to working with African American students and places greater emphasis on institutional influences on student outcomes than preenrollment characteristics. The three-stage model is based on the premise "that the success of African American students at predominantly White institutions is a function of both in-and-out of class experiences" (p. 50), which includes interaction with faculty, staff, students, institutional policies, and academic programs and services.

Stage One: Recruitment

The first stage of the model begins with recruitment. Validation of students' experiences at the recruitment phase entails creating a supportive and non-threatening environment in which prospective students and their families feel comfortable asking questions about the institution. The model recognizes the role parents or significant others play in a student's decision to attend college and encourage that support throughout the student's career at the university (Holmes et al., 2000–2001).

Helpful programs and services in the recruitment phase include offering summer precollege programs, campus visits, and adequate financial assistance. Summer precollege programs, such as Upward Bound, provide a simulated college experience for high school students and provide them with the opportunity to live on campus and take classes in a college setting. Campus visitations are a great opportunity for prospective African American students to obtain an assessment of the campus climate. Current students can share their personal experiences of what it is like to be a person of color on campus. Students can be introduced to campus support structures by interacting with faculty and staff from key areas who can address their expectations of academic and cocurricular life.

Since the family income of many African American students continues to fall below that of White students, expanding financial aid opportunities are available. Alternative funding opportunities, such as need-based aid, can address some access issues for African Americans. However, institutions continue to struggle to find ways to recruit academically talented African American students who have little need for financial aid. Alternative criteria are needed for scholarships targeting those African Americans.

Stage Two: First-Year Experience

Stage two of the model focuses on the first-year experience of the student. An orientation program or summer bridge program, the first component of this stage, that helps African American students become integrated into the campus community provides validation that the student's presence on campus makes a difference. Components of an orientation program should include opportunities for interaction with African American faculty, staff, and students and exposure to cocurricular opportunities, academic policies, and campus resources (Holmes et al., 2000–2001). Summer bridge programs offer credit and noncredit courses taught by supportive faculty in small classroom settings. Students have the opportunity to adjust to the campus community and engage in enrichment opportunities prior to the larger cohort's arrival.

In-class and out-of-class validation are the last two components of stage two. Faculty are key players in providing in-class validation. Student affairs professionals can help faculty understand the background characteristics and learning styles of African American students. Course content, instructional methods, evaluation and feedback, student-faculty interaction, validation of cultural experiences, and reward structures should reflect diverse perspectives (Holmes et al., 2000–2001).

Out-of-class validation, incorporating the needs of African American students into the campus community, is influenced by the following factors: campus climate, residence halls, work experience, peer interactions, academic advising, university recognition, faculty-student interaction outside class, and ethnic minority faculty role models (Holmes et al., 2000–2001). Out-of-class validation is at the very heart of the student affairs profession and should be infused in programs and services for all students. Mentoring programs, involvement in multicultural organizations, rites of passage programs, awards and recognition ceremonies, ethnic residential theme houses, special orientation for African American students, multicultural centers, and multicultural affairs offices contribute to the satisfaction and retention of African American students (Guiffrida, 2003; Patton, 2006; Rhoads, Buenavista, & Maldonado, 2004; Shuford & Palmer, 2004; Smith, 1997; Sutton, 1998; Sutton & Kimbrough, 2001).

Stage Three: Exit Interview

The third stage of the model consists of an exit interview for assessing the effectiveness of the institution's curricular and cocurricular programs (Holmes et al., 2000–2001). The effectiveness of the model is contingent upon the cultural competencies of the faculty and staff, and the campus climate will become more inclusive when faculty and staff work collectively to design curricular, programs, and services that seek to enhance the cultural competencies of students (Howard-Hamilton, Richardson, & Shuford, 1998). Successful programming can occur when practitioners model "the appropriate behavior when teaching others about multiculturalism) (Howard-Hamilton, 2000; Pope, Reynolds, & Mueller, 2004).

In the quest to support African American students, higher education administrators must remember that not all African American students have the same experiences, attitudes, and beliefs; culturally specific programs may not be applicable to all students. Students' individual needs must be taken into account when planning programs and services for African Americans.

Other factors that influence African American students' experiences on campus include focusing them on cross-cultural opportunities with other identity groups. Research on the benefits of diversity (Gurin, Lehman, & Lewis, 2004; Hurtado, Milem, Clayton-Pedersen, & Allen, 1999; Smith, 1997) has revealed a significant benefit for all students. An opportunity for interaction among different racial groups increases understanding. As the world continues to become more diverse, all students, including African Americans, must learn how to appreciate and value cultural differences.

Conclusion

The experience of African Americans in higher education closely parallels their experience in American society. The ability of African Americans to obtain a quality education has been impeded by a social system that has suppressed their legal rights and their human dignity. Despite the obstacles, African Americans have been able to transcend legal and social barriers. Although significant gains have been made in terms of enrollment and acceptance into higher education, inequities still exist. African American students still feel the need to create visible African American communities on PWIs (Person & Christensen, 1996), and these institutions are still wrestling with how to increase the diversity mix of the student population. On the positive side, researchers, business and industry, and higher education administrators are embracing the benefits of diversity. African American students have become valuable players in the higher education arena.

Case Study

Meeting of the Minds

You have just received a letter informing you that you were selected by the president of your university to serve on a team of university administrators from various offices within academic and student affairs. The team has been charged with developing strategies to improve the retention and graduation rates of African American students attending your university (large public 4-year institution). The meeting is scheduled to take place the following week.

When you arrive at the meeting, you see colleagues from throughout the university. The president calls the meeting to order and thanks each team member for his or her commitment to student retention on campus. She also remarks that while she is proud of the progress that has been made to support the intellectual and social development of students on campus, she is firmly committed to student success and engagement for all students and as a result has organized this meeting. She then mentions that the previous semester a campus climate study was commissioned by the university to assess student perceptions of the campus culture and university environment, and a primary finding indicated that African American students felt a sense of alienation on campus and perceived the institution as unwelcoming and hostile.

During her opening remarks, the president asked the team to consider how the Black Cultural Center could better support the educational and social development of African American students and provide cultural programs for all students on campus. In addition, the president asked the team to consider how existing programs and services could be enhanced and new programs developed in cooperation with other offices on campus (e.g., counseling center, learning communities, academic support services, etc.).

Next, the president asked the team to form groups of four to five people to address these and other issues relating to African American student retention. Before taking her seat, she added, "Your mission for this meeting is clear. Use your insight, experience, and expertise to develop strategies and approaches to support the recruitment of African American students, enhance the engagement of African American students in and out of the classroom, and improve graduation rates for African American students attending our university."

Discussion Questions

1. If you were assistant dean of academic advising, given your experience and knowledge of holistic advising and retention initiatives, what strategies and approaches would you recommend to your group? How would your response be different if you were the director of the admissions office? Director of the career resource center? Director of the financial aid office? Director of the multicultural affairs office? Director of the student activities center? Vice provost for academic programs? Associate dean of arts and sciences? Chair of the sociology department?

2. Based on the research literature, student development theory, and your personal experience, what are the major issues affecting African American students at your university?

3. Following a review of research and academic literature that examines strategies, programs, and services designed to support the academic and social development of African American students, what would you perceive to be the most effective interventions or programs that are currently in place on other campuses for African American students? List and examine the feasibility of implementing selected programs and services on your campus.

4. Design an educational program and/or service to support the academic, social, and emotional development of African American students at your university. Also, develop an assessment plan to determine the effectiveness of your educational program or service.

5. Do you believe you could design a campus community where diversity is understood and embraced? Explain your answer.
6. Does your university have an obligation to ensure the success of African American students on campus because of past racial discrimination in American higher education? Explain your answer.
7. How would your answers change to all of the preceding questions if you were advising a small private 4-year university? Two-year college? Women's college? HBI?

References

Ancis, J. R., Sedlacek, W. E., & Mohr, J. J. (2000). Student perceptions of campus cultural climate by race. *Journal of Counseling & Development, 78*(2), 180–185.

Anglin, D. M., & Wade, C. (2007). Racial socialization, racial identity, and Black students' adjustment to college. *Cultural Diversity and Ethnic Minority Psychology, 13*(3), 207–215.

Bowles, F., & DeCosta, F. A. (1971). *Between two worlds: A profile of Negro education.* New York: McGraw-Hill.

Brown v. Board of Educ., 347 U.S. 483 (1954).

Carter, D., & Wilson, R. (1996). *Minorities in higher education. 1995–96 fourteenth annual status report.* Washington, DC: American Council on Education, Office of Minorities in Higher Education.

Cokley, K. (1999). Reconceptualizing the impact of college racial composition on African American students' racial identity. *Journal of College Student Development, 40*(3), 235–246.

Cominole, M., Riccobono, J., Siegel, P., Caves, L., & Rosen, J. (2008). *2008 National postsecondary student aid study: Field test methodology report* (NCES 2008–01). Washington, DC: U.S. Department of Education.

Cross, W. E. (1971). The Negro-to-Black conversion experience: Toward a psychology of Black liberation. *Black World, 20,* 13–27.

Cross, W. E. (1991). *Shades of Black.* Philadelphia, PA: Temple University Press.

Cross, W. E., & Vandiver, B. J. (2001). Nigrescence theory and measurement: Introducing the Cross Racial Identity Scale (CRIS). In J. G. Ponterotto, J. M. Casas, L. M. Suzuki, & C. M. Alexander (Eds.), *Handbook of multicultural counseling* (2nd ed., pp. 371–393). Thousand Oaks, CA: Sage.

Cuyjet, M. J. (1998). Recognizing and addressing marginality among African American college students. *College Student Affairs Journal, 18*(1), 64–71.

Demographics. (2007, August 31). *Chronicle of Higher Education Almanac,* p. 4.

Fleming, J. E. (1976). *The lengthening shadow of slavery: A historical justification for affirmative action for Blacks in higher education.* Washington, DC: Howard University Press.

Garibaldi A. M. (1991). Blacks in college. In C. V. Willie, A. M. Garibaldi, & W. L. Reed (Eds.), *The education of African-Americans* (pp. 93–99). New York: Auburn House.

Goodstein, R., & Ponterotto, J. (1997). Racial and ethnic identity: Their relationship and their contribution to self-esteem. *Journal of Black Psychology, 23*(3), 275–292.

Guiffrida, D. A. (2003). African American student organizations as agents of social integration. *Journal of College Student Development, 44*(3), 305–310.

Gurin, P., Lehman, J. S., & Lewis, E. L. (2004). *Defending diversity.* Ann Arbor: University of Michigan Press.

Harper, S. R. & Quaye, S. J. (2007). Student organizations as venues for black identity expression and development among African American male student leaders. *Journal of College Student Development, 48*(2), 127–144.

Helms, J. (Ed.). (1990). *Black and White racial identity: Theory, research, and practice.* Westport, CT: Greenwood Press.

Helms, J., & Carter, R. (1991). Relationships of White and Black racial identity attitudes and demographic similarity to counselor preferences. *Journal of Counseling Psychology, 38,* 446–457.

Hill, S. T. (1983). *Participation of Black students in higher education: A statistical profile from 1970–71 to 1980–81.* Washington, DC: National Center for Education Statistics. (ERIC Document Reproduction Service No. ED236991)

Holmes, S. L., Ebbers, L. H., Robinson, D. C., & Mugenda, A. G. (2000–2001). Validating African American students at predominantly White institutions. *Journal of College Student Retention, 2*(1), 41–58.

Howard-Hamilton, M. F. (2000). Programming for multicultural competencies. In D. L. Liddell & J. P. Lund (Eds.), *Powerful programming for student learning: Approaches that make a difference* (pp. 67–78). San Francisco: Jossey-Bass.

Howard-Hamilton, M. F., Richardson, B. J., & Shuford, B. (1998). Promoting multicultural education: A holistic approach. *College Student Affairs Journal, 18*(1), 5–17.

Hurtado, S., Milem, J., Clayton-Pedersen, A., & Allen, W. (1999). *Enacting diverse learning environments: Improving the climate for racial/ethnic diversity in higher education* (ASHE//ERIC Higher Education Report, Vol. 26, No. 8). Washington, DC: George Washington University, Graduate School of Education and Human Development.

McEwen, M. K., Roper, L. D., Byrant, D. R., & Langa, M. J. (1990). Incorporating the development of African American students into psychosocial theories of student development. *Journal of College Student Development, 31*(5), 429–436.

Mitchell, S., & Dell, D. (1992). The relationship between Black students' racial identity attitude and participation in campus organizations. *Journal of College Student Development, 33*(1), 39–43.

National Center for Education Statistics. (1993). *Profile of undergraduate students in U.S. postsecondary institutions: 1989–1990.* Washington, DC: U.S. Department of Education.

National Center for Education Statistics. (2002). *Profile of undergraduate students in U.S. postsecondary institutions: 1999–2000.* Washington, DC: U.S. Department of Education.

Nettles, M. T., & Perna, L. W. (1997). *The African American education data book: Higher and adult education* (Vol. 1). Fairfax, Virginia: Frederick D. Patterson Research Institute.

Parham, T., & Helms, J. (1981). The influences of Black students' racial identity attitudes on preferences for counselor's race. *Journal of Counseling Psychology, 28*(3), 250–257.

Parham, T., & Helms, J. (1985a). Attitudes of racial identity and self-esteem of Black students: An exploratory investigation. *Journal of College Student Personnel, 26*(2), 143–146.

Parham, T., & Helms, J. (1985b). Relation of racial identity attitudes to self-actualization and affective states of Black students. *Journal of Counseling Psychology, 32*(3), 431–440.

Parker, W. M., & Flowers, L. A. (2003). The effects of racial identity on academic achievement and perceptions of campus connectedness on African American students at predominantly White institutions. *College Student Affairs Journal, 22*(2), 180–194.

Patton, L. D. (2006). The voice of reason: A qualitative examination of Black student perceptions of Black culture centers. *Journal of College Student Development, 47*(6), 628–646.

Person, D. R., & Christensen, M. C. (1996). Understanding Black student culture and Black student retention. *NASPA Journal, 34(1),* 47–56.

Poindexter-Cameron, J., & Robinson, T. (1997). Relationships among racial identity attitudes, womanist identity attitudes, and self-esteem in African American college women. *Journal of College Student Development, 38*(3), 288–296.

Pope, R. L. (1998). The relationship between psychosocial development and racial identity of Black college students. *Journal of College Student Development, 39(3),* 273–282.

Pope, R. L., Reynolds, A. L., & Mueller, J. A. (2004). *Multicultural competence in student affairs.* San Francisco: Jossey-Bass.

Pounds, A. W. (1987). Black students' needs on predominantly White campuses. In D. J. Wright (Ed.), *Responding to the needs of today's minority students* (pp. 23–38). San Francisco: Jossey-Bass.

Quaye, S. J., Tambascia, T. P., & Talesh, R. A. (2009). Engaging racial/ethnic minority students in predominantly white classroom environments. In S. R. Harper & S. J. Quaye (Eds.), *Student engagement in higher education: Theoretical perspectives and practical approaches for diverse populations* (pp. 157–178). New York: Routledge.

Rhoads, R. A., Buenavista, T. L., & Maldonado, D. E. (2004). Students of color helping others stay in college: A grassroots effort. *About Campus, 9,* 10–17.

Shuford, B. C., & Palmer, C. J. (2004). Multicultural affairs. In F. J. MacKinnon (Ed.), *Student affairs practice in higher education* (pp. 218–238). Springfield, IL: Charles C. Thomas.

Smith, D. G. (1997). *Diversity works: The emerging picture of how students benefit.* Washington, DC: Association of American Colleges and Universities.

Solórzano, D., Ceja, M., & Yosso, T. (2000). Critical race theory, racial microaggressions, and campus racial climate: The experiences of African American college students. *Journal of Negro Education, 69*(1/2), 60–73.

Spring, J. (2001). *Deculturalization and the struggle for equality: A brief history of the education of dominated cultures in the United States* (3rd ed.). New York: McGraw-Hill.

Sutton, E. M. (1998). The role of the office of minority affairs in fostering cultural diversity. *College Student Affairs Journal, 18*(1), 33–39.

Sutton, E. M., & Kimbrough, W. M. (2001). Trends in Black student involvement. *NASPA Journal, 39*(1), 30–40.

Taylor, C., & Howard-Hamilton, M. F. (1995). Student involvement and racial identity attitudes among African American males. *Journal of College Student Development, 36*(4), 330–336.

Thomas, G. E., & Hill, S. (1987). Black institutions in U.S. higher education: Present roles, contributions, future projections. *Journal of College Student Personnel, 28*(6), 496–503.

U.S. Census Bureau. (2001). *The Black population: 2000.* Retrieved May 5, 2003, from http://www.census.gov/prod/2001pubs/c2kbr01-5.pdf

Vandiver, B. J. (2001). Psychological nigrescence revisited: Introduction and overview. *Journal of Multicultural Counseling and Development, 29*(3), 165–173.

Vandiver, B. J., Fhagen-Smith, P. E., Cokley, K. O., Cross, W. E., & Worrell, F. C. (2001). Cross's nigresence model: From theory to scale to theory. *Journal of Multicultural Counseling and Development, 29*(3), 174–199.

Wei, C. C., Berkner, L., He, S., Lew, S., Cominole, M., & Siegel, P. (2009). *2007–08 national postsecondary student aid study (NPSAS:08): Student financial aid estimates for 2007–08: First Look* (NCES 2009–166). Washington, DC: U.S. Department of Education.

Worrell, F. C., Cross, W. E., & Vandiver, B. J. (2001). Nigrescence theory: Current status and challenges for the future. *Journal of Multicultural Counseling and Development, 29*(3), 201–213.

8

AMERICAN INDIAN COLLEGE STUDENTS

Vasti Torres and LeManuel Bitsói

As with many minority groups in the United States, diversity among American Indians is not always recognized by non-Indians. While individual tribes maintain their own customs, language, and traditions, historical and social elements shared by all tribes influence the development of American Indian college students. To attend to this population of students, academe must realize that the issues that have an impact on the developmental process of American Indians are connected to history, self-identification with tribal culture within the institution or community, and the prevalence of Indian culture in the environment. This chapter highlights each of these areas and describes their connection to the student's development during the college years by considering the terminology, historical context, and existing research.

American Indian Terminology

The federal government recognizes 564 Indian tribal nations in the United States, and this number does not include the 70 tribal nations recognized by state governments (Bureau of Indian Affairs [BIA], 2007). Each tribe has a different language and tribal customs, but what is most important is to ascertain how a student self-identifies. It should be noted that tribes have specific requirements for tribal membership, and therefore membership becomes an important aspect in their identity. Diversity among the tribes makes it difficult for college administrators and faculty to understand the experiences of all American Indian tribal members, yet sensitivity and knowledge about tribal expectations is the first step in helping American Indian students succeed in higher education.

Self-identification for indigenous people includes *American Indian* and *Native American*, and the terms are often used interchangeably. While much of the research literature uses American Indian, usage of the term Native American has increased.[1] In some instances, *Native* is often used to refer to native culture, yet among American Indians, their tribal or nation affiliation has greater importance than broad terminology (Herring, 1991). The diversity among tribes makes tribal affiliation a more accurate and descriptive self-identification.

To explore the developmental issues American Indians face in college, this chapter begins with a historical overview of tribal sovereignty and the government-sanctioned oppression of Native cultures in the United States. These two aspects of tribal history continue to have an impact on American Indians today. Once the historical context is set, Indian values are explored, and their connection to student development is explained. After exploring the traditional values of American Indians, the current research on student development theory for American Indians is presented through existing models representing levels of acculturation. To further understand the experiences of these students in higher education, a review of existing research and the critical issues to consider are covered. The chapter ends with a case study to help explore the issues brought forth in this chapter.

Historical Context Affecting American Indians

Understanding the American Indian experience begins with historical issues that influence how American Indians interpret societal expectations and their own environment. The first of two historical issues, which are interconnected, is the need for an appreciation of tribal sovereignty. Sovereignty is critical to American Indians because of the second historical issue: the history of government-sanctioned oppression of Indian culture. By maintaining tribal sovereignty, American Indian nations have been able to overcome deliberate attempts to eliminate their culture and instead have created environments where Native culture is valued and passed on to their descendants. Challenges to the preservation of American Indian culture and language are explained by Spring (2010): "As a result of globalizations and imperialism, indigenous peoples have been forced to undergo extreme cultural change, resulting in many becoming socially and psychologically dysfunctional" (p. 21). Thus, it is no surprise that historically most American Indians were inhumanely deculturalized by their conquerors, and it has taken a combination of civil rights activism and federal legislation to abolish horrific policies that were instituted during the 19th and 20th centuries. Some members of the academy may feel these issues are part of the past, yet issues of sovereignty continue today and influence educational opportunities for many American Indians. Research on ethnic and racial minorities has determined that the developmental process for racial or ethnic identity acknowledges the potential presence of oppression and domination (Evans, Forney, Guido, Patton, & Renn, 2010). Thus, these historical issues become even more relevant to understanding the development of contemporary American Indian college students.

Tribal Sovereignty

Though tribal nations have varying degrees of sovereignty, this privilege provides tribal governments with some degree of independence and the right to self-govern. Tribal sovereignty has its foundation in the assertion that tribal nations held inherent sovereignty before there was a United States government and have never delegated those rights (Lomawaima, 2000). Tribal members take great pride in the notion of sovereignty, and for many it is the "bedrock upon which any and every discussion of Indian reality today must be built" (p. 3). Furthermore, sovereignty is essential to the development of any tribal nation in regard to education, economic development, social services, and health care (Bitsói, 2007). Begay (1997) also asserts that sovereignty places the keys to economic and social development in the hands of tribal governments.

Many American Indian tribal nations use a tribal council that focuses on maintaining the community and promoting the needs of the tribe. However, religious leaders may also assist with tribal leadership. For example, Sandia Pueblo in New Mexico is a federally recognized tribal nation that appoints a governor and lieutenant governor to lead the tribal council, while a warchief and lieutenant warchief are responsible for all religious activities in the Pueblo (Sandia Pueblo, 2010). Perhaps one of the most sophisticated forms of tribal governments is that of the Navajo Nation, which happens to mirror the federal government with its three branches: executive, legislative, and judicial, but tailored to the meet the needs of the Navajo people (Navajo Nation, 2009). An example of the unique tailoring is the world-renowned

Peacemaking Program that is part of the judicial branch of the Navajo Nation government. The program has been referred to as a "horizontal system of justice" since all participants are considered to be equals with the purpose of preserving relationships and restoring harmony among involved parties (Navajo Courts, 2009). In essence, peacemakers are the institutional keepers of the methods and principles of original dispute resolution, culture, and tradition in the Navajo justice system (Navajo Courts). With these examples, it becomes clear that decisions made by tribal governments are at times focused on efforts to maintain their culture and the community values of their tribal nation. These efforts are considered necessary because of the history of the government-sanctioned oppression of Indian culture, language, and forced removal of Native Americans onto reservations.

As previously mentioned, the federal government has made repeated efforts to oppress and deculturalize American Indians, beginning with the Naturalization Act of 1790 that excluded American Indians from being U.S. citizens even though they were indigenous peoples (Spring, 2010). The legal assault that kept American Indians mentally, physically, and emotionally oppressed continued with the Indian Removal Act of 1830, which allowed the government to take tribal lands and forcibly evict indigenous owners. This was followed by the Indian Peace Commission, established in 1867, to determine where Indians would be allowed to live as Whites began moving westward, spreading across American Indian land (Spring, 2010).

Today's American Indian reservations are a result of the federal government's primary motivation to control and socially engineer the assimilation and deculturalization of American Indians into the White educational and cultural systems (Spring, 2010; Takaki, 1993). However, the primary impetus for the establishment of reservations was primarily because of land usage and ownership as asserted by Spring, "Reservations and allotment programs were the responses to the land issue" (p. 32). In addition, this forced removal to specific plots of land was to discourage seasonal migration, because Indian territories (i.e., hunting grounds, fishing waters, agricultural fields, etc.) were coveted by White settlers, and to force Indians to learn how to manage farming-sized tracts of land (Deloria, 2001). The reservation system also allowed the U.S. government to control tribes by using the military, without warning, to strike American Indian bands outside the boundaries of the reservations (Takaki). Furthermore, the early goal of the reservation system was to make sure American Indians did not retain their Native culture and to force their transition onto "the white man's road" (Takaki, p. 233). First created in the 1850s, the reservation system has gone through many policy changes, most of which have focused on socially engineering how American Indians live and on providing the U.S. government with a method for institutionalized oppression.

Subsequent federal policies gradually improved and began regulating land ownership on reservations, enhancing access to educational opportunities and upgrading reservation schools. With the onset of gaming, some American Indian tribal nations have even more authority in controlling schools on their reservations, as well as funding tribal government operations or programs, providing for the general welfare of the Indian tribe and its members, promoting tribal economic development, donating to charitable organizations, and helping fund operations of local government agencies (National Indian Gaming Commission, 2010).

The policies mandated for the reservation system seem to have one ongoing dilemma—which parts of the Native American Indian culture are "safe enough to encourage, and which are too dangerously different to be tolerated" (Lomawaima & McCarty, 2002, p. 287)? Along with other minority groups during the civil rights movement, tribal governments focused on self-empowerment through the control of education. As Wildcat (2001) asserts, "Democracy suggests people have a right to educate children in accordance with their societal values and beliefs," and questions, "Why should we expect less in our Native communities?" (p. 139). These efforts in education have advanced tribal schools and colleges that promote Indian traditions and history. Though changes in federal policies allowed American Indians more rights toward self-determination, it was not until 1988 that the U.S. government reaffirmed its special duty to assist American Indian tribes in offering the best educational opportunities by providing funding for indigenous community schools (Lomawaima & McCarty). While these are relatively recent policy changes, the need to understand the role of governmental oppression on native culture continues to be important.

In addition to improved federal policies governing K–12 schools in regard to bilingual education, the establishment of tribally controlled colleges and universities has assisted in maintaining and sustaining tribal languages and cultures. Tribal Colleges and Universities (TCUs share a common mission that seeks to promote the culture of the tribe and strengthen the economic as well as social status of the tribal community (Belgarde, 1996). Guardia and Evans (2008) also found that part of the mission of TCUs is to preserve tribal language and culture. Safeguarding language and culture led to the establishment of the first tribally controlled community college in the United States—Navajo Community College. Now known as

Diné College (2009), it was established in 1968 on the Navajo reservation. To further the advancement of TCUs, in 1972 the American Indian Higher Education Consortium (AIHEC) was established with five charter colleges. The criteria for AIHEC membership required that the colleges have formal charters from an American Indian tribe, establish an American Indian governing board, have a majority American Indian student body, and provide educational services to the American Indian community (Belgarde). Today these colleges provide a transition from tribal living to the outside educational world and create an educational environment that accepts and rewards traditional American Indian traditions and equips students to pursue more opportunities (Belgarde). Furthermore, TCUs have a vital role in the personal and academic development of American Indian students by providing access to education, personal support, exposure to Native culture and language, and preparation for additional educational opportunities and careers (Guardia & Evans, 2008). According to AIHEC (2009), there are at present 36 tribal colleges and universities in the United States.

Governmental Oppression

The early struggles between the federal government and sovereign tribal nations prompted many regulations that attempted to force the assimilation of American Indians and to oppress Native culture. The most notorious form of this oppression was Richard Henry Pratt's goal to "Americanize" Indians with the development of the Carlisle Indian School and his infamous motto: "Kill the Indian, save the man" (Pratt, 1973). Subsequently, other federally sanctioned forms of oppression and assimilation were carried out by the BIA, the governmental agency responsible for administering and managing lands held in trust by the federal government for Indian people (BIA, 2009).[2] Historically, the BIA also oversaw federal boarding schools where American Indian students were expected to become "White" through various draconian measures:

- In 1903 the BIA issued the Short Hair and Citizenship Dress Order that made it illegal for men to wear long hair or for any Indian to use Native dress (Lomawaima, 2000).
- The mandatory education of American Indian children in federal day schools or federal and mission boarding schools where only White culture and customs were taught lasted through the 1960s (Hyer, 1990; Lomawaima, 2000).

- Various researchers have documented a litany of traumatic events experienced by American Indians in their educational experiences; they were beaten, placed in solitary confinement, had their mouths washed with bar soap, were forced to have their hair cut, had to dress and behave like White people, and were forced to stand for hours holding stacks of books on their heads for speaking their Native language (Lomawaima & McCarty, 2006; Szasz, 2005).
- Many university researchers were allowed to "study" Native culture in a manner that today would be considered unethical. According to one estimate, about 90% of all objects made by American Indians between 1850 and 1950 are in museum collections (Lomawaima, 2000).

These historical examples of sanctioned oppression illustrate the distrust built between tribal culture and the majority White culture. To understand some of the developmental concerns of American Indians today, one must first understand the historical origins of this distrust. For many years, one of the major historical issues of contention between the U.S. government and tribal leaders was the dissonance between the values of the tribes and those of the majority society. The ultimate goal of such ill-advised governmental policies until the mid-1900s was to force American Indians to assimilate and not promote the retention of American Indian culture (Takaki, 1993). As previously mentioned, a primary goal of the reservation system was to control and assimilate American Indians into the White culture. Probably because of the BIA's atrocious track record in educating American Indians, the federal government reorganized the BIA and created the Bureau of Indian Education (BIE) in 2006 with the following mission:

> to provide quality education opportunities from early childhood through life in accordance with a tribe's needs for cultural and economic well-being in keeping with the wide diversity of Indian tribes and Alaska Native villages as distinct cultural and governmental entities. Further, the BIE is to manifest consideration of the whole person by taking into account the spiritual, mental, physical and cultural aspects of the individual within his or her family and tribal or village context (BIE, 2010).

Cultural values help form our identities and dictate behavior, so it is important to look at the connection between cultural values and student development in college.

American Indian Values and the Connection With Student Development

In spite of attempts to assimilate and destroy Native culture, American Indians "insist on surviving on their own terms" (Lomawaima & McCarty, 2002, p. 281). This survival includes maintaining Native culture, language, and values. Ecklund (2005) found that attending college can sometimes have a negative rather than a positive effect on some American Indian students and their commitment to their cultural community. However, Bitsói (2007) found the opposite to be true at an Ivy League institution where Native students strengthened their Native identities and found they could be both Native and scholars. At the core of Indian values are communal concerns (including adherence to tradition), responsibility for family and friends, cooperation, and tribal identification (LaFromboise, Heyle, & Ozer, 1990). These values can at times be in conflict with U.S. majority values of individualism, competitiveness, and amassing property and titles. When working with American Indian students, a clear understanding of the central role these values have must be recognized (LaFromboise & Rowe, 1983). Furthermore, Brown (2005) indicates that it is extremely important to have a place on campus where Native Americans have a sense of comfort and belonging. College administrators and faculty must recognize that American Indians' values and traditions will allow them to be successful and that the choices these American Indian students make can be based on Indian values and may not necessarily be in line with the majority-oriented societal values prevalent in the college environment.

Non-Native traditional student development theory believes that part of developing integrity includes the tearing down of "traditional" values and the rebuilding of a broader understanding of the world that will better suit the student in the future (Chickering & Reisser, 1993). These traditional values as defined by Chickering and Reisser focus on selfish or exploitative behaviors, and the shift in thinking that is needed is to understand how these traditional beliefs can demean the beliefs of others or people as individuals. The opposite is the case for traditional American Indian values. In American Indian culture, communal values begin with an understanding of one's responsibility to the whole (LaFromboise, Heyle, & Ozer, 1990). This core value places American Indian college students at odds with some of the traditional values held by their White counterparts. Furthermore, Guardia and Evans (2008) found the following core values are held by many American Indians: sharing, cooperation, noninterference, present-time orientation, being versus doing, extended-family orientation, respect, harmony and balance, spiritual causes for illness and problems, group dynamics, and the importance of the tribe (pp. 239–241). These types of contrasts with majority cultural values question the process by which American Indians maneuver the development of integrity in the White sense, even though they may know what it means to have integrity within their Native communities. Since congruence between personal and societal values is one of the sequential stages for developing integrity (Chickering & Reisser), American Indian students may experience a different way of viewing and processing concepts of mainstream integrity and competitiveness. This example of the differences between traditional beliefs in White and Native cultures illustrates the limited amount of research on American Indians and existing student development theories. Understanding the experiences of American Indian students is the first step to being able to recognize when theories developed for majority students may not necessarily apply to this student population. Though more research is needed on the developmental issues of American Indian college students, models and research studies can inform practice. Research in other disciplines has focused mainly on issues of identity development among American Indians, and for this reason, the next section focuses on these models in existing research.

American Indian Identity Development

Like many cultures that interact with the majority White culture in the United States, American Indians usually identify first with their cultures while possessing varying degrees of acculturation to the majority culture. This level of acculturation influences self-identification and the development of American Indian college students. While various research studies (Garrett, 1996; Horse, 2001; Sage, 1997) have examined American Indian identity development, two models emerge from the concepts of acculturation that can assist the academy to better understand American Indian college students. The first is Ryan and Ryan's categories of Indianness (as cited in LaFromboise, Trimble, & Mohatt, 1990), and the second is the Health Model Conceptualization of Acculturation by Choney, Berryhill-Paapke, and Robbins (1995).

Building on the work of various researchers (e.g., Ryan & Ryan, 1982), LaFromboise, Trimble, and Mohatt, (1990) classified Indians according to residential patterns, level of tribal affiliation, and extent of commitment to maintaining their tribal heritage. Collectively, they define the five categories of Indianness as

- *Traditional:* These individuals generally speak and think in their native language and know little English. They observe "old-time" traditions and values.
- *Transitional:* These individuals generally speak both English and the Native language in the home. They question basic traditionalism and religion, yet cannot fully accept dominant culture and values.
- *Marginal:* These people may be defensively Indian, but are unable either to live the cultural heritage of their tribal group or to identify with the dominant problems (i.e., socio-economic status, religion, politics, etc.) due to their ethnicity.
- *Assimilated:* Within this group are the people who, for the most part, have been accepted by the dominant society. They generally have embraced dominant culture and values.
- *Bicultural.* Within this group are those who are, for the most part, accepted by the dominant society. Yet they also know and accept their tribal traditions and culture. They can thus move in either direction, from traditional society to dominant society with ease. (p. 638)

Acknowledgment and awareness of the multiple loyalties inherent in American Indian students can assist non-Indians (including students, faculty, and staff) in understanding this group of students (LaFromboise, Trimble, and Mohatt, 1990). It is not clear what developmental process, if any, occurs within these categories, and therefore it is difficult to ascertain if movement (or development) among the categories should be expected. However, these categories can serve as a tool to help describe the diversity among American Indian students.

The second model is the Health Model Conceptualization of Acculturation by Choney et al. (1995), which uses a health approach to acculturation rather than a deficit approach. This pan-Indian model represents four areas of human personality that are in harmony "with the domains of the medicine wheel (a uniquely Indian means of conceptualizing the human condition based on four essential elements)" (p. 85). The four areas of human personality are behavioral, social/environmental, affective/spiritual, and cognitive. Within these areas are concentric circles, with each perimeter of the circle representing a different level of acculturation: traditional, transitional, bicultural, assimilated, and marginal. There is no value judgment "placed on any level of acculturation, nor is any dimension of personality emphasized more than another" (p. 85). A person in each of the levels would respond differently and would illustrate the various ways of coping that result depending on an individual's environmental and societal circumstance. This model does not take a linear approach, and therefore it is feasible that an individual could maintain four different levels of acculturation corresponding to the four personality domains.

This interaction between acculturation and personality domains is important to understand because American Indian college students may respond differently according to the personality domain and their own coping skills. For example, a student who is more acculturated in the cognitive domain yet may be more traditional in the social/environment domain may have few academic difficulties but many outside-of-class (social) stressors. Understanding the interactions among these constructs becomes important to better understand the American Indian experience. This model is useful in conceptualizing the variety of experiences an American Indian college student can face and how his or her reaction may vary.

In addition to understanding these models, it should also be noted that American Indians have values that are similar to other ethnic and racial groups. For example, Asian Americans also value collectivism and the importance of family (Kim, Atkinson, & Umemoto, 2001). In their study, Kim et al. found that valuing "group interests and goals is expected to be promoted over individual interests and goals" (p. 575), and this is similar to Native Americans' valuing tribal traditions and culture over individual accomplishments. In regard to the importance of family, Asian Americans feel a strong sense of obligation to the family as a whole and a commitment to maintaining family well-being. Furthermore, "individual family members are expected to make sacrifices for the family" (p. 577). This finding correlates with the expectation of American Indians to contribute to their families throughout their lives. Another example regarding the value of family can be found in the African American community. Suizzo, Robinson, and Pahlke (2008) found that African American mothers stressed that their children should know they will always have their families to support them. They also found that family history was important as well as knowing the "stories from way back when" (p. 303). In addition, they found that extended families played an active role in rearing children. Knowing that these types of parallels exist between American Indians and other racial or ethnic groups should assist American Indian students in knowing they have more in common with others and that should allow them not to feel as isolated.

Critical Issues for Practitioners in Higher Education

Qualitatively, there has been a trend to examine the success and persistence factors of American Indians in college by Native scholars (e.g., Bitsói, 2007;

Brayboy, 2004; Lowe, 2005; Waterman, 2004). However, much of the quantitative research in diversity studies uses data sets that include very few American Indians, making it difficult to generalize findings for this population. The studies presented in this section provide insight into the American Indian college student and the issues administrators and faculty need to understand. Next, a section on applying the research provides suggestions on how practitioners can help American Indian students develop in college. Though more research is needed, there is sufficient evidence that American Indians perceive their environment in different ways than White students and therefore may experience difficulty in adjusting to predominantly White institutions (PWIs; Ducheneaux, 1999).

Research on American Indians in College

As mentioned previously, inroads have been made in positive research on Native Americans in college, but the focus here is on three areas of study: American Indians at a PWI, attending a TCU versus a state university, and the importance of family. The first area is qualitative and focuses on 13 undergraduate American Indian students who persisted for more than one semester at a large PWI where Taylor (1999) identified factors that affect persistence for American Indian students. The variation among the participants illustrates the diversity of this population. Eight of the participants were first-generation college students, while five considered themselves to be assimilated into the White culture, and three described themselves as more traditional Indians. The factors that emerged from this study indicate that alienation and the reasons for going to college were the major influences in persistence for these students.

The alienation emerged from seven subfactors: stereotypes, hostility, lack of respect, thoughtless comments, aloneness, lack of role models, and lack of institutional support. Misconceptions and stereotypes from majority students promoted students' feelings of not fitting in and what the researcher labeled "the looks" that American Indians were getting that gave them the feeling of not looking like everyone else. The lack of diversity in the student body, as well as in faculty and staff, made students feel alone and illustrated the importance of having others who look like them in the university community. The subfactor dealing with the lack of institutional support spoke to the rhetoric of support and the lack of action directly oriented toward supporting American Indians. General support and financial aid were not interpreted as specifically supporting of American Indians, and annual events to support cultural diversity appeared as "tokenism" to these students (Taylor, 1999, p. 12).

The reasons for going to college were found to be salient because it helped identify the students' ultimate goal. For some of these students, the goal is not simply the desire to go to college, rather it is something "they need in order to survive in a predominantly White society, but do not personally want" (Taylor, 1999, p. 12). A number of these students were pulled to return to their roots, yet the difficulty in finding jobs on rural reservations where they could use their college degrees generated some difficult choices for them. These types of choices further illustrate the complex interrelation the Health Model Conceptualization of Acculturation (Choney et al., 1995) attempts to frame. On the one hand, the students may understand the need for a college degree, but on the other hand the economic conditions on many reservations make it somewhat difficult to meet students' goal of returning to their communities.

In the second area of study comparing the experiences of 48 Plains Indians at two institutions (one tribal college and one state university), Ducheneaux (1999) found that the students attending the state PWI were more "traditional" in their orientation than expected. In previous studies using the Native American College Student Attitude Scale, American Indians at White state institutions were found to be more likely to be bicultural or assimilated in their acculturation level than their tribal college counterparts (Ducheneaux). Though many issues were discussed in regard to why this result emerged, Ducheneaux's study brings to light the issue of assumptions made about students as a result of the institution they choose to attend and the uncertainty of such assumptions being borne out in fact.

In the third area of study, recognizing the importance of family support (Dodd, Garcia, Meccage, & Nelson, 1995) emerged as being very important to success. It should be noted that the family is at the core of American Indian values, and educational programs oriented toward American Indians must incorporate this fact. Ortiz and Heavy Runner (2003) reinforce the findings of these research studies through their factors that affect success in college for American Indians, most of them dealing with family support. These factors include the effects of being first-generation college students, the need for positive role models who have experienced success, support from family members, and an understanding of the familial obligations many American Indian students have. Moreover, Bitsóí (2007) found that all Native American students at Harvard University found a sense of family within the Harvard Native American community, and this was essential to having an even more successful educational experience at Harvard. Thus, on-campus programs and services that focus on forcing students to separate themselves from their ties to their families can be incongruent with traditional American Indian values and cause cultural dissonance rather than enabling student development.

In other studies focusing on the retention of American Indian students, several important factors emerged. Some of the studies found that academic preparation and study habits contribute to academic success (Brown & Robinson Kurpius, 1997; Hulburt, Kroeker, & Gade, 1991). Others using more culturally sensitive surveys found that cultural pressures and prejudice were barriers to success (Dodd et al., 1995; Tate & Schwartz, 1993). The research of Kirkness and Barnhardt (1991) emphasized the importance of the academy's respect for American Indian students and their "need for a higher educational system that respects them for who they are, that is relevant to their view of the world, that offers reciprocity in their relationships with others, and that helps them exercise responsibility over their own lives" (p. 1).

American Indian values are so closely tied to community it is thus natural that Hulburt et al. (1991) found that Native students were more concerned about personal relationships and relevance of subject matter than about study habits. This study recommends learning environments that focus on mutually empowering learning rather than traditional lecture-style teaching. This style of collaborative learning was also suggested as a method to help American Indian students improve their study skills. However, Native scholar Lowe (2005) contends that Native American students are now attending college to learn that "college is yet another school and nothing more" (p. 38). Thus, Native American students are encouraged to enroll in study skill seminars and to actively seek advising to help create collaborative partnerships between academic advisers and American Indian students to increase students' chances of success (Brown & Robinson Kurpius, 1997).

Applying the Research to Help American Indians Develop

Based on task force and conference findings from the U.S. Department of Education and the White House Conference on Indian Education, Butterfield (1994) suggested five systemic reforms that are needed to help American Indian students. The first is fostering intercultural harmony by providing opportunities for positive reinforcement and acceptance of Indian values. The second is improving teacher preparation to better prepare teachers to be appropriate role models for American Indian students and help teachers understand Indian values. The third is developing instructional curricula and strategies that take into account the learning styles of American Indian students. The fourth is to include parents at all levels of education. The fifth is to adopt a new paradigm for evaluation that does not place American Indian students at a disadvantage, as a majority of them are educated in K–12 with culturally inappropriate curricula, emphasis on standardized testing, and substandard educational systems (Butterfield). These reforms speak to all levels of education and should be considered a blueprint to improving the educational opportunities for American Indian students.

The main issue that should emerge for college administrators and faculty from the research presented in this chapter is that colleges and universities hold many stereotypes that more than likely do not pertain to American Indian students on campus. The first step in helping American Indian students develop in college is for student affairs professionals and faculty to educate themselves about the values and traditions of the individual American Indian student. Using one of the models presented, they should attempt to understand how the student self-identifies as an American Indian and help him or her make choices that align with his or her cultural values. Cultural assumptions should not be made with American Indian students, for what can appear "to be adaptive in one culture would be non-adaptive—in fact culturally destructive—in another," as found by LaFromboise & Rowe (1983, p. 589). For this reason, it is important for student affairs practitioners to interact with American Indian students with open minds and recognize the difference between differing value systems.

The second issue to consider is the level of institutional commitment to actively support American Indian students. As for many minority students, active support for the culture includes more than just programs and activities. Understanding how institutional policies and practices either assist or hinder students from making choices consistent with their cultural values is critically important. For instance, if the institutional environment promotes a competitive and individualist culture for students, some sort of assessment should be performed to determine how these values can clash with the traditional values of American Indians.

The final issue to consider is assessing the openness of administrators in determining any cultural differences in the college community. This final issue is perhaps the most difficult because it requires student affairs professionals and faculty to self-reflect and illustrate a commitment to diversity that transcends words. Based on the historical legacy of American Indians in the United States, it is imperative that administrators understand they must go beyond the minimum to gain the trust of and build relationships with American Indian students. Development is more likely to occur in a safe and supportive environment (Evans et al., 2010); therefore, the challenge for student affairs and academic administrators, as well as faculty, is learning what a supportive environment is for American Indians on their campuses.

Since existing research is limited, student affairs professionals and faculty need to pay additional attention to making sure American Indian students succeed. The lack of culturally sensitive information available to help these students can promote behaviors that can eventually hinder success. Taking the time to listen and understand the experiences of American Indian students on campus can help one to understand how student development is being affected. Moreover, the traditional values of respect for elders in the American Indian communities may make it difficult for a student to confront an administrator or faculty member about an unwelcoming environment. Therefore the responsibility and risk needs to lie with the staff and faculty members working with American Indian students.

Environmental factors at each institution vary greatly, and therefore there is no one way to create a positive environment for American Indian students. In *The Renaissance of American Indian Higher Education: Capturing the Dream*, Benham and Stein (2003) provide descriptions of model programs that meet various goals for a positive environment. The programs in this book may provide ideas to help a particular campus create a positive environment for American Indian student success. Another stellar example of helping Native Americans to succeed in college is the seminal book *The American Indian and Alaska Native Student's Guide to College Success* by D. Michael Pavel and Ella Inglebret (2007), which outlines a journey to success in college. In their book, Pavel and Inglebret provide practical information regarding college choice; financial aid; spiritual, mental, and physical well-being; strategies and profiles of successful college graduates; and additional information designed to assist Native American students, their parents and families, and the educators who work with them.

In conclusion, the following case study is presented to prompt discussion and understanding about potential issues American Indian students might face at PWIs.

Case Study

Allison is a transfer student from Tribal College, located on her reservation. She has lived on the reservation for most of her life but left only because she had finished all the available academic courses for her major at Tribal College. She transferred to the nearby State College because it was close to home. Though a PWI, State College is surrounded by several American Indian tribes, and there is a noticeable number (about 5%) of undergraduates who self-identify as American Indians. Allison is living on campus (like the majority of students) because it is easier for her to live at State College than to commute 3 hours each way from her reservation home every day.

In her first semester, Allison is taking an interdisciplinary course called Democracy in Action. The course meets a general education requirement, and because she is a transfer student she feels a bit behind on her general requirements. During a class discussion, the issue of gaming, specifically casinos on American Indian reservations, was brought up as an example of an unwanted business in the state. This prompted further conversation on the issues of tribal sovereignty, and many of the White students felt that sovereignty was not more important than the fact that state law does not allow gambling.

Allison is the only American Indian in the class, and because the instructor did not explain tribal sovereignty or the economic issues tribes face on reservations, she was very uncomfortable speaking up or talking to the instructor. Instead, Allison has approached you, her assigned mentor, for advice and guidance. State College's mentoring program was established to help minority students in their transition to the college environment. Most of the issues you have dealt with were bureaucratic in nature, and by explaining a process or making a phone call, these issues were fixed. However, this issue is more complex since Allison has told you that she does not feel welcome in the class and is worried that the instructor will be biased against her because she is an American Indian and a member of the tribe being discussed. Allison has never been in this situation and is wary about the institutional climate or what support she has available to her. As a result, Allison is discouraged and is considering leaving college because she feels unsupported and uncomfortable.

Consider these questions:

1. Though all individuals in this case need some skill and knowledge enhancement, which ones should be focused on first—the instructor, other students, Allison, or others?
2. What assumptions do the students and faculty at this institution appear to have about American Indians?
3. How can the environment be improved for Allison and other American Indian students?

4. Should someone (an individual or a representative of an on-campus resource agency) intervene to assist Allison?
5. What type of community outreach is needed to better inform the State College community about Native Americans?

Notes

1. The term American Indian has historical significance as well as political. In the 1970s the American Indian Movement (AIM) put the spotlight on American Indian issues of poverty, inequity in education, and lack of the U.S. government's attention to the social needs and heath care of American Indians. Today, the term Native American refers to any indigenous person of the United States and its territories. The term is also used to refer to indigenous people throughout Central and South America (Bitsói, 2007).

2. According to the BIA website, the BIA is "responsible for the administration and management of 66 million acres of land held in trust by the United States for American Indian, Indian tribes, and Alaska Natives. Bureau of Indian Education (BIE) provides education services to approximately 44,000 Indian students" (BIA, 2009).

References

American Indian Higher Education Consortium. (2009). *About AIHEC.* Retrieved on March 30, 2009, from http://www.aihec.org/about/index.cfm

Begay, M. A., Jr. (1997). *Leading by choice, not chance: Leadership education for native chief executives of American Indian nations.* Unpublished doctoral dissertation, Harvard University, Cambridge, MA.

Belgarde, W. L. (1996). History of American Indian community colleges. In C. Turner, M. Garcia, A. Nora, & L. I. Rendon (Eds.), *Racial & ethnic diversity in higher education* (2nd ed., pp. 3–13). Boston: Pearson Custom Publishing.

Benham, M. K. P., & Stein, W. J. (2003). *The renaissance of American Indian higher education: Capturing the dream.* Mahwah, NJ: Erlbaum.

Bitsói, L. L. (2007). *Native leaders in the new millennium: An examination of success factors of Native American males at Harvard College.* Unpublished doctoral dissertation, University of Pennsylvania.

Brayboy, B. M. (2004). Hiding in the ivy: American Indian students and visibility in elite educational settings. *Harvard Educational Review, 72,* 125–152.

Brown, D. L. (2005). American Indian student services at UND. In G. S. McClellan, M. J. T. Fox, & S. C. Lowe (Eds.), *Serving Native American students* (pp. 87–94). San Francisco: Jossey-Bass.

Brown, L. L., & Robinson Kurpius, S. E. (1997). Psychosocial factors influencing academic persistence of American Indian college students. *Journal of College Student Development, 38*(1), 3–12.

Bureau of Indian Affairs. (2007). *Federal Register, 72*(55), 13647–13652.

Bureau of Indian Affairs. (2009). Retrieved August 23, 2010, from http://www.bia .gov/WhatWeDo/index.htm

Bureau of Indian Education. (2010). *Bureau of Indian education.* Retrieved August 12, 2010, from http://www.bie.edu.

Butterfield, R. A. (1994). *Blueprint for Indian education: Improving mainstream schooling.* Charleston, WV: ERIC Clearinghouse for Rural Education and Small Schools. (ERIC Digest No. ED 372 898).

Chickering, A. W., & Reisser, L. (1993). *Education and identity* (2nd ed.). San Francisco: Jossey-Bass.

Choney, S. K., Berryhill-Paapke, E., & Robbins, R. R. (1995). The acculturation of American Indians: Developing frameworks for research and practice. In J. G. Ponterotto, J. M. Casas, L. A. Suzuki, & C. M. Alexander (Eds.), *Handbook of multicultural counseling* (pp. 72–93). Thousand Oaks, CA: Sage.

Deloria, V., Jr. (2001). Property and self-government as educational initiatives. In V. Deloria, Jr., & D. R. Wildcat (Eds.), *Power and Place: Indian Education in America.* Golden, CO: Fulcrum Resources.

Diné College. (2009). *History.* Retrieved March 30, 2009, from http://www.dinecol lege.edu/about/history.php

Dodd, J. M., Garcia, F. M., Meccage, C., & Nelson, J. R. (1995). American Indian student retention. *NASPA Journal, 33*(1), 72–78.

Ducheneaux, T. (1999). *Biculturalism and Native American college students' performance on the WAIS-III.* Unpublished master's thesis, University of North Dakota, Grand Forks.

Ecklund, T. R. (2005). *The relationship between psychosocial development and acculturation among American Indian college students.* Unpublished doctoral dissertation, State University of New York at Buffalo.

Evans, N. J., Forney, D. S., Guido, M., Patton, L. D., & Renn, K. A. (2010). *Student development in college theory, research, and practice* (2nd ed.). San Francisco: Jossey-Bass.

Garrett, M. T. (1996). "Two people": An American Indian narrative of bicultural identity. *Journal of American Indian Education, 36*(1), 1–21.

Guardia, J. R., & Evans, N. J. (2008). Student development in tribal colleges and universities. *NASPA Journal, 45*(2), 237–264.

Herring, R. D. (1991). Counseling indigenous American youth. In C. C. Lee (Ed.), *Multicultural issues in counseling: New approaches to diversity* (2nd ed., pp. 53–70). Alexandria, VA: American Association for Counseling and Development.

Horse, P. G. (2001). Reflections on American Indian identity development. In C. L. Wijeyesinghe & B. W. Jackson III (Eds.), *New perspectives on racial identity: A theoretical and practical anthology* (pp. 91–107). New York: New York University Press.

Hurlburt, G., Kroeker, R. & Gade, E. (1991). Study orientation, persistence and retention of Native students: Implications for confluent education. *Journal of American Indian Education, 30*(3), 16–23.

Hyer, S. (1990). *One house, one voice, one heart: Native American education at the Santa Fe Indian school.* Santa Fe: Museum of New Mexico Press.

Kim, B. S. K., Atkinson, D. R., & Umemoto, D. (2001). Asian cultural values and the counseling process: Current knowledge and directions for future research. *The Counseling Psychologist, 29*(4), 570–603.

Kirkness, V. J., & Barnhardt, R. (1991). First Nations and higher education: The four Rs-respect, relevance, reciprocity, responsibility. *Journal of American Indian Education, 30*(3), 1–15.

LaFromboise, T. D., Heyle, A. M., & Ozer, E. J. (1990). Changing and diverse roles of women in American Indian cultures. *Sex Roles, 22*(7–8), 455–476.

LaFromboise, T. D., & Rowe, W. (1983). Skills training for bicultural competence: Rationale and application. *Journal of Counseling Psychology, 30*(4), 589–595.

LaFromboise, T. D., Trimble, J. E., & Mohatt, G. V. (1990). Counseling intervention and American Indian tradition: An integrative approach. *The Counseling Psychologist, 18*(4), 628–654.

Lomawaima, K. T. (2000). Tribal sovereigns: Reframing research in American Indian education. *Harvard Educational Review, 70*(1), 1–21.

Lomawaima, K. T., & McCarty, T. L. (2002). When tribal sovereignty challenges democracy: American Indian education and the democratic ideal. *American Educational Research Journal, 39*(2), 279–305.

Lomawaima, K. T., & McCarty, T. L. (2006). *To remain an Indian: Lessons in democracy from a century of Native American education.* New York: Teachers College Press.

Lowe, S. (2005). This is who I am: Experiences of Native American students. In G. S. McClellan, M. J. T. Fox, & S. C. Lowe (Eds.), *Serving Native American students* (pp. 33–40). San Francisco: Jossey-Bass.

National Indian Gaming Commission. (2010). *What happens to the profits from Indian gaming operations?* Retrieved August 23, 2010, from http://www.nigc.gov/About_Us/Frequently_Asked_Questions.aspx

Navajo Courts. (2009). *The Navajo Nation peacemaking program.* Retrieved March 30, 2009, from http://www.navajocourts.org/indexpeacemaking.htm

Navajo Nation. (2009). *The Navajo Nation government.* Retrieved March 30, 2009, from http://www.navajo.org/history.htm

Ortiz, A. M., & Heavy Runner, I. (2003). Student access, retention, and success: Models of inclusion and support. In M. K. P. Benham & W. J. Stein (Eds.), *The renaissance of American Indian higher education: Capturing the dream* (pp. 215–240). Mahwah, NJ: Erlbaum.

Pavel, D. M., & Inglebret, E. (2007). *The American Indian and Alaska Native student's guide to college success.* Westport, CT: Greenwood.

Pratt, R. H. (1973). The advantages of mingling Indians with Whites. In F. P. Prucha (Ed.), *Americanizing the American Indians: Writings by the "Friends of the Indian" 1880–1900* (pp. 260–271). Cambridge, MA: Harvard University Press.

Ryan, L., & Ryan, R. (1982). *Mental health and the urban Indian.* Unpublished manuscript.

Sage, G. P. (1997). Counseling American Indian adults. In C. Lee (Ed.), *Multicultural issues in counseling* (pp. 35–52). Alexandria, VA: American Counseling Association.

Sandia Pueblo (2010). *The administration.* Retrieved August 23, 2010, from http://www.sandiapueblo.nsn.us/administration.html

Spring, J. (2010). *Deculturalization and the struggle for equality: A brief history of the education of dominated cultures in the United States* (6th ed.). Boston: McGraw-Hill.

Suizzo, M., Robinson, C., & Pahlke, E. (2008). African American mothers' socialization beliefs and goals with young children: Themes of history, education, and collective independence. *Journal of Family Issues, 29*(3), 287–316.

Szasz, M. C. (2005). I knew how to be moderate. And I knew how to obey: The commonality of American Indian boarding school experiences, 1750s–1920s. *American Indian Culture and Research Journal, 29*(4), 74–94.

Takaki, R. (1993). *A different mirror: A history of multicultural America.* Boston: Little, Brown.

Tate, D. S., & Schwartz, C. L. (1993). Increasing the retention of American Indian students in professional programs in higher education. *Journal of American Indian Education, 33*(1), 21–31.

Taylor, J. S. (1999, November). *America's first people: Factors which affect their persistence in higher education.* Paper presented at the annual meeting of the Association for the Study of Higher Education, San Antonio, TX.

Waterman, S. J. (2004). *The Haudenosaunee college experience: A complex path to degree completion.* Unpublished doctoral dissertation, Syracuse University, Syracuse, NY.

Wildcat, D. R. (2001). The question of self-determination. In V. Deloria Jr., & D. R. Wildcat (Eds.), *Power and place: Indian education in America* Golden, CO: Fulcrum Resources (135–150).

9

BIRACIAL AND MULTIRACIAL COLLEGE STUDENTS

Kristen A. Renn

Biracial and multiracial students—individuals who have parents from more than one racial group—are a growing presence on college campuses.[1] Data from the U.S. Census Bureau indicate that the number of biracial or multiracial college students will increase (Lopez, 2003). Evidence suggests that the development of racial identity among college students who are biracial or multiracial is in some ways similar to that of other students of color but may differ somewhat from racial identity development among their monoracial (i.e., having parents from only one racial group) peers (Renn, 2004; Rockquemore & Brunsma, 2002; Wallace, 2001). How these students make sense of their own racial identities in the context of increasingly diverse college campuses is an important matter for research and professional practice.

This chapter addresses the status and experiences of biracial and multiracial students in U.S. postsecondary education, presents models that describe their identity development, and offers suggestions for higher education professionals working with these students.[2] It concludes with learning activities and discussion questions related to understanding and working with multiracial college students.

Biracial and Multiracial College Students

In the 1990s multiracial students became a visible and vocal presence at a number of colleges and universities (Campus Awareness and Compliance

Initiative, 2005). The increased visibility of mixed-race students on campus coincided with the emergence of a national multiracial movement to advocate for changes in how the federal government defined racial groups and collected data in the census. Beginning with the founding of Interracial Intercultural Pride (I-Pride) in San Francisco in 1978–1979 and accelerating through the 1980s and 1990s, parents of biracial children, individuals in multiethnic relationships, and parents who had adopted children of races other than their own (a process sometimes called *transracial adoption*, see Javier, Baden, Biafora, & Camacho-Gingerich, 2007) joined mixed-race adults and youth in local groups and national organizations such as the MAVIN Foundation (http://www.mavinfoundation.org) and the Association of MultiEthnic Americans (AMEA; http://www.ameasite.org). These groups were central to the movement that resulted in the 1997 decision by the Office of Management and Budget (OMB) to permit census respondents to indicate more than one race.[3] At the same time, student organizations formed locally and connected using technologies facilitated by the emergence of the Internet (Ozaki & Johnston, 2008). Even on campuses without official mixed-race student groups, biracial and multiracial students became more visible to educators who sought to provide programs and services that could accommodate their needs and interests (Wong & Buckner, 2008).

Because federal reporting of data on student race and ethnicity has required that each individual be assigned to only one race, obtaining an exact count of mixed-race students in higher education has not been possible. Changes in federal reporting of data on student race and ethnicity implemented in 2010–2011 should enable a more accurate accounting (Renn & Lunceford, 2004). Starting in 2010–2011, the U.S. Department of Education (2007) requires that all postsecondary institutions collect these data in two steps: Students will indicate if they are Hispanic/Latino or Not Hispanic/Latino, regardless of race, and they will select from one or more of the five federal categories—American Indian or Alaskan Native, Asian, Black or African American, Native Hawaiian or other Pacific Islander, or White. Institutions can collect more specific data on student ethnicity or heritage but must then collapse those data into an unduplicated head count in the five racial categories and a Two or More Races category for reporting to the National Center for Education Statistics' Integrated Postsecondary Data System (IPEDS; Kellogg & Niskodé, 2008). After the 1997 OMB decision to include a more-than-one-race option, the new requirements will create a database that can be used to examine trends within institutions, compare institutions, and link K–12 and postsecondary data systems (Renn, 2009).

In spite of the lack of accessible, accurate data on the number of mixed-race students in higher education, some reasonable estimates can be made. Jones and Smith (2001) reported that 2.4% of the total respondents in Census 2000 were of two or more races (not counting Hispanic/Latino as a racial group), and 4.0% of those under age 18 were of two or more races, indicating that this population is growing. Using Census 2000 data, Lopez (2003) showed that 3% to 4% of the school-age population (ages 5–19) is mixed race, with a larger group (nearly 5%) of preschoolers behind them. In a state-by-state breakdown, Lopez also showed that when Latino was considered on a par with the five federal racial categories, the proportion of mixed-race youth rises from 10% in Rhode Island (lowest) to 41% in Hawaii (highest). The rate of interracial marriages increased from 0.4% in 1960 (U.S. Census Bureau, 1994) to 7.4% in 2000 (Simmons & O'Connell, 2003), and presumably this increase will continue to contribute to increases in the number of multiracial college students. There is no evidence to suggest that mixed-race youth attend college at higher or lower rates than other groups; using Lopez's calculations of the mixed-race youth population as estimates of the college population over the next 5 to 10 years, 10% to 40% of college students may be of more than one racial heritage.

Experiences of Multiracial College Students

It is not enough to know that the number of multiracial students is increasing; it is important also to understand something about their experiences in college. A growing body of literature provides insight into how multiracial youth and college students negotiate the racialized landscape of U.S. high schools and higher education. Research on secondary and postsecondary students (Basu, 2006; Kellogg, 2006; Kilson, 2001; Renn, 2003, 2004; Rockquemore, 2002; Rockquemore & Brunsma, 2002; Tizard & Phoenix, 1993; Wallace, 2001) makes up a substantial part of this literature. Autobiographies and collections of personal narratives (Azoulay, 1997; Camper, 1994; Chao, 1996; Fulbeck, 2006; Funderberg, 1994; Gaskins, 1999; Jones, 1994; Minerbrook, 1996; O'Hearn, 1998; Walker, 2001) bring the voices of mixed-race youth and young adults directly to the reader. Together these works suggest three themes in the experiences of multiracial students: the desire to identify themselves rather than to be placed in categories by others, the role of physical appearance in multiracial identity, and the role of peers and peer culture in school and college experiences related to race.

Self-Identification

The theme of racial self-identification persists in research about and narratives of mixed-race college students. In their studies of biracial college students, Basu (2006), Kellogg (2006), Renn (2003, 2004), and Wallace (2001) noted that the ability to identify themselves rather than be placed in racial categories by others was important to their research participants. In some cases, participants cited Maria Root's (1996) *Bill of Rights for Racially Mixed People,* an often referenced statement of multiracial pride and independence:

> *I have the right*
> > not to justify my existence in this world
> > not to keep the races separate within me
> > not to be responsible for people's discomfort with my physical ambiguity
> > not to justify my ethnic legitimacy
>
> *I have the right*
> > to identify myself differently than strangers expect me to identify
> > to identify myself differently than how my parents identify me
> > to identify myself differently than my brothers and sisters
> > to identify myself differently in different situations
>
> *I have the right*
> > to create a vocabulary to communicate about being multiracial
> > to change my identity over my lifetime—and more than once
> > to have loyalties and identify with more than one group of people
> > to freely choose whom I befriend and love. (p. 7)

Nearly half of these rights specifically refer to self-identification. Many biracial and multiracial college students have taken Root's declaration to heart, identifying themselves differently according to context (see Basu, 2006; Kilson, 2001; Renn, 2003, 2004; Rockquemore & Brunsma, 2002; Wallace, 2001). Whether mixed-race students identify themselves consistently in one way or differently according to context, the central principle at stake is the right and opportunity to self-identify.

With very few exceptions, beginning with filling out admissions applications, students' experiences in college are marked by compulsory identification in racial categories (Renn & Lunceford, 2004). Ninety-eight percent of colleges in a random sample drawn for one study (Renn & Lunceford, 2004) asked applicants to indicate race/ethnicity; the 2% that did not ask on the application were historically Black colleges and universities. To be clear, asking applicants to check boxes to indicate race and ethnicity is not necessarily the same thing as asking for their racial and/or ethnic identity (Brunsma, 2005; Townsend, Markus, & Bergsieker, 2009), yet young people refer to official college forms, including applications, as a location where they can indicate the full diversity of their heritage (King, 2008; Renn, 2000, 2004). Often, however, they have been prevented from doing so by forms that ask them to "check one box only." Padilla and Kelley (2005) found, for example, that 73% of a stratified random sample of 298 4-year and 2-year institutions did not allow students to identify as having mixed heritage. Renn and Lunceford (2004) found that only 17% of 4-year institutions did.

The 1997 decision revising OMB standards for collecting and reporting data on student race and ethnicity required institutions to instruct respondents to indicate all races that apply (from the five racial categories described earlier), yet the requirement to report multiracial students in a merged Two or More Races category in effect reduces the ability of respondents to have their self-identified racial background carried forward in the data. The difference between a student reporting Asian and White heritage and a student reporting Latino and Black heritage will be invisible in the data when both students are reported as Two or More Races. And students will be unable to identify themselves as Multiracial or Biracial, if those are their preferred racial identities. The opportunity to check more than one box, however, is generally seen as a step forward for self-identification (Kellogg & Niskodé, 2008).

Experiences in college, after the admissions application and other forms are completed, also highlight multiracial students' desire to identify themselves rather than be identified by others. Voluntary membership in student organizations and activities focused on race, ethnicity, and culture may provide opportunities for mixed-race students to explore and more closely identify with aspects of their heritages, regardless of how others perceive their identities (Kellogg, 2006; Renn, 2004). For students with a parent who is not a native speaker of English, language classes are sometimes a place for identity exploration and commitment, and study abroad provides some mixed-race students with the opportunity to identify with one of their cultural heritages (Renn, 2004). Other academic activities—class projects, research papers, language dialogues, performing arts—may complement a biracial student's efforts to identify with multiple aspects of his or her racial and ethnic background (Basu, 2006; Renn, 2004). Taken together, curricular and cocurricular involvement in identity exploration provides opportunities for the self-identification many mixed-race students report they are seeking.

Physical Appearance

Physical appearance—skin color, eye shape and color, hair color and texture, body shape—is an enduring factor in research and narratives on the mixed-race experience of high school and college students (AhnAllen, Suyemoto, & Carter, 2006; Chao, 1996; King, 2008; O'Hearn, 1998; Rockquemore, 2002; Wijeyesinghe, 2001). A central theme of this factor is dealing with other people's discomfort with, curiosity about, or attention (welcome or unwelcome) to the ways that many mixed-race people do not fit neatly into societal expectations of what it means to "look White" or Black or Asian. On college campuses where racial dynamics function in part based on appearances, not being readily identifiable to others creates an uncomfortable ambiguity, perhaps prompting other students to project specific identities: "You look Latina. You must speak Spanish," or stereotypes: "Your skin is so light, you must be one of those stuck-up, light-skinned African American women" (King, 2008; Renn, 2004; Rockquemore, 2002).

While it might be tempting in an age of increasing diversity and globalization to dismiss the role of physical appearance—sometimes called *phenotype*—in the experiences of mixed-race students, this theme is one of the most persistent in the literature on multiracial experiences and identities (Azoulay, 1997; Basu, 2006; Fulbeck, 2006; Funderberg, 1994; Gaskins, 1999; Jones, 1994; Kilson, 2001; Renn, 2004; Root, 1996; Walker, 2001; Wallace, 2001; Wijeyesinghe, 2001). Research involving biracial women showed that appearance may be an especially salient factor for their identities and experiences (Basu, 2006; Rockquemore, 2002). Biracial women report that dating culture, popular media (such as beauty magazines), advertising, and the entertainment industry focus attention on women's appearances, portraying light-skinned women of color as "exotic" and more socially desirable than darker-skinned women. Biracial women then face the paradox of being desired by men, sometimes resented by other women of color, yet still subject to societal racism because they are not White.

The importance of physical appearance in others' categorizations of biracial college students interacts directly with the desire to self-identify; identifying oneself as one wishes may be difficult based on how others perceive one's race and ethnicity based on appearance. The opportunity to self-identify may be reduced or made more challenging if others make assumptions about the racial identities of biracial students. Self-identification then becomes a constant process of "coming out" as mixed race (Renn, 2004), a process that may be more or less comfortable based on the individual and his or her circumstances.

Peers and Peer Culture

The role of peers and peer culture on college student outcomes is well documented (see Astin, 1984; Kaufman & Feldman, 2004; Pascarella & Terenzini, 1991, 2005), and there is no evidence to suggest that their influence on the experiences and identities of multiracial students is any less than for monoracial students. Indeed, studies suggest that peers play a substantial part in the identity exploration and racial identities of multiracial students (Basu, 2006; Kellogg, 2006; Renn, 2003, 2004). Groups of multiracial peers create opportunities for multiracial students to find comradeship, and monoracial peers (both White and students of color) create opportunities for identity exploration, support, and challenge (Renn, 2004; Renn & Arnold, 2003).

Research participants have described the role of multiracial peers in providing locations to explore mixed-race identity, to discuss shared experiences about growing up with parents who were from different backgrounds and who were different from the students themselves, and to provide educational activities for the rest of the campus (Kellogg, 2006; Renn, 2004; Wallace, 2001). On some campuses, formal student organizations for mixed-race students form a nucleus for these activities (see Ozaki & Johnston, 2008; Wong & Buckner, 2008), and on others there are informal networks of multiracial students that may or may not coalesce into a formal organization (Ozaki & Johnston, 2008; Renn, 2000). In either case, formal and informal networks of multiracial peers provide locations for identity exploration and commitment.

Monoracial peers also play important roles in the experiences of multiracial students. In some cases, monoracial friends and student organizations (e.g., Black Student Union, Asian/Pacific Alliance, etc.) provide support for multiracial students to explore their different heritage groups and to identify themselves as they choose (Renn, 2004). Often, however, multiracial students report that they encounter resistance from monoracial students based on physical appearance (as noted previously) or a perception that by claiming a multiracial identity, mixed students are somehow "trying to . . . 'escape their Blackness'" or other non-White identity, as one participant in Renn's (2004, p. 119) study claimed. Biracial students experience pressure to be "authentic" in their identities—to be Black enough, Latino/Latina enough, Native American enough, Asian in the right way—and not to appear to be rejecting any one racial identity except, perhaps, White (King, 2008; Renn, 2004; Wallace, 2001). Some biracial students experience peer pressure to choose one heritage group over another (King, 2008; Talbot, 2008) as a way to demonstrate loyalty and authenticity. The dominant role of peers and peer culture in racial identity is not unique to biracial students, but because these students are de facto not part of the monoracial White majority and because they may face additional scrutiny by peers concerned with maintaining communities of students of color, exploring the influence of peers on biracial student experiences is important.

Identity Development Models

The status and experiences of biracial students provide a context and foundation for understanding various identity and identity development models that have been proposed for multiracial students. Largely unexplored until the 1990s, biracial and multiracial identity development has been described in stage models (e.g., Kich, 1992; Poston, 1990) and nonstage models that emphasize identity processes, outcomes, or both (e.g., Renn, 2003, 2004, 2008; Rockquemore & Brunsma, 2002; Root, 1990, 1998; Wijeyesinghe, 2001). Psychological approaches dominated the early models (e.g., Kich, 1992; Poston, 1990; Root, 1990), with sociological and ecological approaches entering the field later (e.g., Kilson, 2001; Renn, 2003; Rockquemore & Brunsma, 2002; Wijeyesinghe, 2001). The models share an assumption that racial identity development for people with mixed heritages can result in healthy racial and overall self-concept, and that there is nothing inherently worse or disadvantageous about being biracial or multiracial than being monoracial.

Inherent in all of these models is the reality that by definition, biracial students have at least some heritage that places them in a nondominant racial or ethnic group in the United States. As such, their identity development is influenced by the dominant White racial ethos that may favor assimilation to the majority culture. For students whose appearance allows them to "pass" as White, no matter what their actual background is, these forces can be especially strong (Renn, 2004). It is important to remember that although biracial identity development processes and patterns may differ from those of monoracial students of color, mixed-race students are still subject to environmental factors and dominant forces of White culture.

Stage Models of Biracial Identity Development: Poston and Kich

Like the stage models proposed for monoracial people of color (e.g., Cross, 1995; Helms, 1995), the biracial identity development stage models trace an individual from early childhood through adolescence into adulthood. Believing that the monoracial models did not accurately depict the development of biracial individuals, Poston (1990) proposed a "new and positive model" (p. 153) that would better describe how biracial people come to have a healthy, positive biracial identity. Renn (2008) summarized Poston's five stages:

1. Personal Identity. Young children hold a personal identity, not necessarily linked to a racial reference group.
2. Choice of Group Categorization. Based on personal factors (such as appearance, cultural knowledge, etc.) and factors defining perceived group status and social support, an individual chooses a multicultural existence that includes both parents' heritage groups or a dominant culture from one background.
3. Enmeshment/Denial. Guilt at not being able to identify with all aspects of his or her heritage may lead to anger, shame, or self-hatred; resolving the guilt and anger are necessary to move beyond this level.
4. Appreciation. Individuals broaden [their] racial reference group through learning about all aspects of their backgrounds, though individuals may choose to identify with one group more than with others.
5. Integration. This level represents a multicultural existence in which the individual values all of her or his ethnic identities.

Although Poston's model shares some limitations of the stage models he rejected (e.g., Cross, 1987; Morten & Atkinson, 1983), his model includes three stages—Choice of Group Categorization, Enmeshment/Denial, and Appreciation—that directly address the experience of biracial people as they come to understand and accept themselves as members of more than one racial group. Poston's model, as with other stage models, contains an endpoint of integration/synthesis in which the individual internalizes and values all aspects of his or her identity. Poston's model was the first to attempt to explain a lifespan approach to healthy biracial identity development.

Based on his 1982 doctoral dissertation, Kich (1992) proposed three stages of biracial, bicultural identity development, tracing development from childhood through adolescence to adulthood (p. 305):

1. An initial awareness of differentness and dissonance between self-perceptions and others' perceptions of them (initially, 3 through 10 years of age)
2. A struggle for acceptance from others (initially, age 8 through late adolescence and young adulthood)
3. Acceptance of themselves as people with a biracial and bicultural identity (late adolescence throughout adulthood)

Though less detailed than Poston's (1990) model, Kich's (1992) model highlights the dynamic between self and others' perceptions, which explains critical aspects of *how* identity develops, not just *what* it develops into. Kich specifically identified school and community settings as the location for the struggle for acceptance, a research finding that has persisted in the 28 years since his dissertation research was conducted (see Kellogg, 2006; Renn, 2004; Wallace, 2001). Together, Poston and Kich provide useful road maps to biracial identity development, but they do not allow for the full range of possible identities that Root's (1996) *Bill of Rights for Racially Mixed People* might suggest are healthy and possible.

Varying Identity Outcomes for Multiracial Individuals

First proposed by Root (1990) as ways to "resolve 'Other' status," varying identity outcomes for multiracial students have become the accepted ways of thinking about biracial student identities. Based on her clinical psychological practice, Root (1990) proposed four potentially positive resolutions of the tension of biracial identity.

1. Acceptance of the Identity Society Assigns. Family and a strong alliance with and acceptance by a (usually minority) racial group provide support for identifying with the group to which others assume the biracial individual most belongs.
2. Identification With Both Racial Groups. Depending on societal support and personal ability to maintain this identity in the face of potential resistance from others, the biracial individual may be able to identify with both (or all) heritage groups.

3. Identification With a Single Racial Group. The individual chooses one group, independent of social pressure to identify in a particular way (as in resolution #1).
4. Identification as a New Racial Group. The individual may move fluidly among racial groups but identifies most strongly with other biracial people, regardless of specific heritage backgrounds.

In keeping with the philosophy of the bill of rights Root (1996) later published, she proposed that an individual might identify in more than one way at the same time or move fluidly among identities.

Though not derived from research, Root's (1990) identity resolutions have persisted in successive studies of biracial identity. Wallace (2001) used them as the basis of her research with high school and college students, finding that students did, in fact, identify in these ways. Kilson (2001) found similar identities among mixed-race young adults, and Rockquemore and Brunsma (2002) noted them as well in their survey-based quantitative study of 177 biracial (Black/White) college students.

Renn (2003, 2004) found an additional identity category in which students chose to opt out of identifying racially. Calling this category "extraracial," she located it among five patterns of racial identity:

1. Student holds a monoracial identity, choosing one of his or her heritages with which to identify (as in Root, 1990, third resolution).
2. Student holds multiple monoracial identities, shifting according to specifics of a situation (Root, 1990, second resolution).
3. Student holds a multiracial identity, electing not one heritage or another, but a distinct, separate category called multiracial, biracial, mixed, etc. (Root, 1990, fourth resolution).
4. Student holds an extraracial identity, deconstructing race or opting out of identification with U.S. racial categories as a means of resistance to what may be seen as artificial or socially constructed categories (not seen in Root, 1990).
5. Student holds a situational identity, identifying differently in different contexts, a fluid identity pattern in which racial identity is stable but some elements are more salient than others depending on context (inherent in Root, 1990).

In a sample of 56 students from six institutions, Renn (2004) found that nearly half (48%) identified in each of the first two patterns, 89% held a multiracial identity, 23% held an extraracial identity, and 61% identified situationally (percents total more than 100 because nearly all students were in more than one pattern). Other researchers (Kilson, 2001; Rockquemore & Brunsma, 2002; Wallace, 2001) found roughly similar proportions, with variations explained by sampling and data collection methods. Critical to all these models is the idea that one way of identifying is not a stage on the way to another, and that individuals may choose to change identities over time. Some models propose factors that may influence identity, typically in a person-environment framework.

Ecological and Person-Environment Approaches to Biracial Identity Development

If accepting an integrated biracial identity is the goal (Kich, 1992; Poston, 1990), or coming to have one or more of the four (Root, 1990) or five (Renn, 2004) identity patterns is considered healthy, understanding how individuals arrive at these identities may enable educators to help students achieve these outcomes. Person-environment or psychosocial processes similar to those implicit in earlier models of racial identity development (e.g., Atkinson, Morten, & Sue, 1979; Cross, 1995; Helms, 1995) have been shown also to contribute to biracial identity development. Ecological approaches (Renn, 2003, 2004; Root, 1998, 1999) have been useful in explaining the processes of multiracial identity development, and Wijeyesinghe's (2001) Factor Model of Multiracial Identity highlights person-environment features that contribute to various identity outcomes.

Developmental and human ecology models typically place an individual in his or her sociohistorical and cultural context to illustrate how the environment influences the person and vice versa. In his Person-Process-Context-Time developmental ecology model, Urie Bronfenbrenner (1993) focused attention on how an individual's developmentally instigative characteristics act to provoke or inhibit various reactions from people and objects through what he called *proximal processes* (Renn & Arnold, 2003). According to Bronfenbrenner's ecology model, some school and college contexts favor individuals with certain characteristics (Renn & Arnold, 2003). Renn (2003, 2004) used this model to show how individual characteristics such as propensity to explore a new environment, initiative to self-label, and family history could affect any of the five identity patterns multiracial college students might choose. For example, a campus featuring many groups for students of different cultural backgrounds could provide a rich context for exploration of multiracial heritages. On the other hand, if that environment also featured very tightly controlled access to those groups—where peers kept strict control over who was "X enough" to belong comfortably—then exploration of multiple heritages might be constrained. The emphasis on the person-environment interaction from proximal processes to more distal influences of broad sociocultural contexts is central to Bronfenbrenner's approach and to Renn and Arnold's adaption of this approach to study college student development.

Root's (1999) ecology approach embeds identity in nested contexts of generation, regional history of race relations, class, and gender systems. Personal characteristics such as inherited influences (e.g., languages at home, parent's heritage, extended family, values, and phenotype) and traits (e.g., temperament, social skills, coping skills, talents) enter social interactions with the community (home, school, work, community, friends, etc.) to influence racial and ethnic identity. Putting identity, rather than the individual, at the center of this model allows Root (1999) to provide detail on personal characteristics most relevant to racial identity, whereas Bronfenbrenner's (1993) model does not specify a domain of development or characteristics most important to that domain. By emphasizing the processes of the person-environment interactions, the ecology models provide a window into the *how* as well as the *what* of multiracial identity development.

Wijeyesinghe (2001) proposed an eight-factor model of multiracial identity, asserting that each of the following factors influenced choice of racial identity.

1. Racial ancestry
2. Early experience and socialization
3. Physical appearance
4. Other social identities (e.g., gender, sexuality, ability)
5. Religion
6. Cultural attachment
7. Political awareness and orientation, and
8. Social and historical context

The Factor Model of Multiracial Identity includes elements of the ecological approaches (Renn, 2003, 2004; Root, 1998, 1999) but does not distinguish between those influences that come from the individual and those that come from the environment or context. Instead, the model emphasizes the effect that each factor has on choice of racial identity, bringing the critical elements of physical appearance, religion, cultural attachment, and political awareness together in ways not found in the other models.

Taken as a group, the ecological approaches and Factor Model bring together key aspects of person-environment theory. They account for factors that have been empirically linked to multiracial identity development in college students, including gender, social class, family and family status, age, spirituality, social awareness and orientation, and geographic region (Renn, 2004; Rockquemore & Brunsma, 2002; Root, 1998, 2003; Shih, Bonam, Sanchez, & Peck, 2007; Wallace, 2003; Wijeyesinghe, 2001). Drawing attention to the proximal processes—the day-to-day, person-to-person (or person-to-media) interactions—that drive human development (Bronfenbrenner, 1993), these models provide a way to understand how biracial college students might move through Poston's (1990) or Kich's (1992) stages, or how they might arrive at one of the four or five identity patterns described by Root (1990), Renn (2003, 2004), Wallace (2001), Kilson (2001), or Rockquemore and Brunsma (2002). The ecology models also suggest to educators ways of designing environments to promote healthy racial identity development among all students, including those of mixed race.

Programs and Services for Multiracial Students in Higher Education

There is no evidence to suggest that multiracial students need programs or services different from those that benefit other students who are in a minority on their campuses. In fact, researchers (e.g., Kellogg, 2006; Renn, 2004; Wallace, 2001) have found that like other students of color, mixed-race students benefit from a campus climate that is culturally open and inclusive, with programs and services that acknowledge differences and similarities among students from all backgrounds. It is also true, however, that for services to be effective for mixed-race students, the *approach to providing* programs and services for students of color must take into account the reality that not all students fit neatly into one race or ethnicity. The importance of changing institutional forms has already been discussed, but there are a number of other opportunities for higher education professionals to improve the learning and developmental environment for multiracial students.

First, conduct an audit of existing programs, services, practices, and offices to see how they deal with students who choose to identify themselves in more than one racial category, in no racial category, or in a stand-alone multiracial category. Do forms require students to indicate one race only? Are the requirements for race-based scholarships clear for biracial students?

If there are offices or professional staff for monoracial groups of color (e.g., Black, Asian, Native American, Latino/Latina), how do multiracial students fit into their mission, programs, and services? Are resources available for monoracial groups of color equally available to a mixed-race student organization? How would the campus look and feel to a student who identified as mixed race? Do ostensibly monoracial students and student groups welcome mixed-race peers?

Second, train professional and paraprofessional staff to look for bias toward monoraciality and to be aware that not all students will identify themselves in a single category. For example, it is not uncommon at some diversity/awareness training activities for the facilitator to ask students to join others of the same race, typically in five monoracial groups (White, Black, Asian, Native American, and Latino/Latina). Where do biracial students go during this exercise? Having frank discussions on the ways physical appearance is an unreliable means of determining racial identity is another strategy; naming skin color, hair texture, and eye and nose shape as unreliable markers of identity creates space for staff to confront their own assumptions about what people from X group or with Y identity look like, and who looks X or Y enough to be part of a certain group.

Third, create and sustain opportunities for mixed-race students to participate in peer groups with other mixed students. Whether or not a campus sustains a biracial student organization, administrators can ensure ongoing visibility of biracial people by sponsoring and supporting activities that draw attention to the fact that not everyone is monoracial (e.g., speakers and films featuring multiracial topics and themes). Hosting discussion groups for multiracial students is another strategy, and helping multiracial students connect with one another online could also help create sustainable peer communities.

Fourth, identify campus and community role models for mixed-race students. In addition to President Barack Obama, a number of prominent biracial public figures come from entertainment (Keanu Reeves, Mariah Carey, Dwayne "The Rock" Johnson, Vin Diesel, and Alicia Keys) and sports (Derek Jeter, Grant Hill, Tiger Woods, Jamila Wideman, and Apolo Anton Ohno). While students can easily point to famous people of mixed heritage, they may benefit from having local mentors and more accessible role models. Tap informal networks of multiracial faculty, staff, and community leaders to lead discussions, participate in educational panels, or advise student groups. While it would be inappropriate to approach someone who "looks biracial" to enlist them in this effort, using campus networks, online social networks, and other means to seek participation would be appropriate.

Fifth, provide opportunities in the curriculum for students to explore and express their racial identities. Mixed-race students in various studies (e.g., Basu, 2006; Renn, 2004) discussed the importance of academic course work in exploring aspects of their heritage and understanding the history and context of race in the United States and other countries. Whether in the occasional course dedicated to the mixed-race experience or in courses where multiracial issues were one topic among many, or even in courses where race was not a central focus but class exercises and assignments allowed for exploration of racial identity, multiracial students took advantage of opportunities to build their knowledge and cultural skills. Language courses and study abroad provided additional opportunities for students to understand their heritages better.

By conducting a campus audit, training staff, creating opportunities for peer and mentor interaction, and providing curricular opportunities to explore racial identity, campus administrators can prepare for increasing populations of multiracial students. Creating an environment that welcomes multiracial students and supports their full participation in intellectual and campus life also creates a context in which multiracial students can contribute to the community by providing monoracial students of different cultural identities, backgrounds, and experiences with opportunities for interactive mutual learning from them as well. The 2010 U.S. Census will provide additional information on the proportion of the population that is Two or More Races—and especially that proportion that is high school and college age. But before census results are released, we already know that by including Latino as a racial category, the mixed-race school age population—the young people who are coming to college in the next 10 years—is somewhere between 10% and 40%, depending on the state (Lopez, 2003). Old systems for collecting data and providing programs and services for a population that is assumed, incorrectly, to be monoracial will need to be changed to accommodate the needs and interests of this growing group.

Learning Activities and Discussion Questions

1. Find your undergraduate institution's admissions application (typically online) and see how applicants are asked to indicate their race and ethnicity. Does the format comply with the OMB (1997) guidelines? Can all students identify themselves as they choose? Then locate the institution's data on student race and ethnicity. Is it clear

how the answers reported on the admissions form are aggregated and reported publicly? How do multiracial students appear in the institutional data? How do international students and those students who choose not to identify themselves appear? Is there an explanation on the admissions application or in institutional data about how missing data are handled? What about students who report more than one race?

2. Choose a higher education institution and see what kinds of student organizations are present. See if there are groups for monoracial students of color and if there is a group for biracial or multiracial students. If there are both, do they appear to receive the same amount of institutional support or recognition? If there is not a group for multiracial students, can you tell to what extent their concerns and interests may be addressed by the monoracial student groups? Do those groups sponsor events geared toward understanding and appreciating mixed race? To what extent does there appear to be cross-group programming (e.g., Black Student Union cosponsoring with Asian/Pacific Alliance)? Be sure when you are looking for multiracial student groups you are finding groups of multiracial students, not groups for students of many races (a multiracial *group,* not a group of multiracial *students*). From what you can find, and recognizing the limitations of what is available online and in published materials, what can you say about the likely climate for students who identify with more than one racial group?

3. Visit the websites of the MAVIN Foundation (http://www.mavin-foundation.org), AMEA (http://www.ameasite.org), and the Mixed Heritage Center (http://www.mixedheritagecenter.org). These sites feature reports, resource links (to books, articles, and films), media, and discussion boards. What resources can you locate that you could use in your work with students, both biracial and monoracial?

4. What are the reasons to include Hispanic/Latino as a racial category—and not separately as an ethnicity—when considering biracial and multiracial students? What are the reasons not to do so? Which calculation is most appropriate to the campus climate at your institution?

5. The OMB changed the check-one-only policy to check all that apply in 1997. Higher education was scheduled to enact this policy sometime in 2010–2011, and a majority of institutions were waiting for guidance from the Department of Education (through IPEDS)

before making changes in data collection (see Renn & Lunceford, 2004). What were the arguments for and against individual institutions making changes on their own before the IPEDS guidelines were issued? What was gained and what was lost by waiting?

6. In what ways do the experiences and identities of multiracial students reflect those of other (monoracial) students of color? In what ways are they similar to monoracial White students? How do the differences and similarities among these three groups—multiracial students, monoracial students of color, and monoracial White students—influence their college experiences?

Notes

1. The U.S. Office of Management and Budget (OMB) defines five racial categories: American Indian/Alaska Native, Asian, Black/African American, Native Hawaiian or Other Pacific Islander, and White, and two ethnic categories: Hispanic/Latino and Not Hispanic/Latino (OMB, 1997). The presence of many students with one or more Hispanic/Latino/Latina parent supports consideration of this category as socially equivalent to the five defined racial categories (Carter, Yeh, & Mazzulla, 2008; Harris & Sim, 2002). Thus, for the purposes of this chapter, *multiracial* includes individuals with, for example, one Latino/Latina and one White parent.

2. Individuals with parents from two or more federal racial categories may be called *biracial, multiracial, multiethnic, mixed race, mixed heritage,* or *mixed.* There is little concurrence on preferred terms among individuals with two or more racial heritages (see MixedFolks, n.d.) or among scholars and professionals who work with these students. The terms are used interchangeably in this chapter.

3. Under the OMB 1997 guidelines, respondents can indicate all categories that apply. Data are aggregated in a category titled Two or More Races (see Jones & Smith, 2001). Competing proposals called for adding a Multiracial category to the existing categories, but the check-all-that-apply strategy was preferred (for a discussion of the multiracial movement, multiracial individuals, the 2000 Census, and the policy process that led to changes in the census, see Perlmann & Waters, 2002; Renn & Lunceford, 2004; Winters & DeBose, 2003).

References

AhnAllen, J. M., Suyemoto, K. L., & Carter, A. S. (2006). Relationship between physical appearance, sense of belonging and exclusion, and racial/ethnic self-identification among multiracial Japanese European Americans. *Cultural Diversity and Ethnic Minority Psychology, 12,* 673–686.

Astin, A. W. (1984). Student involvement: A development theory for higher education. *Journal of College Student Personnel, 25,* 297–308.

Atkinson, D., Morten, G., & Sue, D. W. (1979). *Counseling American minorities: A cross-cultural perspective.* Dubuque, IA: W. C. Brown.

Azoulay, K. G. (1997). *Black, Jewish, and interracial: It's not the color of your skin, but the race of your kin, and other myths of identity.* Durham, NC: Duke University Press.

Basu, A. (2006). *Negotiating social contexts: Identities of biracial college women.* Greenwich, CT: Information Age Publishers.

Bronfenbrenner, U. (1993). The ecology of cognitive development: Research models and fugitive findings. In R. H. Wozniak & K. W. Fischer (Eds.), *Development in context: Acting and thinking in specific environments* (pp. 3–44). Hillsdale, NJ: Erlbaum.

Brunsma, D. L. (2005). Interracial families and the racial identification of mixed-race children: Evidence from the Early Childhood Longitudinal Study. *Social Forces, 84,* 1131–1157.

Camper, C. (Ed). (1994). *Miscegenation blues: Voices of mixed race women.* Toronto, Canada: Sister Vision Press.

Campus Awareness and Compliance Initiative. (2005). *Toolkit, Introduction, College Campus Experiences.* Retrieved May 14, 2008, from http://www.mavinfoundation.org/caci

Carter, R. T., Yeh, C. J., & Mazzulla, S. L. (2008). Cultural values and racial identity statuses among Latino students: An exploratory investigation. *Hispanic Journal of Behavioral Sciences, 30*(1), 5–23.

Chao, C. M. (1996). A bridge over troubled waters: Being Eurasian in the U.S. of A. In J. Adleman & G. Enguidanos-Clark (Eds.), *Racism in the lives of women: Testimony, theory, and guides to antiracist practice* (pp. 33–43). New York: Haworth Press.

Cross, W. E. (1987). A two-factor theory of Black identity: Implications for the study of identity development in minority children. In J. S. Phinney & M. J. Rothertham (Eds.), *Children's ethnic socialization: Pluralism and development* (pp. 117–133). Newbury Park, CA: Sage.

Cross, W. E., Jr. (1995). The psychology of Nigrescence: Revisiting the Cross model. In J. G. Ponterotto, J. M. Casas, L. A. Suzuki, & C. M. Alexander (Eds.), *Handbook of multicultural counseling* (pp. 93–122). Thousand Oaks, CA: Sage.

Fulbeck, K. (2006). *Part Asian, 100% hapa.* San Francisco: Chronicle Books.

Funderberg, L. (1994). *Black, White, other: Biracial Americans talk about race and identity.* New York: William Morrow.

Gaskins, P. F. (1999). *What are you? Voices of mixed-race young people.* New York: Henry Holt.

Harris, D. R., & Sim, J. J. (2002). Who is multiracial? Assessing the complexity of lived race. *American Sociological Review, 67,* 614–627.

Helms, J. E. (1995). An update of Helms's White and people of color racial identity development models. In J. G. Ponterotto, J. M. Casas, L. A. Suzuki, & C. M. Alexander (Eds.), *Handbook of multicultural counseling* (pp. 181–198). Thousand Oaks, CA: Sage.

Javier, R. A., Baden, A. L., Biafora, F. A., & Camacho-Gingerich, A. (Eds.) (2007). *The handbook of adoption: Implications for researchers, practitioners, and families.* Thousand Oaks, CA: Sage.

Jones, L. (1994). *Bulletproof diva: Tales of race, sex and hair.* New York: Doubleday.

Jones, N. A., & Smith, A. S. (2001). *The two or more races population: 2000.* Washington, DC: U.S. Census Bureau.

Kaufman, P., & Feldman, K. A. (2004). Forming identities in college: A sociological approach. *Research in Higher Education, 45*(5), 463–496.

Kellogg, A. (2006). *Exploring critical incidents in the racial identity of multiracial college students.* Unpublished doctoral dissertation, University of Iowa, Iowa City.

Kellogg, A., & Niskodé, A. S. (2008). Policy issues for student affairs and higher education. In K. A. Renn & P. Shang (Eds.), *Biracial and multiracial college students: Theory, research, and best practices in student affairs* (pp. 93–102). San Francisco: Jossey-Bass.

Kich, G. K. (1992). The developmental process of asserting a biracial, bicultural identity. In M. P. P. Root (Ed.), *Racially mixed people in America* (pp. 304–317). Newbury Park, CA: Sage.

Kilson, M. (2001). *Claiming place: Biracial young adults of the post–Civil Rights era.* Westport, CT: Bergin & Garvey.

King, A. R. (2008). Student perspectives: The racial balancing act. In K. A. Renn & P. Shang (Eds.), *Biracial and multiracial college students: Theory, research, and best practices in student affairs* (pp. 33–42). San Francisco: Jossey-Bass.

Lopez, A. M. (2003). Mixed-race school-age children: A summary of census 2000 data. *Educational Researcher, 32,* 25–37.

Minerbrook, S. (1996). *Divided to the vein: A journey into race and family.* New York: Harcourt, Brace.

MixedFolks. (n.d.). *Names for MixedFolks.* Retrieved June 10, 2007, from http://www.mixedfolks.com/names.htm

Morten, G., & Atkinson, D. R. (1983). Minority identity development and preference for counselor race. *Journal of Negro Education, 52,* 156–161.

Office of Management and Budget. (1997). *Revisions to the Standards for the Classification of Federal Data on Race and Ethnicity.* Retrieved May 7, 2008, from http://www.whitehouse.gov/omb/fedreg/ombdir15.html

O'Hearn, C. C. (1998). *Half and half: Writers on growing up biracial and bicultural.* New York: Random House.

Ozaki, C. C., & Johnston, M (2008). The space in between: Issues for multiracial student organizations and advising. In K. A. Renn & P. Shang (Eds.), *Biracial and multiracial college students: Theory, research, and best practices in student affairs* (pp. 53–62). San Francisco: Jossey-Bass.

Padilla, A., with Kelley, M. (2005). *One box isn't enough: An analysis of how U.S. colleges and universities classify mixed heritage students.* Retrieved January 11, 2006, from http://www.mavinfoundation.org/projects/obie_report_110905.pdf

Pascarella, E. T., & Terenzini, P. T. (1991). *How college affects students.* San Francisco: Jossey-Bass.

Pascarella, E. T., & Terenzini, P. T. (2005). *How college affects students: A third decade of research.* San Francisco: Jossey-Bass.

Perlmann, J., & Waters, M. C. (Eds.). (2002). *The new race question: How the census counts multiracial individuals.* New York: Russell Sage Foundation.

Poston, W. S. C. (1990). The biracial identity development model: A needed addition. *Journal of Counseling and Development, 69,* 152–155.

Renn, K. A. (2000). Patterns of situational identity among biracial and multiracial college students. *Review of Higher Education, 23,* 399–420.

Renn, K. A. (2003). Understanding the identities of mixed-race college students through a developmental ecology lens. *Journal of College Student Development, 44,* 383–403.

Renn, K. A. (2004). *Mixed race college students: The ecology of race, identity, and community.* Albany, NY: SUNY Press.

Renn, K. A. (2008). Research on bi- and multiracial identity development: Overview and synthesis. In K. A. Renn & P. Shang (Eds.), *Biracial and multiracial college students: Theory, research, and best practices in student affairs* (pp. 13–22). San Francisco: Jossey-Bass.

Renn, K. A. (2009). Education policy, politics, and mixed heritage students in the United States. *Journal of Social Issues, 65*(1), 165–184.

Renn, K. A., & Arnold, K. D. (2003). Reconceptualizing research on peer culture. *Journal of Higher Education, 74,* 261–291.

Renn, K. A., & Lunceford, C. J. (2004). Because the numbers matter: Transforming postsecondary education data on student race and ethnicity to meet the challenges of a changing nation. *Education Policy, 18*(5), 752–783.

Rockquemore, K. A. (2002). Negotiating the color line: The gendered process of racial identity construction among Black/White biracial women. *Gender & Society, 16*(4), 485–503.

Rockquemore, K. A., & Brunsma, D. L. (2002). *Beyond black: Biracial identity in America.* Thousand Oaks, CA: Sage.

Root, M. P. P. (1990). Resolving "Other" status: Identity development of biracial individuals. *Women and Therapy, 9*(1–2), 185–205.

Root, M. P. P. (1996). A Bill of Rights for racially mixed people. In M. P. P. Root (Ed.), *The multiracial experience: Racial borders as the new frontier* (pp. 3–14). Newbury Park, CA: Sage.

Root, M. P. P. (1998). Experiences and processes affecting racial identity development: Preliminary results from the Biracial Sibling Project. *Cultural Diversity and Mental Health, 4*(3), 237–247.

Root, M. P. P. (1999). The biracial baby boom: Understanding the ecological constructions of racial identity in the 21st century. In R. H. Sheets & E. R. Hollins (Eds.), *Racial and ethnic identity in school practices: Aspects of human development* (pp. 67–90). Mahwah, NJ: Erlbaum.

Root, M. P. P. (2003). Racial identity development and persons of mixed race heritage. In M. P. P. Root & M. Kelley (Eds.), *Multiracial child resource book: Living complex identities* (pp. 34–41). Seattle: MAVIN Foundation.

Shih, M., Bonam, C., Sanchez, D. T., & Peck, C. (2007). The social construction of race: Biracial identity and vulnerability to stereotypes. *Cultural Diversity and Ethnic Minority Psychology, 13,* 125–133.

Simmons, T., & O'Connell, M. (2003). *Married-couple and unmarried-partner households: 2000.* Washington DC: U.S. Census Bureau.

Talbot, D. M. (2008). Exploring the experiences and self-labeling of mixed-race individuals with two minority parents. In K. A. Renn & P. Shang (Eds.), *Biracial and multiracial college students: Theory, research, and best practices in student affairs* (pp. 23–32). San Francisco: Jossey-Bass.

Tizard, B. & Phoenix, A. (1993). *Black, white or mixed race? Race and racism in the lives of young people of mixed parentage.* London: Routledge.

Townsend, S. S. M., Markus, H. R., & Bergsieker, H. B. (2009). My choice, your categories: The verification or denial of multiracial identities. *Journal of Social Issues, 65*(1), 185–204.

U.S. Census Bureau. (1994). *Table 1: Race of wife by race of husband: 1960, 1970, 1980, 1991, and 1992.* Retrieved May 8, 2008, from http://www.census.gov/population/socdemo/race/interractab1.txt

U.S. Department of Education. (2007). Final guidance on maintaining, collecting, and reporting racial and ethnic data to the U.S. Department of Education. *Federal Register.* Retrieved May 5, 2008, from http://www.ed.gov/legislation/FedRegister/other/2007–4/101907c.html

Walker, R. (2001). *Black, White and Jewish: Autobiography of a shifting self.* New York: Putnam.

Wallace, K. R. (2001). *Relative/outsider: The art and politics of identity among mixed heritage students.* Westport, CT: Ablex.

Wallace, K. R. (2003). Contextual factors affecting identity among mixed heritage college students. In M. P. P. Root & M. Kelley (Eds.), *Multiracial child resource book: Living complex identities* (pp. 87–92). Seattle: MAVIN Foundation.

Wijeyesinghe, C. L. (2001). Racial identity in multiracial people: An alternative paradigm. In C. L. Wijeyesinghe & B. W. Jackson III (Eds.), *New perspectives on racial identity development: A theoretical and practical anthology* (pp. 129–152). New York: New York University Press.

Winters, L. I., & DeBose, H. L. (2003). *New faces in a changing America: Multiracial identity in the 21st century.* Thousand Oaks, CA: Sage.

Wong, M. P. A., & Buckner, J. (2008). Multiracial student services come of age: The state of multiracial student services in the United States. In K. A. Renn & P. Shang (Eds.), *Biracial and multiracial college students: Theory, research, and best practices in student affairs* (pp. 43–52). San Francisco: Jossey-Bass.

10

WHITE COLLEGE STUDENTS

B. Afeni McNeely Cobham

In this chapter, racism is defined as a personal ideology sustained by systemic policies and practices of oppression based on the belief that a racial group is either biologically or culturally inferior, and the use of such beliefs to rationalize a racial group's treatment in society (Bulmer & Solmos, 1999; Tatum, 2000). In the past few decades, there has been an influx of research on how systemic racism remains embedded in American values vis-à-vis White privilege (Dyer, 1988; Feagin, 2001; Helms, 1992; McIntosh, 1989).

The privilege of Whiteness or being White can arguably mean that "affiliation with the dominant side of power systems" (Wildman & Davis, 2000, p. 53) bestows standards of normalcy, qualifications, achievement, and cultural values from an insular White perspective. Conversely, some might argue that White subgroups (i.e., women, poor, queer, ethnic, uneducated or nonprotestant) are not beneficiaries of such privileges. While it is true that these multiple-identity White communities endure intragroup discrimination, any attempt to engage in "oppression sweepstakes," which pits one form of oppression against another (Smith, Yosso, & Solorzano, 2007), would undermine the daily experiences of groups marginalized because of their race, language, culture, phenotype, accent, immigrant status, and surname (Smith et. al).

Researchers have suggested that understanding the identity development of White American students will assist college administrators and faculty in creating a campus environment that fosters cultural competence (Carter,

The author and editors wish to acknowledge the contributions of Elizabeth Broughton in the development of this chapter.

213

1990; King & Shuford, 1996; Ortiz & Rhoads, 2000). The purpose of this chapter is to provide a historical and sociological perspective of White Americans who attend colleges and universities and to discuss research relevant to their experiences in higher education.

To that end, a portion of this chapter touches upon critical areas that shape White American identity development. The first section addresses the social construction of race in the United States. The second considers how the social construction of race determines White peoples' social, economic, and political status in U.S. culture. In summation, the third section illustrates how this status influences White American college students' intercultural engagement with non-White peers, faculty, and administrators. This chapter also introduces best practices to assist educators working with White American college students, and offers recommendations to administrative and academic professionals.

Brief History of White Americans

On most campuses, issues of racism or racist attitudes are generally explored from the perspective of underrepresented students as racism's target or the oppressed. Incidents of racism, whether enacted consciously or subconsciously, are seldom investigated from the perspective of White students' ethnic/racial identity. Most White Americans rarely explore their status or attitudes as racial beings (Carter, 1990; Hardiman, 1994), in part because they are viewed, or in some cases perceive themselves, to be from one European ancestry (Takaki, 1993). To date, there are 53 categories of European Americans in the United States, the largest ones being German American, English, and Irish American (Giordano & McGoldrick, 1996). Many White ethnics maintain a rich history of their ancestry, thus their heritage and influence on American culture cannot be underestimated in understanding White identity.

The sentiment of cultural and racial superiority among early colonists in America was reflective of the beliefs they brought with them from England. As a result, White ethnics (including Catholics and Jews) who fell outside White Anglo-Saxon Protestant (WASP) values were labeled as inferior and were subjected, in many cases, to oppressive hostility.

The blueprint for WASP indoctrination was implemented in several ways: English imperialism in Europe, Asia, and Africa; the acculturation of WASP values through education; and the colonization of North America with the intent of creating a "land . . . primarily inhabited by Whites" (Spring, 2007, p. 5). The first naturalization laws restricted citizenship to "free White persons," as Spring pointed out. The legal interpretation of the Naturalization Act of 1790 profoundly defined one's race according to skin color. While the law was exclusive to phenotype, it was inclusive of White ethnic immigrants from eastern and central Europe. This was not the intention of the WASP leadership, in fact, it was an oversight. Jacobson (1998) writes:

> So natural was the relationship of whiteness to citizenship that, in the debate which followed, nowhere did they pause to question the limitation of naturalized citizenship to "white persons. . . . probably because legislators at the time were so consumed by legal problems posed by slavery, whiteness, and blackness. Consequently, whiteness in the early decades of the republic remained a legislative and conceptual monolith that left the gates open to all European comers. (pp. 22, 40)

The idea of White citizenship justified social, economic, and political inequalities as natural, underlining the belief that systemic racial practices in American government, education, and laws were necessary to govern those labeled as inferior. Specifically, the values, lifestyle, and language White immigrants in America were judged by were those of White Anglo-American Protestants. These standards constructed current social and political institutions, and continually shape social and political forces of privilege (Giordano & McGoldrick, 1996).

White Ethnic Groups Stories

It's important to note that this section of this chapter is not an attempt to vet the complex and in-depth history of White people in America. By providing a snapshot into the immigration experiences of three White ethnic groups, a pattern in the American psyche is revealed. Racism, as defined in this chapter, and racist practices have always been shaped and carried out by those with the political, economic, and social power to inform policy and relegate other racial groups to disempowered status. As a consequence, the quest for access and equal opportunity in America often meant that many White ethnics had to abandon their traditions, values, language, and lifestyle in an effort to assimilate with the dominant group.

The Irish. More than a half million Irish immigrated to America to flee a famine crisis and the oppressive laws of the English that left them deprived of civil rights, exploited, stripped of their language, and subjected to hangings, slavery, or deportation for trivial offenses. As a result, many Irish immigrants brought the trauma of their experiences to America (Shannon, 1964). Similar to other ethnic Whites, the Irish worked as manual laborers and builders for dismally low wages. Whenever possible they clustered in dilapidated housing communities, often living with disease, fire, violence, alcoholism, and crime. White Anglo-Americans viewed immigrants from Ireland as inferior and prohibited them from equal opportunity and access. Sowell (1981) wrote, "The native public's reaction to the Irish included moving out of neighborhoods en masse as the immigrants moved in; stereotyping them all as drunkards, brawlers, and incompetents; and raising employment barriers exemplified in the stock phrase, 'No Irish need apply'" (p. 17).

The Germans. German immigration to America was gradual in 1620, however, by the early 18th century emigration from Germany surged. Many Germans came as indentured servants, bound by contract to work for 3 to 7 years to pay off their transportation to America. Sowell (1981) offered an illustration of the Germans' transatlantic voyage:

> Indentured servants were packed into small, ill-ventilated quarters on small ships. . . . The weakness and dehydration produced by seasickness made the ill-fed passengers particularly vulnerable to disease. . . . after a vessel docked in an American port . . . the indentured servants were brought out of their quarters, walked up and down to let the buyers see them, and sometimes feel their muscles and talk to them to form some opinion of their intelligence and submissiveness. (p. 48)

For many White Anglo-Americans, the trade in human beings whom they perceived as inferior caused no moral shame. When World War I began, anti-German sentiment was polarized by the removal of German books from libraries, the cancellation of German language courses in public schools, and boycotts of German American cultural institutions (Huebener, 1962; Sowell, 1981).

The Italians. Prior to laws that slowed down massive immigration to America (such as the Reed-Johnson Immigration Act of 1924), ancestors of Italian Americans emigrated from southern Italy at a rate of 200,000 per year. According to Sowell (1981), those who came to America were typically poor agricultural laborers who suffered economic setbacks because of infertile agricultural terrains. In addition, because of a social cast system primarily built around literacy and class, southern Italians were "poor, powerless, and despised" by their northern compatriots (Sowell, p. 104). Crispino (1980) found that Italian immigrants' primary reason for coming to America was to better themselves economically and then return to Italy. Those who remained in the United States worked in jobs the Irish immigrants held before them (i.e., railroad building, construction, etc.). Others were able to secure white-collar jobs as seamen, tailors and shoemakers, barbers, and masons, but they earned less annually than White Americans. Sentiment toward Italians as a group ranged from accusations of being inferior and criminal-minded to lacking ambition and being difficult to communicate with. Discriminatory practices increased as Italian immigrants expressed concerns over their children being subject to a curriculum of "Americanization" often found in public schools. Kaestle (1983) supported this idea by asserting that the establishment of public schools in the early 19th century was specifically designed to protect the ideology of an Anglo-American Protestant culture.

Who Is White? The Politics of Assimilation

Although the architects of the U.S. Constitution were divided over immigration policy, there was widespread consensus that the privileges associated with citizenship could only be granted to those who would strengthen the concept of a homogenous White population (Jacobson, 1998; Kaufmann, 2004; Spring, 2007). As the number of White ethnics in America began to outpace "pure-blooded" White Anglo-Americans, some groups transformed into dominant minorities. The political and economic implications of a population shift were a threat to the dominant WASP culture. As such, the assimilation of White ethnics became a necessity for the dominant culture to remain in control. Assimilation is the process by which one cultural group is absorbed by another (Schwean, Mykota, Robert, & Saklofske, 1999). Taken further, assimilation for White ethnics meant completely dissolving their ethnicity into the White Anglo-American way of living. The White Anglo-American Protestant ethic emphasized individual hard work, the amassment of property and wealth, and a nuclear family structure (Spring, 2007). For some White ethnics, succumbing to the principles of White Anglo-American culture was an abandonment of their racial and cultural identity. According to Crispino (1980), for example, Italian Americans value the nuclear family as well as "relationships with extended family members related by blood and in-laws up to the fourth degree" (p. 20). Furthermore,

Italian Americans and other White ethnics often developed grassroots organizations that helped new immigrants from their homeland in the transition and adjustment to America. These organizations were a threat to White Anglo-American philosophies on self-reliant hard work and success, though such principles seem contradictory based on the exploited labor of African slaves, conquered Native Americans, and indentured Asian and White servants.

The Americanization/assimilation movement demanded that White ethnic immigrants and their children speak English only, abandon cultural aspects of their homeland, and relinquish membership or involvement in ethnic organizations and social institutions that fostered ethnic identity. The Americanization of White ethnics received full support from White Americans as well as prominent political leaders. Woodrow Wilson often spoke unfavorably of "hyphenated Americans" (Sowell, 1981) and is credited with saying that "ethnic identity was not compatible with being a thorough American" (Kaufmann, 2004, p. 30). Many White ethnic groups responded to this criticism by removing their ethnic designation from the word American. Intergroup relations among White Americans and White ethnics grew through intermarriages, interracial neighborhoods, military service in all-White units, and attending the same schools and churches. Furthermore, some gained access to American political and social structures through coalition voter blocks and membership in all-White athletic and social clubs. The longevity of White ethnics in America increased their numbers, and as a result, their children (second and third generations) adopted cultural aspects of the United States including, but not limited to, ideological positions on privilege. Specifically, White ethnics who faced oppression from White Anglo-American Protestants adopted similar attitudes that discriminatingly rejected non-European groups (Yancey, 2003). Thus, the ideological transformation and physical appearance of White ethnic groups made their gradual acceptance among White Americans seamless.

In turn, a component of White privilege identity is the perception that non-English descendants believe they are members of the majority group and subsequently are entitled to all privileges that come with majority-group affiliation. For that reason, ethnic White people's outlook of being a part of the majority culture is usually stronger than their sentiment of belonging to a separate ethnic group. Campus administrators may be contributing to empty rhetoric about race, privilege, and the impact of systemic social hierarchy on college campuses by not fully understanding White students as racial beings, the politics of White privilege, and White identity development.

White Privilege

"I don't think about race" is a commonly shared sentiment held by a majority of White Americans. For White people, indifference about race or the systemic implications of racism is an inherent privilege rooted in the history of American culture. W. E. B. DuBois (1903/1996), a prolific 20th-century American scholar, described the psychosocial complexity of Blacks living in the United States as *double consciousnesses* where one exists in two worlds (a Black world and a White world). In stark contrast, most White Americans are not plagued by double consciousness because they do not identify themselves as racial beings. Dyer (2002) asserted, "As long as race is something only applied to non-White peoples, as long as White people are not racially seen and named, they/we function as a human norm. Other people are raced; we [White people] are just people" (p. 10). Accordingly, when the topic of race is brought up in classroom settings, campus newspapers, and during programming initiatives, for many White American college students the topic triggers thoughts and feelings that are uncomfortable, painful, fearful, or all too often, indifferent. Reflecting on this phenomenon, Doane (1997) argued that the dominant group's acceptance of systemic privilege often leads to passive rhetoric that denies race or racism as an important factor in the social hierarchy. In fact, the platform of "White Nationalism," which Swain (2002) defines as "repacked, relabeled, and transformed White supremacy," espouses a culturally hegemonic worldview that posits White privilege as an inheritance bestowed upon Whites by their "God-given natural right to their distinct cultural, political, and genetic identity as white Europeans" (p. 16). The privilege of Whiteness allows one to respond to incendiary, racist beliefs in several ways: through *silent racism* (Trepagnier, 2006), which advances subconscious racist assumptions so entrenched in American culture that challenges to the status quo would not have an impact; through active resistance where Whites serve as nonpaternalistic social justice advocates and antiracist activists; through cultural hegemony (Schwean et al., 1999) in which representatives of a racial group impose their social reality on another group in a menacing way; or through the presumption that the experiences of people of color in America are monolithic.

The author recalls a conversation with a White female student who shared her blueprint for helping "underprivileged" Hispanic/Latino/Latina American teenagers as part of a required community service initiative sponsored by the student's sorority. After patiently and politely listening, the author asked the student if her strategic plan was based on conversations with the students or their parents/guardians, or was her course of action rooted in her assumptions about the needs of Hispanic/Latino/Latina teenagers. Regrettably, the student took offense to the question, but this situation underscores the fundamental importance of nonpaternalistic advocacy. The underprivileged Hispanic/Latino/Latina teenagers the student spoke of came from middle-class backgrounds. Therefore, these students were not economically or socially underprivileged, but they were in need of female college-aged mentors to reinforce the importance of academic pursuits and achievement. Although it was unintended and not malicious, the White student exhibited a patronizing attitude toward Hispanic/Latino/Latina teenagers.

It is important for well-meaning White people to consistently assess White privilege and how it shapes their view of others. Author and antiracist activist Tim Wise (2009) supports this position in his charge for an honest dialogue about race in America. Participating on a CNN panel on racial profiling, Wise asserted that White people must "admit that [they] have been conditioned to have [prejudicial] reactions" toward people who are not White. Furthermore, Wise said he believes that these beliefs and knee-jerk reactions can be effectively addressed, but not if White people do not acknowledge them. Building on this argument, White privilege allows White people to avoid or not respond to opportunities of multicultural competence in which one can develop or enhance knowledge, skills, and attitudes about another's race, identity, and experiences (Howard-Hamilton, 2000). According to McIntosh (1989), White students are often taught that racism places individuals at a disadvantage, but they are not taught that racism places White people at an advantage as a member of the dominant group. Specifically, many White Americans have been socialized to view racism as men in white sheets carrying out individual acts of cruelty, not "invisible systems of conferring dominance on White people as a group" (McIntosh, p. 10). Christine Sleeter further demonstrates this point during an interview on the topic of multiculturalism in Miner and Peterson (2000–2001):

> My grandfather was a painter and wallpaper hanger who did fairly well buying property, renovating it, and then selling it. I grew up with the family story that he only had a second-grade education and "look how well he did." Yet he was buying property at a time in which property ownership was much easier for white people. As a part of Roosevelt's New Deal legislation, money for low-cost federal subsidized housing loans [was] made available to white families and not to families of color, because southern senators wanted to keep African Americans working as sharecroppers. Part

of that New Deal legislation was specifically crafted so that people like my grandfather could buy property. I have inherited then, the benefits of that piece of systemic, historic white racism. (pp. 1–2)

Complete immersion into the complexity of privilege may lead White students to unpack issues of race and identity from an antiracist point of view. Trepagnier (2006) referred to antiracism as an unwavering position against racism that is active not passive. Trepagnier takes this idea further by asserting that "antiracism . . . interrupts racism in all its forms, whether personal or institutional, blatant or routine, intended or unintended. . . . If one claims to be antiracist but takes no action against racism, the claim is false" (p. 104). Practitioners must play a role in shifting White students' paradigms to help them understand (if they do not already do so) and unpack privilege from a systemic point of view that illuminates how advantages for one group can and has often led to economic, social, or political advantages for individual members of that group.

White American College Students

The characteristics of colonial college students reveal a range of economic backgrounds. Brubacher and Rudy (1997) pointed out that in spite of poverty, eager students were presented with opportunities to attend college. However, a caste system did exist in the halls of higher education. In the student catalogs of Harvard and Yale during colonial times, students were ranked on the basis of their family wealth or social position. In terms of students' temperament, Handlin and Handlin (1970) referred to the young men as "lads" who viewed their transition to manhood and ultimately the workforce as a burden they did not want to contend with. The authors note how "college was a refuge where with communal approbation young men could separate themselves from their fathers and begin to chart independent courses through life" (p. 23). For many years, college administrators and faculty debated with students over issues of independence. Faculty saw their role as educator and surrogate parent. Students, on the other hand, were staunchly against the in loco parentis philosophy and began to rebel to make their feelings known. As a result, the inclusion of cocurricular student life in academia began. Several student organizations sprung up on college campuses, none more formidable than secret societies or fraternal organizations. These groups were often criticized for their exclusivity because membership was reserved for wealthy students. Handlin and Handlin illustrated the exclusiveness of these groups through their observation of documented recruitment practices: "The criterion for admitting a new member [entailed the question] 'would you want your sister to marry him?' This showed the relationship students desired. They sought a surrogate family, that intimate group life out of which . . . lifelong friendships grow" (p. 40).

As the college system moved into the 19th and 20th centuries, Greek-lettered organizations grew in numbers and stature yet continued the practice of exclusive membership. Members of other student groups such as sororities, athletic teams, literary societies, and campus newspapers also segregated themselves into smaller homogenous campus cultures. These early examples of comfort zones or group identity clusters shaped campus silos found in many colleges and universities today. In the years following the Civil War, demographics of college students attending predominantly White institutions (PWIs) began to shift slightly with the enrollment of women and students of color. White students' response toward coeducation and integration often embodied the exclusive baggage of their colonial predecessors, thus treatment of the new student body varied from deep-seated resentment to cautious acceptance. Legislation such as the Morrill Act of 1862, *Brown v. Board of Education* (1954), the Civil Rights Act of 1964, Affirmative Action (1965), and Title IX (1972) mandated access and equity in colleges and universities but had no impact in eradicating discriminatory practices and beliefs often found in institutional polices, student life, and the curriculum. For that reason, "it became apparent that PWIs were not created to facilitate a holistic educational experience for non-Whites, [women] or immigrant people of color" (Cobham & Parker, 2007, p. 88). Building on this argument, although PWIs yielded to desegregation, the systemic integration of non-White American values, standards, culture, and the meaning of achievement has yet to have a prominent place in the ivory tower. The ensuing outcome was the formation of support structures that represented and addressed the needs of students' multiple identities (i.e. gender, race, sexual identity, class, religion, etc.) as alternatives to general acceptance within the larger campus community.

Many White students and their advocates bemoan identity-based groups as college-sponsored double standards. As individuals or as a group, some White Americans claim disenfranchisement over the absence of designated scholarships for White students, a White student alliance, White history month, White cultural centers, or White studies departments. These sentiments illustrate the profound need for administrative and academic practitioners to address the perception of special treatment deprivation within the context of White identity development. This could be accomplished, in part, through antiracist curricular and cocurricular initiatives that examine Whites as racial beings with multiple subgroup identities, the impact of racism on White people, and inherent privileges embedded in the White American psyche if left unchallenged.

Research on White College Students

Several studies conducted at predominantly White research institutions have examined the cognitive development (Perry, 1968), identity development (Chickering, 1969), moral development (Gilligan, 1982; Kohlberg, 1976), and ethnographic behavior (Moffatt, 1989) of college students. While these theories are valuable approaches for working with students, some researchers have questioned their relevance to other students who are not White (Evans, Forney, & Guido-DiBrito, 1998; Pascarella, & Terenzini, 1998). In fact, in a compilation of major studies that measured the impact of college on students, Pascarella and Terenzini concluded that the studies were conducted on "traditional, White, undergraduate college students ages 18–22 who attended four-year institutions full-time, who lived on campus, who didn't work, and had few, if any family responsibilities" (p. 152). A portion of Moffatt's ethnographic research analyzed student cultures with a focus on race/ethnicity and gender. From his field-based observations and in-depth research, Moffatt estimated that "between a tenth and a quarter" of the White students attending his research site were racists (p. 164). He concluded that "most of these White racists probably never acted on their attitudes, but it only took a few of them acting out [these attitudes] to generate the intermittent racist hassles that Black students" contend with (p. 164). Moffatt observed that many White students simply wanted everyone to be human and to assimilate so that racism would no longer exist. These observations illustrate the cultural hegemonic paradigm of White students and how they form and perpetuate cultural attitudes and behaviors that bell hooks (1989) identifies as White superiority. hooks refers to White supremacy as subconscious, internalized values that maintain domination, even if some Whites do not openly support or demonstrate overt forms of discrimination or prejudice. Specifically, the White students who participated in Moffat's study lacked familiarity with privilege, White identity development, and an effective approach to confronting racism. Feagin, Vera, and Imani (1996) correlated subconscious supremacy to symbols that create for many White alumni of PWIs a sense of belonging or "nostalgia" (p. 53). The authors asserted that conventional practices such as campuswide activities and publications (i.e., homecoming, yearbook, sporting events, and campus newspaper) "glorified white life and recreational activities," that focused on white student traditions (p. 54).

As American higher education moves deeper into the 21st century, new political, economic, and demographic forces will further affect the challenges academic professionals face when dealing with White college students. The majority of research on race usually compares race/ethnic groups' perception of campus climate and adjustment (Ancis, Sedlacek, & Mohr, 2000; Strage, 2000), student involvement (DeSousa & King, 1992), and educational gains (Astin, 1993). Increasingly, though, more researchers are examining White college student attitudes toward White identity development and racism. Carter (1990) explored White identity attitudes and racism among 100 White college students. The results indicated that White women were found to be more intellectually and emotionally understanding of racial differences than White men. Pope-Davis and Ottavi (1994) replicated the study with a larger sample size and found that White women and older students were psychologically more advanced in accepting racial differences than the men or younger students who participated in the study. Pope-Davis and Ottavi attributed these findings to Carter's (1990) observation of White women's experience with gender discrimination and their ability to correlate such experiences to racial discrimination. Furthermore, the significant age gap regarding racial identity attitudes illustrated that racial awareness and acceptance could be attributed to age maturity. Martin, Krizek, Nakayama, and Bradford (1996) explored White students' preferences for racial self-labels. Although some respondents were resistant to the idea of self-labeling, most preferred to be identified as White. When the respondents were asked to define White, several replied "White is White" (p. 139). These findings demonstrate the indistinguishable position of Whiteness as a powerful function in one's having the choice (or privilege) to claim ethnic or nonethnic labels.

These sociological approaches demonstrate the significant organizational, historical, cultural, and social factors that shape, influence, and perpetuate a privileged hierarchy on college and university campuses. Accordingly, campus administrators must be attentive to these empirical findings when advocating for an inclusive campus environment. Failure to do so will continue to promote superficial diversity initiatives that fall short of addressing deep-seated racial issues that create an undercurrent of mistrust, unethical and disrespectful behavior, and exclusionary practices.

White Identity Development

Several scholars have examined the process of White identity development through the sociological lens of Hardiman's (1982) White Identity Development model, Helms's (1984) White Racial Identity model, and Ponterotto's (1988) White Racial Consciousness Development model. Because the stages of each approach are analogous, Sabnani, Ponterotto, and Borodovsky (1991) integrated the models to illustrate the inclusivity of each framework and developed a White Racial Identity model comprising the following five stages.

Preexposure/precontact. White people in this stage have not explored their own race/ethnic identity, nor are they aware of their social position in society based on historical and systemic racism. There is also "an unconscious identification with Whiteness and an unquestioned acceptance of stereotypes about minority groups" (Ponterotto, Utsey, & Pedersen, 2006, p. 101). The attitudes of White people in this stage could be further explained in Reason and Evan's (2007) position on racial apathy, which the authors describe as Whites' indifference to issues of discrimination.

Conflict. This characteristic centers on emotional conflict about the impact of Whiteness in a racist society. Awareness about race relations is facilitated through interactions with members of underrepresented groups and information obtained from various sources (family, friends, academic courses, etc.). A key component of the conflict stage is the confusion, guilt, anger, and depression White people undergo in trying to decide if they want to relent to majority group norms or engage in antiracist values. For example, a White person may be offended by certain racist activities and participate in a social protest against this injustice, yet simultaneously be less than enthusiastic if a member of his or her family dates a person of color.

Pro-minority/Antiracism. This trait is situated in one of two outcomes from the emotional conflict of stage 2. White people immerse themselves in antiracist thinking and practices as a way to hold themselves and their own culture accountable for racial problems. Furthermore, in this stage White people unpack "self-focused anger and continuing guilt over their previous conformity to White Eurocentric socialization" (Ponterotto et al., 2006, p. 102).

Retreat into White culture. This phase is probably the most complex of the five. While some White people deal with the conflict stage through immersion into minority experiences, others would prefer to retreat from situations that challenge their knowledge and awareness of White privilege, racial identity, and systemic racism. The retreat is characterized by taking deliberate means to avoid interracial contact so one can remain in the "comfort, security, and familiarity of same-race contacts" (Ponterotto et al., 2006, p. 102). An important aspect of this stage is confrontation. White peers who view advocacy of minority issues as "disloyal or a betrayal" to the White race (stage 3), and minority peers who are skeptical about Whites' "newfound supportive (pro-minority) attitude" may cause Whites who endure these confrontations to retreat into a world where "over identification with Whiteness and defensiveness about White culture" serves as their emotional crutch (Ponterotto et al., p. 102).

Redefinition and integration. During this stage, White people focus their energy inward to explore their own racial group identity and privilege. According to Ponterotto et al. (2006), Whites "acknowledge their responsibility for maintaining racism and at the same time identify with a White identity that is non-racist and healthy" (p. 102). Based upon this recognition, Whites consciously avoid ethnic and racial generalizations and begin to apply their newly defined sense of values, beliefs, and behaviors to all aspects of their lives. This new behavior is considered healthy and fosters interest in becoming "agents of change rather than liberal bystanders" (Hardiman, 1994, p. 129).

The fundamental hypothesis of White Identity Development is to examine the effects of racism on Whites, how Whites' development is influenced by life experiences, and how these experiences are linked to their interaction with group (same-race) members and nongroup members in a multicultural society. Movement between stages is fluid and varies for each individual. Furthermore, an individual can stay in one stage for a long period of time; therefore, campus faculty and staff working with White students should not be discouraged if little progress is made during the students' tenure at an institution. Transition to each stage usually occurs as the cumulative result of events, maturity, and lived experiences. Notwithstanding, the reality of measured progress should not deter administrative and academic professionals from strategically creating opportunities that foster genuine intercultural engagement among White students and their non-White peers.

Best Practices for Intercultural Engagement

The historical and political issues that plague America as a whole exist as microcosms on college and university campuses. Academic professionals should not expect students to tackle these issues on their own. Assessment of institutional practices, policies, environments, and commitment to diversity can provide important indicators for developing effective initiatives that foster intercultural engagement among White students and their non-White/ethnic peers.

Theory. Topics centered on race, privilege, and the affects of racism have often been described as *difficult dialogues*. Watt (2007) defined difficult dialogues as written or verbal exchanges that may arouse feelings of discomfort between individuals who have different beliefs and values. More than likely, higher education professionals will be on the frontline of facilitating difficult dialogues between students in academic and cocurricular settings as well as among themselves. In an effort to engage people in effective discussions, Watt introduced the Privileged Identity Exploration (PIE) model to assist professionals in assessing and managing the defensive behaviors displayed when people are protecting their existence as privileged. The PIE model describes eight defensive reactions when people are "recognizing, contemplating, or addressing privileged identity" (p. 119). *Denial* can be identified when someone argues that a societal injustice does not exist. Watt asserted that a person might concede that injustice occurs but make conflicting statements that illustrate his or her difficulty accepting the injustice as a reality. A *Deflection* defense circumvents the reality of any social injustice by shifting the focus away from the core issue to a broader or nonintimidating target. Similarly, individuals who display what they believe to be logical responses to why racism or discrimination occurs are enacting a *Rationalization* defense. An *Intellectualization* defense is a person's attempt to "avoid feeling dissonant" (p. 121) by providing intellectual arguments about why injustices exist.

The *Principium* defense is when a person avoids exploring discrimination based on "religious or personal principle" (Watt, 2007, p. 121). Some individuals may try a different approach to aversion through a *False Envy* defense, which is superficial admiration for a person or group in an effort to avoid or deny "deeper exploration [into] the complexities of race in society" (p. 122). Watt states that a *Benevolence* defense avoids exploration into the powerlessness of a marginalized group through outward acts of charity (i.e., writing a check), and that a *Minimization* defense might be displayed through a person's resolution to diminish the enormity of social injustice issues.

White students often ask with frustration, "When are we going to move beyond race?" The empathetic response is that moving beyond race requires an honest confrontation about race and many other forms of marginalization instead of typical acts of avoidance. Thus the overarching concept of difficult dialogues can arguably be connected to the *Conflict* stage of the White Racial Identity model in which one struggles through emotional conflict on the journey toward multicultural competence. However, the lot of difficult dialogues does not exclusively belong to White students or White higher education professionals. Both these groups' awareness about entrenched issues on race, privilege, and identity should be explored.

Assessment. Higher education professionals have to be aware of transparent and ambiguous barriers to having difficult dialogues. A key component of intercultural engagement is an institution's climate. In their study of students' perception about the campus racial climate at five PWIs, Harper and Hurtado (2007) discovered the following nine themes (in italics). Research participants revealed *cross-race consensus over the institution's negligence* in fostering meaningful racial understanding by avoiding *difficult dialogues about racism and racial injustice.* There has been a long-standing debate about *segregation along racial comfort zones* and the double standard of critics who reject these campus silos. Harper and Hurtado shed light on this by noting the difference between the visibility of "ethnic neighborhoods" by students of color, and the unawareness of such communities when White students also selectively congregate in student groups, athletic teams, dining halls, and residential settings. Furthermore, some White respondents offered a rationalization defense in accusing minority student organizations as being the cause of intercultural barriers and segregated spaces. As a consequence, other emerging themes revealed *gaps among racial groups' satisfaction* with social opportunities. Moreover, White respondents *overestimated their racial counterparts' satisfaction* with the institution and were oblivious to the diametrically different views their minority peers held about the institutional climate. The authors point out that an institution's *reputation for racism* may explain respondents' displeasure with the campus climate. Therefore, it would seem difficult to challenge this perception if the *pervasiveness of Whiteness*, another theme found in the study, permeated campus space, curriculum, and activities. The complexities of students' racial experiences at PWIs were illuminated in the study's last two findings. *Minority professionals felt a "conscious powerlessness"* in addressing racism because they feared retaliation from senior administrators and lack of support. Furthermore, the institutions studied had not *conducted any formal climate assessments.* As a result, the lack of empirical evidence about the campus environment hampered efforts from campus administrators to initiate or promote intercultural dialogues and engagement.

Curricular and cocurricular resources. Ponterotto, Utsey, and Pedersen (2006) offered comprehensive examples of exercises, case studies, survey instruments, books, and films on the topic of multicultural awareness and prejudice reduction. These resources could be instrumental in beginning or enhancing a multicultural competence curriculum. The pedagogical strategy of *recursive loop* can reveal other innovative methods for dealing with difficult dialogues in the classroom. Rich and Cargile (2004) described three components of this form of teaching: one, public sharing of students' voices to make theoretical ideas real; two, connecting student's racial experiences to each others so that "White students see how color does indeed provide a standpoint for viewing race" (p. 354); and three, creating opportunities for substantive conversation that reconsiders White identity through constructive conflict. Such dialogue can illuminate the way White students' discourse has "historical roots in White supremacy and the resistance of White supremacy" (p. 354). This approach advances the importance of allowing students to hear opposing views and various opinions in an educational and developmental way.

The University of Oregon (2007) assists faculty in the classroom through the Teaching Effectiveness Program, which offers various workshops under the teaching to diversity curriculum. The website includes a series titled, "What Does Being White Have to Do With Diversity?" The resource links are plentiful and provide exercises that probe the prejudices of higher education professionals and students. Some of the resources include links to discussions on models of White Identity Development, components of White cultural values and beliefs, questions in an exercise that probes students' internal prejudices titled "What About Me?", tactics for combating racism, faculty engagement exercises that ask faculty what makes them nervous about raising issues of racism in their classroom, and references and selected resources for continuing difficult dialogues.

In settings outside the classroom, higher education professionals are called upon to continue learning opportunities that foster well-rounded college experiences. Einfeld and Collins (2008) discovered that students involved in college-sponsored service-learning programs increased their awareness of societal inequality, felt a sense of empowerment, and became more cognizant of their privilege. The authors also found that the length of time spent in the service-learning site was a contributing factor in the development of multicultural competence. At the University of Denver, the

Citizen-Athlete Community Outreach Program deepens student athletes' understanding of civic engagement and social change through initiatives that serve underrepresented communities in the Denver metro area. According to former program director Anthony "TD" Daniels, participants and coaches were more insightful and aware of issues of social inequality and appreciative of the opportunity to develop cross-cultural relationships with various community partners.

Conclusion

Several experts project that in the year 2050 a major demographic shift will occur in America and subsequently in American social and political institutions. For many this will not mean much if higher education professionals and students fail to genuinely address race, privilege, and identity by conforming to defense modes such as "deflection, minimization, and rationalization" (Watt, 2007) or incorrectly perceiving 21st-century race matters as a postracial era (Yancey, 2003). The election of the nation's first Black (or biracial) president did not mean that race became irrelevant; in stark contrast, racial realities were heightened leaving ample opportunity for students to discuss topics that would often be treated as taboo. Confronting issues of race in academia will not be an easy process for students or campus administrators, particularly when such efforts are often deterred by claims that the campus climate, institutional practices, groups, and individuals are or should be color blind. While some view color-blindness as a righteous campaign toward multiculturalism, restricting the exploration of privilege to color-blind theory advances the idea that issues of race and identity are unworthy of consideration, dialogue, and ultimately change. Hitchcock (2001) argued that if one is not able to see race, one cannot see the impact of racism, and if people are blind to systemic racism based on racial hierarchy, they are incapable of changing the system they fail to see.

Difficult dialogues will require considerable self-reflection, shifting the paradigm of Whiteness as a racial construct, recognizing and acknowledging ambiguous and unambiguous forms of privilege, and being courageous at times beyond our own comfort to challenge long-standing systemic racism that has shaped individual racist attitudes. This process can begin with identifying students' common interests and issues.

Among the commonalities White students have with their non-White counterparts is the influence socialized environments have on students' comfort with cross-racial interactions and the subsequent anxiety of going to college and interacting with peers not of one's race. This viewpoint is supported in Smith, Bowman, and Hsu's (2007) study of racial attitudes among Asian and White college students. The authors discovered that participants were more comfortable interacting with members of their own race, in part because of the lack of contact they had with people from other races prior to attending college. Saenz, Ngai, and Hurtado (2007) found that engagement with diverse peers in high school provided research participants with experiences and skills in fostering cross-cultural relationships in college. Villalpando (2002) discovered that satisfaction with college was enhanced for research participants when they were provided opportunities to attend cultural awareness workshops or were exposed to diverse pedagogical curricula and practices. These findings illustrate the importance of higher education professionals' creating opportunities that go beyond superficial intercultural engagement. Chang (2007) describes this engagement as intentional and active initiatives that affect continuous cross-racial interaction among our students.

Case Study: The Campus Newspaper

The president of the Latino/Latina Student Alliance (LSA) leaves you a voice-mail message requesting a meeting. The president states that yesterday's edition of the campus newspaper featured a political cartoon that was offensive to members of the student body. She goes on to say that the newspaper has continually offended students of color and would like to meet with you in an attempt to understand why the issue of racial insensitivity continues to be a problem among the predominantly White newspaper staff. As faculty adviser you normally review the paper before it goes to print, but you were out of town on business and did not have the chance to peruse the issue now under fire. Before returning the president's phone call you look through yesterday's paper and discover the following:

> The cartoon depicts a White male student in stereotypical nerd attire looking at the subject next to him in bewilderment as he holds a sign that reads: perfect SAT score, 12 points. Standing next to the White male is a Black male student who looks in the other direction, blasé, whistling, and holding a sign that reads: minority status, 20 points. Next to these two images is a third sign that reads: Affirmative Action, pointless.

At first glance you do not view the cartoon as offensive. In an effort to obtain other opinions you ask the editorial staff to meet with you to discuss the matter further. The cartoon was featured on the opinion page, so you direct your inquiry to the editor and assistant editor of that page. The opinion page editor, the lone person of color on staff, states that he did not choose the cartoon, nor did the assistant editor inform him that the cartoon would be placed in the paper. The editor goes on to share with his peers that recent conversations with the leadership of the LSA revealed that the cartoon is being perceived as racist because it implies that students of color attending the university do not have to work hard to be admitted, and once enrolled do not work just as hard as their White peers to succeed academically.

After hearing the comments of the opinion page editor, the assistant editor defends his decision to run the cartoon as free speech and an opinion shared by the majority in America and on the campus. He goes on to say that the minority students at the school are hypersensitive, eager to call someone racist, and always complaining. The meeting progressed into a heated debate with the editorial staff divided on offering a public apology to the campus community.

The following day you receive an e-mail from the dean of students who wants to know why the president of LSA has demanded a meeting with the dean, the editor of the campus newspaper, the LSA adviser, and yourself.

Discussion Questions

1. What are the issues or problems presented in this case? Be specific.
2. As adviser, how should you approach this situation with the editorial staff?
3. What intervention might you consider based on student development theory and White identity development?
4. Should university administrators intervene in this issue? Why or why not? Also discuss who should address the issue and how it should be addressed.
5. Should the editorial staff offer a public apology to the campus community? Why or why not?
6. What impact would an apology (or no apology) have on the campus climate?
7. Should a campus newspaper staff (and adviser) be responsible for fostering cultural or racial sensitivity? Why or why not?
8. If the assistant editor and most of the students on staff were people of color, would this make the issue less contentious? Why or why not?

References

Ancis, J. R., Sedlacek, W. E., & Mohr, J. J. (2000). Student perceptions of campus cultural climate by race. *Journal of Counseling and Development, 78*(2), 180–185.

Astin, A. W. (1993). *What matters in college: Four critical years revisited.* San Francisco: Jossey-Bass.

Brown v. Board of Education, 349 U.S. 294 (1954).

Brubacher, J. S., & Rudy, W. (1997). *Higher education in transition: A history of American colleges and universities* (4th ed.). Piscataway, NJ: Transaction.

Bulmer, M., & Solomos, J. (1999). *Racism.* New York: Oxford University Press.

Carter, R. T. (1990). The relationship between racism and racial identity among White Americans: An exploratory investigation. *Journal of Counseling and Development, 69*(1), 46–53.

Chang, M. J. (2007). Beyond artificial integration: Reimagining cross-racial interactions among undergraduates. In S. R. Harper & L. D. Patton (Eds.), *Responding to the realities of race on campus* (pp. 25–37). San Francisco: Jossey-Bass.

Chickering, A. W. (1969). *Education and identity.* San Francisco: Jossey-Bass.

Civil Rights Act of 1964, Pub. L. No. 88–352, 78 Stat. 241 (1964).

Cobham, B. A., & Parker, T. L. (2007). Resituating race into the movement toward multiculturalism and social justice. In S. R. Harper & L. D. Patton (Eds.), *Responding to the realities of race on campus* (pp. 88–93). San Francisco: Jossey-Bass.

Crispino, J. A. (1980). *The assimilation of ethnic groups: The Italian case* (1st ed.). New York: Center for Migration Studies.

DeSousa, D. J., & King, P. M. (1992). Are White students really more involved in collegiate experiences than Black students? *Journal of College Student Development, 33,* 363–369.

Doane, A. W. (1997). Dominant group ethnic identity in the United States: The role of hidden ethnicity in intergroup relations. *Sociological Quarterly, 38*(3), 375–397.

Dubois, W. E. B. (1996). *The souls of black folk.* New York: Penguin Books. (Original work published 1903)

Dyer, R. (1988). White. *Screen, 29*(4), 44–64.

Dyer, R. (2002). The matter of Whiteness. In P. S. Rothenberg (Ed.), *White privilege: Essential readings on the other side of racism* (pp. 9–13). New York: Worth.

Einfeld, A., & Collins, D. (2008). The relationships between service-learning, social justice, multicultural competence, and civic engagement. *Journal of College Student Development, 49*(2), 95–109.

Evans, N. J., Forney, D. S., & Guido-DiBrito, F. (1998). *Student development in college.* San Francisco: Jossey-Bass.

Exec. Order No. 10925, 3 C.F.R. 339, (1964–1965 Comp.).

Feagin, J. (2001). *Racist America: Roots, current realities, and future reparations.* New York: Routledge.

Feagin, J. R., Vera, H., & Imani, N. (1996). *The agony of education: Black students at White colleges and universities.* London: Routledge.

Gilligan, C. (1982). *In a different voice.* Cambridge, MA: Harvard University Press.

Giordano, J., & McGoldrick, M. (1996). European families: An overview. In M. McGoldrick, J. Girodano, & J. K. Pearce (Eds.), *Ethnicity and family therapy* (2nd ed., pp. 427–439). New York: Guilford Press.

Handlin, O., & Handlin, M. F. (1970). *The American college and American culture.* New York: McGraw-Hill.

Hardiman, R. (1982). *White identity development: A process oriented model for describing the racial consciousness of White Americans.* Unpublished doctoral dissertation, University of Massachusetts, Amherst.

Hardiman, R. (1994). White racial identity development in the United States. In E. P. Salett & D. R. Koslow (Eds.), *Race ethnicity and self* (pp. 117–140). Washington, DC: National Multicultural Institute Publications.

Harper, S. R., & Hurtado, S. (2007). Nine themes in campus racial climates and implications for institutional transformation. In S. R. Harper & L. D. Patton (Eds.), *Responding to the realities of race on campus* (pp. 7–24). San Francisco: Jossey-Bass.

Helms, J. E. (1984). Toward a theoretical explanation of the effects of race on counseling: A Black and White model. *Counseling Psychologist, 12*(4), 153–165.

Helms, J. E. (1992). *A race is a nice thing to have.* Topeka, KS: Content Communications.

Hitchcock, J. (2001). *Unraveling the white cocoon.* Dubuque, IA: Kendall/Hunt.

hooks, b. (1989). *Talking back: Thinking feminist, thinking Black.* Boston: South End Press.

Howard-Hamilton, M. F. (2000). Programming for multicultural competencies. In D. L. Liddell & J. P. Lund (Eds.), *Powerful programming for student learning: Approaches that make a difference* (pp. 67–78). San Francisco: Jossey-Bass.

Huebener, T. (1962). *The Germans in America.* Philadelphia: Chilton.

Jacobson, M. F. (1998). Whiteness of a different color: European immigrants and the alchemy of race. Cambridge, MA: Harvard University Press.

Kaestle, C. F. (1983). *Pillars of the republic: Common schools and American society, 1780–1860.* New York: Hill and Wang.

Kaufmann, E. P. (2004). *The rise and fall of Anglo-America.* Cambridge, MA: Harvard University Press.

King, P., & Shuford, B. (1996). A multicultural view is a more cognitively complex view: Cognitive development and multicultural education. *American Behavioral Scientist, 40*(2), 153–164.

Kohlberg, L. (1976). Moral stages and moralization: The cognitive-developmental approach. In T. Lickona (Ed.), *Moral development and behavior: Theory, research, and social issues* (pp. 31–53). New York: Holt, Rinehart & Winston.

Martin, J. N., Krizek, R. L., Nakayama, T. K., & Bradford, L. (1996). Exploring Whiteness: A study of self labels for White Americans. *Communication Quarterly, 44*(2), 125–144.

McIntosh, P. (1989). White privilege: Unpacking the invisible knapsack. *Peace and Freedom, 1*(1), 10–12.

Miner, B., & Peterson, B. (2000–2001). Diversity vs. White privilege: An interview with Christine Sleeter. *Rethinking Schools Online, 15*(2), 1–6.

Moffatt, M. (1989). *Coming of age in New Jersey: College and American culture.* New Brunswick, NJ: Rutgers University Press.

Morrill Act of 1862, 7 U.S.C. § 301 et seq.

Naturalization Act of 1790, Pub. L. 2–3, 1 Stat. 103 (1790).

Ortiz, A. M., & Rhoads, R. A. (2000). Deconstructing Whiteness as part of a multicultural educational framework: From theory to practice. *Journal of College Student Development, 41*(1), 81–93.

Pascarella, E. T., & Terenzini, P. T. (1998). Studying college students in the 21st century: Meeting new challenges. *The Review of Higher Education, 21,* 151–165.

Perry, W. G., Jr. (1968). *Forms of intellectual and ethical development in the college years: A scheme.* New York: Holt, Rinehart & Winston.

Ponterotto, J. G. (1988). Racial consciousness development among White counselor trainees: A model. *Journal of Multicultural Counseling and Development, 16,* 146–156.

Ponterotto, J. G., Utsey, S. O., & Pedersen, P. B. (2006). *Preventing prejudice: A guide for counselors, educators, and parents* (2nd ed.). Thousand Oaks, CA: Sage.

Pope-Davis, D. B., & Ottavi, T. M. (1994). The relationship between racism and racial identity among White Americans: A replication and extension. *Journal of Counseling and Development, 72*(3), 293–297.

Reason, R. D., & Evans, N. J. (2007). The complicated realities of Whiteness: From color blind to racially cognizant. In S. R. Harper & L. D. Patton (Eds.), *Responding to the realities of race on campus* (pp. 67–75). San Francisco: Jossey-Bass.

Reed-Johnson Immigration Act of 1924, Pub. L. 68–139, 43 Stat. 153 (1924).

Rich, M. D., & Cargile, A. C. (2004). Beyond the breach: Transforming White identities in the classroom. *Race, Ethnicity and Education, 7*(4), 351–365.

Sabnani, H. B., Ponterotto, J. G., & Borodovsky, L. G. (1991). White racial identity development and cross-cultural counselor training: A stage model. *Counseling Psychologist, 19,* 76–102.

Saenz, V. B., Ngai, H. N., & Hurtado, S. (2007). Factors influencing positive interactions across race for African American, Asian American, Latino, and White college students. *Research in Higher Education, 48*(1), 1–38.

Schwean, V. L., Mykota, D., Robert, L., & Saklofske, D. H. (1999). Determinants of psychosocial disorders in cultural minority children. In V. L. Schwean & D. H. Saklofske (Eds.), *Handbook of psychosocial characteristics of exceptional children* (pp. 147–170). New York: Springer.

Shannon, W. V. (1964). *The American Irish* (2nd ed.). New York: Macmillan.

Smith, T., Bowman, R., & Hsu, S. (2007). Racial attitudes among Asian and European American college students: A cross-cultural examination. *College Student Journal, 41*(2), 436–443.

Smith, W. A., Yosso, T. J., & Solorzano, D. G. (2007). Racial primes and Black misandry on historically White campuses: Toward critical race accountability in educational administration. *Educational Administration Quarterly, 43*(5), 559–585.

Sowell, T. (1981). *Ethnic America.* New York: Basic.

Spring, J. (2007). *Deculturalization and the struggle for equality: A brief history of the education of dominated cultures in the United States* (5th ed.). New York: McGraw-Hill.

Strage, A. A. (2000). Predictors of college adjustment and success: Similarities and differences among Southeast-Asian American, Hispanic, and White students. *Education, 120*(4), 731–740.

Swain, C. M. (2002). *The new White nationalism in America: Its challenge to integration.* Cambridge, UK: Cambridge University Press.

Takaki, R. (1993). *A different mirror: A history of multicultural America.* Boston: Little, Brown.

Tatum, B. (2000). Defining racism: "Can we talk?" In M. Adams, W. J. Blumenfel, R. Castaneda, H. W. Hackman, M. L. Peters, & X. Zuniga (Eds.), *Readings for diversity in social justice: An anthology on racism, anti-Semitism, sexism, heterosexism, ableism, and classism* (pp. 418–421). New York: Routledge.

Title IX, Education Amendments of 1972, 20 U.S.C. §§ 1681–1688.

Trepagnier, B. (2006). *Silent racism: How well-meaning White people perpetuate the racial divide.* Boulder, CO: Paradigm.

University of Oregon. (2007). *Teaching effectiveness program: Be free to teach.* Retrieved April 30, 2008, from http://tep.uoregon.edu/index.html

Villalpando, O. (2002). The impact of diversity and multiculturalism on all students: Findings from a national study. *NASPA Journal, 40*(1), 124–144.

Watt, S. K. (2007). Difficult dialogues, privilege and social justice: Uses of the Privileged Identity Exploration (PIE) model in student affairs practice. *The College Student Affairs Journal, 26*(2), 114–126.

Wildman, S. M., & Davis, A. D. (2000). Language and silence: Making systems of privilege visible. In M. Adams, W. J. Blumenfel, R. Castaneda, H. W. Hackman, M. L. Peters, & X. Zuniga (Eds.), *Readings for diversity in social justice: An anthology on racism, anti-Semitism, sexism, heterosexism, ableism, and classism* (pp. 79–82). New York: Routledge.

Wise, T. (2009, July 26). *Racial profiling in America: Real or imagined?* Retrieved August 1, 2009, from http://www.cnn.com/video/data/2.0/video/us/2009/07/26/nr.racial.profiling,cnn.html

Yancey, G. (2003). *Who is White? Latinos, Asians, and the new Black/nonBlack divide.* Boulder, CO: Lynne Rienner.

II

INTERNATIONAL COLLEGE STUDENTS

Sevan G. Terzian and Leigh Ann Osborne

On August 1, 1946, U.S. President Harry S. Truman signed the Fulbright Act into law. This provision funded foreign student study in the United States for a prescribed period of time, and it marked the beginning of a steady rise in the number of international students pursuing undergraduate and graduate degrees at American institutions of higher education. In 1953, for example, less than 34,000 international students studied at roughly 1,600 American colleges and universities. These students made up about 1.4% of the total student population. By the 1964–1965 academic year, 82,045 international students enrolled from all regions of the world, with students from southern and eastern Asia being the largest group. This figure continued to increase dramatically, ballooning to 154,580 in 1974–1975, 342,113 in 1984–1985, 453,787 in 1995–1996, and 623,805 in 2007–2008, totaling 3.5% of the entire student population on American campuses (Institute of International Education, 2009).

A number of factors have contributed to this growth. For example, the Fulbright-Hays Act of 1961 (also called the Mutual Educational and Cultural Exchange Act opened more sources of federal funding for student and faculty exchanges. Nearly all international students are classified as nonimmigrant and need to obtain a student visa to study in the United States. Today, these prospective students can come to the United States only if they are accepted by an academic institution accredited by the Department of Homeland Security. The applicant must show the acceptance letter, certificate of eligibility, evidence of financial support, and proficiency in English to a consular official during a personal visa interview at a U.S. consulate abroad. The federal government regulates three classes of visas for international students. The F-1 visa is the most common and is primarily for students at degree-granting institutions and language schools. The M-1 visa applies to students attending vocational and nonacademic trade schools. The J-1 visa was created by the Mutual Educational Exchange Act of 1961 for exchange visitors, and it targeted professors and research scholars who intended to visit for an extended period of time. In addition to the scholar category, the J visa is also used for exchange students and students receiving government funding such as Fulbright grants. Although part-time on-campus employment is permitted, employment restrictions on these visa categories generally prohibit F, M, and J holders from obtaining full-time jobs while studying. Spouses of J visa holders can apply for employment, but spouses of F and M visa holders cannot—a distinction that holds significant financial implications for married international students. Thus, one important variable that can influence the rate of international student growth in the United States involves policies concerning granting and renewing student visas (U.S. Department of State, 2010; U.S. Immigration and Customs Enforcement, 2007).

Other factors have affected this rate as well. The proliferation of secondary schools in developing nations has produced many graduates who are qualified to enter college. But in many instances, the higher education system of these nations cannot meet the growing demand. As a result, many secondary school graduates seek admission abroad. The comprehensive and diverse nature of American institutions of higher education, often with extensive educational resources, attract many students from abroad, particularly those from countries without well-developed educational infrastructures (Charles & Stewart, 1991). Political uncertainty in the home country or ethnic minority status may encourage students from various nations to study abroad as well (Cummings, 1992).

Although the United States has historically hosted the greatest number of international students, there are signs that the country faces significant challenges if it is to maintain its position as the destination of choice. Roughly 40% of the world's international students attended U.S. schools in the early 1980s, but this fell to 32% by the mid-1990s, and slipped even further to 25% by mid-2000 (Bevis & Lucas, 2007). Several factors account for this decline. Competition for international students has increased drastically as other countries have recognized the potential academic, cultural, and financial contributions these students bring to their universities. English-speaking nations such as Australia, Canada, and the United Kingdom have developed coordinated national strategies to welcome sojourning students.

Western European countries have increased the number of English-taught degrees at their universities and are recruiting heavily around the world (Labi, 2007). China, India, and South Korea have also expanded access to higher education that was previously unavailable, particularly at the graduate level (Council of Graduate Schools, 2008).

In addition to external competition, changes in American higher education internally and in governmental polices have played a role. The proliferation of online degree programs and the growth of branch campuses have allowed thousands of foreign students to obtain a U.S. degree without leaving home. Several prominent American universities have established branch campuses in locations such as Qatar, Singapore, and the United Arab Emirates (Altbach & Knight, 2007; Lewin, 2008).

Numerous scholars have suggested that government policies enacted in the name of national security explain America's weakened dominance as an educational destination. These policies restricted visas and increased monitoring of foreign students. Particularly in the wake of the 1993 World Trade Center bombing and the terrorist attacks of September 2001, public debate intensified about whether to restrict the granting of visas to international students and to monitor their activities (Altbach, 2004; Bennell & Pearce, 1998; Bevis & Lucas, 2007; Coppi, 2007; Kiernan, 1999). However, questions about policies regarding international students are not unique to the terrorism concerns of recent years; the United States has historically expressed a degree of ambivalence about hosting international students (Terzian & Osborne, 2006).

Although the United States remains the top destination of international students, enrollment figures for 2003–2004 dropped for the first time in more than three decades. The decline in international students continued until 2006–2007, when enrollments showed the first signs of an upward turn, increasing 3% from the previous year. The 2007–2008 data show further signs of recovery with a 7% increase, which for the first time surpasses the total number of students enrolled in 2002–2003. Despite these improvements, the United States lacks a comprehensive national policy on the importance of international students. Beyond the federal process of granting student visas, the policies of American institutions of higher education remain relatively decentralized. Each academic institution pursues a distinct agenda in setting admissions criteria, offering financial aid and resources, and providing student services. Many graduate programs, particularly in the sciences, rely heavily on international students, as fewer American students pursue such disciplines each year. Restrictions on international students can have a dramatic effect on the future of those academic programs, as well as the scientific and technological supremacy the United States has enjoyed for decades (Anders, 2007; Institute of International Education, 2009).

In addition to their significant academic contributions, international students added an estimated $15.5 billion to the U.S. economy in 2007–2008. In that academic year, 62% of the 632,805 international students in the United States paid for their education through personal and family resources. Only 26% of all international students studying in the United States received funding from the host college or university (Institute of International Education, 2009). These figures indicate that increases in college tuition or the implementation of various fees can affect whether a student can study in the United States. Thus, as college tuitions have continued to rise significantly, a growing number of international students have chosen to study at 2-year colleges, which often have lower tuition rates and reduces students' time spent in the United States (with its concomitant living expenses) in half. Whether enrolling for intensive training in the English language or for brief training in a specialized discipline, international students have found 2-year colleges increasingly appealing. Indeed, enrollments doubled between 1988 and 1998. In the 2007–2008 academic year, 86,683 international students attended community colleges. It is important to note, however, that large research universities still host the greatest number of international students (Desruisseaux, 1998; Institute of International Education, 2009; McCormack, 2007).

India sent the most students to the United States in the 2007–2008 academic year: 94,563, which was 15.2% of the international student population. China and South Korea were the second and third most represented countries of origin, with 13% and 11%. In the 2007–2008 academic year, 110,906, or 19.6% of all international students in the United States, studied business and management, while 96,133, or 17%, studied engineering. Physical and life sciences was the third most popular area of study for international students, with 9.3% of the total (Institute of International Education, 2009).

In addition to these generalizations, however, it is important to acknowledge that significant differences prevail among international students: "A married graduate student from East Asia is likely to have very different priorities and interests from those of an unmarried Latin American undergraduate. Regarding both as foreign students implies that they have more in common than they do" (Bulthius, 1986, p. 22).

Research on International Students

Despite a plethora of scholarly research on international students on American campuses, no meta theories have emerged to help guide policies for counselors and academic institutions. Some have noted that most studies on international students employ convenient samples at nearby universities (Leong & Chou, 1996; Yoon & Portman, 2004). Moreover, most research focuses on adjustment problems and outcomes, "without exploring the dynamics or process of adjustment itself" (Pedersen, 1991, p. 14). Researchers have devoted much more attention to the client (i.e., international student) than the role of the counselor or the process of counseling. On the one hand, some scholars suggest that a more sophisticated understanding of international students cannot be achieved without increasingly specific studies that take into account their social class, places of origin, gender, and undergraduate or graduate status. Spouses and children of international students have been largely ignored in this body of research and warrant greater attention (Chittooran & Sankar-Gomes, 2007). On the other hand, some scholars have lamented the specific nature of research on the experiences of international students and have called for investigations beyond the social, psychological, and academic dimensions of adjustment. Instead of discussing the problems of individuals at single institutions, broader analyses of issues and practices must occur for effective policy making to take place. For example, comparative studies of international and domestic students can demonstrate whether problems of adjustment are unique to the sojourn experience. Furthermore, studies based on admissions data can reveal which factors predict the success of international students. Research on academic progress can indicate how well international students move through a program of study and how well the curriculum matches their needs. Studies of faculty members can identify their attitudes toward international students. Demographic studies can highlight cultural variations; follow-up studies can reveal an institution's costs and benefits of hosting international students (Altbach, 1989; Yoon & Portman).

In other words, there is a pressing need for research on international student experiences in more specific studies that take into account greater numbers of variables, as well as a need for more general studies with larger samples considering a wider range of factors of adjustment. Still, the existing literature offers some theoretical consideration of some of the challenges facing these students.

Patterns of Student Adjustment to the Host Country and Academic Institution

Lysgaard (1955) proposed a U-curve hypothesis to describe the phases of acculturation. According to this theory, the sojourner enters the host culture with initial feelings of elation and optimism that soon lead to frustration and depression upon encountering various difficulties in the new society. After some time for adjustment, these feelings give way to growing confidence and satisfaction. The sojourner has learned to adapt to the specific demands of the host culture. Gullahorn and Gullahorn (1966) suggested that a W-curve more accurately accounts for the stages of sojourner adjustment— that the period of reentry to the home culture involves the same movement from initial elation to frustration and then readjustment. Bulthius (1986) developed a comparable model of adjustment for student sojourners with stages of spectating (exhaustion upon arriving in the host country but excited to be there), adaptation (participation in the host culture conflicts with native values leading to a form of culture shock), coming to terms (reconciliation as the sojourner rejects some aspects of the host culture but accepts others), and predeparture (preparation for returning home).

Numerous scholars have criticized the U-curve hypothesis of sojourner adjustment for a number of reasons. Some have argued that such a monolithic model cannot adequately account for so many different cultures, social classes, and situations involved in the sojourner experience. Church (1982) cited varied results from different sojourners and myriad dependent variables that may affect the adjustment pattern, such as homesickness, depression, and loneliness. Nash (1991) noted that most empirical research does not support the U-curve hypothesis. He suggests that it does not account for those international students who do not adapt to the host culture and return home before finishing their studies. Although Ward, Bochner, and Furnham (2001) observed an increase in longitudinal research, most empirical studies of international student adjustment are not longitudinal nor do they use control groups to show whether the stages of adjustment are unique to sojourners. Even Bulthius (1986) qualified her stages of adjustment by urging student personnel to consider that

> many traditional student development theories may not apply to foreign students whose value systems differ dramatically from those of Americans. Americans value independence, self-reliance, autonomy, efficiency, time management, and entrepreneurship. Our theories of student development tend to promote such values, character traits, and life patterns. (p. 26)

Some researchers have offered different models for understanding international student development. Furnham and Bochner (1982) questioned the tendency to view the problems of sojourners in medical terms, which implies there is some deficiency in them. Their problems are not necessarily pathological but may be symptoms of a lack of familiarity or knowledge of the host culture. Therefore, according to Bochner's cultural learning model, instead of assuming the goal of counseling is to help sojourners assimilate into the host culture, they should be encouraged to understand the new culture and navigate within it without losing their identity. Along these lines, Berry (1980) offered four categories of stances a sojourner can take when in a host culture: integrationist (preserving one's native culture and mixing in elements of the host culture), assimilationist (abandoning one's native culture and embracing the host culture wholesale), separationist (rejecting the values of the host culture and holding true to the native culture), and marginalist (abandoning one's native culture but not adopting another in its place). Hull's (1981) modified cultural contact hypothesis suggests that foreign students who interact with people from the host country tend to become more satisfied with their overall academic experience than those who do not. According to this theory, such contact can bridge language barriers and mitigate the social and academic isolation of international students. Arthur (2004) suggested that the difficult period of adjusting to the host culture, known as culture shock, should also be recognized for its productive potential: "Culture shock is therefore a double-sided feature of cross-cultural transition; it is the most stressful and the most motivating aspect of living and learning in a new environment" (p. 29).

Sources of Stress

Some scholars have suggested that expectations for international students to play multiple roles tend to confuse and stress them. For instance, Bochner (1972) said that international students are expected to act as foreigners, university students, young adults, and cultural ambassadors—and these roles often conflict with one another. Furnham and Bochner (1982) separated the problems of international students into four groups: those common to anyone living in a foreign culture, those common to late adolescents and early adults, academic stress, and pressure to represent one's home country well. Indeed, international students often find themselves in the difficult position of being mediator between the home and host countries, particularly when international relations may be strained. Paige (1990) proposed that international students studying in the United States find that others perceive them as having inferior language, academic, and analytical skills, and a naive understanding of the American educational system; serving as cultural resources to enrich the lives of Americans; serving as financial resources by enrolling and paying full tuition; and playing the role of outsider/other. Pedersen (1991) drew on this idea and argues that these myriad expectations render it particularly difficult for international students to fulfill stereotypes. Ironically, perhaps even scholarly research on international students stigmatizes them further as a group. Yoon and Portman (2004) criticized the "overgeneralization of research findings to all international students and the underemphasis of within-group differences" (p. 35). As a result, one must account for individual factors in studying these groups.

Theories of cultural difference also attempt to explain the nature of international students' difficulties. Oropeza, Fitzgibbon, and Baron (1991) identified culture shock, changes in social and economic status, expectations about academic performance, isolation and discrimination, and family problems as sources of stress. Taft (1977) constructed a framework to suggest that coping for an international student depends upon the size of the gap between the home and host cultures and the extent to which the host culture allows room for the sojourner to find a niche that complements his or her home values. Similarly, Chapdelaine and Alexitch (2004) concluded that the larger the cultural gap between the student's home and host culture the more decreased the amount of interaction is with individuals from the host culture. Social customs and ways of communicating may be out of place and contribute to an international student's frustration. In some instances, international students exacerbate the stress that results from these factors. Aubrey (1991) cited the tendency of international students to repress stress and to be unwilling to admit they are unhappy in the host country, as such an admission would be shameful. As a result, international students tend to internalize their emotional problems. Alexander, Klein, Workneh, and Miller (1976) anticipated this theory in stating that numerous stresses place international students at high risk for emotional problems, and that they tend to seek medical rather than counseling help. Misra and Castillo (2004) found that international students report lower levels of self-imposed academic stress than American students. Similarly, Hanassab and Tidwell (2002) noted that international students ranked academic and career needs higher than psychological and individual needs. Rather than concluding that international students experience less stress or have minimal personal concerns, however, the investigators said their findings support the notion that many international students do not admit to feelings of stress because of their home culture's stigmatization of such admissions. Furnham and Bochner (1982) cautioned that international students may view emotional problems differently from Americans, and the viable options for addressing those problems may differ.

Common Issues of International Students

Academic Adjustments

International students encounter a host of academic challenges. To a large degree, these worries stem from the problem of adjusting to a distinct educational system with explicit and implicit expectations. For example, many American institutions of higher education place a heavy emphasis on the intellectual as well as the personal growth of their students. As a result, American colleges and universities typically allow students more freedom in selecting courses and expect their students to demonstrate their learning in the form of class discussions and open-ended essay examinations.

To many international students, these expectations can present tricky problems. According to Charles and Stewart (1991), the liberal arts ideal of intellectual breadth may be confusing to international students, and they "may not be accustomed to the competitive environment of many American colleges and universities" (p. 179). Various studies of Asian international students, for instance, reveal apprehension about voicing their ideas in a class discussion. Partly this behavior results from a lack of confidence in speaking English, but it also reflects differences in educational systems and cultural values. In many Asian societies, the professor is viewed as the definitive authority on a matter, and silence is viewed as a sign of respect. Class meetings are often conducted in lecture format, and students are expected to memorize and repeat the relevant information. There is relatively little room for students to question the views of the instructor or to develop their own understanding of a particular topic. By contrast, faculty in many American institutions of higher education tend to value autonomy and self-assertiveness and thus expect their students to engage in independent and creative assignments such as essay responses. Such standards can be difficult for many international students who are often unaccustomed to having such freedom and can be acutely afraid of speaking in class. Such discrepancies can result in feelings of alienation and lower grades (Leong & Sedlacek, 1989; Lin & Yi, 1997; Mori, 2000; Sheehan & Pearson, 1995).

Although much of the literature suggests that Asian students in particular struggle to adjust to the U.S. classroom, some scholars caution against stereotyping Asian students as passive individuals. Liu (2001) found that cross-cultural differences in the classroom can lead to misunderstandings between American and Asian students: "For Asian students, especially those who do not speak English very well, the momentary silence in class may give them an opportunity to formulate in English what they want to say, but this desire may be subverted by American students' eagerness to break what they perceive as an uncomfortable silence" (p. 198). Pursuing this point, Hsieh (2007) argued that attributing the relative silence of Asian international students in U.S. classroom settings to cultural differences alone is shortsighted. In an analysis of the experiences of a female Chinese student, the investigator calls attention to the potentially "disempowering nature" of the American classroom because of American classmates' "assumption of cultural superiority" (p. 390).

English Language Difficulties and Social Isolation

If international students do not possess a proficient command of the English language, they can experience a host of frustrating situations on American campuses. The Test of English as a Foreign Language (TOEFL) is required of most prospective international students before admission to a U.S. higher education institution. Prior to 2005 the TOEFL measured reading and writing abilities but neglected speaking skills. Thus, a high score on the TOEFL did not necessarily indicate fluency or an understanding of different English dialects, idioms, or cultural nuances. In response to numerous criticisms of the TOEFL design, the Educational Testing Service developed an Internet-based TOEFL that also measures speaking abilities. The addition of a speaking requirement caused concern among Asian students, in particular, because many English instruction curricula do not emphasize conversation skills (Associated Press, 2005; Bollag, 2005).

Although the TOEFL changes may lead to improvements in English instruction worldwide and provide a more accurate predictor of a student's English skills, international students with marginal English abilities will still face linguistic challenges in the U.S. classroom. Many such students tend to have more difficulty in understanding class lectures, participating in class discussions, preparing oral presentations, and studying for essay examinations. While a number of academic institutions offer intensive English for Speakers of Other Languages (ESOL) classes, international students may overestimate their English language proficiency upon arrival and eschew that option—a choice that can overburden them and cause inordinate stress as the semester progresses and they fall behind in their course work. As some international students are hired as teaching assistants, moreover, the language barrier can become particularly acute. Undergraduate students may complain they do not understand their instructor, and in response the instructor may become defensive. These difficult situations can be prevented if academic advisers encourage their international students to take English support courses and carry a lighter academic course load as they begin their studies at the host institution (Charles & Stewart, 1991; Lin & Yi, 1997; Mori, 2000; Pedersen, 1991). In addition, supervising professors and domestic classmates can make adjustments to improve the learning environment for all students. For example, Halleck (2008) constructs a role-play exercise for international teaching assistants and their undergraduate students to "confront culturally embedded attitudes and values" (p. 137).

Language barriers can also exacerbate the already stressful elements of transition by socially isolating international students on American campuses. A number of studies have proposed that meaningful social contact between international and domestic students can significantly improve the English language skills of nonnative speakers. The best way to overcome language difficulties is to have a native-speaking friend. In many cases, however, such relationships appear difficult to establish: "Generally speaking, host students neither make themselves available nor make an effort great enough to create a bridge for international friendship" (Hayes & Lin, 1994, p. 12). As a result, the initiative is often left to the international student, and while many are eager to learn English and gain a better understanding of American culture, numerous misperceptions and preconceptions can hinder such developments. A lack of common understanding of social mores from different cultures can hinder cross-cultural interaction. Other barriers can include a paucity of university-sponsored programs to facilitate such relations, poor publicity of existing programs, and not having access to a car. For many international students, moreover, social activities are far less important than academic achievement. The safer alternative for many non-English-speaking international students, therefore, is to associate in culturally homogenous groups (Fritz, Chin, & DeMarinis, 2008; Sheehan & Pearson, 1995).

A number of scholars have found that international students on American campuses tend to experience social isolation because of an unfamiliarity and general discomfort with main currents of American culture. Trice (2004) concluded that Western European students and those with a high proficiency in English had more frequent social interactions with American students than other international student groups. While Middle Eastern and African students interacted the least with Americans, these groups were less concerned about this lack of interaction than students from East and Southeast Asia. The geographic distance separating international students from their native country is indicative of the sense of "social loss" they are likely to feel. Far away from friends and family, these students find themselves removed from their familiar social support networks: "As a consequence, they often feel less confident, sense unremitting tension, take less time off, enjoy it even less, and become confused over how to have fun" (Hayes & Lin, 1994, p. 8). Unfamiliarity with American social customs and culture can lead to isolation, homesickness, performance anxiety, sleeping and eating problems, among other physical ailments—all of which can enervate international students' motivation to work toward their primary goal of academic achievement. Further, discrimination or lack of interest from American students can discourage international students from actively seeking Americans as friends.

It is important to recognize that this social "Balkanization" does not constitute pathological behavior; it represents a rational response to difficult circumstances. Staff of international student affairs offices and other campus resources can work to mollify the feelings of isolation many international students endure.

Pressures From Abroad and Returning Home

International students tend to experience a host of pressures stemming from their native countries. For example, most finance their education using family resources or sponsoring agents in their home country. Economic or political developments at home can dramatically affect the availability of funding, so many international students have particular incentives to finish their academic programs as quickly as possible, which can lead to academic overload. In many cases, international students bear the burden of high expectations of academic achievement from their families and peers back home, which can exacerbate stress if the student encounters initial difficulties in coping with linguistic and cultural transitions. Indeed, the worst possible scenario would be to return home as a result of failing in school and not receiving the degree, which can be "the ultimate disaster for many, if not most, foreign students" (Pedersen, 1991, p. 38).

Many international students want to return home on their own terms; others may seek employment in their host country. This latter desire can lead to the brain drain phenomenon and siphon the intellectual resources of a nation. Those who do return home face an array of potential challenges such as reverse culture shock with symptoms like excessive concerns over food and drinking water; impatience with inconveniences; paranoia of being cheated, robbed, or injured; and obsession with minor pains, among others. The international student has inevitably changed in some respects during his or her sojourn and may find it difficult to adjust to life in the home country. The initial elation upon returning may soon change to frustration. The returning sojourner may have trouble finding peer networks for sharing experiences in the foreign culture. He or she may return home with feelings of accomplishment, confidence, and independence—which may not be appreciated back home. Finally, there is the tricky problem of finding a job in the home country that reflects the higher education training the student received abroad. This constitutes a particularly difficult task in developing nations with volatile economies and possibly fewer opportunities for specialized careers (Arthur, 2004, 2007; Bevis & Lucas, 2007; Pedersen, 1991; Spencer-Rodgers, 2000).

Financial Concerns

Financial restrictions also concern international students studying in the United States. The vast majority of international students hold F-1 visas from the U.S. Citizenship and Immigration Service (USCIS, formerly known as the Immigration and Naturalization Service [INS]). This means that to remain in the country legally, the student must stay enrolled and take a full course load at the approved institution. These students can be employed by the school for up to 20 hours per week, although no such limits exist when the school is not in session. After completing their program of study, international students on F-1 visas can engage in temporary off-campus employment known as Optional Practical Training. This work must occur in the student's field of study, and the student must apply to the USCIS for approval at a cost of $340. Spouses of F-1 visa holders, moreover, cannot seek employment. These rules limit the extent to which an international student can supplement his or her income and can lead to inordinate stress. Immigration regulations that limit opportunities for outside employment or for federal financial aid make accelerating students' academic progress a viable option. Although international students can request exceptions for special circumstances, they generally cannot take courses part-time or drop out without forfeiting their student visas (Bulthius, 1986; Charles & Stewart, 1991; Mori, 2000).

Discrimination and Stereotyping

International students can also encounter problems regarding racial discrimination upon entering the host country and throughout their sojourn. Several scholars have investigated the effects of racial discrimination and stereotyping on international students. Hanassab and Tidwell's (2002) findings substantiated the research of Sodowsky and Plake (1992) who found that African students perceived more prejudice and discrimination than other international student groups surveyed. The impact of racial discrimination can be profound. Rahman and Rollock (2004) illustrated a link between feelings of prejudice and levels of depression among South Asian international students. Perceptions of discrimination can also serve as an obstacle to meaningful social interaction in the host community. Domestic students may attach particular stigmas to the international student, based on his or her country of origin. Indeed, as international developments alter the balance of foreign relations, students from different countries of origin may become susceptible to hostile treatment in the United States (Hayes & Lin, 1994; Lee & Rice, 2007). The status of international students as minorities further complicates their relationship with the majority culture in the United States. For some students who are part of the majority culture or ethnicity in their home countries, their minority status in the United States may be the first time they have ever experienced discrimination (Arthur, 2004; Bulthius, 1986; Johnson & Sandhu, 2007; Yoon & Portman, 2004). Further, several researchers have called attention to the complexities of gender discrimination and the female international student experience (Bonazzo & Wong, 2007; Cole & Ahmadi, 2003; Green & Kim, 2005; Hsieh, 2007).

Defining International Student Problems

Although the literature on international students generally focuses on the problems unique to them and contrasts the differences between international and domestic students, there are problems that are common for all college students. These include adjusting to a new setting, academic demands, social and family pressures, financial concerns, and anxiety about future career plans. While the sources of stress in the college experience may be similar, the reactions to these stressors differ significantly between international and domestic students (Misra & Castillo, 2004; Mitchell, Greenwood, & Guglielmi, 2007; Yoon & Portman, 2004; Zhao, Kuh, & Carini, 2005). In addition, most international students face concerns that do not apply to the majority of domestic students, such as navigating through a new culture, adjusting to the U.S. educational system, overcoming language difficulties, and comprehending complex immigration rules. Despite the difficulties international students experience, many find ways to cope successfully and thus achieve significant accomplishments during their sojourns. Arthur (2004) lamented the lack of research on the fortitude of this population: "Agendas that are focused on problems give the implicit message that international students are problem-laden. This ignores the major contributions that international students make to the internationalization of educational institutions" (p. 125). International students have the greatest chance of succeeding if university personnel lead them to "see their strengths and view their cross-cultural studying experience in an explorative and experiential fashion, like a journey" (Lin & Pedersen, 2007, p. 297).

Institutional Policies Affecting International Students

Institutional and Governmental Policies

Although the decision to grant or deny a visa to prospective international students lies with the U.S. Department of State, admissions decisions are made at the campus level. The Association of International Educators (NAFSA) laments the decentralized nature of this process and recommends a uniform national effort to increase the United States' share of international students via more deliberate recruiting and internationalizing campus facilities and resources. At many institutions, the international student adviser has little input on admissions decisions, as a graduate college often ensures that a candidate has met the minimum requirements. Additional criteria often include an applicant's academic transcript and results from the TOEFL and SAT or GRE exams. Admissions officers often try to gauge the language proficiency, social/psychological readiness, and potential research-development projects of the prospective student. As interviews are rarely feasible, however, such questions are usually left unanswered (Desruisseaux, 1999).

NAFSA urges admissions officers to consider numerous factors when recruiting and evaluating applications from prospective international students. These include ensuring the goals and policies for international students are congruent with the larger mission of the academic institution. In addition, it is incumbent on such officials to communicate timely and accurate information regarding matters such as cost of living expenses, English language requirements, and the particular demands of the academic program in question (NAFSA, 2002). These deliberate considerations are particularly important, for as Thackaberry and Liston (1986) noted, "The consequences of failure for this population are far higher both financially and emotionally than for Americans" (p. 34). Common abuses in recruiting and admitting international students can include using placement agencies (headhunters who charge a fee and are more interested in profit than finding a good match for the applicant and the institution), recruiting international students without having proper support services on campus, misrepresenting the institution in brochures, misusing immigration forms, employing poorly trained foreign admissions advisers, and misleading an applicant into thinking that success in an intensive ESOL program will guarantee admission to an academic program. Indeed, admissions personnel hold an ethical responsibility to portray their institution fairly to prospective international students. They must also give honest and clear information about financial and living expenses, sponsors' funding requirements, and restrictions about holding jobs (El-Khawas, 1994; Neuberger, 1992; Thackaberry & Liston, 1986).

Administrators of higher education institutions must also navigate the complex governmental requirements inherent to hosting international students. In the mid- to late 1990s, the INS developed a plan called the Coordinated Interagency Partnership Regulating International Students (CIPRIS) to use fingerprints and detailed computer records to track the activities of international students on American campuses. The idea arose in the wake of the World Trade Center bombing of 1993 and was seen by some as a potential defense against future terrorist acts. In the fall of 1997 the INS tested its program in Alabama, Georgia, North Carolina, and South Carolina. Under the plan, academic institutions would be required to notify the INS when an international student dropped a course (to ensure that the student was taking at least the minimum allowed to remain in residence). University administrators and advocates for international education, such as the Institute of International Education, the American Council on Education, and NAFSA, criticized the plan for the reporting burdens it placed upon colleges and universities. In addition, these groups opposed the fees that students would be required to pay to support the system (Bevis & Lucas, 2007; Urias & Yeakey, 2008).

After the terrorist attacks of September 2001, government scrutiny of international students intensified and led to the swift creation of a successor to CIPRIS: the Student and Exchange Visitor Information System (SEVIS). Although only one of the nineteen terrorists involved in 9/11 entered the United States on a student visa to study English at a language school, the news that two others received student visa approvals posthumously exposed the need for better coordination and oversight of the INS. The Patriot Act of 2001 allocated more than $36 million to implement an Internet-based tracking system. The act required all academic institutions with international students to report information about these students to the SEVIS system by January 30, 2003 (U.S. Immigration and Customs Enforcement, 2002). The government's rapid implementation of SEVIS led to a dramatic shift in the role of student personnel responsible for advising international students. Formerly charged primarily with providing support services and cultural programming, these professionals now faced the dilemma of advocating for students while simultaneously ensuring their institution's compliance with federal regulations. In a national survey of international student and scholar advisors (ISSAs), 86% of respondents "believed that SEVIS required them to focus more on regulatory compliance than student programming" (Rosser, Hermsen, Mamiseishvili, & Wood, 2007, p. 532).

While university administrators worked to implement the government's rapid changes to student visa policies, they also faced a backlash against international students that persisted in varying degrees after the events of September 11, 2001. Although the exact number of physical assaults and threats against international students after 9/11 is unknown, the perception of the United States as an unwelcoming place lingered. Students from the Middle East in particular experienced feelings of uneasiness and suspicion as well as pressure from families to return home (Klein & DeGregory, 2001; McMurtrie, 2001; Morgan, 2002; Wilkinson, 2002).

Campus officials addressed the needs of international students after 9/11 by offering discussion forums between international and domestic students and bolstering counseling and support services. Student organizations for international students were also instrumental in working with staff to address concerns. Some university presidents wrote statements declaring the importance of international students and calling for sensitivity. Harvard University's Civil Rights Project (2003) published a guide to help international students identify and respond to hate crimes and racial profiling. In addition to addressing the potential hostility toward international students on campus and in the community, administrators were also met with visits from federal investigators seeking information about specific students. FBI agents visited more than two hundred institutions to gather information that led to personal interviews of numerous international students. This FBI presence on campus, not seen since the Cold War, forced higher education officials to balance government mandates for information with the need to protect the rights of their students and safeguard them against racial profiling (Marklein, 2003; Steinberg, 2001; Urias & Yeakey, 2008; Wilkinson, 2002).

The perception of an unwelcoming climate, coupled with the increased visa woes and government scrutiny, left many advocates for international education worrying about the effect on international student enrollments. Some institutions responded by offering to pay the government's mandatory SEVIS fee for students committing to enroll or pay for the express shipment of their immigration documents to speed the visa process. Others developed recruitment strategies for attracting international students to their institutions.

Guidelines for Student Affairs Personnel and Faculty

In discussing viable goals and strategies for campus personnel, Pedersen (1991) admitted that administrators "are still not sure how to define success in counseling international students" (p. 45). Despite a general lack of research on counseling foreign students, according to Dalili (1982) the fact remains that the implications can be dramatic: "The long-term success of foreign students' stays in the U.S. will depend on their successful adjustment, which may in turn depend on the success of the advising/counseling process" (p. 11). Pedersen recommended that counselors identify specific skills for international students to use to help them cope with problems in adjusting to American culture and campus life. He also suggested that counselors encourage international students to reflect on their changing values and worldviews and to develop relationships with conationals while negotiating the host culture. A continuous process of orientation and counseling, including follow-up contacts after the international student has returned home, can help to mitigate tensions often associated with cultural transitions (Dalili; Fritz et al., 2008; Pedersen).

Campus administrators must find ways to initiate contact with international students—publicize their services through ESOL programs, for instance. It is also important to have a frontline counseling staff from a variety of cultural backgrounds who are able to empathize with the international student and then refer him or her to a counseling expert.

Campus Programs

To help facilitate the adjustment of international students to campus life, orientation programs can begin even before they arrive in the host country. International student advisers at the receiving institution can send students prearrival information about academics, housing, health insurance, transportation, and other matters. Alumni groups in foreign countries can host receptions and information sessions to provide prospective students with useful insights about the institution and community. It is also beneficial for student personnel staff or students to meet the arriving sojourner at the airport or bus station. Upon arriving at campus, a series of orientation programs can welcome the new students and offer essential information that will acquaint them with the campus, inform them about immigration rules, familiarize them with the American system of higher education, describe various aspects of American culture and values, and identify some of the challenges involved in cross-cultural adjustment. More specific topics can include advising, community, and other available campus services, and how to manage finances and understand the U.S. health care system. It is especially important to make the new students aware of the myriad student services that exist on campus, as many sojourners may not even imagine they would be in place. These orientation sessions can include small-group lectures and discussions, slide presentations, and films. It is crucial to match the program to the English proficiency level of the international students as best as possible (Reiff & Kidd, 1986).

Residential life staff must also recognize the particular needs of various international students and acknowledge their own cultural assumptions. Orientation programs through residential life offices can help all campus residents appreciate differences. Furthermore, while nearly all international undergraduate students are unmarried, some graduate students bring their dependents with them. Orientation programs for the entire sojourning family can address transportation, schools, recreational facilities, shopping, and safety issues to abet academic success for the student and smooth cultural adjustment for the family. Thus, staff members who have experience working with families and children are needed (Chittooran & Sankar-Gomes, 2007; Neuberger, 1992).

Programs for intercultural exchange have been found to facilitate international students' adjustment to campus life. These include international coffee hours, talent shows, events forums (in which the entire campus learns about a particular culture), and international film nights. In addition, various peer programs in which international students are matched with American students have yielded beneficial results on social adjustment as well as academic performance. For example, intercultural communication workshops have included small groups of international and American students using role playing, case studies, and communication exercises to address the various cultural backgrounds of the participants. The goal was to lead all participants along a path of awareness to deeper understanding to appreciation, and ultimately to accepting cultural differences or similarities. In another example, a Collaborative Cultural Exchange Program at one institution arranged year-long practicums for U.S. graduate students in counseling programs who paired up with sojourning students and assisted them in locating housing, shopping areas, and appropriate clothing for changing seasons. The popularity of these programs reveals that international students value social relations in addition to academic achievement (Jacob & Greggo, 2001).

A significant but frequently overlooked aspect of international student adjustment entails the transition upon returning to the home country. Various recommendations for host colleges and universities include establishing a job-placement office. As most international students studying in the United States come from countries with developing and volatile economies, such services are especially important. Counseling practices, moreover, can help international students to prepare for their return via workshops. Counselors need to be aware that the international student has inevitably changed during his or her sojourn and perhaps may find it difficult to readjust to the cultural traditions and customs of the home country. Such dissonance can lead to stress but can be mitigated in counseling sessions in which the international student is encouraged to articulate his or her expectations about returning home. Marks (1987) cited the ambivalence many international students may encounter:

> Students may . . . feel stress from either their desire or their lack of desire to return home, from a feeling or lack of feeling of accomplishment in what they have done during their stay in the host country, and from the opportunity or lack of opportunity to discuss their experiences with those who have had similar ones. (p. 126)

Again, campus workshops can allow returning students to anticipate these potential problems and to equip them with practical strategies on how to cope with reverse culture shock, different cultural values, issues of economic development, and how their American education can translate into new opportunities in other countries (Arthur, 2007; Reynolds & Constantine, 2007).

Case Study

Mountain State University (MSU) is a public institution with 35,000 undergraduate and graduate students. It is situated in a state that has witnessed unprecedented population and economic growth over the past 30 years. During that time, MSU has undergone a transformation from a regional and academically marginal school into a leading research university with a wideranging international reputation. Its student body has reflected the changing demographics of the state, and nearly 5% of its undergraduate and graduate students come from other nations.

Mohammad Shafqat is a first-year graduate student in economics from Iran. Although his TOEFL score met the university's minimum requirement, his oral English skills are marginal at best. This has hurt his ability to fulfill his duties as a teaching assistant (TA); the undergraduate students in his section have often experienced difficulty deciphering his limited English. Students have steadily complained to the economics department about this. In addition, their scores on the standard examinations for the course have been significantly below those of students in other sections with different TAs. A few weeks into the term, the professor and coordinator of the course met with Mohammad to see if there was anything she could do to help him. Mohammad was embarrassed by his lack of speaking abilities, and he merely responded by saying that everything was fine.

Sometime during the last month of class in the fall term, administrators of the economics department indicated that if the complaints about Mohammad's teaching continued, they would alleviate him from his duties as TA, which was his only source of income. Faced with the pressure and potential shame of returning to his home country without having earned his degree, Mohammad began to devote intense hours each night trying to improve his English by studying books of grammar. This had a marginal effect on his performance.

During a review session preceding the final exam, some of the students in Mohammad's section became frustrated because they could not understand his answers to their questions. Mohammad began to lose control of the class as angry students started talking over one another. Mohammad overheard one student say loudly to another, "Why's this guy here anyway? He's probably a terrorist!" Despite his own difficulty at articulation, Mohammad understood the student's words completely. At that point, he announced that the review session was over and left the room.

Later that day, as the resident adviser of Mohammad's floor in the graduate student dormitory, you pass Mohammad in the hallway outside his door and notice his intense expression—bleary-eyed, confused, and disoriented. When you ask him if you can help, he recounts his semester-long ordeal to you for the first time.

Discussion Questions

1. How do you respond—and why?
2. What resources would you use to help this student?
3. What measures could university administrators take to remedy this particular situation and to prevent this from happening to other international students?

References

Alexander, A. A., Klein, M. H., Workneh, F., Miller, M. H. (1976). Psychotherapy and the foreign student. In P. B. Pedersen, J. G. Draguns, W. J. Lonner, & M. H. Miller (Eds.), *Counseling Across Cultures* (pp. 227–243). Honolulu: University Press of Hawaii.

Altbach, P. G. (1989). Foreign student adjustment: Issues and perspectives. In K. Ebuchi (Ed.), *Foreign students and internationalization of higher education: Proceedings of OECD/Japan Seminar on Higher Education and the Flow of Foreign Students* (pp. 173–182). Hiroshima, Japan: Research Institute for Higher Education.

Altbach, P. G. (2004). Higher education crosses borders: Can the United States remain the top destination for foreign students? *Change, 36*(2), 18–24.

Altbach, P. G., & Knight, J. (2007). The Internationalization of higher education: Motivations and realities. *Journal of Studies in International Education, 11*(3–4), 290–305.

Anders, J. (2007). *U.S. Student visas reach record numbers in 2007.* Retrieved from http://www.america.gov/st/washfile-english/2007/November/20071116123904zjsrednao.5665552.html

Arthur, N. (2004). *Counseling international students: Clients from around the World.* New York: Kluwer Academic/Plenum.

Arthur, N. (2007). International students' career development and decisions. In H. Singaravelu & M. Pope (Eds.), *A handbook for counseling international students in the United States* (pp. 37–56). Alexandria, VA: American Counseling Association.

Associated Press. (2005, September 25). An English test is changed, and some foreign students worry. *New York Times*, p. 23.

Aubrey, R. (1991). International students on campus: A challenge for counselors, medical providers, and clinicians. *Smith College Studies in Social Work, 62,* 280–284.

Bennell, P., & Pearce, T. (1998). *The internationalisation of higher education: Exporting education to developing and transitional economies.* IDS Working Paper 75. Brighton, UK: Copyright Institute of Development Studies.

Berry, J. W. (1980). Acculturation as varieties of adaptation. In A. Padilla (Ed.), *Acculturation: Theory, models, and some new findings* (pp. 9–25). Boulder: Westview.

Bevis, T. B., & Lucas, C. J. (2007). *International students in American colleges and universities: A history.* New York: Palgrave Macmillan.

Bochner, S. (1972). Problems in culture learning. In S. Bochner & P. Wicks (Eds.), *Overseas students in Australia.* Sydney, New South Wales, Australia: New South Wales Press.

Bollag, B. (2005). New test of English as a foreign language puts an emphasis on speaking. *Chronicle of Higher Education, 52*(7), A49.

Bonazzo, C., & Wong, Y. J. (2007). Japanese international female students' experience of discrimination, prejudice, and stereotypes. *College Student Journal, 41*(3), 631–640.

Bulthius, J. D. (1986). The foreign student today: A profile. In K. R. Pyle (Ed.), *Guiding the development of foreign students* (pp. 19–29). San Francisco: Jossey-Bass.

Chapdelaine, R. F., & Alexitch, L. R. (2004). Social skills difficulty: Model of culture shock for international graduate students. *Journal of College Student Development, 45*(2), 167–183.

Charles, H., & Stewart, M. A. (1991). Academic advising of international students. *Journal of Multicultural Counseling and Development, 19,* 173–181.

Chittooran, M. M., & Sankar-Gomes, A. (2007). The families of international students in U.S. universities: Adjustment issues and implications for counselors. In H. Singaravelu & M. Pope (Eds.), *A handbook for counseling international students in the United States* (pp. 113–136). Alexandria, VA: American Counseling Association.

Church, A. T. (1982). Sojourner adjustment. *Psychological Bulletin, 91,* 540–572.

Cole, D., & Ahmadi, S. (2003). Perspectives and experiences of Muslim women who veil on college campuses. *Journal of College Student Development, 44*(1), 47–66.

Coppi, C. (2007). The changing landscape of international student advisement. In H. Singaravelu & M. Pope (Eds.), *A handbook for counseling international students in the United States* (pp. 3–11). Alexandria, VA: American Counseling Association.

Council of Graduate Schools. (2008). *Findings from the 2008 CGS International Graduate Admissions Survey, Phase 1: Applications.* Retrieved from http://www.cgs net.org/portals/0/pdf/R_IntlAppso8_I.pdf

Cummings, W. K. (1992). Global trends in overseas study. In D. McIntire & P. Willer (Eds.), *Working with international students and scholars on American campuses* (pp. 159–180). Washington, DC: National Association of Student Personnel Administrators.

Dalili, F. (1982). *Roles and responsibilities of international student advisors and counselors in the United States.* Akron, OH: University of Akron.

Desruisseaux, P. (1998). 2-year colleges at crest of wave in U.S. enrollment by foreign students. *Chronicle of Higher Education, 45*(16), A66–A68.

Desruisseaux, P. (1999). Foreign students continue to flock to the U.S. *Chronicle of Higher Education, 45*(36), A57–A59.

El-Khawas, E. (1994). Toward a global university status and outlook in the United States. *Higher Education Management, 6,* 90–98.

Fritz, M. V., Chin, D., & DeMarinis, V. (2008). Stressors, anxiety, acculturation and adjustment among international and North American students. *International Journal of Intercultural Relations, 32*(3), 244–259.

Fulbright Act of 1946, Pub. L. No. 58422, U.S.C.A. § 245 et seq.

Fulbright-Hays Act of 1961, Pub. L. No. 87–256, 75_Stat._

Furnham, A., & Bochner, S. (1982). Social difficulty in a foreign culture: An empirical analysis of culture shock. In S. Bochner (Ed.), *Cultures in contact* (pp. 161–198). New York: Pergamon.

Green, D. O., & Kim, E. (2005). Experiences of Korean female doctoral students in academe: Raising voice against gender and racial stereotypes. *Journal of College Student Development, 46*(5), 487–500.

Gullahorn, J. T., & Gullahorn, J. E. (1966). American students abroad: Professional versus personal development. *Annals, 368,* 45–59.

Halleck, G. B. (2008). The ITA problem: A ready-to-use simulation. *Simulation Gaming, 39*(1), 137–146.

Hanassab, S., & Tidwell, R. (2002). International students in higher education: Identification of needs and implications for policy and practice. *Journal of Studies in International Education, 6*(4), 305–322.

Harvard University Civil Rights Project. (2003). *Know your rights on campus: A guide on racial profiling, and hate crime for international students in the United States.* Cambridge, MA: Harvard University. (ERIC Document Reproduction Service No. ED476894)

Hayes, R. L., & Lin, H. R. (1994). Coming to America: Developing social support systems for international students. *Journal of Multicultural Counseling and Development, 22,* 7–16.

Hsieh, M. H. (2007). Challenges for international students in higher education: One student's narrated story of invisibility and struggle. *College Student Journal, 41*(2), 379–391.

Hull, F. W. (1981). A modified culture contact hypothesis and the adaptation of foreign students in cross-cultural settings. In S. C. Dunnett (Ed.), *Factors affecting the adaptation of foreign students in cross-cultural settings* (Special Studies Series No. 134). Buffalo, NY: University at Buffalo, Council on International Studies.

Institute of International Education. (2009). *Open doors 2008: Report on international educational exchange.* New York: Author

Jacob, E. J., & Greggo, J. W. (2001). Using counselor training and collaborative programming strategies in working with international students. *Journal of Multicultural Counseling and Development, 29,* 73–88.

Johnson, L. R., & Sandhu, D. S. (2007). Isolation, adjustment, and acculturation issues: Intervention strategies for counselors. In H. Singaravelu & M. Pope (Eds.), *A handbook for counseling international students in the United States* (pp. 13–35). Alexandria, VA: American Counseling Association.

Kiernan, V. (1999). Congressional panel seeks to curb access of foreign students to U.S. supercomputers. *Chronicle of Higher Education, 45*(4), A57–A59.

Klein, B., & DeGregory, L. (2001, October 1). Muslim students emerge concerned. *St. Petersburg Times,* p. 1B.

Labi, A. (2007). Europe challenges U.S. for foreign students. *Chronicle of Higher Education, 54*(5), A29–A30.

Lee, J. J., & Rice, C. (2007). Welcome to America? International student perceptions of discrimination. *Journal of Higher Education, 53,* 381–409.

Leong, F. T. L., & Chou, E. L. (1996). Counseling international students. In P. B. Pedersen, J. G. Draguns, W. J. Lonner, & J. E. Trimble (Eds.), *Counseling across cultures* (4th ed., pp. 210–242). Thousand Oaks, CA: Sage.

Leong, F. T. L., & Sedlacek, W. E. (1989). Academic and career needs of international and United States college students. *Journal of College Student Development, 30,* 106–111.

Lewin, T. (2008, February 10). Universities rush to set up outposts abroad. *New York Times,* p. A1.

Lin, A. S. P., & Pedersen, P. B. (2007). Multi-national competencies of international student service providers. In H. Singaravelu & M. Pope (Eds.), *A handbook for counseling international students in the United States* (pp. 285–298). Alexandria, VA: American Counseling Association.

Lin, J. G., & Yi, J. K. (1997). Asian international students' adjustment: Issues and program suggestions. *The College Student Journal, 31,* 473–479.

Liu, J. (2001). Asian students' classroom communication patterns in U.S. universities: An emic perspective. Westport, CT: Ablex.

Lysgaard, S. (1955). Adjustment in a foreign society: Norwegian Fulbright grantees visiting the United States. *International Social Science Bulletin, 7,* 45–51.

Marklein, M. (2003, January 20). INS database worries colleges. *USA Today,* p. 6D.

Marks, M. S. (1987). Preparing international students in the United States for reentering the home country. *Journal of Multicultural Counseling and Development, 15,* 120–128.

McCormack, E. (2007). Number of foreign students bounces back to near-record high. *Chronicle of Higher Education, 54*(12), A1.

McMurtrie, B. (2001). Arab students in U.S. head home, citing growing hostility. *Chronicle of Higher Education, 48*(6), A42.

Misra, R., & Castillo, L. (2004). Academic stress among college students: Comparison of American and international students. *International Journal of Stress* *1*(2), 132–148.

Mitchell, S. L., Greenwood, A. K., & Guglielmi, M. C. (2007). Utilization of counseling services: Comparing international and U.S. college students. *Journal of College Counseling, 10*(2), 117–130.

Morgan, R. (2002). An international-student adviser faces rumors, fear, and prejudice. *Chronicle of Higher Education, 49*(2), A6.

Mori, S. (2000). Addressing the mental health concerns of international students. *Journal of Counseling & Development, 78*, 137–144.

NAFSA (2002). *NAFSA's principles of good practice for the recruitment and admissions of international students.* Retrieved from http://www.nafsa.org/about.sec/governance_leadership/ethics_standards/nafsa_s_principles_of/

Nash, D. (1991). The course of sojourner adaptation: A new test of the u-curve hypothesis. *Human Organization, 50*, 283–286.

Neuberger, C. G. (1992). Working with international students on our campuses. In D. McIntire & P. Willer (Eds.), *Working with international students and scholars on American campuses* (pp. 124–138). Washington, DC: National Association of Student Personnel Administrators.

Oropeza, B. A. C., Fitzgibbon, M., & Baron, A., Jr. (1991). Managing mental health crises of foreign college students. *Journal of Counseling and Development, 69*, 280–284.

Paige, R. M. (1990). International students: Cross-cultural psychological perspectives. In R. W. Brislin (Ed.), *Applied cross-cultural psychology* (pp. 161–185). Newbury Park, CA: Sage.

Pedersen, P. B. (1991). Counseling international students. *The Counseling Psychologist, 19*, 10–58.

Rahman, O., & Rollock, D. (2004). Acculturation, competence, and mental health among South Asian students in the United States. *Journal of Multicultural Counseling and Development, 32*, 130–142.

Reiff, R. F., & Kidd, M. A. (1986). The foreign student and student life. In K. R. Pyle (Ed.), *Guiding the development of foreign students* (pp. 39–49). San Francisco: Jossey-Bass.

Reynolds, A. L., & Constantine, M. G. (2007). Cultural adjustment difficulties and career development of international college students. *Journal of Career Assessment, 15*(3), 338–350.

Rosser, V. J., Hermsen, J. M., Mamiseishvili, K., & Wood, M. S. (2007). A national study examining the impact of SEVIS on international student and scholar advisors. *Journal of Higher Education, 54*, 525–542.

Sheehan, O. T. O., & Pearson, F. (1995). Asian international and American students' psychosocial development. *Journal of College Student Development, 36*, 522–530.

Sodowsky, G. R., & Plake, B. S. (1992). A study of acculturation differences among international people and suggestions for sensitivity to within-group differences. *Journal of Counseling and Development, 71*, 53–59.

Spencer-Rodgers, J. (2000). The vocational situation and country of orientation of international students. *Journal of Multicultural Counseling and Development, 28*, 32–49.

Steinberg, J. (2001, November 12). A nation challenged: The students: U.S. has covered 200 campuses to check up on Mideast students. *New York Times*, p. A1.

Taft, R. (1977). Coping with unfamiliar cultures. In N. Warren (Ed.), *Studies in cross-cultural psychology* (pp. 120–135). London: Academic Press.

Terzian, S. G., & Osborne, L. (2006). Postwar era precedents and the ambivalent quest for international students at the University of Florida. *Journal of Studies in International Education, 10*(3), 286–306.

Thackaberry, M. D., & Liston, A. (1986). Recruitment and admissions: Special issues and ethical considerations. In K. R. Pyle (Ed.), *Guiding the development of foreign students* (pp. 31–38). San Francisco: Jossey-Bass.

Trice, A. G. (2004). Mixing it up: International graduate students' social interactions with American students. *Journal of College Student Development, 45*(6), 671–687.

Urias, D., & Yeakey, C. C. (2008). Analysis of the U.S. student visa system: Misperceptions, barriers, and consequences. *Journal of Studies in International Education, 13*(1), 72–109.

U.S.A. Patriot Act of 2001, H.R. 3162, 107th Cong. (2001–2002).

U.S. Department of State. (2010). *Exchange visitors*. Retrieved from http://travel .state.gov/visa/temp/types/types_1267.html#1

U.S. Immigration and Customs Enforcement. (2002). *Final rule implementing SEVIS: Highlights*. Retrieved from http://www.ice.gov/pi/news/factsheets/ 0212FINALRU_FS.htm

U.S. Immigration and Customs Enforcement. (2007). *Becoming a nonimmigrant student in the United States*. Retrieved from http://www.ice.gov/sevis/becoming_ nonimmigrant_student_5200 7.htm#_Toc129683761

Ward, C., Bochner, S., & Furnham, A. (2001). *The psychology of culture shock* (2nd ed.). Philadelphia: Taylor & Francis.

Wilkinson, C. K. (2002). *September 11, 2001*. In C. K. Wilkinson & J. A. Rund (Eds.), *Addressing contemporary campus safety* (pp. 87–96). San Francisco: Jossey-Bass.

Yoon, E., & Portman, T. A. A. (2004). Critical issues of literature on counseling international students. *Journal of Multicultural Counseling and Development, 32*, 33–44.

Zhao, C., Kuh, G. D., & Carini, R. M. (2005). A comparison of international student and American student engagement in effective educational practices. *Journal of Higher Education, 76*(2), 209–231.

12

MEN AND WOMEN COLLEGE STUDENTS

Merrily Dunn

Multicultural issues related to gender have traditionally centered on women. This view originates from the fact that males have historically been the primary recipients of college degrees and the primary population used in the studies that undergird theories of college student development. A complete exploration of multicultural issues related to gender or sex requires the inclusion of men and women. To do less provides a picture of only part of our world and ignores the important understandings gained from studying the interplay between women and men.

Judith Lorber (1994) wrote that "the building blocks of gender are *socially constructed statuses*" (p. 17). The term *sex* is not interchangeable with the term *gender* despite numerous examples of such usage in our professional literature, program presentations, and popular press. Whereas sex is biologically determined, gender is not (Pryzgoda & Chrisler, 2000). Gender is a social construction; the specific content of which varies among cultures and periods in history. Time, place, class, ethnicity, education, religion, language, power relations, and any number of other factors influence what we know about being male and being female. Gender can be viewed as the melding of the personal and cultural and how an individual makes meaning of them (Chodorow, 1995). Gender is fluid, changeable, and sometimes difficult to identify, and some academics argue that the delineation of it from sex is a limiting factor for the study of each (Harrison, 2006). However, it has been argued that in the United States, gender identity is so pervasive and so strongly aligned with being biologically female or male that in this culture gender is, in reality, biologically determined (Devor, 2002). As a result, the culture sees male aggressiveness and competition as natural and women's instincts toward nurturing as the way women will behave by virtue of being female (Devor, 2002). It is increasingly clear that for many individuals gender is not static, nor is it necessarily aligned with biological sex.

History of Women in Higher Education

In many ways, the history of women and men in higher education is the history of the education of White men, and initially only those of substantial means. Since the mid-19th century women and people of color have become players in the higher education arena through coeducation and integration and through the development of separate institutions. When studying the participation of women in what was initially a very male system, it is important and useful to keep in mind two overarching and prevailing themes. Whether as students, faculty, staff, or administrators, women's participation is always reconciled with their roles in the dominant culture. Second, women are allowed to fill traditional male roles when men are not available to fill them. Wars, economic depressions, and less dramatic economic downturns have meant opening up higher education to women, though often reluctantly (Arlton, Lewellen, & Grissett, 1999; Goree, 1993).

Higher education in the United States began in 1636 with the founding of Harvard, which was modeled on the English universities of Oxford and Cambridge. In the years after the Revolutionary War, a number of states primarily in the South established their own colleges, moving toward nonsectarianism (Rudolph, 1990). The precursor of women's higher education was also established during this period with the creation of The Young Ladies' Academy in Philadelphia; Emma Willard's female seminary in Troy, New York; and Mary Lyon's Mount Holyoke College (Solomon, 1985).

The years between 1790 and 1850, characterized by the Enlightenment and the second Great Awakening, laid the foundation for the evolution of women's higher education in the United States through the reform impetus from these prevailing ideologies. These two movements combined to make a strong case for the necessity of women's education (Kerber, 1980; Solomon, 1985). Catherine Beecher, Emma Willard, and Almira Phelps responded by establishing seminaries for women that expanded educational opportunities while working within the accepted parameters defined by the prevailing ideologies of the time (Solomon). During this period the first normal schools appeared (Cohen, 1998). While teaching is often associated with women and was one of the first professions women entered and eventually dominated, the development of normal schools and the roles played by women in them is complicated. Women often taught at the elementary or secondary level without what would currently be considered a college degree. The earliest normal schools ranged from single-sex institutions considered part of a secondary school to distinct institutions to an academic track within a university (Thelin, 2004).

The first Morrill Act of 1862 set aside federal lands, allowing each state to establish land-grant institutions dedicated to teaching agricultural and mechanical arts (Jencks & Riesman, 1968; Johnson, 1997). While these areas were certainly the focus of the act and the initial curricula, the field of education had the largest growth in student enrollment and in jobs after graduation (Thelin, 2004). This act had the effect of creating colleges in every state. The first Morrill Act was expanded upon and enhanced by the second Morrill Act in 1890 (Brubacher & Rudy, 1997), resulting in the creation of a system of land grant colleges and universities that not only educates a large percentage of undergraduate students, making it a model of egalitarianism, it also produces two thirds of all doctoral recipients. This conglomerate of land grant institutions trains the largest number of researchers in the country (Johnson). These institutions, so often understood in terms of the practicality of their initial courses of study, were actually created by reformers striving for an egalitarian ideal—providing educational opportunities for the men and women often overlooked by the more elitist institutions (Johnson). In the long run these reformers provided through the two Morrill Acts an avenue to higher education for women, as well as for working-class men (Dunn, 1993; Goree, 1993; Rosenberg, 1982).

The 20th century ushered in the Progressive Era, characterized by reform movements and a growing sense of the need for community and unity of purpose as well as trust in science and technology (Gordon, 1997; Gruber, 1997), which provided increased opportunities for women students. Many women found a way to be of service and to be socially responsible by working with social service organizations, and studying and working in the evolving fields of social work and home economics (Gordon; Solomon, 1985). While college men were also involved from the beginning, women students, primarily those of the middle and upper classes, embraced social work and integrated it into their lives and identities (Solomon). The development of social work created a route to professionalism for women and added a pathway to education and medicine as occupations requiring postgraduate education (Bledstein, 1976; Gordon).

An even greater number of women and men students flooded college campuses in the decades between the world wars. An increasingly racially, ethnically, and economically diverse group of women and men saw higher education as the means to a successful future (Solomon, 1985). Radical feminists of this era were hopeful that coeducation would mean the end of traditional gender roles (Tyack & Hansot, 2002). College women of this era were different from their predecessors who fought for the right to vote and established settlement houses to aid immigrants and other socially disadvantaged individuals in urban areas. Those earlier collegians looked for and found ways to use their education, giving meaning to lives that could have simply been spent in privileged leisure. While the younger women understood and appreciated the actions of those who had gone before, they were focused on their youth and the possibilities and pleasures available to them because of it. They were no longer pioneers in higher education; they were collegians who had more in common with their male counterparts than the women preceding them in academe (Solomon).

While the war years presented women with new opportunities in educational fields previously dominated by men and new occupational challenges in the broad range of jobs necessary to support the war effort, most gains were lost at the end of World War II. After a period dominated first by an economic depression and then a world war, the United States was a nation craving normalcy, a return to domesticity and traditional family life (Rosenberg, 1992). This desire, coupled with a strong national sense of the debt owed to returning servicemen, created a culture where women entered college in smaller numbers (Solomon, 1985), with two thirds eventually leaving before graduating. They married younger and had more children than women in the previous generation (Rosenberg). Despite these trends, college women were a much more diverse group (Levine, 1995).

Although many believe the feminist activity of the 1960s was a new phenomenon, it was actually a heightened level of activism that had continued in quieter form since the fight for women's suffrage was won in 1920 (Levine, 1995; Rupp & Taylor, 1987). A variety of factors combined to spur the revival of the American women's movement during the 1960s. The civil rights, antiwar, and free speech movements challenged societal norms and mores. The intense questioning of social and institutional structures at the heart of these movements led women to question those same structures. This experience mirrors that of the earliest feminists who started as part of the abolitionist movement (Tyack & Hansot, 2002). Again, women asked the fundamental question: Were they not also being oppressed? Two branches of an organized feminist movement emerged from this inquiry. The women's rights movement was characterized by organizations pledged to reorder existing social structures and institutions, while women's liberation, was more focused on deconstructing existing structures. Both movements were present on college campuses, serving different purposes and demanding different changes. Higher education was changed as a result of these groups' work. By the late 1960s and early 1970s women students were no longer governed by the plethora of rules and regulations that had governed their lives previously. Additionally, they no longer had the structured, institutionalized support provided by large staffs (typically under the umbrella of the dean of women) devoted solely to their well-being (Dunn, 1993). Options for women and men inside the classroom changed and expanded in this period as well. Women's studies, courses devoted to the study of gender and women's experiences in fields from history and psychology to anthropology and languages, blossomed on college campuses across the nation during the late 1960s (Howe, 1984), even though courses on women's history had been taught as early as the 1940s (Rupp & Taylor, 1987).

Educational opportunities for women and men continued to expand throughout the final decades of the 20th century. Women's studies broadened the curriculum of universities while working to eliminate institutionalized sexism and the oppression of women in the broader society (Bastedo, 2005; Brubacher & Rudy, 1997). Women of all races, ethnicities, and classes have continued to enter all types of higher education institutions. At the beginning of the 21st century women constituted more than half the population of our nation's colleges and universities.

According to the 2010 Almanac issue of the *Chronicle of Higher Education*, women comprise 52.4% of students enrolled in higher education institutions in the United States. In the most recent data available (2007–08), this group earned 62% of associate degrees, 57% of bachelor's degrees, 60% of master's degrees, and 51% of doctoral degrees. Women earned 50% of all professional degrees awarded (*Chronicle of Higher Education,* 2010).

Sociological Context of the Cultural Group

Longitudinal data show that college students, male and female, have declined in traditionalism, with women having more egalitarian views than male students (Bryant, 2003). As shown by the demographic data, women students are fully represented at all levels of higher education, including the most traditionally male fields, at the doctoral level and in professional schools. An examination of women's participation in administrative and faculty roles shows a different picture. As of 2007, college presidents were 55% male and 84% White (*Chronicle of Higher Education*, 2008). As of the fall of 2007 women made up 42% of full-time faculty but only 26% of full professors, 39% of associate professors, 47% of assistant professors, and 54% of instructors and lecturers (*Chronicle of Higher Education*, 2009). While the number of women in higher education continues to grow, females are concentrated in lower ranks and, to some degree, have lower salaries (Altbach, 2005).

While women's place in higher education seems guaranteed, egalitarian male and female roles on campus have not evolved as fully. The sweeping social change promised by the movements of the 1960s has perhaps changed higher education in superficial ways. Fundamental structural changes, which could have resulted in a natural change from a reconstructed system, did not occur. It is arguable that academic feminism, a daring social movement striving to change the structure of higher education as well as the content of the curriculum since the late 1960s, has itself been changed by the very institution it set out to reconstruct. Social activism has evolved into academic disciplines intellectualizing the issues the movement sprang from. Can academic feminism be most influential from within the disciplines or standing alone in women's studies or gender studies (Hemmings, 2006)? Decades of research also highlight the difficulty inherent in understanding gender in ways that move beyond stereotyping either gender (Bozin & Yoder, 2008). While male perceptions, understandings, characteristics, and point of view were once the standard for a variety of disciplines, academic feminism has evolved into, through, and from the naming and study of gender, questioning the male norm. When the female is made visible then the male becomes a contrasting construct, not just a norm. While not a corollary, it can be said that studies on men and masculinities expands and enhances the discourse on gender (Bannon & Correia, 2006; Hearn & Kimmel, 2006).

Women are present in the classroom in larger numbers than men, but many argue that the classroom environment has not changed to reflect differences in the way women communicate and learn. Education intended and designed to meet women's educational needs has only begun to emerge since the mid-1980s. Even now the question remains of how schooling at primary, secondary, and postsecondary levels defines, transmits, and maintains ideas about gender and its role across generations and class lines (Arnot, 2002). It is only with the advent of feminist pedagogies that this issue has been addressed (Tisdell, 2000). Studies such as those conducted by Maher and

Tetreault (1994, 2001) grew out of awareness of the significant changes to higher education beginning in the late 1960s. The two most pervasive and far-reaching changes were radically evolving student demographics and the resulting increased desire for an inclusive curriculum and pedagogies. Maher and Tetreault's work, along with that of other scholars, yielded scholarship detailing women's learning and pedagogies reflective of feminist philosophies (Hayes & Flannery, 2000; Mayberry & Rose, 1999). These pedagogies are not without controversy, even within women's studies. Some scholars argue that they abandon intellectual rigor and the transmission of knowledge from faculty to students in their efforts to allow all voices to be validated, and in so doing they may be in danger of the indoctrination they sought to overcome in more traditional academic disciplines (Patai, 2008; Patai & Koertge, 2003).

Research conducted in the early 1980s discovered a chilly climate for women in the classroom, characterized by male students' being treated differently than women who experienced a sense of being less valued than men (Sandler & Hall, 1986). In contrast, Drew and Work's study published in 1998 shows that this may no longer be the case as women students report more interaction with faculty members and more class participation than male classmates. While the authors suggest the classroom environment may have changed since the chilly climate study, they do recognize that their results also show women students are less likely to spend time with faculty outside class and less likely to engage in research with faculty members—activities crucial to academic success and the progression to graduate education (Drew & Work). However, the literature in this area is not consistent with other authors documenting ongoing issues in this area (Martin, 2000; Morris & Daniel, 2008). Bell, Morrow, and Tastsoglou (1999), in advocating the use of feminist pedagogies, believed the issue is twofold: Students are used to and have been schooled in a hierarchical educational system where they are the recipients of objective knowledge, and second, they may be invested in the dominant culture and find threatening those pedagogies designed to encourage students to critique, question, and construct their own knowledge. Carse and DeBruin (2002) concur and add that this classroom volatility and resistance is "testimony both to the growing authority and power of feminist and liberatory ideas and perspectives, and to the continued vulnerability of these ideas and perspectives, particularly when they come from marginalized and historically underprivileged thinkers" (p. 182).

In the past 40 years there has been an influx of women and numerous underrepresented groups onto our campuses. However, as previously noted, the curriculum continues to be structured around Western models of knowledge, emphasizing independence, achievement, and objectivity over cooperation and collaboration (Maher & Tetreault, 1994). While during this period women's studies and African American studies have experienced growth, there has also been a backlash against the perceived affront to the ideals of Western civilization and the emphasis on personal and subjective over objective truth (Bell et al., 1999; Bloom, 1987; D'Souza, 1991; Stake, 2006; Superson & Cudd, 2002). Given the growth of such academic disciplines one would also expect to see a parallel growth in research related to how women learn in order to provide the theory necessary to inform pedagogy. Such research is limited (Hayes, 2000). An understanding of the existing research relevant to women's development provides ample evidence that the way courses are structured and taught may not be consistent with the ways students (male and female) make meaning and understand. Authors advocating pedagogies designed to maximize women's education acknowledge running the risk of marginalizing their work or in effect declaring that separate can be equal (Davis, Crawford, & Sebrechts, 1999). Perhaps one solution is a broader understanding of how women and men learn, acknowledging the complexity of learning in each sex and the reality that there are no learning styles specific to men or women but rather patterns and perspectives that seem to fit one better than the other but may overlap. This greater understanding and willingness to explore the most effective pedagogies for women and men seem to present the greatest likelihood of success in the classroom.

Campuses still struggle with sexual harassment. While progress has been made there still appears to be confusion over definitions, and little attention is paid to the sexual harassment of men (Dziech & Hawkins, 1998). Efforts to define hostile environments as a tool for the identification and elimination of sexual discrimination have produced a backlash in the name of free speech (Cudd, 2002). The explosion of technologies on campuses has been felt in this area; e-mail has become a tool for sexual harassment and stalking (Harmon, 2001). Social networking sites, text messaging, and other forms of communication via the Internet provide forums for harassment that have yet to be effectively dealt with legally or through policy development. These different modes of communication carry with them different forms of expression, different cues, and different policy implications. It requires those responsible for a response to think differently about this type of harassment (Dalaimo, 1997; Geach & Haralambous, 2009). As sex roles have evolved beyond the traditional, heterosexual women run up against the conflicts inherent in the interplay between sexuality and power—what is exploitation and harassment versus sexuality and desire? They struggle with their own sexuality and desire while contemplating the fine line dividing harassment from desired and mutual expressions of this sexuality and desire (Phillips, 2000; Roiphe, 2001).

Sexual assault, ranging from unwanted touching to rape (by acquaintances and strangers), is a continuing issue on campuses. Male rape is also being acknowledged as a significant problem (King, 1992, Scarce, 2000). While undesired sexual behavior is the symptom, the quest for power and control and gender role stereotyping of both genders are the root causes of sexual harassment and sexual assault. Compounding the problem is a lack of agreement and consistent understanding of what constitutes rape among female and male students (Clark & Carroll, 2008).

The book *Just Sex: Students Rewrite the Rules on Sex, Violence, Activism, and Equality* (Gold & Villari, 2000) details the activist movements made over the past three decades at understanding, naming, constructing, and deconstructing meaning regarding gender, sex, and sexual assault. Educators argue that teaching students about sexual assault in the context of gender allows them to think critically about culture, solve problems in context, and be better equipped to see how behaviors fit into the larger picture (Kilmartin & Berkowitz, 2005). According to the current state of student voices in this conversation, it is interesting to see the progress made toward the understanding that violence against women does not have to be some sort of accepted rite of passage for women and men students. Gender roles for members of both sexes are being challenged and myths are being taken apart in an effort to create environments consistent with the values and norms of young adults born and raised after the dramatic social changes brought by the movements of the 1960s and early 1970s. These are students who have always lived in a society that at least on some level argued for equality even when what they saw and experienced may have been inconsistent with that message.

Copenhaver, Lash, and Eisler (2000) investigated the combination of men strongly committed to traditional male roles and alcohol use and abuse. This study found that when in situations of perceived threat to their masculinity such men often turn to substance abuse as a means to managing insecurities. Further, in such cases they were more likely to have engaged in abusive behavior with intimate female partners. Campus administrators repeatedly link sexual assault and similar crimes with the abuse of alcohol and other substances, anecdotal data that are supported by research (Krebs, Lindquist, Warner, Fisher, & Martin, 2009; Marchell & Cummings 2001;

Ullman, Karabatsos, & Koss, 1999). Alcohol abuse by men and women is problematic, with one study finding that women who binge drink underestimate their risk of sexual assault (McCauley & Calhoun, 2008). A greater prevalence of casual sex adds further complexity to the issue and greater ambiguity over how best to address these issues educationally (Littleton, Tabernick, Canales, & Backstrom, 2009).

When looking at the issue of sexual assault from a change perspective and from the perspective of evolution of understanding and response, the presence of men as change agents becomes apparent. Within the movement to not only stop sexual assault but to change societal structure, men are working with women and other men through education, training, and social activism. There is evidence of a growing understanding of the positive, proactive role men can play in changing the culture that allows sexual assault and in some ways promotes it (Montagna, 2000). Conversely, other authors write of male culture that still allows sexual assault as a response to the powerlessness many men feel in relation to women. Additionally, this same culture silences those men who might speak against or stop the actions of others (Kimmel, 2008; Messner, 1997).

The existence of these issues on campuses underscores the fact that while women are present in large numbers, their presence is still unacceptable to many. College and university campuses are microcosms of the larger society. In the United States sexual assault and sexual harassment remain significant societal issues. That being said, it is not surprising that higher education continues to mirror the larger society through the presence of these crimes. Student affairs professionals are often the staff called on to address these problems and issues. While reactive measures address negative behaviors and the consequences, proactive responses often cause the greatest change. Sexual assault; sexual harassment; drugs, alcohol, and other abused substances; growing mental health concerns; and eating disorders are some of the issues compelling student affairs professionals to gain a greater understanding of the problems and their effects on students. Educational program design, implementation, and assessment play an ever-stronger role in divisions of student affairs as staff members continue to search for effective responses to these problems.

Current Research, Trends, Issues Affecting the Cultural Group

The work of many theorists, such as Chickering and Reisser (1993), Kohlberg (1984), and Perry (1970), often studied as part of a student development curriculum, was based on primarily male and often White samples, generalized to the entire population. In part, as a reaction to the reality that such generalizations often led to defining women's development as deficient, Carol Gilligan's (1982) methodology sought to paint a more complete picture. The theory presented in her work, *In a Different Voice*, relied on a sample of women engaged in the process of making morally demanding decisions in real-life settings. From her findings she proposed a theory of women's moral development. Belenky, Clinchy, Goldberger, and Tarule (1986) also sought greater understanding in their study of the intellectual development of women, *Women's Ways of Knowing*. The work of these theorists stands with that of a number of researchers studying women. Goldberger, Tarule, Clinchy, and Belenky (1996) believe gender to be a major category playing a role in the choices made by women in all cultures and communities.

Feminist research, of which these theories are examples, traces its roots to the contemporary women's movement and its manifestation on college campuses. While women's rights activists were involved in struggles for affirmative action, equal pay, and similar issues, women's liberation activists focused in part on the higher education curriculum. This work led to the beginnings of women's studies as an academic field of study and feminist scholarship as a method of knowledge creation and dissemination. Early goals included consciousness-raising (of students and faculty), compensatory courses to add women to a variety of disciplines, creating a mass of research about women, and changing the curriculum to reflect all of humanity (Howe, 1984).

This research also grew from a desire to understand women and women's experiences as separate from the experiences of men rather than always in connection to men. This research is also reflective of the reality that women's learning takes place in a wide variety of contexts, public, private, formal, informal, and in settings intimate and isolating (Hayes, 2000). Howe (1984) describes how it is feasible to "study cohorts of half the human race in their own contexts and their own terms, without reference to the other half" (p. 277). She argues that only after doing this can one effectively conduct comparative studies involving women and men. It is ironic that while Howe writes eloquently and effectively of the need to separate women to study them in their own context, the strongest themes among the women who did separate women to study them in their own contexts are connectedness and relationship (Gilligan, 1982).

Carol Gilligan

Carol Gilligan, Harvard University colleague of Erik Erikson and Lawrence Kohlberg, pioneered the exploration of how girls and women come to understand and make meaning of their experiences. Studying and writing about understandings and articulations of rights, care, and justice, Gilligan explores how children learn to differentiate themselves from primary caregivers, to understand what it means to be female and male, and, ultimately, how this is manifested in decisions made regarding moral dilemmas (Gilligan, 1982; Gilligan & Attanucci, 1988). Gilligan's theory was initially detailed in *In a Different Voice*. While studying women she learned about a theme, a voice, rather than about gender. She makes no claims that the voice she writes of is solely female.

Gilligan (1982) presents a model based on research conducted with women confronted with real-life moral dilemmas. Members of her ethnically and socioeconomically diverse sample of 29 women, aged 15–33, were referred by abortion and pregnancy counseling services. Gilligan's results yielded a model of women's meaning-making structures, how women make decisions on moral questions. Data gathered in Gilligan's interviews with these women revealed three moral perspectives with two transitions, the development of which was measured by the way women used moral language such as *should, ought, good, bad*, and the way participants thought about their behavior. Changes in their thinking and judgments about their behaviors were also studied.

Applications of the theory are seen in a variety of places in the lives of students, as illustrated by relevant literature. One example is in the impact of family obligations on decision making by young women as they make the transition to college. This study was grounded in ecological systems theory, which examines differences among women from a variety of ethnicities (Sy & Brittian, 2008). The study found that Latina students were more likely than Asian American or European American students to be influenced in choices about where to live and how many hours to work either by perceptions of the need to fulfill family obligations or demands that they do so. This example illustrates Gilligan's (1982) finding that women make decisions based on how they make meaning within the context of their relationships. For the women in this developmental position, the perception of familial obligation, perceived or real, frames how they make meaning and their subsequent choices.

Women's Ways of Knowing

Belenky et al. (1986), like Gilligan (1982), do not claim a theory describing women but rather a theory developed as a result of the study of women, which may apply to women or men. In a volume of essays inspired by *Women's Ways of Knowing* (Belenky et al.) 10 years after its publication, Goldberger, Tarule, Clinchy, and Belenky (1996) argue that there has been a significant misunderstanding and criticism of their work as pertaining only to women. Their decision to study only women reflected a desire to more clearly understand women's perspectives, so often distorted by "masculinist psychology" (p. 7). The study and theory presented in *Women's Ways of Knowing* (Belenky et al.) is about how women come to know, how they construct knowledge, and thus are able to order their own sense of the world. It describes cognitive-structural development. Interestingly, one subsequent quantitative study (Ryan & David, 2003) challenging the presence of gender-related knowing styles found these styles to be more dependent on social context than gender.

Belenky et al. (1986) draw on the work of William Perry (1970),whose book *Forms of Intellectual and Ethical Development in the College Years* provided a developmental framework for understanding cognitive and moral meaning making. Belenky et al. designed their study to allow the clarity of women's voices to be heard. Research subjects were recruited from a variety of places, formal and more informal, where the authors judged education took place. This selection was based on their belief that women often learn how to think outside the boundaries of formal educational settings.

After analysis of extensive interviews conducted with 135 women, their perspectives were grouped into five epistemological categories. Belenky et al. (1986) offer a number of qualifiers including the understanding that these are not fixed, universal categories; they are abstract categories and as such do not completely convey the complexities in all women's ways of thinking; these are not specific only to women; and others could understand the data differently and draw different conclusions. The five categories are silence, received knowledge, subjective knowledge, procedural knowledge, and constructed knowledge. The authors also caution that the small number of subjects falling into the silence perspective makes their finding regarding this category especially preliminary, underscoring their belief in the necessity of further research.

Marcia Baxter Magolda

Marcia Baxter Magolda's (1992) cognitive-structural theory of gender-related patterns in intellectual development is outlined in *Knowing and Reasoning in College*. Evolving from extensive research related to William Perry's (1970) theory of intellectual and moral reasoning, Baxter Magolda describes reasoning patterns that emerged from her analysis of a large number of student interviews related to how they come to know in college. Her own evolution in the process of interpreting the students' stories is an especially interesting example of the process of knowledge creation. In this process, Baxter Magolda gradually realizes that she has to remain aware that while the stories are the students', the understanding she draws from them is a combination of their stories and her interpretation of them. Their truth is told through her understanding of it. She also writes about her shift from seeing the stories from the perspective of relevant, existing literature to viewing them from the frames of reference of their authors.

Baxter Magolda (1992) outlines four reasoning patterns, ways of knowing, of justifying thoughts, used by women and men. A primary finding of this study and a guiding assumption of the author is that these patterns of reasoning are associated with gender, but they are not determined by gender. Similar to the theories presented by Carol Gilligan (1982) and Belenky et al. (1986), these are not structures assigning a place to women and men based on their sex. Women and men tend to be present in greater numbers in some patterns and tend to prefer the use of some patterns rather than others. Gender differences are seen in three of the four patterns presented in this study. Another crucial assumption guiding Baxter Magolda is that these patterns are fluid social constructions. As a result, students are not fixed in the ways in which they know. Because they are constructing these patterns, the ways they are used can change given circumstances, context, or varying experiences. Baxter Magolda stresses that these are continuums rather than dichotomies.

At the center of Baxter Magolda's (1992) *Knowing and Reasoning in College* is the Epistemological Reflection Model. It comprises four ways of knowing, and the gender-related patterns of knowing are present in three of these. The four ways of knowing include absolute knowing, transitional knowing, independent knowing, and contextual knowing. Inherent in each are the domains of evaluation, nature of knowledge, and the roles of learner, peer, and instructor (Baxter Magolda).

The models presented in *Women's Ways of Knowing* (Belenky et al., 1986) and *Knowing and Reasoning in College* (Baxter Magolda, 1992) address epistemology as well as its relationship to gender. This topic, and the models outlined here, served as the catalyst for a variety of studies relevant to students. Brownlee's (2001) research with female and male preservice teacher education students draws empirical connections between Perry (1970), Belenky et al., and Baxter Magolda. Further, it provides useful ideas for any educator who wants to engage with students on complex, big ideas, challenging not only the content of their thinking but the structure and sophistication of it as well. In an investigation of women returning to the study of mathematics, the models developed by Belenky et al. and Baxter Magolda were integrated. Study results supported this integration and provided a possible structure for teaching in a way that is not only effective but works to build self-confidence in a collaborative environment (Brew, 2001). While these examples are classroom specific their implications for learning have applicability far beyond that setting.

Womanist Identity

There is a natural progression for women, and for men studying women, from identification and understanding of oppression to studying the addition of women to studying the construct of gender and all it implies. This progression of thought and study has also led to the study of women's identity development. Often associated with Black identity development, this can be a confusing theoretical area. Misunderstandings occur often on the distinctions and differences among feminism, Black feminism, African feminism, African womanism, and Walker's term *womanist*, which denotes a black feminist or woman of color feminist (Alexander-Floyd & Simien, 2006). In this chapter the discussion relates to womanist identity development as articulated by Helms and detailed in Ossana, Helms, and Leonard (1992).

According to Watt (2006), Helms structures her model in a fashion similar to Cross's model of racial identity development, outlining four stages: womanist preencounter, encounter, immersion-emersion, and internalization). In the preencounter stage, women believe the societal notions of gender that hold men in greater esteem and women in positions lower than men's. As a result of some encounter that challenges these ideas, women begin to question societal norms and see alternative views of womanhood in the encounter stage. As is true in Cross's model, immersion-emersion is characterized by a strong identification with the group and a very positive view of self. Finally, in internalization, the positive sense of self based on experiences with other women and self-determined ideals is incorporated into the identity (Watt). This model is similar to the Downing and Roush model (as described in Boisnier, 2003) of feminist identity development, which was also heavily influenced by Cross. However, it is important to note one crucial difference. The Downing and Roush model ultimately leads to a feminist identity. Helms's model of womanist identity development allows for a more personal internalized identity. It could be feminist, but it could as easily be anything that serves as a meaningful definition of womanhood for any woman moving through Helms's stages This is one reason Helms's model is often more descriptive of the experiences of African American women (Boisnier, 2003).

Best Practices to Assist This Cultural Group

A survey of websites devoted to gender-related programs reveals extensive programmatic efforts on behalf of women at campuses across the country. Far less prevalent are programs designed to address men's issues. The content of these pages also highlights the variety of issues students encounter as they pursue higher education. Programs, organizations, support groups, and referral information in this section cover many topics one would expect from women's or women's and men's centers, such as sexual assault, disordered eating, single parenthood, and questioning sexuality. The scope of many centers include other topics, including the needs of women reentering college, White women against racism, aging parents, body acceptance, self-acceptance, and support for those experiencing anxiety.

Links to college and university websites, blogs, and social networking site profiles and groups relevant to women's centers and women's and men's centers throughout the United States can be found at http://www.nwsa.org/centers/socialwebsites.php. This resource is one component of the National Women's Studies Association (http://www.nwsa.org), dedicated to leadership in the fields of women's and gender studies. While the list on this site is not exhaustive and addresses few men's centers, it is useful. Although still limited, there are resources online that specifically address men's issues, masculinities, and men's studies. However, growth is evident as seen through the Men's Studies Press (http://www.mensstudies.com/home/main.mpx), the American Men's Studies Association (http://www.mensstudies.org/, and websites such as the first national conference for campus programs related to gender equity and antiviolence groups (http://www1.csbsju.edu/menscenter/projects/equality.htm). These sites also serve as resource centers and information clearinghouses.

The following programs illustrate the instructive nature of material for student affairs professionals looking for examples in working with women and men on campus. These include the University of Michigan's Center for the Education of Women, the New Leadership Program at Rutgers University, the Men's Resource Center at Lakeland Community College in Ohio, the Men's Health Clinic at the College of William and Mary, and the Men's Center for Leadership and Service at the College of Saint Benedict and Saint John's University.

The Center for the Education of Women at the University of Michigan (http://www.cew.umich.edu/index.htm) is one of the oldest university women's centers in the United States. Founded in 1964 its mission includes research, publication, advocacy and policy development, counseling and internships, as well as extensive programming. The center focuses on undergraduate women, faculty and staff women, community women, and women with special needs such as graduate students who are single parents. Separate from this center, the University of Michigan also sponsors and supports the Women in Science and Engineering Residence Program (http://www.lsa.u mich.edu/wiserp) that provides a mechanism for women from similar disciplines to live together and learn from each other with additional support provided by the institution. These programs are especially helpful for women in nontraditional majors.

The goal of an initiative from the Center for American Women and Politics at Rutgers University (http://www.cawp.rutgers.edu/NEWLead ership/), titled National Education for Women's Leadership (NEW Leadership), is "to educate and empower the next generation of women leaders." This three-part program includes the residential institute, NEW Leadership, a training institute, and an educational website. NEW Leadership includes a summer, weeklong residential program for college women combined with periodic daylong workshops and ongoing leadership projects or experiences during the academic year. The training institute uses the program at Rutgers as a model to train other universities in establishing similar programs as well as providing seed grants to assist in these efforts. The eventual outcome will be the creation of college women's leadership programs in all regions of the country.

Lakeland Community College in Ohio created the Men's Resource Center (http://www.lakelandcc.edu/comeduc/men/) in 1996 as a tool to meet the educational needs of men, including the recruitment and retention of men, and especially the needs of those who are thinking about or are in midlife or career transitions. Located near Cleveland, this institution fills the need for a male-focused counterpart to the Women's Center. The programs' themes are similar to what a women's center would offer, such as programs on jobs and career development, parenting, health issues, and entry or reentry of older adults into a higher education environment. It also provides referrals and connections to a variety of external agencies. This is all carried out in the context of focusing on men themselves rather than on men in the context of their relationship to women.

The Student Health Center at the College of William and Mary (http://www.wm.edu/offices/healthcenter/services/menshealth/index.php) offers a Men's Health Clinic, which is a well-researched, comprehensive program that seeks to combat the effects of gender stereotypes that potentially lead men to neglect and disregard good health and good health practices. The website links to descriptions of the data supporting the need for the program and provides extensive information related to men's health.

Finally, the Men's Center for Leadership and Service at the College of Saint Benedict and Saint John's University (http://www1.csbsju.edu/menscenter/) focuses on men as they search for a greater understanding of their masculinity in a safe and respectful environment that also encourages women to join the conversation as men come to a greater awareness of themselves as men. This center is guided in its mission of seeking a greater understanding of patriarchy to "create a more enlightened concept of manhood." Founded in 2001 as the first men's center on a liberal arts campus, its history is detailed in Kellom and Raverty (2006).

Recommendations, Implications, Future Trends Affecting This Cultural Group

While great strides have been made generally in higher education in the full integration of women into the academy, the academy has not changed as drastically as one would expect. Women's studies and the new scholarship relative to women have gained space for women at colleges and universities but have failed to change the structure of higher education to be more responsive to the differences they highlight (Stromquist, 2001). The time for studying women as additive to men has passed. The knowledge gained from the multitude of scholarship on women must transform what we know and how we think. Women constitute the majority of college students at the undergraduate level and earn an increasingly significant number of the degrees conferred at nearly all other levels of graduate and professional education (*Chronicle of Higher Education,* 2010). The next logical stage of growth needs to be the exploration of how higher education will be further transformed. How do academic programs evolve to take into account the results of the past 30 plus years of research? How do such programs make sense of what is commonly taught when the context has been altered by additional knowledge that may confront and contradict what has commonly been considered truth? How can higher education be most responsive to the needs of women and men? When placed in the context of a student body that is older and has numerous competing claims, what does the academy of the future look like? How does it maintain its relevance in the lives of students? How are student services structured to be of most service to students?

Surveying the websites of programs for women on college campuses reveals that many of them have been long out of date with a clear lack of funding or adequate resources given the size of their campuses and the presence of women students. This finding leads one to believe there is little interest in or support for women's programs, and it also reveals a sense of nonchalance—that the time has passed for feminism and social justice activity, that the struggle is irrelevant. It would be tempting to accept that conclusion in the face of a general societal notion that women have achieved some acceptable level of equality that is really enough. However, when viewing websites about programs like the ones described in the best practices section of this chapter, the reality of a different level of work is apparent. The programs described—simple, complex, elegant, and straightforward—are indicative that new needs are being met in ways that make sense in their own contexts. The University of Michigan is a strong research institution; its Center for the Study of Women in Education is reflective of that and of its commitment to serving all constituents. Lakeland Community College has found a way to reach a male audience with effective, informative information. Rutgers University developed a strong program and then responded to the needs of others by making it available in a variety of ways. William and Mary found a proactive, sound educational practice to meet the health needs of the women and men on its campus. The program at Saint John's University brings men and women students together to study gender, masculinity, and the roles these play in the lives of students in a way that is congruent with the Catholic tradition of that institution.

Higher education has moved beyond the days of "add women and stir." We are beyond the surface issues, beyond the glaring omissions and the unfathomable levels of sexism. We are in perhaps a more difficult place. We have made progress, and it becomes easy to rest on our accomplishments and grow complacent. We are in a place of far greater subtlety. Now is not the time to stop. Now is the time to understand what the lessons of the past 30 plus years mean to a generation of students who have grown up in a world forever different because of social movements that forced us to examine who we are, what we know, and why we believe what we do. Now is the time for reordering and discovering new meanings, structures, and ways of being and knowing that involve the interplay between men and women living in the same world, learning in the same academy, and looking toward the same future.

Discussion Questions

1. What does it mean to say that gender is a social construction? How do you see that actualized in your environment?
2. Why is it important to study gender as a construct or as a way we make meaning about our environment, who we are, and what we know?
3. Women are currently the majority of undergraduate students enrolled in postsecondary education. As a group they also have a history of being marginalized and at times excluded from educational opportunities. How would you characterize the status of women today? Give examples. Why do you think this way?
4. Which of the developmental theories outlined in this chapter seem the most relevant as you think about the students you work with? Why?
5. What aspect of the development of male and female students do you think should be studied but hasn't been?
6. What do you think of the theories that describe developmental differences between women and men? Do you think they're accurate, or have they overstated the case of difference? Why or why not?
7. As you think about the curriculum of colleges and universities several decades after the beginning of women's studies, do you think there's still a need for courses focused on women and gender? Is there a need for men's studies? Why or why not?
8. Why do you think campuses still have problems with sexual assault and sexual harassment? How have the technologies we've all come to depend on played a role in these issues?

References

Alexander-Floyd, N. G., & Simien, E. M. (2006). Revisiting "What's in a name?"- *Frontiers, 27*(1), 67–89.

Altbach, P. G. (2005). Harsh realities: The professorate faces a new century. In P. G. Altbach, R. O. Berdahl, & P. J. Gumport (Eds.), *American higher education in the twenty-first century: Social, political, and economic challenges* (2nd ed., pp. 287–314). Baltimore: Johns Hopkins University Press.

Arlton, D., Lewellen, A., & Grissett, B. (1999). Social systems barriers of women in academia: A review of historical and current issues. In M. McCoy & J. Di-Georgio-Lutz (Eds.), *The woman-centered university: Interdisciplinary perspectives* (pp. 61–70). Lanham, MD: University Press of America.

Arnot, M. (2002). *Reproducing gender? Essays on educational theory and feminist politics.* London: Routledge-Falmer.

Bannon, I., & Correia, M. C. (Eds.). (2006). *The other half of gender: Men's issues in development.* Washington, DC: World Bank.

Bastedo, M. N. (2005). Curriculum in higher education: The historical roots of contemporary issues. In P. G. Altbach, R. O. Berdahl, & P. J. Gumport (Eds.), *American higher education in the twenty-first century: Social, political, and economic challenges* (2nd ed., pp. 462–485). Baltimore: Johns Hopkins University Press.

Baxter Magolda, M. B. (1992). *Knowing and reasoning in college: Gender-related patterns in students' intellectual development.* San Francisco: Jossey-Bass.

Belenky, M. F., Clinchy, B. M., Goldberger, N. R., & Tarule, J. M. (1986). *Women's ways of knowing: The development of self, voice, and mind.* New York: Basic.

Bell, S., Morrow, M., & Tastsoglou, E. (1999). Teaching in environments of resistance: Toward a critical, feminist, and antiracist pedagogy. In M. Mayberry & E. C. Rose (Eds.), *Meeting the challenge: Innovative feminist pedagogies in action* (pp. 23–46). New York: Routledge.

Bledstein, B. J. (1976). *The culture of professionalism: The middle class and the development of higher education in America.* New York: Norton.

Bloom, A. D. (1987). *The closing of the American mind.* New York: Simon & Schuster.

Boisnier, A. D. (2003). Race and women's identity development: Distinguishing among Black and White women. *Sex Roles, 49,* 211–218.

Bozin, M. A., & Yoder, J. D. (2008). Social status, not gender alone, is implicated in different reactions by women and men to social ostracism. *Sex Roles, 58,* 713–720.

Brew, C. (2001). Women, mathematics and epistemology: An integrated framework. *International Journal of Inclusive Education, 5*(1), 15–32.

Brownlee, J. (2001). Epistemological beliefs in pre-service teacher education students. *Higher Education Research & Development, 20*(3), 281–291.

Brubacher, J. S., & Rudy, W. (1997). *Higher education in transition: A history of American colleges and universities* (4th ed.). New Brunswick, NJ: Transaction.

Bryant, A. N. (2003). Changes in attitudes toward women's roles: Predicting gender-role traditionalism among college students. *Sex Roles, 48,* 131–142.

Carse, A. L., & DeBruin, D. A. (2002). Transforming resistance: Shifting the burden of proof in the feminist classroom. In A. M. Superson & A. E. Cudd (Eds.),

Theorizing backlash: Philosophical reflections on the resistance to feminism (pp. 181–199). Lanham, MD: Rowman & Littlefield.

Chickering, A. W, & Reisser, L. (1993). *Education and identity* (2nd ed.). San Francisco: Jossey-Bass.

Chodorow, N. J. (1995). Gender as a personal and cultural construction. *Signs: Journal of Women in Culture and Society, 20*(3), 516–544.

Chronicle of Higher Education. (2008). Characteristics of senior college administrators by type of institution, 2007. Retrieved from http://chronicle.com/article/Characteristics-of-Senior/23135

Chronicle of Higher Education. (2009). Number of full-time faculty members by sex, rank, and racial and ethnic group, fall 2007. Retrieved from http://chronicle.com/article/Number-of-Full-Time-Faculty/47992

Chronicle of Higher Education. (2010). Almanac of higher education: Degrees conferred by racial and ethnic group, 2007–8. Retrieved from http://chronicle.com/article/Degrees-Conferred-by-Racial/124006

Clark, M. D., & Carroll, M. H. (2008). Acquaintance rape scripts of women and men: Similarities and differences. *Sex Roles, 58,* 616–625.

Cohen, A. M. (1998). *The shaping of American higher education: Emergence and growth of the contemporary system.* San Francisco: Jossey-Bass.

Copenhaver, M. M., Lash, S. J., & Eisler, R. M. (2000). Masculine gender-role stress, anger, and male intimate abusiveness: Implications for men's relationships. *Sex Roles, 42*(5–6), 405–414.

Cudd, A. E. (2002). When sexual harassment is protected speech: Facing the forces of backlash in academe. In A. M. Superson & A. E. Cudd (Eds.), *Theorizing backlash: Philosophical reflections on the resistance to feminism* (pp. 217–243). Lanham, MD: Rowman & Littlefield.

Dalaimo, D. M. (1997). Electronic sexual harassment. In B. R. Sandler & R. J. Shoop (Eds.), *Sexual harassment on campus: A guide for administrators, faculty and students* (pp. 85–103). Boston: Allyn & Bacon.

Davis, S. N., Crawford, M., & Sebrechts, J. (Eds.). (1999). *Coming into her own: Educational success in girls and women.* San Francisco: Jossey-Bass.

Devor, H. (2002). Becoming members of society: Learning the social meanings of gender. In N. P. McKee & L. Stone (Eds.), *Readings in gender and culture in America* (pp. 26–47). Upper Saddle River, NJ: Prentice Hall.

Drew, T. L., & Work, G. G. (1998). Gender-based differences in perception of experiences in higher education. *Journal of Higher Education, 69*(5), 542–555.

D'Souza, D. (1991). *Illiberal education: The politics of race and sex on campus.* New York: Free Press.

Dunn, M. S. (1993). *Separation and integration: Women at the Ohio State University 1960–1975.* Unpublished doctoral dissertation, Ohio State University, Columbus.

Dziech, B. W., & Hawkins, M. W. (1998). *Sexual harassment in higher education: Reflections and new perspectives.* New York: Garland.

Ferguson, A. (1988). Woman's moral voice: Superior, inferior, or just different? In J. M. Faragher & F. Howe (Eds.), *Women and higher education in American history: Essays from the Mount Holyoke College sesquicentennial symposia* (pp. 183–197). New York: Norton.

Geach, N., & Haralambous, N. (2009). Regulating harassment: Is the law fit for the social networking age? *Journal of Criminal Law, 73,* 241–257.

Gilligan, C. (1982). *In a different voice.* Cambridge, MA: Harvard University Press.

Gilligan, C., & Attanucci, J. (1988). Two moral orientations. In C. Gilligan, J. V. Ward & J. M. Taylor (Eds.), *Mapping the moral domain: A contribution of women's thinking to psychological theory and education* (pp. 73–86). Cambridge, MA: Center for the Study of Gender, Education and Human Development, Harvard University Graduate School of Education.

Gold, J., & Villari, S. (Eds.). (2000). *Just sex: Students rewrite the rules on sex, violence, activism, and equality.* Lanham, MD: Rowman & Littlefield.

Goldberger, N., Tarule, J., Clinchy, B., & Belenky, M. (Eds.). (1996). *Knowledge, difference and power: Essays inspired by women's ways of knowing.* New York: Basic.

Gordon, L. D. (1997). From seminary to university: An overview of women's higher education, 1870–1920. In L. F. Goodchild & H. S. Wechsler (Eds.), *ASHE reader series on the history of higher education* (2nd ed., pp. 473–498). Old Tappan, NJ: Pearson Custom Publishing.

Goree, C. T. (1993). *Steps toward redefinition: Coeducation at Mississippi State College, 1930–1945.* Unpublished doctoral dissertation, Mississippi State University, Mississippi State.

Gruber, C. S. (1997). Backdrop. In L. F. Goodchild & H. S. Wechsler (Eds.), *ASHE reader series on the history of higher education* (2nd ed., pp. 203–221).. Old Tappan, NJ: Pearson Custom Publishing.

Harmon, A. (2001). Caltech student's expulsion over content of e-mail raises concerns. In L. LeMoncheck & J. P. Sterba (Eds.), *Sexual harassment: Issues and answers* (pp. 124–127). New York: Oxford University Press.

Harrison, W. C. (2006). The shadow and the substance: The sex/gender debate. In K. Davis, M. Evans, & J. Lorber (Eds.), *Handbook of gender and women's studies* (pp. 35–52). Thousand Oaks, CA: Sage.

Hayes, E. (2000). Creating knowledge about women's learning. In E. Hayes & D. D. Flannery (Eds.), *Women as learners: The significance of gender in adult learning* (pp. 217–245). San Francisco: Jossey-Bass.

Hayes, E., & Flannery, D. D. (Eds.). (2000). *Women as learners: The significance of gender in adult learning.* San Francisco: Jossey-Bass.

Hearn, J., & Kimmel, M. S. (2006). Changing studies on men and masculinities. In K. Davis, M. Evan, & J. Lorber (Eds.), *Handbook of gender and women's studies* (pp. 53–70). London: Sage.

Hemmings, C. (2006). The life and times of academic feminism. In K. Davis, M. Evan, & J. Lorber (Eds.), *Handbook of gender and women's studies* (pp. 13–34). London: Sage.

Howe, F. (1984). *Myths of coeducation: Selected essays.* Bloomington: Indiana University Press.

Jencks, C., & Riesman, D. (1968). *The academic revolution.* Garden City, NY: Doubleday.

Johnson, E. L. (1997). Misconceptions about the early land-grant colleges. In L. F. Goodchild & H. S. Wechsler (Eds.), *ASHE reader series on the history of higher education* (2nd ed., pp. 222–233). Old Tappen, NJ: Pearson Custom Publishing.

Kellom, G. E., & Raverty, A. (2006). Introduction: The center for men's leadership and service at Saint John's University. *The Journal of Men's Studies, 14,* 265–268.

Kerber, L. K. (1980). *Women of the republic: Intellect and ideology in revolutionary America.* Chapel Hill: University of North Carolina Press.

Kilmartin, C., & Berkowitz, A. D. (2005). *Sexual assault in context: Teaching college men about gender.* Mahwah, NJ: Erlbaum.

Kimmel, M. (2008). *Guyland: The perilous world where boys become men.* New York: HarperCollins.

King, M. B. (1992). Male sexual assault in the community. In G. C. Mezey & M. B. King (Eds.), *Male victims of sexual assault* (pp. 1–12). Oxford, UK: Oxford University Press.

Kohlberg, L. (1984). *Essays on moral development: Vol. 2. The psychology of moral development.* San Francisco: Harper & Row.

Krebs, C. P., Lindquist, C. H., Warner, T. D., Fisher, B. S., & Martin, S. L. (2009). College women's experiences with physically forced, alcohol- or other drug-enabled, and drug-facilitated sexual assault before and since entering college. *Journal of American College Health, 57,* 639–649.

Levine, S. (1995). *Degrees of equality: The American Association of University Women and the challenge of twentieth-century feminism.* Philadelphia: Temple University Press.

Littleton, H., Tabernick, H., Canales, E., & Backstrom, T. (2009). Risky situation or harmless fun? A qualitative examination of college women's bad hook-up and rape scripts. *Sex Roles, 60,* 793–804.

Lorber, J. (1994). *Paradoxes of gender.* New Haven, CT: Yale University Press.

Maher, F. A., & Tetreault, M. K. T. (1994). *The feminist classroom.* New York: Basic Books.

Maher, F. A., & Tetreault, M. K. T. (2001). *The feminist classroom: Dynamics of gender, race, and privilege.* Lanham, MD: Rowman & Littlefield.

Marcell, T., & Cummings, N. (2001). Alcohol and sexual violence among college students. In A. J. Ottens & K. Hotelling (Eds.), *Sexual violence on campus: Policies, programs, and perspectives* (pp. 30–52). New York: Springer.

Martin, J. R. (2000). *Coming of age in academe: Rekindling women's hope and reforming the academy.* New York: Routledge.

Mayberry, M., & Rose, E. C. (Eds.). (1999). *Meeting the challenge: Innovative feminist pedagogies in action.* New York: Routledge.

McCauley, J. L., & Calhoun, K. S. (2008). Faulty perceptions? The impact of binge drinking history on college women's perceived rape resistance efficacy. *Addictive Behaviors, 33,* 1540–1545.

Messner, M. A. (1997). *Politics of masculinities: Men in movements.* Thousand Oaks, CA: Sage.

Montagna, S. (2000). Men-only spaces as effective sites for education and transformation in the battle to end sexual assault. In J. Gold & S. Villari (Eds.), *Just sex: Students rewrite the rules on sex, violence, activism, and equality* (pp. 181–188). Lanham, MD: Rowman & Littlefield.

Morris, L. K., & Daniel, L. G. (2008). Perceptions of a chilly climate: Differences in traditional and non-traditional majors for women. *Research in Higher Education, 49,* 256–273.

Ossana, S. H., Helms, J. E., & Leonard M. M. (1992). Do "womanist" identity attitudes influence college women's self-esteem and perceptions of environmental bias? *Journal of Counseling and Development, 70*(3), 402–408.

Patai, D. (2008). *What price utopia? Essays on ideological policing, feminism, and academic affairs.* Lanham, MD: Rowman & Littlefield.

Patai, D., & Koertge, N. (2003). *Professing feminism: Education and indoctrination in women's studies.* Lanham, MD: Lexington Books.

Perry, W. G., Jr. (1970). *Forms of intellectual development in the college years: A scheme.* New York: Holt, Rinehart and Winston.

Phillips, L. M. (2000). *Flirting with danger: Young women's reflections on sexuality and domination.* New York: New York University Press.

Pryzgoda, J., & Chrisler, J. C. (2000). Definitions of gender and sex: The subtleties of meaning. *Sex Roles, 43*(7–8), 553–569.

Roiphe, K. (2001). Reckless eyeballing: Sexual harassment on campus. In L. LeMoncheck & J. P. Sterba (Eds.), *Sexual harassment: Issues and answers* (pp. 249–259). New York: Oxford University Press.

Rosenberg, R. (1982). *Beyond separate spheres: Intellectual roots of modern feminism.* New Haven, CT: Yale University Press.

Rosenberg, R. (1992). *Divided lives: American women in the twentieth century.* New York: Hill and Wang.

Rudolph, F. (1990). *The American college and university: A history.* Athens: University of Georgia Press.

Rupp, L. J., & Taylor, V. (1987). *Survival in the doldrums: The American women's rights movement, 1945 to the 1960s.* New York: Oxford University Press.

Ryan, M. K., & David, B. (2003). Gender differences in ways of knowing: The context dependence of the attitudes toward thinking and learning survey. *Sex Roles, 49*(11–12), 693–699.

Sandler, B. R., & Hall, R. (1986). *The campus climate revisited: Chilly for women faculty, administrators and graduate students.* Washington, DC: Association of American Colleges and Universities.

Scarce, M. (2000). Male-on-male rape. In J. Gold & S. Villari (Eds.), *Just sex: Students rewrite the rules on sex, violence, activism, and equality* (pp. 39–46). Lanham, MD: Rowman & Littlefield.

Solomon, B. M. (1985). *In the company of educated women: A history of women and higher education in America.* New Haven, CT: Yale University Press.

Stake, J. E. (2006). Pedagogy and student change in the women's and gender studies classroom. *Gender and Education, 18,* 199–212.

Stromquist, N. P. (2001). Gender studies: A global perspective of their evolution contribution, and challenges to comparative higher education. *Higher Education, 41*(4), 373–387.

Superson, A. M., & Cudd, A. E. (Eds.), (2002). *Theorizing backlash: Philosophical reflections on the resistance to feminism.* Lanham, MD: Rowman & Littlefield.

Sy, S. R., & Brittian, A. (2008). The impact of family obligations on young women's decisions during the transition to college: A comparison of Latina, European American, and Asian American students. *Sex Roles, 58,* 729–737.

Thelin, J. R. (2004). *A history of American higher education.* Baltimore: Johns Hopkins University Press.

Tisdell, E. J. (2000). Feminist pedagogies. In E. Hayes & D. D. Flannery (Eds.), *Women as learners: The significance of gender in adult learning* (pp. 155–183). San Francisco: Jossey-Bass.

Tyack, D., & Hansot, E. (2002). Feminists discover the hidden injuries of coeducation. In *Jossey-Bass reader on gender in education* (pp. 12–48). San Francisco: Jossey-Bass.

Ullman, S. E., Karabatsos, G., & Koss, M. P. (1999). Alcohol and sexual aggression in a national sample of college men. *Psychology of Women Quarterly, 23,* 673–689.

Watt, S. K. (2006). Racial identity attitudes, womanist identity attitudes, and self-esteem in African American college women attending historically Black single sex and coeducational institutions. *Journal of College Student Development 47*(3), 319–334.

13

LESBIAN, GAY, BISEXUAL, AND TRANSGENDER COLLEGE STUDENTS

Tony Cawthon and Vicki Guthrie

The lesbian, gay, bisexual, and transgender (LGBT) college student population has been referred to as the invisible minority (Sanlo, 1998). This group is not typically as easily identifiable as many other cultural groups on a college campus, yet its members constitute a significant student subpopulation meriting intentional efforts in education and support.

It is a common misconception that LGBT students "belong to a single, amorphous group when in fact there are many differences among lesbian, gay, bisexual, and transgender people" (Worthington, McCrary, & Howard, 1998, p. 141). By definition, gender identity and sexual orientation are two completely different constructs. Yet, three primary concerns "unite sexual orientation and gender identity in distinct ways: overlapping identities, mistaken identities, and the sexual orientation of transgendered people" (Carter, 2000, p. 272). According to Chestnut (1998), the issue of being gender different is "inextricably a gay issue simply because of the radical inseparability of gender and gayness: significant numbers of gay people always have been and probably always will be gender different" (p. 1). She asserted that at any gathering of more than a half dozen gay people, a substantial minority of gays, lesbians, and bisexuals, perhaps as many as a third, differ visibly from the norm in their expression of gender. This chapter describes commonalities and differences among LGBT individuals.

Historically, little research has been conducted on the LGBT student population. D'Augelli (1989) and D'Augelli and Rose (1990) said that this lack of scholarly research reflected evidence of the LGBT population's invisibility. Furthermore, research has focused only on lesbian and gay students, largely to the exclusion of bisexual and transgender students. A noticeable increase in research on the undergraduate student experience occurred in the 1990s, but it still focused on lesbian and gay students (D'Augelli, 1991; Evans & Levine, 1990; Evans & Wall, 1991; Liddell & Douvanis, 1994; Rhoads, 1995a; 1995b). While a review of the literature produced studies regarding bisexual and transgendered individuals, it revealed no research on the campus lives of bisexual or transgender students. D'Aguelli (1996) reported that it is more common for bisexual and transgender individuals to be "lumped in" with lesbian and gays. Robin and Hamner (2000) stated that often these two identities are simply added on to the title of the research being conducted without even being included in the sample. Thus, the number of bisexual and transgender students and their campus experiences remain ill defined.

On most campuses, student affairs professionals take the lead in educating the campus community on diversity and multicultural efforts. Marszalek and Goree (1995) reported that at many colleges and universities student affairs professionals were making sincere efforts to provide supportive environments for LGBT students. As the general population learns and understands more about the gay community, there is strong evidence that the visibility of LGBT students is improving (D'Emilio, 1991; Herdt, 1992). Further, as the number of LGBT students increased, the influence of these students grew (D'Augelli, 1992; Rhoads, 1994, 1997). However, research suggests that this growing acceptance of diversity on campuses in not uniform and that many LGBT students report that campuses are not tolerant, supportive, or accepting (Levine, 1992; Liddell & Douvanis, 1994; Rankin, 2003).

This chapter begins with an investigation of the terminology associated with this cultural group. A basic understanding of these terms is essential to fully support LGBT students. The sections on history, demographics, and sociological context explore dimensions of the significant changes for the LGBT population. An examination of contextual issues relative to LGBT students and current research and trends accompanies an exploration of best practices and exemplary programs. The chapter concludes with specific recommendations for working with and addressing the needs of LGBT students on the college campus, followed by a case study and discussion questions.

Terminology

One way student affairs professionals help reduce the stereotypes and prejudices toward LGBT students is by promoting an understanding of the associated terminology. Grasping the subtle differences in terminology is not as easy as it might seem. For example, the literature illustrates that although distinct meanings can be attributed to terms such as *gay, homosexual, sexual orientation, sexual identity, transgender* and *transsexual,* they are often used interchangeably. Therefore, a common understanding of the terms is essential.

Sexuality is a term with three components: sexual behavior, sexual identity, and sexual orientation. Often these are used interchangeably, but in fact they have significantly different meanings. *Sexual behavior* refers to what one does sexually, one's actions. *Sexual identity* can incorporate several types of identity—gender identity, sex roles identity, physical identity, and sexual orientation identity (Ryan & Futterman, 1998). *Gender identity* refers to whether the individual identifies as male or female, how individuals perceive themselves and what they choose to call themselves. This may or may not agree with their biological sex or societal gender role. *Sex roles* are expectations that result from biological sex (i.e., physical makeup as determined by chromosomes, hormones, reproductive organs, and body parts), such as pregnancy or facial hair growth. *Physical identity* (also known as *gender role identity*) refers to socially constructed expectations associated with being masculine or feminine.

Sexual orientation not only involves a person's choice of sexual partners (Patterson, 1995), but also emotional attraction to others (Coleman, 1990; Shively & DeCecco, 1993). These sexual partners and emotional attractions could involve same-sex individuals (homosexuality), opposite-sex individuals (heterosexuality), or same- and opposite-sex individuals (bisexuality). Identity (or how one identifies oneself) is only one component of our *sexual orientation*. This along with attraction, choice of sexual partners, *and* commitment to the majority or minority group allow for a full understanding of the gay, bisexual, or heterosexual identity. For example, gay identity refers to possessing an emotional attraction to the same sex, engaging in same-sex behaviors, and developing a connection to others with similar characteristics (Cass, 1990). Although gay is commonly used to refer to homosexual men and women, "*gay men*" and "*lesbians*" have become the preferred terms. Closely related to the issue of sexual orientation is *affectional orientation*.

Affectional orientation (Lambert, 2005) is an alternative term for sexual orientation that refers to a broader range of sexuality, and it assumes that an individual's sexual orientation is characterized by whom he or she is prone to fall in love with, with sexuality only being a portion of his or her range of experiences and attractions.

The term homosexual first appeared in 1869 (Mondimore, 1996), although it did not appear in an American text until 1892 (Fone, 2000). Historically, the homosexual was associated with the idea of something deviant, unnatural, or sick. This belief was reflected in the American Psychiatric Association's classification of homosexuality as a mental disorder until 1973.

Similarly, the word *queer* was historically a derogatory slang word used to identify homosexuals. However, it has been "embraced and reinvented as a positive, proud, political identifier when used by homosexuals among and about themselves" (Lesbian, Gay, Bisexual Transgender Center, 2010, para 32), and often extends to include bisexuals and transgender individuals within its broad span. Queer is sometimes used as shorthand for LGBT.

Bisexual identity and behavior are also not the same. There are multiple definitions and uses of the term *bisexual.* Robin and Hamner (2000) defined bisexuality as erotic and sexual interest in or attraction to men and women. Barret and Logan (2001) defined bisexuality as the "experience of erotic, emotional, and sexual attractions to a person of the same and other-gender" (p. 110). The difficulty with defining bisexuality is twofold—many individuals engage in sexual behavior *primarily* with one gender, and even though they engage in same- and opposite-sex behaviors, they may identify themselves as homosexual, gay, bisexual, lesbian, heterosexual, transgender, or none (Firestein, 1996). To clarify, Dworkin (2000) offered the definition of bisexual identity as a "self-label" individuals select when they are attracted to men and women and see the possibility of becoming involved with either.

The term gender identity describes an individual's internal sense of self as male, female, or somewhere between or outside these two categories (Bilodeau & Renn, 2005). Transgender focuses on individuals whose gender identity conflicts with biological sex assignment. It encompasses a wide array of gender nonconforming identities and behaviors. Transgender challenges the idea that there are only two genders—male and female. Ekins and King (1996) defined a transgender individual as one who blends or bends genders. This umbrella term embraces transsexuals, transvestites, cross dressers, male and female impersonators, and gender benders. Because transgender refers to gender identity and not to sexual orientation, transgender people may be heterosexual, homosexual, bisexual, or asexual. Feinberg (1996) reported that the majority of transgender people are heterosexual, although they are largely considered homosexual by the general public.

Two other terms professionals must understand are *heterosexism* and *homophobia*. Weinberg (1972) first used homophobia. It is defined as irrational fear, intolerance, and discomfort with people who are gay, lesbian, or bisexual (*Alyson Almanac*, 1994–1995). Heterosexism refers to maintaining beliefs that heterosexuality is superior to all other types of sexual orientation. Discrimination and prejudice against LGBT students are often the result of homophobia and heterosexism. Unfortunately, LGBT students may also internalize these prejudices and stereotypes, resulting in self-hatred. Thus, dealing with homophobia and heterosexism is a daily struggle for LGBT students on the college campus.

History

Although the gay movement began in Germany, gay organizations have existed in the United States since the 18th century (Bullough, 1979). While the first formally organized gay group in the United States was the Society for Human Rights in 1924, the gay rights movement publicly emerged in the United States after World War II with the Mattachine Society in 1951, ONE in 1952, and Daughters of Bilitis in 1955 (Adam, 1987). Despite the birth of these groups, a repressive atmosphere continued to exist throughout the 1950s as gay individuals were routinely abused and blackmailed.

In 1961 Illinois became the first state to decriminalize homosexual behavior between consenting adults; the first television special on homosexuality, "*The Rejected*," was aired; and the Society for Individual Rights was founded (later becoming a leading advocacy group). In 1965 the American Civil Liberties Union proposed changes in laws dealing with homosexuals, and in 1968, the North American Conference of Homophile Organizations was attended by 26 gay-related groups (*Alyson Almanac*, 1994–1995). Another important expression of societal change was the founding of the Metropolitan Community Church in Los Angeles (http://mccchurch.org) in 1968 as a global Christian church with an open, inclusive, and loving message for gays, lesbians, bisexuals, transgenders, and all people (today the church has 250 congregations in 23 countries).

The gay rights movement was forever changed on June 28, 1969, when a routine police raid of the Stonewall Inn, a gay bar, in New York City, was met by a core group of customers who fought back and started a three-day riot during which the bar was set on fire. Though similar raids had regularly occurred years before in Los Angeles, by the end of the Stonewall riot, the gay movement was born. Soon organized gay groups demanded protection and became a political force.

Despite attacks by religious conservatives in the 1970s, progress was still made. In 1970 the Unitarian Church revised its view of homosexuality and passed the first of multiple resolutions in support of LGBT people. Since the 1970s the United States has elected its first openly gay politicians, the American Psychiatric Association and the American Psychological Association removed homosexuality from its list of disorders, and the first major Christian denomination ordained an open lesbian minister (*Alyson Almanac,* 1994–1995).

During the 1980s and 1990s the gay and lesbian movement strengthened, and bisexuals and transgender individuals gained increased visibility (Fone, 2000). In 1993 the U.S. Supreme Court ruled that laws against hate crimes were constitutional, and in 1996 the court ruled that states could not enact legislation to deny civil rights or deny due process to gay men and lesbians. Today, gay pride marches are held in most major cities, increasing numbers of companies extend benefits to domestic partners of their employees, and healthy role models exist for gay individuals in sports, politics, and entertainment. However, despite these positive changes, the Human Rights Commission said the United States lags behind other countries in gay rights (Brown, 1999).

In the past 30 years the number of LGBT groups on college campuses has grown significantly, as well as educational resources for them. A common perception is that the growth in LGBT student organizations on colleges and universities occurred after the Stonewall riots of 1969. The reality is that the struggle for visibility started on campuses a few years prior to the Stonewall riot. For example, in 1967 the Student Homophile League, the first LGBT student organization, was founded at Columbia University, and within a year student chapters of the Student Homophile League were established at Cornell, New York University and Massachusetts Institute of Technology (Beemyn, 2003). After Stonewall, the number increased significantly, and whereas the first organizations were influenced by the Student Homophile League, groups after 1969 were influenced by the Gay Liberation Front (founded in New York). By 1971 gay liberation groups existed in every major city and campus in the United States (Adam, 1987). At the University of Minnesota in 1971, Jack Baker became the first openly gay person elected student body president at a major university, and with his partner, they became the first American gay couple to seek a marriage license (*Alyson Almanac*, 1994–1995).

Barol (1984) described the late 1980s as a time when colleges recognized gay and lesbian student organizations, allowed gay dances, granted tenure to openly gay faculty, and began offering academic courses on homosexuality. The inaugural gay fraternities and lesbian sororities were charted at the University of California Los Angeles in 1988. Berrill (1989) estimated in 1989 there were about 300 gay student organizations in existence, which Slater (1993) said was a typical method for providing services to LGBT populations even though they were staffed with volunteers and had few financial resources. These organizations served several purposes on campuses: They provided social interaction, served as political entities, offered educational resources, provided services and support, and allowed students opportunities for leadership development (Scott, 1991).

As LGBT campus student organizations have grown in number and impact, so has the attention devoted to them. A significant number of court cases since the early 1970s have revolved primarily around the issues of freedom of speech, freedom of association, due process rights, and right of equal protection.

LGBT Campus Resource Centers and offices, another development on college campuses, provide student services and programs; offer campuswide support to LGBT students, faculty, staff, their friends, and families; and work to offer opportunities for growth for entire institutions (Sanlo, 2000a). The website for the Consortium of Higher Education LGBT Resource Professionals (http://www.lgbtcampus.org/) notes that the first office of LGBT affairs opened at the University of Michigan in 1971, but the majority of these offices opened in the 1990s. A 2006 survey conducted by the consortium (2008–2010) indicated that 100 colleges and universities have resource centers with varying names and are staffed primarily by paid professional staff.

Four of the national organizations and programs designed to assist campuses in serving LGBT students are described briefly in the following.

Founded in 1971, the *National Queer Student Coalition* (NQSC) is one of the oldest national LGBT student organization. NQSC is an affiliate of the U.S. Student Association (USSA, 2007). Founded and run by students, USSA's primary purpose is organizing, advocating for, and providing networking for LGBT students and disseminating to its members copies of federal legislation affecting LGBT students.

Safe Zone is a national program designed to equip heterosexual individuals with skills and resources to assist them to become advocates for the LGBT student population as *allies*. The program exists under names such as Safe Space, Safe on Campus, and Safe Harbor. The general idea of these groups is to allow LGBT allies to place a "safe" symbol in a high-visibility area to identify that area as a safe place for LGBTs (http://www.montana.edu/wwwcc/docs/safezone.html)

The Center for Lesbian and Gay Studies (CLAGS) at the Graduate Center of the City University of New York was founded in 1991 as the first university-based research center dedicated to the comprehensive study of historical, cultural, and political issues of LGBT individuals. CLAGS offers membership opportunities, public programs and conferences, and serves as the national center for the promotion of scholarship that fosters social change (http://web.gc.cuny.edu/clagsl/).

Campus Pride is the only national nonprofit organization for student leaders and campus groups working to create a safer college environment for LGBT students. It is a volunteer-driven network of student leaders whose primary objective is to develop resources, programs, and services to support LGBT and ally students on U.S. college campuses. Campus Pride was founded in 2001 and started out as an online community and resource clearinghouse (http://www.campuspride.org).

Demographics

Compared with other chapters in this book, describing the demographics of LGBT students on the college campus, a "largely invisible minority group" (Fassinger, 1998, p. 15), is difficult. To begin with, the question of "how many homosexuals are there" is politically charged. Michael, Gagnon, Laumann, and Kolata (1994) stated, "Some religious conservatives, for example, would like the number to be very low, so they can argue that homosexuality is a perversion and should not be tolerated, that the overwhelming majority of Americans would never dream of indulging in such behavior" (p. 171). On the other hand, "many gay groups would like the number to be large, so they can argue that homosexuals are a force to be reckoned with" (p. 171).

Numerous studies and researchers have attempted to determine the number of gay individuals. Doing so is a problem because of a number of measurement issues that make a clear, definitive answer to the numbers question difficult at best. How the concept of homosexuality is defined is key, and herein lie several challenges. Michael et al. (1994) note three primary issues. "First, people often change their sexual behavior during their lifetimes, making it impossible to state that a particular set of behaviors defines a person as gay" (p. 172). For example, an individual who currently has sex with others of the same sex, may not have done so 5 or 10 years ago. The second issue is that "there is no set of sexual desires or self identification that uniquely defines homosexuality. Is it sexual desire for a person of the same gender, is it thinking of yourself as a homosexual, or is it some combination of these behaviors that make a person a homosexual?" (p. 172). Third, "homosexuality is not easily measured. . . . the history of persecution has a lasting effect both on what people are willing to say about their sexual orientation and on what they actually do" (p. 172).

Katchadourian (1989) asserted, "Individuals who are attracted to both sexes are even harder to define" (p. 365). First, they have received considerably less attention than those who are exclusively homosexual or heterosexual. In addition, depending on the definition used, bisexuality may unintentionally be swept into the category of the "majority of the gay population" (p. 365) whose members have had some heterosexual experience, or grouped with heterosexuals who have had an early same-sex experience or who choose homosexual behavior "only under certain circumstances, as substitutes, when heterosexual outlets are unavailable," for example, in prisons, or single-sex boarding schools (p. 365). Klein (1993) indicated that bisexuals outnumber homosexuals with estimates ranging between 5 and 10 times the number.

The transgender population is not homogeneous; there is incredible diversity and the extreme social stigma attached to the expression of transgender behavior makes getting an accurate estimate of the number of transgender individuals extremely difficult. Lees (1998) reported that some transgender individuals pass as lesbian, gay, or bisexual, but greater numbers pass as straight, hiding their transgender concerns. Transsexuals who seek sex reassignment surgery were estimated to make up less than .01% of the U.S. population, yet, according to Brown and Rounsley, "it is reasonable to assume that there were scores of unoperated cases for every operated one" (as cited in Carter, 2000, p. 274).

Nevertheless, there are a number of sources of statistics regarding the general population. Many have accepted the widely quoted figure that 10% of the American population is homosexual. This figure is attributed to the Kinsey studies in the late 1940s (Kinsey, Pomeroy, & Martin, 1948). However, a careful analysis of Kinsey's work revealed his strong conviction that a single measure of homosexuality did not exist as it is not possible to classify sexual orientation in two distinct categories—homosexual and heterosexual. Michael et al. (1994) concluded that "the 10% number has been repeated more often than it has been examined. . . . [If] interpreted as meaning that one in ten adults in the United States is exclusively homosexual, it is higher than Kinsey himself stated" (p. 173).

Thoresen (1998) said that "lesbian and gay people are variously estimated to make up from 4 to 12 percent of the population of the United States, using data from the original studies by Kinsey, Pomeroy, and Martin (1948), and more recent data by Weinberg and Williams (1974), Bell and Weinberg (1978), and Paul, Weinrich, Gonsiorek, and Hotvedt (1982)" (p. 262). She further noted that these numbers "can be, and have been argued endlessly, both in the scholarly and the popular media" (p. 262). Her position was to "select numbers that [she] believed to be competently and professionally derived" (p. 262) and concluded "about 10% of the general population, and probably an equal percentage of [college] students is lesbian or gay" (p. 255).

Singer and Deschamps (1994) have estimated that 7.2 million Americans under age 20 are lesbian or gay. As for the number of LGBT college students, Sherrill and Hardesty (1994) reported that studies estimate that one in six college students is LGBT. Carter (2000) said that there will likely be a few transgender students on most college campuses. "Despite the inability to arrive at universally accepted, verifiable numbers and percentages, LGBT individuals are a visible presence in American society and an integral student subculture on the college campus. There are also "LGBT people who serve as faculty, staff, administrators, maintenance support, residence staff, campus clergy, campus police—people in every area of our institutions, a small few of whom are willing to share their identities" (Sanlo, 1998, p. xvii). There-fore, student affairs professionals need to be conscious of and attentive to this only partially visible minority on the college campus. While their pro-portions may be debatable, their certain presence in substantive numbers is not.

Sociological Context

The prevailing societal assumption that "heterosexuality is normal, natural, and preferable as a sexual orientation" (O'Brien, 1998, p. 31) creates a hetero-sexist culture in which individuals are assumed to be heterosexual and are treated as though they are. This culture routinely "denies the existence and contributions of LGBT individuals" (Worthington et al., 1998, p. 136). Homophobia in both forms—the fear and hatred of homosexuality in others and the fear of homosexuality in oneself—permeates our society and affects LGBT and heterosexual individuals alike, constituting a form of oppression.

Heterosexism and homophobia in the larger American society is mirrored in its college and university campuses. For LGBT individuals, homophobia is "not just an abstract societal challenge, [but a] critical, concrete, daily health issue . . . [that] infiltrates the lives, relationships, hope, dreams of LGBT students" (Keeling, 1998, p. 148). Despite the strides that have been made in fostering increased acceptance of LGBT people and the increasing numbers of institutional policies prohibiting discrimination on the basis of sexual orientation, researchers have documented pervasive prejudice, derogatory comments, verbal and physical harassment, and violence against LGBT individuals on college and university campuses (Croteau & Lark, 1995). A study by Rankin (2003) of 1,669 self-identified LGBT individuals on 14 campuses indicated that more than 36% of LGBT undergraduates have experienced harassment on campus, and in 79% of the cases by other students. The danger present in the environment is illustrated all too clearly by the horrific 1998 murder of Matthew Shepard, a gay student at the University of Wyoming.

Throughout history, many individuals condemning and attacking LGBT people have claimed religious justification (Kraig, 1998). DuMontier (2000) said, "The Bible, particularly its literal interpretation, has often been used as a means of justifying prejudice and discrimination" (p. 331). Many private colleges and universities have a religious affiliation that shapes their approach to serving LGBT students, and LGBT college students come from a broad range of religious traditions. DuMontier described faith development and LGBT identity development as "parallel processes" (p. 322) and underscores that "there are points in which the evolution of gay identity development may be connected and integral to faith development" (p. 327).

In the past two decades, theories of LGBT identity development have been formulated; they "are grounded in the assumption that oppressive contextual influences exert impact on normative developmental processes" (Fassinger, 1998, p. 14). In other words, the stress of college is exponentially greater for young people developing an identity as an LGBT person. Thus, the lifelong process of developing a positive LGBT identity (which may well have begun prior to college) collides head-on during the college years with the developmental trajectory of the college student. The result is that the

LGBT student is often put "at considerable disadvantage in terms of achieving successful resolution of developmental tasks" (Fassinger, p. 19).

Coming out is another critical aspect of LGBT identity development, "and one that is distinct from that of heterosexuals" (Newman, 1998, p. 163). Coming out involves the development of an LGBT identity and the public expression (to varying degrees) of this identity. The LGBT student must come out to three primary populations—oneself, other LGBT people, and heterosexuals (Evans & Broido, 1991). In addition, being out is not always an either/or process

> but can be understood as a "continuum from not being out to oneself . . . to being explicitly out in every setting. Some midway points include being out to oneself, but not to others; being out to a few trusted others; being out selectively to friends; and assuming that everyone [knows], often because of visibility. (p. 663)

A number of methods can be used to come out to others. Individuals may assume that others will ascertain their sexual orientation by recognizing certain symbols such as a pink triangle or rainbow displayed on their backpack, clothing, jewelry, car, or residence hall room door, or by hearing them discuss their lives as if their being gay, lesbian, or bisexual were common knowledge (Evans & Broido).

According to Moses and Hawkins, one motivation for coming out is "a desire to be closer to others, to validate one's own self-worth, and to stop having to hide" (as cited in Evans & Broido, 1991, p. 658). However, Evans and Broido's research revealed that the motivation to come out "often had to do with environmental circumstances as much as internal pressures" (p. 663). Henchen and O'Dowd said that peers who are already out may exert pressure for others to come out as well (as cited in Evans & Broido). Encouragement from supportive individuals, a perception of a receptive climate, and having LGBT role models are additional factors that motivate this important decision. Coming out is "usually understood as psychologically beneficial, in that LGBT people eliminate, or lessen, the dissonance caused by the lack of congruence between public and private personas (Newman, 1998, p. 164). Students have reported the advantages of "feelings of pride, authenticity, and relief . . . [as well as] appreciating being able to be open about who they are" (Evans & Broido, p. 664).

However, coming out into a hostile environment may result in additional stressors such as increased social ostracism or loss of social support

(Newman, 1998). It is for precisely such reasons that many LGBT students choose to remain in the closet and to pass as heterosexuals. Rankin (2003) indicated that LGBT people of color are more likely than White LGBT people to conceal their sexual orientation or gender identity to avoid harassment. Research has shown that students perceive distinct disadvantages to being out:

> feelings of concern for others who might be indirectly hurt by the student's being out (e.g., closeted friends, family), distress at being labeled, fears and actual experience of harassment and rejection, needing to limit behaviors to avoid unsafe situations, and negative effects on academic performance because of involvement in LGB activities. (Evans & Broido, 1991, p. 664)

Compounding the difficulties of isolation and the barriers to involvement are the pockets of heterosexism and homophobia, which may be found to be more intense in certain areas of the campus—particularly those that are single sex, such as athletic programs and Greek organizations. "LGBT athletes are often fearful of derision if they come out, and straight athletes are frequently afraid of falsely being labeled as gay if they do not participate in oppressive acts" (Salkever & Worthington, 1998, pp. 193–194). A similar dynamic can be seen among members of some sororities and fraternities. The result is that LGBT students become silenced within their own teams and organizations and are often forced to suffer the assault of homophobic remarks unknowingly made by teammates, fraternity brothers, or sorority sisters.

There is evidence that fraternities and sororities are becoming more tolerant. Case's (1998) research indicated that

> despite fears to the contrary, most GLBT [*sic*] fraternity and sorority *initiated* members receive a relatively supportive response from the majority of their members when they voluntarily reveal their sexual orientation. . . . [however,] the probability of a negative response is much greater if the member is involuntarily outed. (p. 69)

An indication of positive change is the 1990 Resolution on Heterosexism Within the Greek Community that was passed by the Association of Fraternity Advisors and encourages chapters "to implement sexual orientation awareness, education, and sensitivity programs for the Greek community [and] to challenge Greek chapter or member behaviors or attitudes that are heterosexist in nature" (as cited in Case, p. 72).

Specific Contextual Issues for Bisexual Students

There is no one accepted definition of bisexuality; its diversity and complexity challenges our notion of dichotomous sexuality and identity and "confuses, unnerves, and creates suspicion among lesbian, gay, and heterosexual people" (Pope & Reynolds, 1991, p. 206). Many heterosexuals see bisexuals as gay and extend homophobia and heterosexism to incorporate this population as well, while "many lesbian and gay people suspect individuals of choosing bisexuality as a means of maintaining heterosexual privileges" (p. 207). *Biphobia* is a term for prejudice based on the fear and distrust of bisexual people and feelings; it has at its core "the ultimate marginalizing question, 'Does bisexuality really exist?'" (p. 207).

In addition to these definitional and conceptual issues, O'Brien (1998) stated, "For bisexual people, there is no large-scale or widespread 'bisexual subculture,' no bisexual Mecca (as San Francisco is, for example, for gays). Bisexuals depend largely on individual support and understanding for their affirmation" (p. 31). Klein (1993) found that the average age individuals first identify as bisexual is 24 and may be delayed because of the resistance from the straight and gay communities. What bisexual students wanted most, according to O'Brien (1998), was unbiased and considerate treatment that does not marginalize them based on their sexual orientation or assume they are abnormal.

Specific Contextual Issues for Transgender Students

Confusion surrounds the term transgender. Few individuals can accurately define it, neither can they fathom what it might be like "not to be comfortable living within the confines of the social stereotypes of gender as applied to themselves" (Lees, 1998, p. 37). According to Lees, "The process of educating the wider community about transgender issues can be difficult: Most transsexual people choose to live a quiet life not identified as having 'changed sex'" (p. 43). Perhaps this is at least partially because transgender people are more vulnerable to random homophobic attacks than lesbian, gay, or bisexual people (Carter, 2000).

For many students who are questioning their gender identity, "the time away at college is often the first chance to challenge the gender role assigned at birth and to decide how to integrate transgenderness into life as an adult" (Lees, 1998, p. 37). Lees explains, "the path of self-discovery often involves going from one gender extreme to the other, then settling down somewhere in between" (p. 38). The college years are considered an optimal time for a transsexual individual to make a transition (Lees). Reitz said that across the nation transgender students have been demanding comfortable living space, representation in organizations, and support from higher education administration and staff (as cited in Carter, 2000).

Not all transgender people are comfortable being a part of the LGBT conglomeration. After all, gender identity is not the same as sexual orientation, and many transgender individuals identify as heterosexual. Not only do they not consider themselves lesbian, gay, or bisexual, "some transgender people would be happier without this tie being made in the public mind . . . [yet] this is currently the only place in which to provide public recognition to transgender people" (Lees, 1998, p. 40).

Current Research, Trends, Issues

To be effective, student affairs professionals must be knowledgeable about current research affecting LGBT individuals. It is imperative they understand gay identity development since many students begin questioning their sexuality, coming out to themselves and others, during the college years (Evans & D'Augelli, 1996).

Researchers writing about identity development use the terms *homosexual identity* and *gay identity* interchangeably; few studies clearly delineate what is meant by the concept (Cass, 1983–1984). Cass identified five different uses of these terms: "(1) defining oneself as gay, (2) developing a sense of self as gay, (3) possessing an image of self as homosexual, (4) knowing the way a homosexual person is, and (5) exhibiting consistent behavior in relation to homosexual-related activity" (p. 108). From these differing definitions, it is apparent that identity can be defined individually, intrapersonally, or as both. Regardless of which specific definition is being used, Warren (1974) said that most researchers agreed that the process toward identity development is answering the questions "Who am I? and Where do I belong?" (p. 145).

Extensive attention to homosexual or gay identity development began in the 1970s. The early theories on gay identity development were primarily sociological in perspective and explored gay identity and related issues. Early studies included those of Dank (1971), Hammersmith and Weinberg (1973), Weinberg (1978), and Bell and Weinberg (1978).

Building upon the work of gay identity research, gay identity development models followed. These models focus on the process gay men and lesbians go through to become aware and accepting of their gay identities. The early models are developmental in nature, involving a series of stages that are linear in thought and reflect a social, psychological, or psychosocial perspective (Levine & Evans, 1991). Examples include social (Lee, 1977; Coleman, 1981), psychological (Minton & McDonald, 1984; Plummer, 1975; Troiden, 1979), and psychosocial (Cass, 1979).

In recent years, these models have been criticized for not allowing for differences in identity development among gay men and lesbian women, ignoring identity development in bisexuals and transgender individuals, and assuming that identity formation occurs in sequential stages. Thus, new theories are evolving to address the differences in the LGBT community. Examples of recent research include Sophie's (1986) lesbian identity development; D'Augelli's (1994) model of lesbian, gay, and bisexual development; McCarn and Fassinger's (1996) lesbian identity development; Fassinger and Miller's (1996) lesbian/gay identity formation; Weinberg, Williams, and Pryor's (1994) bisexual identity development; and Bolin's (1993) transgender identity development. Moses and Hawkins (1986) reported great variance in the age that gay men and lesbians become aware of same-sex feelings. DeMonteflores and Schultz (1978) said that men typically disclose their homosexual identity earlier than women. Troiden (1988) established that lesbians' identity is tied to an emotional relationship whereas gay men's identity is tied to their sexual relationships. Morales (1990) criticized most homosexual identity models as being based on the experiences of upper-class White lesbians and gay men. McCarn and Fassinger (1996) further noted that existing models do not consider the multiple aspects of identity.

To understand students' development and assist with their growth, student affairs professionals need to be knowledgeable about those theories. As it is beyond the scope of this chapter to discuss each theory or model, four are presented below. The reader is also referred to Bilodeau and Renn (2005) for an excellent comparison of sexual orientation and gender identity development theories.

Cass's Model of Homosexual Identity Formation

Vivienne Cass's work (1979, 1983–1984, 1984) formed the basis for conceptualizing homosexual development for men and women starting in the late 1970s. Cass proposed a stage model of homosexual identity development with six stages that assume a movement in self-perception from heterosexual to homosexual. The first stage is identity confusion, in which the individual first perceives his or her thoughts of, feelings about, and attractions to others of the same sex. The second is identity comparison, where the individual perceives and must deal with social stigmatization and alienation. Cass's third stage is identity tolerance, in which individuals, having acknowledged their homosexuality, begin to seek out other homosexuals. Stage four is identity acceptance in which positive connotations about being homosexual foster even further contacts and friendships with other gays and lesbians. In the fifth stage, identity pride, the individual minimizes contact with heterosexual peers to focus on issues and activities related to his or her homosexual orientation. In identity synthesis, the final of Cass's stages, there is less of a dichotomy of individual differences between the heterosexual and nonheterosexual communities or aspects of the individual's life; the individual judges himself or herself on a range of personal qualities not just upon sexual identity.

Savin-Williams's Stages

Ritch Savin-Williams (1990, 1995, 1998) is another influential stage theorist of gay identity development. Building from his earlier work with gays and lesbians (1990), he postulated differing developmental trajectories that spring from turning points (developmental challenges or presses). Savin-Williams (1998) outlined eight chronological stages in which the trajectories reflect identity development tied to specific phenomenological and/or cognitive responses at the turning points:

> awareness of same-sex attractions, occurrence of first gay sexual experience, occurrence of first heterosexual sexual experience, labeling oneself as gay or bisexual, disclosing one's sexuality to others (but not family members), experiencing one's first gay romantic relationship, disclosing one's sexuality to family members, and fostering a positive identity. (p. 15)

While not every marker might be experienced by a gay youth, nor might the markers always be in this particular order, Savin-Williams (1998) noted that the markers do form a common pattern of identity development for young gay men. Significantly for student development professionals, the means and ranges of ages of experience place these developmental processes within the traditional collegiate years. Savin-Williams's main contribution is describing the broad range of developmental distinctions in these progressive stages or levels of gay identity development.

Fassinger's Model

Ruth Fassinger (1998), whose work is perhaps less well known than Cass's or Savin-Williams's by student affairs professionals, developed an inclusive model of lesbian/gay identity formation. It too is stage-based, but it is multi-faceted, reflecting dual aspects of development—individual sexual identity and group membership identity. The first of Fassinger's four stages is aware-ness—from an individual perspective, of being different from heterosexual peers, and from a group perspective, of the existence of differing sexual orientations among people. The second stage is exploration—on an individual level, of emotions and erotic desires for people of the same sex, on the group level, of how one associates with gay people as a social class. The third level is a deepening commitment to this changing notion of identity—on an individual level it is a personalization of the knowledge and beliefs about same-sex sexuality, and on the group level, it is personal involvement with a nonheterosexual reference group, and realizing the existence of oppression and the potential consequences of identifying and socializing with non-heterosexuals. The final stage, internalization/synthesis, is an integration of same-sex sexuality into one's overall identity—from a collective perspective, it conveys one's identity as a member of a minority group in all social contexts.

D'Augelli's Life Span Model of Sexual Orientation Development

Anthony D'Augelli's (1991, 1994) model of sexual orientation development incorporates social contexts in ways the earlier stage models did not and presents human development as "unfolding in concurring and multiple paths, including the development of a person's self-concept, relationships with family, and connections to peer groups and community" (Bilodeau & Renn, 2005, p. 28). The model addresses the effect environmental and biological factors have on the fluidity or fixed nature of one's sexual orientation and contains six identity processes that operate, not as ordered stages but more or less independently: exiting heterosexuality—recognizing that one is not heterosexual and beginning to tell others that one is lesbian, gay, or bisexual; developing a personal lesbian, gay, or bisexual identity—a "sense of personal socio-affectional stability that effectively summarizes thoughts, feelings, and desires" (D'Augelli, 1994, p. 325) in which internalized myths about lesbian, gay, or bisexual roles are challenged in settings and with others who confirm what it means to be nonheterosexual; developing a lesbian, gay, or bisexual social identity—creating a social support network that supports a lesbian, gay, or bisexual identity and recognizing that determining others' true reactions takes time; becoming a lesbian, gay, or bisexual offspring—

disclosing one's lesbian, gay, or bisexual identity to parents (or others who provide familial type support), redefining relationships, and establishing a positive relationship with parents through education and patience; developing a lesbian, gay, or bisexual intimacy status—engaging in the complex process of forming an intimate relationship given the invisibility of nonheterosexual couples; and entering a lesbian, gay, or bisexual community—making a commitment to some degree of social and political action, which can be at significant personal risk (D'Augelli).

Key interrelated variables in the formation of identity are personal subjectivities and actions—perceptions and feelings about sexual identity, sexual behaviors, and the meanings attached to them; interactive intimacies—influences of family, peers, intimate partnerships; and sociohistorical connections—social norms, policies, and laws relevant to one's geographical location, culture, values of the historical period (Renn, Dilley, & Prentice, 2003).

Chen-Hayes and Haley-Banez (2000) expanded this model to include transgender people and gender identity/expression. The six developmental tasks were revised as follows: exiting heterosexuality and traditionally gendered identities, developing a personal LGBT identity status, developing an LGBT social identity, becoming an LGBT offspring, developing an LGBT intimacy status, and entering an LGBT community.

Bisexual Identity Development, Transgender Identity Development

Bisexuality has surfaced of late as a separate cultural identity from lesbian, gay, and heterosexual identity. It is no longer simply assumed that bisexual individuals progress toward a healthy bisexual identity that follows the lesbian, gay, and bisexual development models.

Research by Klein (1993), Rust (1993), Fox (1995) and Weinberg et al. (1994) suggests there are distinct developmental patterns of bisexual identity development. Weinberg et al. proposed a four-stage model that contradicts earlier perspectives of bisexual identity development as simply a stage between heterosexual and gay and lesbian identification (Fox) or as a form of foreclosed identity (Cass, 1990). Fox concluded that bisexual identity development is a complex process, one that includes homosexual and heterosexual perspectives. Factors such as environment, relationships, and degree of openness influence this development. Weinberg et al. added that for most people who self-identity as bisexuals, this identity occurs later in life for lesbian and gay males and after they have developed a heterosexual identity.

While bisexuality challenges the idea that there are only two sexual orientations, transgender challenges the idea of only two genders. Limited research has been conducted examining issues facing transgender individuals (Carter, 2000) and little research has been available on transgender students until a few years ago. In 2006 the *Journal of Gay & Lesbian Issues in Education* published a special issue on trans youth containing several qualitative studies examining the experiences of undergraduate and graduate students who self-identify as transgender. As reported by D'Augelli, (1990), the size of the population of transgender individuals on campus remains unknown, and Carter stated that when thinking of students and the development of their identities, gender is not usually considered. A review of the literature revealed only one study focused on transgender identity development: Bolin (1993) examined male-to-female transsexuals who ultimately moved toward sex-conversion surgery and proposed a four-stage model.

Best Practices

This section offers a brief overview of three of the numerous best practices for working with LGBT students: LGBT Campus Resource Centers (CRCs), the 2 in 20 Program at the University of Massachusetts Amherst, and the Lavender Graduation at the University of California, Los Angeles. Readers can go to http://www.lgbtcampus.org for other examples of best practices.

LGBT CRCs

Perhaps the ultimate in best practices to support and enrich the lives of LGBT students and make the campus climate LGBT affirmative is to provide an LGBT CRC. The mission of these centers is to serve the campus community "in matters related to sexual orientation and gender identity, although the primary focus is on providing services for LGBT students, faculty, staff, and their friends and families, [and] in some cases, . . . the local community" (Sanlo, 2000a, p. 486). The Consortium of Higher Education LGBT Resource Professionals has a directory that lists over 157 registered campus offices or centers, many with a full-time professional director (see http://www.lgbtcampus.org/directory/). Other offices are managed on a part-time basis by faculty, staff, or graduate assistants.

While the large majority of LGBT CRCs are housed in student affairs departments, others are located in campus gender or cultural centers or in academic affairs. Centers vary not only in staffing and reporting structures but on budget as well. Some CRCs are "funded to provide programming, others are funded strictly to provide information, referral, support, and advocacy. Some are funded to provide services to students only or to students, faculty, and staff, and, at some institutions, to the local community as well" (Sanlo, 2000a, pp. 490–491).

Ideally these centers will eventually become commonplace on college campuses, but many campuses have established other successful programs to address LGBT students' issues of sexual orientation and gender identity. The following are examples of successful approaches by divisions of student affairs in the absence of or in conjunction with an established LGBT CRC.

University of Massachusetts Amherst's 2 in 20 Program

In the fall of 1992 the University of Massachusetts Amherst created a space in a residence hall on one of the floors for students interested in LGBT concerns to accommodate student needs and improve the campus climate for LGBT students. Though similar proposals have resulted in controversy on some campuses, several institutions, including Rutgers University, University of California-Santa Cruz, University of Maine at Orono, and Wesleyan University in Connecticut, have established similar special-interest housing programs (Herbst & Malaney, 1999).

Herbst and Malaney (1999) said that "the residence hall experience is central to improvement of campus climate for GLBT [sic] students" (p. 109). They underscore Bourassa and Shipton's (1991) opinion that a minimal requirement for a residence hall environment is "having a residence life staff that is not homophobic" (Herbst & Malaney, 1999, p. 109). Although special-interest housing is a visible statement of support for the LGBT community and provides a supportive environment for students and a safe space on campus, Shea stated that "some administrators believe it can hinder the mission to educate the larger population regarding gay issues because the special interest housing isolates the GLBT [sic] students" (as cited in Herbst & Malaney, p. 109). However, Herbst and Malaney said that "with proper programming, it should be possible for the residence life staff to create a sense of inclusiveness in the general community as well as provide the opportunity for special interest students to have a comfortable and safe place to share their lives with people who have common interests and concerns" (p. 109).

The 2 in 20 Program (named after the popularized statistic that 1 in every 10 people is gay) opened in the fall of 1992. Eventually, it "became more visible and students increasingly wanted to move in" (Herbst & Malaney, 1999, p. 110). A community room/lounge was created on the floor that is reserved for the program, in addition to "a 'response room' for students from other residence halls in need of temporary relocation due to harassment based on their sexual orientation" (p. 110). The following year, 2 in 20 adopted a charter and constitution that officially added transgender students and allies to the residential program and required that the resident assistant for the floor and the residence director for the building "be strong, 'out' members of the GLBT [sic] community" (p. 110).

Herbst and Malaney (1999) found an overall positive reaction to the program saying that it provides students "with some fundamental experiences that are important for their development and growth, such as a safe and supportive place to live and be themselves" (p. 115). The residents and the residence hall staff involved with the space were positive about the personal safety and comfort of the residents in the program and showed an enormous commitment to continuing to strengthen the program. While Herbst and Malaney generally assess the floor community to be a just and caring one, there seems to be some peer pressure on the floor for residents to be activists involved in the student LGBT group and in addressing LGBT issues on campus (e.g., fighting homophobia). The respondents also identified a need for floor residents to learn more about LGBT history and LGBT issues and causes. The 2 in 20 floor has received positive national attention and has been described as a "prototype for other campuses to emulate" (p. 117).

Lavender Graduation at the University of California, Los Angeles

According to Weiss, in addition to institution-wide commencement ceremonies, a number of campuses hold special celebrations based on specific ethnic identities at which students are acknowledged for their academic achievements and their cultural heritages (as cited in Sanlo, 2000b). Lavender Graduation is a university-supported celebration of the lives and achievements of LGBT students at the culmination of their academic careers, which, by 2001, was being held by at least 45 institutions (see http://www.1809lgbtalumni.org/mission/lavendergrad.htm).

The original Lavender Graduation was designed by Sanlo in 1995 while working as the director of the LGBT CRC at the University of Michigan.

The color lavender has been claimed by the LGBT civil rights movement in the 1950s and 1960s, and it represents pride and kinship in the LGBT community. Jay and Young (1994) reported that the color was selected because it represented a mixture of light blue and pink (colors stereotypically associated with boys and girls). In recent years, pink has become more associated with the gay community as it represented the pink triangle that gay men were forced to wear in German concentration camps (Sanlo, 2000b).

Lavender Graduation is intended to "support an institution's mission of excellent service that embraces, enhances, and celebrates the academic achievement of LGBT students. It is a cultural celebration that recognizes LGBT students of all races and ethnicities and acknowledges their achievements and contributions to the university" (Sanlo, 2000b, p. 645). The ceremony brings together many people of the university community to recognize LGBT students with greetings, speeches, leadership awards, and rainbow-colored tassels for their caps, followed by a reception for the graduates, their families, friends, and guests. Surveys indicate that graduating students have positive reactions to the event, and family, friends, and other nonstudent participants also respond positively (Sanlo). Other outcomes of the ceremony include "an opportunity for institutions to provide a graceful exit for students . . . [and] to develop an entire cadre of giving alumni" (p. 646). But, most importantly, it is "an opportunity to tell LGBT students they matter" (p. 646).

Recommendations, Implications, Trends

Ensuring that LGBT college students have a safe, supportive, and conducive environment for pursuing their educational goals must be an institutional and student affairs priority requiring institutional and individual allies. As the moral conscience of the campus (Brown, 1985), student affairs staff should be at the forefront of efforts in creating an LGBT-affirmative campus climate and should serve as role models for others in the campus community. Please note that while the authors do not assume all the readers of this volume are heterosexually oriented, this section primarily addresses heterosexual student affairs professionals out of particular concern with assisting this group in becoming more competent in addressing the needs of LGBT students.

Institutional Support

An institutional ally as described by Lucozzi (1998) is a college or university that intentionally creates and sustains an environment that supports the actions of individual allies on behalf of LGBT students. It recognizes the harmful effects of homophobia not only on LGBT students but on heterosexuals as well. For example, a study by Sherrill and Hardesty (1994) showed that "31% of GLBT students left school for one semester or longer and 33% dropped out or transferred because of coming out or harassment issues prior to coming out" (p. 269). Perhaps less obvious, according to Blumenfeld, is the fact that "homophobia is energy draining; it diverts energy from constructive endeavors" (as cited in Lucozzi, p. 49). Lucozzi, based on work by DeVito (1979) and Schoenberg (1989), offers the following recommendations for campus administrators who must

1. Go to the source, find out what LGBT students need or want by communicating with them.
2. Be proactive by moving forward with policies or programming that validate LGBT students and express the institution's commitment to being an ally.
3. Recognize and confront institutional homophobia.
4. Educate the campus community on the connections between other oppressions and homophobia.
5. Become familiar with the developmental issues of LGBT students and integrate them into the curriculum and services.
6. Support LGBT employees through domestic partner benefits and sensitive employee policies.
7. Provide positive role models for LGBT students by attracting LGBT faculty, staff, and administrators.
8. Be sure all levels of the institution are involved.

Since the early 1970s, and especially the mid-1990s, more than 500 colleges and universities have added sexual orientation to their nondiscrimination policies (Sanlo, 1998). Kraig (1998) noted,

> Institutions that create policies through which LGBT members are made to feel welcome, safe from discrimination, and affirmed will probably be rewarded with LGBT faculty and staff who serve the communities' needs well. Such policies are not sufficient, however, if they are not accompanied

by public and constant statements of support for LGBT members of the campus. (p. 251)

Renn (1998) reported that faculty play an important role in the LGBT student experience. "How college faculty address, or fail to address, issues of sexual orientation in their classrooms has a significant impact on the learning environment" (p. 231). Sometimes it is the faculty's passivity rather than conscious acts of aggression and overt victimization that create negative experiences for LGBT students, and "by not acting to interrupt the pattern of LGBT victimization [they] are contributing to it" (p. 232). An institution acting in an ally role can provide development opportunities for faculty, because even if faculty are inclined to want to learn more about LGBT issues, too many colleges and universities fail to provide opportunities for them to do so.

At some institutions an academic department or program of LGBT/ queer studies "benefits LGBT and questioning young people on college campuses not only intellectually but psychologically and emotionally as well" (Chesnut, 1998, p. 222). This field has "made enormous contributions to our understandings of sexuality within history and culture; it has also produced information of enormous benefit in countering myths and misinformation about LGBT people today" (p. 222). Colleagues in the area of LGBT/queer studies make excellent collaborators and resources in supporting LGBT students on campus, which should not be "the work of student affairs professionals alone" (p. 228).

Individual Support

On the individual level, student affairs professionals must continually and intentionally seek to learn about the wide-ranging needs of LGBT students and issues pertinent to their development (Worthington et al., 1998). "Because students frequently begin coming out during the college years, student affairs administrators need to be familiar with this developmental process and ways to be supportive as students begin to disclose their sexual identity to themselves and others" (Evans & Broido, 1991, p. 658).

While it is fundamental to understand issues faced by LGBT individuals and be able to make a difference in their educational experience, "it is equally important to consider their own development in becoming an LGBT-affirmative person" (Worthington et al., 1998, p. 136). Gelber and Chojnacki said that to become effective in working with the LGBT population, individuals must "1) be realistic about the limitation imposed on them by their socialization into homophobic, heterosexist practices, 2) make a commitment to overcome that socialization, and 3) actively pursue experiences that facilitate their own movement toward that goal" (as cited in Worthington et al., p. 136). For individuals interested in learning more about how to be an ally, Fahy (1995) outlined 50 ways to be one. Washington and Evans (1991) and Broido (2000) also offer specific recommendations for becoming an effective ally. It is important to understand that a certain amount of moral courage is required. "Being morally courageous means being vocal, condemning harassment and discrimination, and advocating for the rights of the GLBT community," Tierney said (as cited in Watkins, 1998, p. 273).

Underhile and Cowles (1998) urged, "After opening your mind, open your space and make sure its safe" (p. 176). Signs and symbols such as rainbow flags and stickers, pink triangles, and buttons proclaiming "straight, but not narrow" convey to students that it is acceptable to be who they are. Make sure the office environment provides visual signs that heterosexuality is not the only acceptable culture. This can be done by displaying LGBT-affirmative materials such as books, newspapers, magazines, or pamphlets. The artwork in the office can also convey powerful messages.

Other efforts include providing educational programs to develop student affairs staff competencies in working with LGBT students and educating other elements of the campus community (faculty, administrators, support personnel) to create a more LGBT-affirmative campus climate and to make additional allies for the LGBT population. Educational programs can include forum presentations, speakers, group discussions, panels, ally training, problem-solving sessions, films, and workshops. Key to success are participation and involvement. Indeed, "as knowledge is gained, ignorance and prejudice can be lessened, providing a more sensitive atmosphere" (Salkever & Worthington, 1998, p. 199).

The provision of support services—including advising, peer support groups, mentoring, and resource referral—for LGBT students is essential. Keeling (1998) underscored the importance of

> services that do not presume that the fact of the sexuality is the only or dominant psychological issue for LGBT students . . . [but] that do, on the other hand, take into account the specific needs created by being gay, lesbian, or bisexual, and the context that sexuality creates for other psychological and spiritual concerns. (p. 150)

The services should be flexible and able to assist students who may be at varying stages of their identity development and coming out process. The staff in these areas should be knowledgeable and LGBT affirmative. Keeling (1998) added,

> It is simply not adequate to have one, or a few, clinicians, educators, or counselors who are 'known' to LGBT students as caring, skilled, empathic providers; LGBT students should expect that *any and every* clinician, counselor, and educator will be humane, caring, and interested in their concerns. (p. 154)

Optimally, programs and services could be centralized in or coordinated with an LGBT CRC to be used by all members of the college and university community. Watkins (1998) said that this office would

> serve as the primary clearinghouse for GLBT educational resources, such as videos, books, and pamphlets, would provide support services for GLBT individuals, sponsor GLBT cultural events, compile GLBT hate crime statistics, and conduct training sessions for the campus community on GLBT issues and heterosexism. (p. 275)

"LGBT students struggle with many of the same issues that confront heterosexual students" (Worthington et al., 1998, p. 140). Therefore, student affairs practitioners need to be able to "recognize sexual orientation is peripheral to the issue at hand to respond accordingly" (p. 140). They should realize the limitations of their training and expertise in working with LGBT students. Their primary goal is to listen, express concern and support, and help students "consider and evaluate her or his needs for services without presuming that the student will want or need additional help" (Salkever & Worthington, 1998, p. 200). If the student desires additional help, it is essential to have a list of appropriate referrals to campus and community resources.

Case Study: The Shower

You are Marie Santos, dean of students at Valley University, a public university of 20,000 students in a small rural town in the Midwest. A large protest on campus has been scheduled that day because the campus is divided on issues stemming from an incident that occurred in the residence halls several weeks before.

Donna Smith, a freshman resident of one of the all-women's halls on campus, stayed in her room one Saturday night because she was feeling ill. All of her friends, in fact most of the residents of the hall, were out at a home football game that was followed by a concert by a popular band. Entering the restroom down the hall, feeling nauseated for the third time that evening, she was surprised to hear voices coming from one of the shower stalls. She stayed in the restroom for several minutes fighting the urge to be sick again and then decided to brush her teeth. She was startled when Marcy from two doors down the hall emerged from the shower stall followed closely by her roommate, Jane. Playful flirtation was obvious between the two who were equally startled to see Donna in the restroom. Donna blushed, stammered, and made a quick exit concluding that the rumors about the two being lesbians certainly seemed to be true.

Several days later, the campus community became aware of the incident through Donna's opinion piece in the student newspaper. Donna's purpose was to talk about the diversity on campus and how grateful she was to have the opportunity to be exposed to so many different people, even though the incident itself had been uncomfortable at first. She pledged her support to gay and lesbian students on campus as an ally and urged other students to do the same. Though Donna did not include names, residents of her floor were quick to identify the two women and started to avoid Marcy and Jane. Several residents of the floor went to the resident assistant and the resident director appalled that nothing had been done to address the situation disciplinarily. The "inequity" outraged a number of students who said that the university was discriminating against heterosexual students who were not allowed to shower with their boyfriends in the floor's common bathroom or to live with their boyfriends.

The protest involves several conservative student groups on campus that believe the university should take strong action against promoting this lifestyle in the residence halls. A street preacher who visits campus, regularly condemning homosexuality on religious grounds, has been called in by some of the religious groups. A bill has been introduced in the Student Senate that would ban homosexual students from being able to be roommates in campus residence facilities, although no enforcement mechanism has been specified. The campus ally organization plans a counter protest, although the group is somewhat divided over the inequity question.

The LGBT student group on campus, Queer Students Association (QSA), has been largely silent on the issue. Mostly a support group sponsoring a few social events each year and one highly publicized fund-raiser, a drag show, QSA has not been involved in political or advocacy issues for LGBT students. Some of the QSA members are highly frustrated with the leadership of the group in this crucial situation.

The protest is marked on your calendar for noon in addition to a meeting with Chris Stevens, a male-to-female transgender resident of the floor in question who lives in a single room and who is increasingly uncomfortable and is sure she will be outed in this process; a meeting with Pat Clark, a student affairs staff member who is adviser to the QSA to discuss the schism occurring in that organization; and a meeting with the resident hall's resident director and the director of residence life to discuss the situation in the hall and the disciplinary actions that should be taken, if any.

Discussion Questions

1. What are the issues or problems presented in this case? Be specific.
2. What resources are available to you to address this issue? How would you include other entities on campuses to assist you?
3. What primary issues or actions would you anticipate for each of your scheduled meetings and the protest? How would you approach these events?
4. Weigh the issue of whether LGBT students should be allowed to be roommates in campus facilities. What is your position?
5. Explain the roles each person (i.e., director of residence life, residence director, Donna, Jane, Marcy, etc.) and organization (QSA, Student Government, Residence Hall Association, campus newspaper, etc.) have in resolving this issue.
6. Using your knowledge of LGBT identity development, what interventions would you recommend for participants and organizations involved?
7. Discuss the roles allies can play in assisting the campus to eliminate homophobia and discrimination faced by LGBT students.
8. Explain how a student affairs professional can best contribute to establishing an environment and campus community that is open and accepting of all students and its constituents.

References

Adam, B. D. (1987). *The rise of a gay and lesbian movement.* Boston: Twayne.
Alyson Almanac: The factbook of the lesbian and gay community. (1994–1995). Boston: Alyson Publications.
Barol, B. (1984, May). The fight over gay rights. *Newsweek on Campus,* pp. 4–10.
Barret B., & Logan, C. (2001). *Counseling gay men and lesbians.* Pacific Grove, CA: Brooks/Cole.

Beemyn, B. G. (2003). The silence is broken: A history of the first lesbian, gay, and bisexual college student groups. *Journal of the History of Sexuality, 12*(2), 205–223.

Bell, A. P., & Weinberg, M. S. (1978). *Homosexualities: A study of diversity among men and women.* New York: Simon & Schuster.

Berrill, K. (1989). *Report of the campus project of the National Gay and Lesbian Task Force.* Washington, DC: National Gay and Lesbian Task Force.

Bilodeau, B. L., & Renn, K. A. (2005). Analysis of LGBT identity development models and implications for practice. In R. L. Sanlo (Ed.), *Gender identity and sexual orientation: Research, policy, and personal perspectives* (pp. 25–39). San Francisco: Jossey-Bass.

Bolin, A. (1993). Transcending and transgendering: Male-to-female transsexuals, dichotomy, and diversity. In G. Herdt (Ed.), *Third sex, third gender: Beyond sexual dimorphism in culture and history* (pp. 447–486). New York: Zone Books.

Bourassa, D., & Shipton, B. (1991). Addressing lesbian and gay issues in the residence hall environment. In N. Evans & V. A. Wall (Eds.), *Beyond tolerance: Gays, lesbians and bisexuals on campus* (pp. 167–178). Alexandria, VA: American College Personnel Association.

Broido, E. M. (2000). Ways of being an ally to lesbian, gay, and bisexual students. In V. A. Wall & N. J. Evans (Eds.), *Toward acceptance: Sexual orientation issues on campus* (pp. 345–369). Washington, DC: American College Personnel Association.

Brown, L. (1999, April 15). U.S. lags behind world in gay rights. *Southern Voice, 1,* 28–29.

Brown, R. D. (1985). Creating an ethical community. In H. J. Canon & R. D. Brown (Eds.), *Applied ethics in student services.* San Francisco: Jossey-Bass.

Bullough, V. L. (1979). *Homosexuality: A history.* New York: New American Library.

Carter, K. A. (2000). Transgenderism and college students: Issues of gender identity and its role on our campuses. In V. A. Wall & N. J. Evans (Eds.), *Toward acceptance: Sexual orientation issues on campus* (pp. 261–282). Washington, DC: American College Personnel Association.

Case, D. N. (1998). Lesbian, gay, and bisexual issues within the Greek community. In R. L. Sanlo (Ed.), *Working with lesbian, gay, bisexual, and transgender college students: A handbook for faculty and administrators* (pp. 67–78). Westport, CT: Greenwood.

Cass, V. C. (1979). Homosexual identity formation: A theoretical model. *Journal of Homosexuality, 4*(3), 219–235.

Cass, V. C. (1984). Homosexual identity formation: Testing a theoretical model. *Journal of Sex Research, 20,* 143–167.

Cass, V. C. (1983–1984). Homosexual identity: A concept in need of definition. *Journal of Homosexuality, 9,* 105–126.

Cass, V. C. (1990). The implications of homosexual identity formation for the Kinsey model and scale of sexual preference. In D. P. McWhirter, S. A. Sanders, & J. M. Reinisch (Eds.), *Homosexuality/heterosexuality: Concepts of sexual orientation* (pp. 239–266). New York: Oxford University Press.

Chen-Hayes, S. F., & Haley-Banez, L. (2000). *Lesbian, bisexual, gay and transgendered counseling in schools and families (1,2)* [DVD]. Hanover, MA: Microtraining Associates.

Chestnut, S. (1998). Queering the curriculum or what's Walt Whitman got to do with it? In R. L. Sanlo (Ed.), *Working with lesbian, gay, bisexual, and transgender college students: A handbook for faculty and administrators* (pp. 221–230). Westport, CT: Greenwood.

Coleman, E. (1981). Developmental stages of the coming out process. *Journal of Homosexuality, 7,* 31–43.

Coleman, E. (1990). Toward a synthetic understanding of sexual orientation. In D. P. McWhirter, S. A. Sanders, & J. M. Reinisch (Eds.), *Homosexuality/heterosexuality: Concepts of sexual orientation* (pp. 267–276). New York: Oxford University Press.

Consortium of Higher Education LGBT Resource Professionals (2008–2010). *Self studies: A 2006 Self Study.* Retrieved August 23, 2010, from http://www.lgbt.campus.org/about/studies

Croteau, J. M., & Lark, J. S. (1995). A qualitative investigation of biased and exemplary student affairs practices concerning lesbian, gay, and bisexual issues. *Journal of College Student Development, 36*(5), 472–482.

Dank, B. M. (1971). Coming out in the gay world. *Psychiatry, 34,* 180–197.

D'Augelli, A. R. (1989). Homophobia in a university community: Views of prospective resident assistants. *Journal of College Student Development, 30,* 546–552.

D'Augelli, A. R. (1991). Gay men in college: Identity process and adaptations. *Journal of College Student Development, 32,* 140–146.

D'Augelli, A. R. (1992). Lesbian and gay male undergraduates' experience of harassment and fear on campus. *Journal of Interpersonal Violence, 7*(3), 383–395.

D'Augelli, A. R. (1994). Identity development and sexual orientation: Toward a model of lesbian, gay, and bisexual development. In E. J. Trickett, R. J. Watts, & D. Birman (Eds.), *Human diversity: Perspectives on people in context* (pp. 312–333). San Francisco: Jossey-Bass.

D'Augelli, A. R. (1996). Enhancing the development of lesbian, gay, and bisexual youths. In E. D. Rothblum & L. A. Bond (Eds.), *Preventing heterosexism and homophobia* (pp. 124–150). Thousand Oaks, CA: Sage.

D'Augelli, A. R., & Rose, M. L. (1990). Homophobia in a university setting: Attitudes and experiences in heterosexual freshmen. *Journal of College Student Development, 31,* 484–491.

D'Emilio, J. (1991). The campus environment for gay and lesbian life. *Academe, 76*(1), 16–19.

DeMonteflores, C., & Schultz, S. J. (1978). Coming out: Similarities and differences for lesbian and gay men. *Journal of Social Issues, 34,* 180–197.

DeVito, J. A. (1979, November). *Educational responsibilities to the gay and lesbian student.* Paper presented at the 65th annual meeting of the Speech Communication Associates, San Antonio, TX.

DuMontier, V. L., II (2000). Faith, the Bible, and lesbians, gay men, and bisexuals. In V. A. Wall & N. J. Evans (Eds.), *Toward acceptance: Sexual orientation issues on campus* (pp. 321–341). Washington, DC: American College Personnel Association.

Dworkin, S. H. (2000). Individual therapy with lesbians, gays, and bisexuals. In R. M. Perez, K. A. DeBord, & K. J. Bieschke (Eds.), *Handbook of counseling and therapy with lesbians, gays, and bisexuals*. Washington, DC: American Psychological Association.

Ekins, R., & King, D. (1996). Blending genders: An introduction. In R. Ekins, & D. King (Eds.), *Blending genders: Social aspects of cross dressing and sex-changing* (pp. 1–4). New York: Routledge.

Evans, N. J., & Broido, E. M. (1991). Coming out in college residence halls: Negotiation, meaning making, challenges, supports. *Journal of College Student Development, 40*(6), 658–668.

Evans, N. J., & D'Augelli, A. R. (1996). Lesbians, gay men, and bisexual people in college. In R. C. Savin-Williams & K. M. Cohen (Eds.), *The lives of lesbians, gays, and bisexuals: Children to adult* (pp. 201–226). Fort Worth, TX: Harcourt Brace.

Evans, N. J., & Levine, H. (1990). Perspectives on sexual orientaton. In L. V. Moore (Ed.), *Evolving theoretical perspectives on students* (pp. 49–58). San Francisco: Jossey-Bass.

Evans, N. J., & Wall, V. A. (Eds.). (1991). *Beyond tolerance: Gays, lesbians, and bisexuals on campus*. Alexandria, VA: American College Personnel Association.

Fahy, U. (1995). *How to make the world a better place for gays and lesbians*. New York: Warner.

Fassinger, R. E. (1998). Lesbian, gay, and bisexual identity and student development theory. In R. L. Sanlo (Ed.), *Working with lesbian, gay, bisexual, and transgender college students: A handbook for faculty and administrators* (pp. 13–22). Westport, CT: Greenwood.

Fassinger, R. E., & Miller, B. A. (1996). Validation of an inclusive model of sexual minority identity formation on a sample of gay men. *Journal of Homosexuality, 32*, 53–78.

Feinberg, L. (1996). *Transgender warriors*. Boston: Beacon.

Firestein, B. A. (Ed.). (1996). *Bisexuality: The psychology and politics of an invisible minority*. Thousand Oaks, CA: Sage.

Fone, B. (2000). *Homophobia: A history*. New York: Henry Holt.

Fox, R. C. (1995). Bisexual identities. In A. R. D'Augelli & C. J. Patterson (Eds.), *Lesbian, gay, and bisexual identities over the lifespan: Psychological perspectives* (pp. 48–86). New York: Oxford University Press.

Hammersmith, S. K., & Weinberg, M. S. (1973). Homosexual identity: Commitment, adjustment, and significant others. *Sociometry, 36*(1), 56–79.

Herbst, S., & Malaney, G. D. (1999). Perceived value of a special interest residential program for gay, lesbian, bisexual, and transgender students. *NASPA Journal, 36*(2), 106–119.

Herdt, G. (1992). *Gay culture in America: Essays from the field*. Boston: Beacon.

Jay, K., & Young, A. (1994). *Lavender culture*. New York: New York University Press.

Katchadourian, H. A. (1989). *Fundamentals of human sexuality* (5th ed.). Fort Worth, TX: Holt, Rinehart and Winston.

Keeling, R. P. (1998). Effective and humane campus health and counseling services. In R. L. Sanlo (Ed.), *Working with lesbian, gay, bisexual, and transgender college students: A handbook for faculty and administrators* (pp. 147–157). Westport, CT: Greenwood.

Kinsey, A. C., Pomeroy, W. B., & Martin, C. E. (1948). *Sexual behavior in the human male.* Philadelphia: Saunders.

Klein, F. (1993). *The bisexual option*. Binghamton, NY: Harrington Park Press.

Kraig, B. (1998). Exploring sexual orientation issues at colleges and universities with religious affiliations. In R. L. Sanlo (Ed.), *Working with lesbian, gay, bisexual, and transgender college students: A handbook for faculty and administrators* (pp. 245–254). Westport, CT: Greenwood.

Lambert, S. (2005). The experience of gay male and lesbian faculty in counselor education departments: A grounded theory. *Dissertation Abstracts International, 66* (06A), 2113. (UMI No. 3177885)

Lee, J. A. (1977). Going public: A study in the sociology of homosexual liberation. *Journal of Homosexuality, 3,* 49–78.

Lees, L. J. (1998). Transgender students on our campuses. In R. L. Sanlo (Ed.), *Working with lesbian, gay, bisexual, and transgender college students: A handbook for faculty and administrators* (pp. 37–44). Westport, CT: Greenwood.

Lesbian, Gay, Bisexual Transgender Center. (2010). *Definitions and information.* Retrieved August 20, 2010, from http://www.ohio.edu/lgbt/resources/Definitions _and_Information.cfm

Levine, A. (1992). A time to act. *Change, 24*(1), 3–4.

Levine, H., & Evans, N. (1991). The development of gay, lesbian and bisexual identities. In N. Evans, & V. Wall (Eds.), *Beyond tolerance: Gay, lesbians and bisexuals on campus.* Washington, DC: American College Personnel Association.

Liddell, D. L., & Douvanis, C. J. (1994). The social and legal status of gay and lesbian students: An update for colleges and universities. *NASPA Journal, 31,* 121–129.

Lucozzi, E. A. (1998). A far better place: Institutions as allies. In R. L. Sanlo (Ed.), *Working with lesbian, gay, bisexual, and transgender college students: A handbook for faculty and administrators* (pp. 47–52). Westport, CT: Greenwood.

Marszalek, J. F., III, & Goree, C. T. (1995). Practicing what we preach? Gay students' perceptions of student affairs. *College Student Affairs Journal, 15*(1), 80–86.

McCarn, S. R., & Fassinger, R. E. (1996). Re-visioning sexual minority identity formation: A new model for lesbian identity and its implications for counseling and research. *The Counseling Psychologists, 24,* 508–534.

McNaron, J. A. (1989). Mapping a country: What lesbian students want. In C. Pearson, D. L. Shavelik, & J. G. Touchton (Eds.), *Educating the majority: Women challenging transitions in higher education* (pp. 102–113). New York: Macmillan.

Michael, R. T., Gagnon, J. H., Laumann, E. O., & Kolata, G. (1994). *Sex in America: A definitive survey*. Boston: Little, Brown.

Minton, H. L., & McDonald, G. J. (1984). Homosexual identity formation as a developmental process. *Journal of Homosexuality, 9,* 91–104.

Mondimore, F. M. (1996). *A natural history of homosexuality*. Baltimore, MD: John Hopkins University Press.

Morales, E. S. (1990). Ethnic minority families and minority gays and lesbians. In F. W. Bozett, & M. B. Sussman (Eds.), *Homosexuality and family relations*. Binghamton, NY: Harrington Park Press.

Moses, A. E., & Hawkins, R. O. (1986). *Counseling lesbian women and gay men: A life-issues approach*. New York: Glencoe/McGraw-Hill.

Newman, P. A. (1998). Coming out in the age of AIDS: HIV prevention on campus. In R. L. Sanlo (Ed.), *Working with lesbian, gay, bisexual, and transgender college students: A handbook for faculty and administrators* (pp. 159–170). Westport, CT: Greenwood.

O'Brien, K. M. (1998). The people in between: Understanding the needs of bisexual students. In R. L. Sanlo (Ed.), *Working with lesbian, gay, bisexual, and transgender college students: A handbook for faculty and administrators* (pp. 31–35). Westport, CT: Greenwood.

Patterson, C. J. (1995). Lesbian and gay parents and their children: A summary of research findings. In American Psychological Association (Ed.), *Lesbian and gay parenting: A resource for psychologists* (2nd ed.). Washington, DC: Author.

Plummer, K. (1975). *Sexual stigma: An interactionist account*. London: Routledge & Kegan Paul.

Pope, R. L., & Reynolds, A. L. (1991). Including bisexuality: It's more than just a label. In N. J. Evans & V. A. Wall (Eds.), *Beyond tolerance: Gays, lesbians, and bisexuals on campus*. Washington, DC: American College Personnel Association.

Rankin, S. R. (2003). *Campus climate for gay, bisexual, lesbian, and transgender people: A national perspective*. Washington, DC: National and Gay Lesbian Task Force Policy Institute.

Renn, K. A. (1998). Lesbian, gay, bisexual, and transgender students in the college classroom. In R. L. Sanlo (Ed.), *Working with lesbian, gay, bisexual, and transgender college students: A handbook for faculty and administrators* (pp. 231–237). Westport, CT: Greenwood.

Renn, K. A., Dilley, P., & Prentice, M. (2003). Commonalities, differences and complementarities. In J. C. Smart (Ed.), *Higher education: Handbook of theory and research* (Vol. 28, pp. 191–262). Norwell, MA: Kluwer.

Rhoads, R. A. (1994). *Coming out in college: The struggle for a queer identity*. Westport, CT: Bergin & Garvey.

Rhoads, R. A. (1995a). The cultural politics of coming out in college: Experiences of male college students. *The Review of Higher Education, 19,* 1–23.

Rhoads, R. A. (1995b). Learning from the coming out experiences of college males. *The Journal of College Student Development, 36,* 67–74.

Rhoads, R. A. (1997). Implications of the growing visibility of gay and bisexual male students on campus. *NASPA Journal, 34,* 275–286.

Robin, L., & Hamner, K. (2000). Bisexuality: Identities and community. In V. A. Wall & N. J. Evans (Eds.), *Toward acceptance* (pp. 245–259). Lanham, MD: University Press of America.

Rust, P. C. (1993). "Coming out" in the age of social constructionism: Sexual identity formation among lesbian and bisexual women. *Gender and Society, 7,* 50–77.

Ryan, C., & Futterman, D. (1998). *Lesbian and gay youth.* New York: Columbia University Press.

Salkever, K., & Worthington, R. L. (1998). Creating a safe space in college athletics. In R. L. Sanlo (Ed.), *Working with lesbian, gay, bisexual, and transgender college students: A handbook for faculty and administrators* (pp. 193–202). Westport, CT: Greenwood.

Sanlo, R. L. (Ed.). (1995). *Gender identity and sexual orientation: Research, policy and personal perspectives.* San Francisco: Jossey Bass.

Sanlo, R. L. (1998). *Working with lesbian, gay, bisexual, and transgender college students: A handbook for faculty and administrators.* Westport, CT: Greenwood.

Sanlo, R. L. (2000a). The LGBT campus resource center director: The new profession in student affairs. *NASPA Journal, 37*(3), 485–495.

Sanlo, R. L. (2000b). Lavender graduation: Acknowledging the lives and achievements of lesbian, gay, bisexual, and transgender college students. *Journal of College Student Development, 41*(6), 643–647.

Savin-Williams, R. C. (1990). *Gay and lesbian youth: Expressions of identity.* Washington, DC: Hemisphere.

Savin-Williams, R. C. (1995). Lesbian, gay, male and bisexual adolescents. In A. R. D'Augelli & C. J. Patterson (Eds.), *Lesbian, gay, and bisexual identities over the life span: Psychological perspectives* (pp. 165–189). New York: Oxford University Press.

Savin-Williams, R. C. (1998). *And then I became gay: Young men's stories.* New York: Routhledge.

Schoenberg, R. (1989). Lesbian/gay identity development during the college years. (Doctoral dissertation, University of Pennsylvania, 1989). *Dissertation Abstracts International, 50,* 27 52243.

Scott, D. (1991). Working with gay and lesbian student organizations. In N. J. Evans & V. A. Wall (Ed.), *Beyond tolerance: Gays, lesbians, and bisexuals on campus* (pp. 117–130). Alexandria, VA: American College Personnel Association.

Sherrill, J. M., & Hardesty, C. A. (1994). *The gay, lesbian, and bisexual students' guide to colleges, universities, and graduate schools.* New York: New York University Press.

Shively, M. G., & DeCecco, J. P. (1993). Components of sexual identity. In L. D. Garnets & D. C. Kimmel (Eds.), *Psychological perspectives on lesbian and gay male experiences* (pp. 80–88). New York: Columbia University Press.

Singer, B. L., & Deschamps, D. (Eds.). (1994). *Gay & lesbian stats: A pocket guide of facts and figures.* New York: New Press.

Slater, B. R. (1993). Violence against lesbians and gay male college students. In L. C. Whitmaker & J. W. Pollards (Eds.), *Campus violence: Kinds, causes, and cures* (pp. 171–202). New York: Haworth Press.

Sophie, J. (1986). A critical examination of stage theories of lesbian identity development. *Journal of Homosexuality, 12,* 39–51.

Thoresen, J. H. (1998). "Do we have to call it that?!" Planning, implementing, and teaching an LGBT course. In R. L. Sanlo (Ed.), *Working with lesbian, gay, bisexual, and transgender college students: A handbook for faculty and administrators* (pp. 255–263). Westport, CT: Greenwood.

Troiden, R. R. (1979). Becoming homosexual: A model of gay identity acquisition. *Psychiatry, 42,* 362–373.

Troiden, R. R. (1988). Homosexual identity development. *Journal of Adolescent Health, 9,* 105–113.

Underhile, R., & Cowles, J. R. (1998). Gay, lesbian, bisexual, and transgender students with disabilities: Implications for faculty and staff. In R. L. Sanlo (Ed.), *Working with lesbian, gay, bisexual, and transgender college students: A handbook for faculty and administrators* (pp. 171–177). Westport, CT: Greenwood.

U.S. Student Association. (2007). *Welcome to USSA!* Retrieved August 22, 2010, from http://www.usstudents.org/

Warren, C. A. B. (1974). *Identity and community in the gay world.* New York: Wiley.

Washington, J., & Evans, N. J. (1991). Becoming an ally. In N. J. Evans & V. A. Wall (Eds.), *Beyond tolerance: Gays, lesbians, and bisexuals on campus* (pp. 195–204). Washington, DC: American College Personnel Association.

Watkins, B. L. (1998). Bending toward justice: Examining and dismantling heterosexism on college and university campuses. In R. L. Sanlo (Ed.), *Working with lesbian, gay, bisexual, and transgender college students: A handbook for faculty and administrators* (pp. 267–276). Westport, CT: Greenwood.

Weinberg, G. (1972). *Society and the healthy homosexual.* New York: Anchor/ Doubleday.

Weinberg, G. (1978). On "doing" and "being" gay: Sexual behavior and homosexual male self-identification. *Journal of Homosexuality, 4*(2), 143–156.

Weinberg, M. S., & Williams, C. J. (1974). *Male homosexuals: Their problems and adaptations.* London: Oxford University Press.

Weinberg, M. S., Williams, C. J., & Pryor, D. W. (1994). *Dual attraction: Understanding bisexuality.* New York: Oxford University Press.

Worthington, R. L., McCrary, S. I., & Howard, K. A. (1998). Becoming an LGBT affirmative career adviser: Guidelines for faculty, staff, and administrators. In R. L. Sanlo (Ed.), *Working with lesbian, gay, bisexual, and transgender college students: A handbook for faculty and administrators* (pp. 135–143). Westport, CT: Greenwood.

14

NONTRADITIONAL COLLEGE STUDENTS

Fiona J. D. MacKinnon and Rosiline D. Floyd

Adult learners add a welcome dash of maturity and character to college campuses. They enrich the college classroom with their wide-ranging backgrounds and diverse perspectives; they are varied in age, gender, color, political persuasion, and socioeconomic class. The stereotype of college as an experience for the young is still pervasive within society at large, and on many campuses so many adults feel sensitive about their status. Even the name most institutions use to describe adult learners–*nontraditional students*—has negative implications. Fortunately, some colleges and universities, particularly community colleges, urban institutions, and liberal arts colleges with specially designed niches for returning adults, create environments in which all multicultural adult learners are not only accepted but also appreciated and respected.

Historically, students and teachers came to universities from the same privileged social backgrounds, sharing similar values and principles (Hermida, 2009). Thus teachers' and students' perspectives were the same. Because of this cultural climate, the differences and needs of diverse populations and the role of educators in meeting the needs of all students were not acknowledged or understood. Throughout most of U.S. educational history, adults have not been welcomed by institutions of higher education, even though veterans have been tolerated following major wars. Multicultural adults and women have had an even more difficult time gaining access to continued education. Race, class, age, and gender have been the primary factors leading to disparities in access. In spite of rhetoric that voices empowerment and equal access, the reality denies the sentiment (Merriam & Caffarella, 1999).

Many multicultural academics challenge collegiate educational providers to create environments that are engaging and supportive for all students (Bell, 1992; Guy, 1999; Wilson, 1987). Higher education administrators, faculty, and student affairs professionals can play important roles in changing society for the betterment of all. All educational stakeholders must carefully examine their own views of mainstream American culture and the European American ethnic identity that prevails in most colleges and universities to enhance the learning experience of multicultural adult learners (Guy). Higher education is a very patriarchal environment with a strong European tradition. Traditionally, African Americans, Native Americans, Hispanic Americans, and Asian Americans who frequently have been relegated socially, politically, and economically to the margins of society have also been marginalized as adult learners by higher education. The reality of the higher education experience for adult learners is not always evident to student affairs professionals who must not make assumptions about the institutional culture or physical or psychological environment in which learning is taking place (Knowles, 1984). Professionals must listen and assess carefully the stories or narratives adult students tell about their experiences. Instead of expecting adult learners to adapt, stakeholders in education must adapt to the needs of the students.

Demographic Background

The rate of adult involvement in formal learning has grown enormously since the stream of veterans into higher education after World War II. During the 1960s and 1970s the growth in participation of adults in organized learning activities grew at twice the growth rate of their population (Kett, 1994). The label nontraditional was first applied to adult women. This term was also later applied to any college students older than the traditional 18- to 22-year-olds (Kett). Throughout the 1950s and 1960s colleges and universities were "male bastions," (Kett, 1994, p. 429) but by the latter half of the 1970s the number of women students rose by 25%, and the number of men remained unchanged (Kett). The increased enrollment of adult women who took advantage of the easing of age requirements in the 1970s, paved the way for other adults. Voorhees and Lingenfelter (2003) offered one of the most encompassing definitions of the adult learner in postsecondary education:

someone 25 years of age or older involved in postsecondary learning activities. This definition along with the term nontraditional students will be used throughout this chapter. The numbers of nontraditional college students continues to increase. From 1985 to 1996 there was an estimated 65% percent increase in enrollment of students 35 years of age and older, from 1.7 million to 2.9 million (National Center for Education Statistics [NCES], 1996). Using age as the criterion to define *adult learner*, 43% (or 14 million) of students in U.S. higher education are 25 or older (National Center for Higher Education Management Systems [NCHEMS], 2007). The percentage of 25- to 29-year-olds completing a bachelor's degree or higher increased from 17% to 29% between 1971 and 2000 and was 31% in 2008. Women accounted for 57% percent of the bachelor's degrees conferred and 62% of all associate's degrees awarded in the 2006–07 academic year (NCES, 2009).

Overall, the nontraditional student population has grown rapidly. According to NCES, adult learners represented a staggering 6.8 million college students in 2009 (Headden, 2009). Headden further contended adult learners or nontraditional students made up about 70% of enrollment on most college campuses that year. "Those numbers are expected to climb rapidly as colleges look for pools of students—and tuition income—to replace the cohort of 18–22 year olds that will start shrinking when the current baby boomlet trails off " (p. 4). Significant demographic changes are occurring in society, and the population is diversifying culturally and ethnically. Projections indicate that by the year 2050, minorities will account for 47% of the population, yet "minority adults . . . are disproportionately represented among the unemployed, the low-income stratum and the less educated. These characteristics are correlated with low rates of participation in organized adult education" (Merriam & Caffarella, 1999, p. 9). This underdevelopment of talent is a great loss to the nation that benefits when all citizens are educated and productively employed.

Community college administrators have been diligent in recruiting nontraditional populations (Cohen & Brawer, 1996). Community colleges have larger percentages of nontraditional, low-income, and minority students than 4-year institutions. Adult learners made up about 43% of total enrollment at community colleges, and represent 12% of all postsecondary education students (Council for Adult and Experiential Learning [CAEL], 2008). As we enter the second decade of the 21st century, community colleges account for about half the total enrollment in higher education, and 47% of ethnic minority students. Community college student populations tend to reflect the makeup of the local community indicating the openness and readiness of the community college system to welcome students of all backgrounds (Cohen & Brawer).

Retaining nontraditional learners is still a challenge in higher education, with 38.9% dropping out of college compared to traditional-age full-time students (18.2%) (Headden, 2009). Moreover, "the retention rate for nontraditional students age 30 or older is 65.4 percent, and the graduation rate is an abysmal 10.8 percent" (p. 4). In an attempt to reverse poor retention trends, scores of colleges, 2- and 4-year institutions, have committed to focusing on this population. This commitment includes improving outreach, loosening schedules, accelerating courses, granting interim certificates, offering more online classes, providing better advising, improving developmental education, and awarding credit for life and work experience, all radical reforms in how educational institutions serve nontraditional adults.

Educators did not foresee the dramatic economic downturn in this country that started at the beginning of this century. This systemic shift in the nation's economy created an effect similar to a ripple in a pond, with individuals from every generation seeking admittance to our higher education institutions to catch up on the latest trends, find a skill set to meet the needs of today's industries, and in some cases, compete with students half their age.

Nontraditional Students in the 21st Century

Fifty-nine million people, or 30%, of the U.S. adult population, have never entered postsecondary education—and in 35 states, more than 60% of the population does not have an associate's degree or anything higher (CAEL, 2008). Minorities and nontraditional adult learners disproportionately enroll in community colleges and for-profit institutions (NCES, 2009). Kelly (2001) stated that

> a growing number of traditional colleges and universities—under pressure to be more responsive to the needs of students, parents, employers and communities—are turning to some of the same entrepreneurial, customer-oriented approaches that have been used so successfully by for-profit institutions. (p. 4)

To compete globally, we must seek to develop the untapped potential of the millions of working adults who have not completed a 4-year degree. Their success is essential to themselves, their families, and communities, and to the health and security of the nation (Headden, 2009). These people are from different backgrounds—the previously well-paid, now laid-off factory worker, the single parent struggling with three children, the high school dropout or GED recipient who now realizes a future without an education is bleak, the immigrant with limited English skills, the corporate executive who was downsized, and the honored military veteran. All face the transition of returning to school for survival. Some say this population might hold the key to America's future. In the early 21st century a record numbers of jobs were eliminated in manufacturing and the industries that support manufacturing. Technology now drives an increasingly global economy. As companies reinvent themselves for profitability, displaced workers are forced to either find new careers or make adjustments for new career options. Stakeholders in education must be proactive in committing resources to assist in these transitions.

Headden (2009) concluded that today's adults need higher levels of academic and technical knowledge to remain employable in an information and service economy characterized by frequent job and career change. The United States must produce 64 million individuals with college degrees between 2005 and 2025 to remain competitive with leading nations and meet labor force needs. At the current degree-awarding rate, a gap of 16 million degrees is anticipated (NCHEMS, 2007). Increasing global economic competition and the rapid pace of technological change are revolutionizing the skills and educational qualifications necessary for individual job success and national economic well-being. To meet this demand, adults from a variety of backgrounds find themselves returning to school. With this increasing population, colleges and universities around the country must now adapt to the influx of adult learners who have different expectations and perspectives from traditional college students. Postsecondary education once viewed as a luxury is increasingly needed for economic survival.

Having fought wars in Afghanistan and Iraq, soldiers in increasing numbers are returning from war seeking career opportunities. Over the next few years, the United States will welcome more than 2 million veterans returning from Iraq and Afghanistan (Headden, 2009). The new Post 9/11 GI Bill offers generous educational benefits to many of these veterans, as well as those still serving in the active, reserve, and National Guard components of the armed forces. These veterans are expected to enroll in higher education to enhance their job prospects, achieve career goals, expand their knowledge and skill sets for personal and career enrichment, and facilitate their transition to civilian life. Like many other adult students, they return as outsiders to a campus of e-mails, iPods, and social networking sites like Facebook, and Twitter.

Who Are Adult Learners?

Adult learners, or what CAEL (2000) described as the transition from 18–21-year-olds to an older undergraduate population that is now the majority, have a greater understanding of the impact of education on their lives and different expectations from courses and professors than traditional students have. Research on adult education shows adult learners have different expectations for the college experience (Strange, 2008). In a study of adult learners versus traditional-age students, adult learners described their ideal professor and ideal course as organized and flexible.

These learners are typically 25 or older and oftentimes are independent with families. Higher education research tells us that adults learn best when they are actively engaged in the learning experience, that the curriculum is most effective when it builds upon the life experiences and interests of the adult learner, and that there is a need for flexibility in student services (e.g., evening office hours and electronic access; Cross, 1981; Chickering & Reisser, 1993; Headden, 2009; Merriam & Caffarella, 1991).

Despite having an understanding of the values of adult learners, the Commission for a Nation of Lifelong Learners concluded ill-adapted higher education practices pose barriers to participation, including a lack of flexibility in calendars and scheduling, academic content, modes of instruction, and availability of learning services (NCHEMS, 2007). This disconnect resonates as adult learners or nontraditional students drop out of college at a much higher rate, 38.9%, than traditional full-time students (18.2%). The retention rate for nontraditional students age 30 or older is 65.4%, and the 6-year graduation rate is an abysmal 10.8% (Pusser et al., 2007).

In an attempt to reverse these trends some colleges, including 2- and 4-year institutions, have accepted that nontraditional adults learn very differently from younger adults and have adapted their methods accordingly. Many if not most college instructors will say they actually prefer teaching adult students. According to Pusser et al. (2007), older students are generally more engaged, motivated, and focused than younger students. Their expectations are higher, and adult students are more vocal and interactive in class and online. However, unlike younger learners, they have less tolerance for abstract concepts, and they want to use education to help solve problems.

As an instructor of adult learners, one of the authors of this chapter has encountered students who were forced to return to school to receive government benefits. These women sometimes had to bring children to class or leave them outside the door during class. On more than one occasion, the instructor fed or walked a baby so a student could take a test. One memorable African American male student was a laid-off factory worker whose income had dropped from over $80,000 to closer to $20,000 in unemployment and union benefits; he had lost his home, his nice car, and his dignity. There was also the soldier who served two tours in Iraq, had left his wife and four kids in another city, and was attending class from 8 a.m. to noon on Saturday mornings attempting to earn a degree in heating and air-conditioning. Returning to school has physical and psychological effects for these students. Adult learners enter classrooms where chalkboards have been replaced by smart boards, and technology permeates all aspects of college, from registration to ordering textbooks. Many adults are astounded to find themselves carrying or rolling a backpack like other college students when they expected their career choices to last a lifetime without the benefit of additional schooling. They enter these campuses disenfranchised by the lack of economic opportunities and determined to change their futures. Thomas (2005) contended that adult learning programs are all too often marginalized, neglected, and left out of a college or university's mission. However, budget-conscious administrators of colleges and universities must recognize the need and benefits of catering to this increasing population. These students seek more than an instructor; they want a compassionate understanding ear, and they clearly understand the urgency of an education for future employment.

Adult students lead full lives balancing family responsibilities, jobs, and community responsibilities. They cannot place their roles as parents or workers on hold while they attend college to better their lives for themselves and their families. NCES surveys consistently indicate the primary reason adults consider continued learning is for job-related reasons (Kim, Collins, Stowe, & Chandler, 1995). Merriam and Caffarella (1999) cited a United Nations Educational, Scientific, and Cultural Organization (UNESCO) survey in which 91% of the respondents indicated professional or career upgrading for participation in adult education activities. Women without college degrees, industrial workers facing layoffs, and the poor who have not had a chance to further their education are interested in preparing for jobs that will help them support their families (Merriam & Caffarella). College graduates who are already established in careers but wish to advance in the early and middle years of their work life frequently seek advanced education. The economically, politically, and socially disadvantaged who have not had the opportunity for postsecondary education and, in fact, may have received a poor elementary and secondary education foundation also pursue higher education for job-related reasons. Education is frequently the means to meaningful career goals, or at least a reasonable paycheck.

Adult learning is often triggered by life events and transitions (Aslanian & Brickell, 1980; Merriam & Clark, 1991; Schlossberg, Waters, & Goodman, 1995). Life transitions create periods of uncertainty and opportunity that require sustained attention for resolution. Adults report that when they are faced with transitions, like having a baby, changing jobs, or being laid off from work, they are likely to seek informal and formal learning opportunities to develop skills or gain knowledge (Aslanian & Brickell). For example, a person laid off from the health care industry may view the transition as an opportunity to pursue a different career and return to higher education to acquire a certificate or degree in accounting, social work, or computer programming. Transitions or any drastic changes in general are particularly distressing for adults.

Headden (2009) reports the number of adult learners age 25 and older in the United States is expected to climb as colleges seek more students, and careers require more education (p. 4). Academic administrators, faculty, and student affairs professionals all need to work together to provide adult learners with convenient and affordable access, flexible subsidies, and innovative planning tools to increase student success (Headden).

Much research exists on meeting the needs of traditional students (Astin, 1998; Pascarella & Terenzini, 1998; Tinto, 2008). However, one size fits all does not accommodate the different learning styles of adult learners or address the different issues they face. The transition hurdles adult learners face include the technology gap, part-time and reenrollment issues, family and financial commitments, and inadequate initial skills.

Developmental Theories

The Adult Persistence in Learning Model

The Adult Persistence in Learning (APIL) Model provides a road map to help faculty and administrators structure instruction and services for adults (MacKinnon-Slaney, 1994), and it identifies survival skills adults must master to be able to negotiate the occasionally stormy waters of higher education. The model contains three components (personal issues, learning issues, and environmental issues) that combine to direct the success or failure of adults to survive in formal learning environments. Personal issues can be separated into five groups of factors that are heightened when adults are faced with new learning experiences at matriculation or at the start of each term. Factors such as self-awareness, willingness to delay gratification, clarification of career and life goals, mastery of life transitions, and a sense of personal competence allow adult learners to feel ready to accept learning challenges. One factor in particular, academic self-efficacy, plays a continuing role in multicultural adults' ability to persevere in the face of challenge. If faculty and administrators use these concerns as a checklist for problem solving with learners, adults can better face their fears and move ahead.

The second constellation of factors focuses on learning issues. When adult learners return to the classroom they are faced with increased concerned about their educational competence. Relearning how to learn is critical to success in the classroom. A simple suggestion from a faculty member to read a study skills book or take a test to determine favored learning styles can make a difference and help allay classroom jitters. Intellectual and political awareness in the classroom are also important skills.

The third group of factors concentrates on the university or college environment. Many adults, particularly those who are first-generation college students, simply do not know what questions to ask. They do not understand the specialized vocabulary such as *bursar, elective, major,* and *prerequisite.* Adult learners have many unanswered questions about how to access information from the registrar, the bursar, their adviser, the course schedule, and so on. They also want to know about special opportunities available to them and the challenges they will face. And they are concerned with their own comfort level in the environment: comfort with faculty, with student colleagues, and with administrators and staff. Students want to know they matter to the institution and can find a comfortable place for themselves within the university system (Schlossberg, Lynch, & Chickering, 1989). Also, direction and support from professionals can help multicultural adults examine the environment and resolve issues.

A Model for Educating Adult Learners: The Sequence of Student Educational Services

Schlossberg et al. (as cited in Evans, Forney, Guido, Patton, & Renn, 2010) describes the process of adult learners as needing services and support during pivotal stages in their college years from the entry phase, engagement phase of course work, and on-campus transitions as they successfully matriculate and graduate. This approach provides direction for student services professionals and outlines the needs of adult learners. At each stage of moving in, moving through, and moving on the model directs the professional to learner needs, institutional responses, payoffs for learners, and payoffs for institutions. As learners move into the college environment they need to learn the ropes, which involves getting help with such issues as financial aid and planning, admissions procedures, orientation to the institution, availability of student employment, registration, assessment of prior learning, and developmental assessment. The moving through phase focuses on hanging in there through supportive educational services such as career development, life and personal counseling, health services, child care, family care, and developmental mentoring. Finally, the moving on phase centers on planning next steps such as internships and co-op learning, academic review and integration, placement services, job search, and developmental transcript review (Schlossberg et al., 1989). The model ensures that all necessary services will be provided at the right time for returning adults.

Ecological Systems Approach

As student affairs professionals listen to the stories of adult learners, specifically those historically underserved or multicultural adults, they need a method to sensitively analyze the life space of multicultural adults who are embarking on formal learning experiences (Evans et al., 2010). The analysis should reflect the multiple responsibilities of complex lives. Simple, linear models of development or environmental structure are not adequate for the task of understanding how multicultural adults cope with the university experience as well as their already daunting everyday tasks. What is needed is a way in which student affairs professionals can sort and sift through the factors that challenge, or enhance, persistence in learning. Analytical tools that offer an ecological systems approach provide valuable assistance to professionals as they search for appropriate guidance to respond to multicultural adult learners.

Bronfenbrenner's (1993) ecological systems approach provides administrators with insight into the constellation of environments any individual adult lives in. The focus of analysis is on the adult's perceptions of the interconnected reality of life—home, grandparents, in-laws, the neighborhood, the children's school, the classroom, the campus, as well as the values of the larger society. The ecology of human development entails the study of the developing, ever-changing person within the continually varying settings and larger context surrounding that person (Gardiner & Kosmitzki, 2002). Adult learners juggle multiple responsibilities and lead complicated lives that affect their dedication to the college experience. Simple models of development or environment do not capture the essence of their existence.

The ecology systems approach divides the ecological environment into *nested systems*: micro system, mesosystem, exosystem, macrosystem, and chronosystem. The microsystem, the first level of analysis, includes "a pattern of activities, roles, and interpersonal relations experienced . . . in the immediate environment" (Bronfenbrenner, 1993, p. 15). This level of analysis is helpful for understanding the adult's relationships to spouse, partner, children, and parents. If the adult learner is a single parent the student affairs professional can find out answers to such questions as the following: Who takes care of the laundry? Who cooks? Who picks up the children at the day care center? Is there enough money for food? The dynamics of the microsystem have a great impact on the learner's ability to focus on educational responsibilities.

The mesosystem is the second level of analysis and "recognizes that the individual microsystems in which the individual functions are not independent but are closely interrelated and influence each other" (Gardiner & Kosmitzki, 2002, p. 22). The mesosystem consists of two or more microsystems (home and day care, day care and college, college and family, for example). Attitudes and information from one microsystem filter into the other and modify behavior and development accordingly. For example, if daycare is not available when the English class is held then the adult learner either scrambles to find suitable care or leaves the child at home alone. Professionals can help advocate for services that will help adults meet their learning agendas.

The exosystem consists of settings in which the adult may not be a participant but nevertheless influence development in particular ways. For example, the local school board or the welfare system or even extended family, like aunts and uncles, may not be part of the adult's immediate microsystem but yet can have an impact on processes that affect the adult. When the school administration calls for a snow day, the adult learner is left trying to determine how to cope with children at home; when corporate headquarters decide to close the factory, then the adult faces being laid off and termination of any tuition reimbursement plan agreement with the employer. By understanding the linkages between the microsystem and the exosystem administrators can seek solutions to problems that seem overwhelming to the adult learner.

The macrosystem is most complex and provides the societal context for the individual's life space. This system is composed of societal "customs, values, and laws considered important in the individual's culture" (Gardiner & Kosmitzki, 2002, p. 23) According to Bronfenbrenner (1993), the macrosystem

> consists of the overarching pattern of micro-, meso-, and exosystems characteristic of a given culture, subculture, or other extended social structure, with particular reference to the . . . belief systems, resources, hazards, lifestyles, opportunity structures, life course options and patterns of social interchange that are embedded in such overarching systems. (p. 25).

Societal perspectives, biases, and stereotypes that relate to race, ethnicity, disability, and other realities of life can be examined intentionally through the analysis of the macrosystem. These factors are important for multicultural adult learners to recognize and understand so they may overcome barriers frequently placed in their way.

Finally, the chronosystem chronicles the nested systems over time and introduces the possibility of examining the influence of sociohistorical conditions. Often, developmental perspectives or environmental theories only take into account one particular point in time and do not consider the changes in settings, processes, influences, and development that occur over time. For example the terrorists' acts that devastated the World Trade Center in 2001 have sensitized society to the importance of family and relationships, and families may have changed their ways of interacting with each other because of the attacks of 9/11. Neighborhood violence has devastated many lives in the inner city creating awareness over time of the inability of the police or government authorities to act—this, in turn, has spurred on many neighborhood groups to take matters into their own hands for the sake of their children. It is important for student affairs professionals to teach the ecological systems approach to adults so they can make their own judgments and decisions about life experiences in the present and in the future.

Student affairs professionals must intentionally seek the knowledge, skills, and dispositions required to facilitate the learning experience of multicultural adult learners. The central adult issues of identity, purpose, intimacy, and integrity are of continuing concern throughout the life span and not just at the young adulthood stage (Chickering & Reisser, 1993; Gardiner & Kosmitzki, 2002; Helms, 1994; Kegan, 1994). Professionals must come to understand and not take for granted the issues that trigger reflection and response as multicultural adults seek to manage their complex lives with dignity and grace. An empathetic response, an ability to reframe issues, and knowledge of pragmatic techniques that help adults control their own learning experiences are critical skills. Student affairs professionals must recognize that adults take a brave step to return to the educational setting. Adult learners are looking for support for their learning agendas and for opportunities that will provide them with ways of coping. Professionals can help learners transform their dreams into reality.

Institutional Support for Nontraditional Students

American higher education continues as a work in progress nudged by federal policy such as the Post-9/11 GI Bill, stretched by community needs, and pushed by lifelong learning and the learning society. Community colleges have responded to society's cry for continued learning for adults, but 4-year institutions of higher learning have been reluctant to follow suit. In spite of voicing interest and accepting adults to make up for the shortfall of 18- to 22-year-olds, 4-year colleges and universities have not necessarily been hospitable sanctuaries of learning. Nevertheless, adult students continue to seek learning opportunities.

President Barack Obama believes the key to the economic future of this country is education (Fuller, 2010). The $787 billion economic stimulus law of 2009 provided $1.7 billion for adult employment services, including education and training. Also, in mid-July 2009, President Obama announced a $12 billion federal initiative to aid community colleges—a move intended to increase opportunities for many adult students at 2-year institutions and prompt some of these students to transfer to 4-year institutions.

The Lumina Foundation report *Adult Ed Grows Up* (2009) identified several areas of concern regarding America's growing numbers of adult learners. The report contended the higher education community must seek to develop the potential of the more than 54 million working adults who lack a college degree. Initially, higher education institutions must recognize adult learners as a diverse and complex set of individuals. Adult learners need convenient and affordable access to education as these students increasingly choose entrepreneurial postsecondary programs and institutions (Headden, 2009).

Adults transferring from a community college can merge their extensive real-world skills with relevant career interests, they have work experience and life experience that will provide an immediate benefit to the employer. Unlike traditional-age students, adult learners believed instructors were resources to help them learn. These learners said they would more readily ask questions to clarify material. Adult students' self-profiles more closely matched those of their college faculty than those of traditional-age students (Feldman, 1988).

Educational institutions must reconstruct their mission to serve all students including adult learners. Meeting the needs of the adult learner population will require faculty and administrators to respect the diversity of age, gender, race, and social class of adult students; appreciate that academic, professional, and personal goals greatly influence continuing education for most adult learners; implement practices that respect the years of experience adult learners bring to class; ensure that rigorous adult degree programs are accessible, flexible, and practical; and ensure that serving the adult learner population is included in the overall mission of the university (Thomas, 2005).

Rethinking Practice

A paradigm shift to include adult learners in the design of all aspects of postsecondary education needs to occur. This mandate is necessary for all involved including federal and state policy makers, student affairs professionals, postsecondary educators, and postsecondary administrators. Faculty, academic administrators, and student affairs professionals must review their respective policies and practices with a reflective eye making sure their approach signals culturally relevant adult learning. This starts with an understanding of the power influences of the dominant group and of the complexity of biculturalism. "Biculturalism is a mechanism of survival that constitutes forms of adaptive alternatives in the face of hegemonic control and institutional oppression" (Guy, 1999, p. 13). A consistent focus on biculturalism is the only way to ensure the cultural democracy that creates a culturally relevant learning environment.

In particular, four aspects of the learning environment require scrutiny: the student affairs professional's cultural identity, the learners' cultural identity, the curriculum and support in class and out of class, and instructional methods and processes of practice (Guy, 1999). Student affairs professional or instructor cultural self-awareness involves scrutiny of personal values, norms, and dispositions along with an understanding and respect for cultural differences (Kegan, 1994). On the part of the professional, this necessitates going beyond stylistic differences to the developmental constructivist understanding of self in relation to others and a willingness to suspend personal ethnocentric beliefs to concentrate on the meaning derived by learners (Kegan).

Understanding the learners' culture is the second aspect that requires attention from effective professionals. Professionals must begin by acknowledging the culture of their learners and coming to know that culture in a personal way through their relationships with their learners especially in the classroom. So, instead of pushing nontraditional students to adopt North American mainstream academic skills, disciplinary perspectives, and thought processes, we should open our classroom doors to teaching disciplinary content and academic skills from a wide array of diverse traditions so that every student will feel included. This will prepare mainstream and minority students to succeed as interculturally knowledgeable citizens in a globalized world (Schuerholz-Lehr, 2007).

The third component involves examination of the curriculum in and out of class. "Course content that stereotypes the very learners it is designed to serve does those learners an injustice. Insensitive or unknowing teachers can overlook material that learners may find offensive or simply irrelevant to their daily lives" (Guy, 1999, p. 15).

Some educators have attempted to integrate adult learners into instruction and curriculum design. Instead of adjusting to the needs of these students, most of these initiatives are remedial in nature, that is, they aim at equipping nontraditional students with the academic skills and knowledge of mainstream students and teachers (Tinto, 2008). Not surprisingly, these actions have proved inadequate to empower most minority students to succeed, as these measures neglect to acknowledge and incorporate the diverse values, beliefs, and skills, nontraditional students bring to the classroom. Educators must strategically consider all diverse populations, including adult learners, in the development and administration of curriculum, instructional styles, and interactions with students. No longer should nontraditional students be viewed as underprepared; rather, faculty must develop an understanding that their preparation responds to a different way of seeing themselves and understanding the world that derives from their own cultures and traditions. This different way of seeing the world has repercussions in most academic areas (Hermida, 2009). Siebert (2000) contends that instructors must be prepared for this challenge by recognizing that teaching adult learners requires more advanced teaching skills than teaching traditional students. He cites research that consistently shows adult students begin college classes with more fears and concerns than younger students. The role of the instructor is reducing the fears and concerns and then developing strong intrinsic interest in the course by connecting each student's plans for the future and past experiences with the course material. He further explains that an instructor needs many diverse skills to facilitate learning in adult students, including creating a noncompetitive atmosphere that encourages cooperative learning.

Finally, instructional methods and processes of practice may inadvertently include or exclude learners. Adult education approaches to learning, such as andragogy, traditionally require instructors and professionals to share power with learners. In formal learning environments power customarily resides with the instructor or administrator, negating the learner's past experience and ability to direct aspects of the learning agenda (Brookfield, 1995; Guy, 1999; Knowles, 1984). Inclusive teaching acknowledges and incorporates diverse knowledge modes, thought processes, and expressive styles into the classroom (Hermida, 2009).

Recommendations to Benefit Nontraditional-Age Students

Creating services and programming to enhance the postsecondary experiences of adult learners and increase success requires incorporating their needs into the mission of the institutions. In alignment with Siebert's (2000) assertion that the colleges most effective in attracting, retaining, and graduating adult students are those that are highly resilient and responsive to the needs of the students, instructors must be adaptable and flexible. Instructors should respect life experiences of adult learners and include their experiences in curriculum design and in-class activities. Instructors must recognize adult learners have diverse learning styles and design curriculum and present information using visual and auditory methods (Siebert; Hermida, 2009). Adult learners seek relevancy, thus instructors should align their courses so that the assessment and teaching and learning activities match intended learning outcomes (Biggs, 2003). Diversity should be included in assessment by going beyond exams, research papers, and group presentations to include tools used in other cultures, such as informal dialogues, holistic evaluation of student performance throughout the course, or self-evaluation (Hermida, 2009). Biggs (2003) contends assessments that actually evaluate whether and how well students have mastered a wide array of knowledge modes, diverse academic skills, and nontraditional disciplinary perspectives will likely achieve intended learning outcomes.

Programmers of cocurricular activities can also employ understanding of the importance of these four factors—adult learners' significant life experiences, diverse learning styles, need for relevance to their lives, and different communication styles—in planning and executing events and programs that will be attractive to this population. To facilitate success for adult learners, student affairs professionals must become active listeners, and by listening to adult students' stories, identify the developmental tasks that need to be accomplished and provide referral to services and programs that help adults master needed skills, knowledge, and attitudes for successful learning ventures.

Discussion Questions

1. Who are adult learners and why are they returning to school? How do adult learners differ from traditional students in learning styles and in expectations of their experience?
2. Discuss the impact of adult learners on other students, the institution, and society.
3. Identify strategies university administrators, student affairs professionals, and classroom instructors can use to actively engage and facilitate success for adult learners. Include in this discussion incorporating diverse populations into a traditional Eurocentric model and differing models for success.
4. What are some barriers to success for adult learners from the learners themselves and the institution? How can both groups work to limit the impact of these barriers? Discuss models of success for adult learners. Include in this discussion the evolution of technology and how it can hinder or assist adult learners with their transition.

References

Aslanian, C. B., & Brickell, H. M. (1980). *Americans in transition: Life changes as reasons for adult learning.* New York: College Entrance Examination Board.

Astin, A. W. (1998). *The changing American college student: Thirty-year trends 1966–1996.* San Francisco: Josey-Bass.

Bell, D. A. (1992). *Faces at the bottom of the well: The permanence of racism.* New York: Basic.

Biggs, J. (2003). *Teaching for quality learning at university* (2nd ed.). Buckingham, UK: Open University Press.

Bronfenbrenner, U. (1993). *The ecology of human development: Experiments by nature and design.* Cambridge, MA: Harvard University Press.

Bronfenbrenner, U. (1995). Developmental ecology through space and time: A future perspective. In P. Moen, G. H. Elder, & K. Luscher (Eds.), *Development in context: Acting and thinking in specific environments* (pp. 619–647). Washington, DC: American Psychological Association.

Brookfield, S. (1995). *Becoming a critically reflective teacher.* San Francisco: Jossey-Bass.

Chickering, A. W., & Reisser, L. W. (1993). *Education and identity* (2nd ed.). San Francisco: Jossey-Bass.

Clark, M. C., & Caffarella, R. S. (1999). Theorizing adult development. In M. C. Clark & R. S. Caffarella (Eds.), An Update on adult development: New ways of thinking about the life course. *New Directions for Adult and Continuing Education.* San Francisco: Jossey-Bass.

Cohen, A. M., & Brawer, F. B. (1996). *The American community college* (3rd ed.). San Francisco: Jossey-Bass.

Council for Adult and Experiential Learning. (2000). *Serving adult learners in higher education: Principles of effectivenss.* Retrieved from http://www.cael.org/pdf/publication_pdf/Summary%20of%20Alfi%20Principles%20of%20Effectiveness.pdf

Council for Adult and Experiential Learning. (2008). *State policies to bring adult learning into focus.* Retrieved from http://www.cael.org/pdf/State_Indicators_Monograph.pdf

Cross, K. P. (1981). *Adults as learners.* San Francisco: Jossey-Bass.

Evans, N. J., Forney, D. S., Guido, F. M., Patton, L. D., & Renn, K. A. (2010). *Student development in college: Theory, research, and practice* (2nd ed.). San Francisco: Jossey-Bass.

Feldman, K. (1988). Effective college teaching from the students and faculty's view: Matched or mismatched priorities. *Research in Higher Education, 28*(4), 291–344.

Fuller, A. (2010). Obama reaffirms support for community colleges at signing of student-loan bill. *Chronicle of Higher Education.* Retrieved from http://chronicle.com/article/Obama-Reaffirms-Support-for/64877

Gardiner, H. W., & Kosmitzki, C. (2002). *Lives across cultures: Cross-cultural human development* (2nd ed.). Boston: Allyn & Bacon.

Gibbs, G. (1983). Changing students' approaches to study through classroom exercises. In R. M. Smith (Ed.), *Helping adults learn how to learn* (pp. 83–96). San Francisco: Jossey-Bass.

Guy, T. C. (1999). Culture as context for adult education: The need for culturally relevant adult education. In T. C. Guy (Ed.), *Providing culturally relevant adult education: A challenge for the twenty-first century* (pp. 5–18). San Francisco: Jossey-Bass.

Headden, S. (2009). *Adult ed grows up.* Indianapolis, IN: Lumina Foundation for Education.

Helms, J. E. (1994). The conceptualization of racial identity and other "racial" constructs. In E. J. Trickett, R. J. Watts, & D. Birman (Eds.), *Human diversity: Perspectives on people in context* (pp. 285–311). San Francisco: Jossey-Bass.

Hermida, J. (2009). *Inclusive teaching strategies to promote non-traditional student success. Tomorrow's Professor.* Retrieved May 1, 2010, from http://ctl.stanford.edu

Horn, L. (1996). *Nontraditional undergraduates, trends in enrollment from 1986 to 1992 and persistence and attainment among 1989–90 beginning postsecondary students* (NCES 97–578). Washington, DC: U.S. Government Printing Office.

Kegan, R. (1994). *In over our heads: The mental demands of modern life.* Cambridge, MA: Harvard University Press.

Kelly, K. F. (2001). *Meeting needs and making profits: The rise of for-profit degree-granting institutions.* Denver, CO: Education Commission of the States.

Kett, J. F. (1994). *The pursuit of knowledge under difficulties: From self-improvement to adult education in America, 1750–1990.* Stanford, CA: Stanford University Press.

Kim, K., Collins, M., Stowe, P., & Chandler, K. (1995). *Forty percent of adults participate in adult education activities: 1994–95.* Washington, DC: National Center for Education Statistics.

Knowles, M. (1984). *The adult learner: A neglected species* (3rd ed.). Houston: Gulf.

Lumina Foundation Focus. (2009). *Colleges and universities take a mature approach to serving adult students.* Retrieved from http://www.luminafoundation.org/publications/focus_archive/Focus_Fall_20 09.pdf

MacKinnon-Slaney, F. (1994). The adult persistence in learning model: A road map to counseling services for adult learners. *Journal of Counseling and Development, 72,* 268–275.

Merriam, S. B., & Caffarella, R. S. (1999). *Learning in adulthood: A comprehensive guide* (2nd ed.). San Francisco, CA: Jossey-Bass.

Merriam, S. B., & Clark, M. C. (1991). *Lifelines: Patterns of work, love, and learning in adulthood.* San Francisco: Jossey-Bass.

National Center for Education Statistics. (1996). *Nontraditional undergraduates: Trends in enrollment from 1991 to 1992 and persistence and attainment among 1989–90 beginning postsecondary students* (NCES 97–578). Washington, DC: U.S. Department of Education.

National Center for Education Statistics. (2009). *The condition of education 2009* (NCES 2009–081). Washington, DC: U.S. Government Printing Office.

National Center for Higher Education Management Systems. (2007). *Adding up: State challenges for increasing college access and success.* Retrieved from http://makingopportunityaffordable.org

Pascarella, E. T., & Terenzini, P. T. (1998). Studying college students in the 21st century: Meeting new challenges. *Review of Higher Education, 21*(2), 151–165.

Pusser, B., Breneman, D., Gansneder, B., Kohl, K. J., Levin, J. S., Milam, J. H., et al. (2007). *Returning to learning: Adults' success in college is key to America's future.* Indianapolis: Lumina Foundation.

Schlossberg, N. K., Lynch, A. Q., & Chickering, A. W. (1989). *Improving higher education environments for adults: Responsible programs and services from entry to departure.* San Francisco: Jossey-Bass.

Schlossberg, N. K., Waters, E. B., & Goodman, J. (1995). *Counseling adults in transition* (2nd ed.). New York: Springer.

Schuerholz-Lehr, S. (2007). Teaching for global literacy in higher education: How prepared are the educators? *Journal of Studies in International Education, 11*(2), 180–204.

Siebert, A. (2000). *The instructor's role in retaining adult learners and increasing their chances of success in college.* Paper presented at the National Conference on the Adult Learner 2000, Atlanta, Georgia. Retrieved from http://www.adultstudent.com/eds/articles/teaching.html

Strange, A. (2008). Traditional and non traditonal college students' descriptions of the ideal professor and the ideal course and perceived strengths and limitations. *College Student Journal, 42*(1), 225–231.

Thomas, E. (2005). The adult learner: Here to stay. *Black Issues in Higher Education, 22*(6), 1–4.

Tinto, V. (2008). *Moving beyond access: College success for low-income, first-generation students.* Washington, DC: Pell Institute for the Study of Opportunity in Higher Education.

Understanding the New Post 911 GI Bill. Retrieved from http://images.military.com/media/education/pdf/post-911-gi-bill.pdf

Voorhees, R. A., & Lingenfelter, P. E. (2003). *Adult learners and state policy.* Denver, CO: State Higher Education Executive Officers Association and the Council for Adult and Experiential Learning.

Wilson, W. J. (1987). *The truly disadvantaged: The inner city, the underclass, and public policy.* Chicago: University of Chicago Press.

15

COLLEGE STUDENTS WITH DISABILITIES

Martha E. Wisbey and Karen S. Kalivoda

"Over the last two decades we all [colleges and universities] have seen increasing access to higher education for a growing number of minority groups. What has kept us from including students with disabilities in that access—and from recognizing how they contribute to our [campus] community?" (McCune, 2001, p. 11). New student populations on campuses include growing numbers of students who are female, adult, people of color, part-time, disadvantaged, and first generation. Participation in higher education of students with disabilities has also increased since the passage of the Americans With Disabilities Act (ADA, 1990). In 1985 the American Council on Education revealed that 7.7% of college freshmen self-reported having a disability (Ivory, 1986). A decade later, a survey showed that this number increased to 9% for first-year students arriving on college campuses (Henderson, 1995). In 2004 data from the National Center for Education Statistics (NCES) revealed 11.3% of students reported a disability, however, the NCES research included all undergraduates and not just college freshmen (Horn & Nevill, 2006). As the participation of students with disabilities increases, it is anticipated that faculty and student development professionals will encounter more students with disabilities involved in curricular and cocurricular activities. Passage of the ADA (1990) gave people with disabilities the same rights as the rest of the population who were legally protected from discrimination based on race, color, sex, national origin, religion, or age. Although the regulations of the ADA may have contributed to providing opportunities for students with disabilities at institutions of higher education, critical issues of inclusion are paramount to true equal access. Students with disabilities are not participating in postsecondary education at the level they should be, and the barriers inhibiting their access must be examined (Getzel & Wehman, 2005).

Federal Regulations

The 1990 passage of the ADA mandates civil rights for people with disabilities and provides equal access for students with disabilities at institutions of higher education. This victory did not come about easily. People with disabilities fought for years for civil rights protection while carefully refraining from claiming the role of victim. The goal of the disability movement was for integration and an equal opportunity to facilitate successful matriculation (Shapiro, 1993). The disability rights movement, referred to as a hidden power by Shapiro, is compared to other minority group movements as follows:

> Given the sweep of the ADA, it seemed a formidable task to win passage. For one thing, disability rights constituted a stealth civil rights movement. Although its activists pointed to the black, women's and gay rights movements as models, unlike those causes, the disability rights movement had never filled the streets with tens of thousands of protesters. It had no Martin Luther King, Jr. to bring it together, no Betty Friedan to write its manifesto. It had no unifying touchstone moment of courage or anger like the Montgomery Bus Boycott, the Freedom Rides, or the Stonewall riots. There was virtually no attention from the public or press. The fight for disability civil rights was a largely invisible, almost underground, movement. (p. 117)

People with disabilities have a variety of mental and physical impairments and constitute a fragmented group. The disability community differs in comparison to other identifiable underrepresented groups on campuses that have a common characteristic (like race or ethnicity) because individual disabilities vary greatly in type and severity.

Definition of Disability

The ADA's (1990) legal definition of disability is a physical or mental impairment that substantially limits one or more major life activities, such as walking, seeing, breathing, working, and learning. Examples of disabilities listed in the federal regulations include but are not limited to orthopedic, visual, speech and hearing impairments, cerebral palsy, epilepsy, muscular dystrophy, multiple sclerosis, cancer, heart disease, diabetes, emotional illness, specific learning disabilities, and HIV disease (Non-discrimination on the Basis of Disability in State and Local Government Services Final Rule, 1991). Types of disabilities commonly found among college and university students can be visible or nonobvious, such as traumatic brain injuries, attention deficit hyperactivity disorders (ADHD), blindness and low vision, chronic illnesses, deafness and being hard of hearing, learning disabilities, mobility impairments, and psychological disorders. Typical disabilities seen more frequently on many college and university campuses include orthopedic (25.4%), psychological (21.9%), health impairments (17.3%), and attention deficit hyperactivity disorders (11%; Horn & Neville, 2006).

However, these disabilities are not all inclusive. To determine if someone qualifies as disabled, the degree to which he or she is substantially limited in major life activities must be taken into consideration. In fact, the U.S. Supreme Court has made several rulings that have further defined the ADA's definition of disability. In 1999 the courts narrowed the definition of disability by considering *mitigating measures* (*Murphy v. United Parcel Service,* 1999; *Sutton v. United Air Lines,* 1999). That is, one who uses a mitigating measure such as taking medication for a health condition or wearing eyeglasses to correct vision may not meet the substantially limiting requirement of the definition of disability. In January 2002 the Supreme Court established a more specific definition of major life activities in *Toyota Motor MFG., KY v. Williams* (2002). This employment-related ruling stated that Williams was not substantially limited in performing manual tasks because she was able to successfully participate in activities of central importance to most people's daily lives. The court provided examples of daily living activities (e.g. brushing teeth, household chores, and bathing) that Williams could still perform and concluded that she did not qualify as a person with a disability. While this case may offer new challenges for higher education professionals in establishing which students are protected, it also reinforces the institutional obligation to provide educational opportunities to qualified students.

Many college students who do not have an obvious disability are faced with the problem of disclosing it. Considering the Supreme Court decisions, combined with the stringent documentation requirements of many institutions of higher education, it is understandable that some students may not want to disclose a disability, especially one that is not readily apparent. Typically, disability service programs in higher education require recent and thorough documentation from a qualified health professional to substantiate a disability. If the documentation presented is outdated (more than 3 years old), students may be required to seek more current documentation at their own expense. Some institutions are more flexible as long as the documentation states the diagnosis and adequately addresses the student's level of functioning and accommodations needed (Jarrow, 1997). Although federal regulations support a system in which students are required to present adequate documentation of disability, additional concerns regarding disability legitimacy issues and cost factors for obtaining that documentation may deter a college student from revealing a disability. Once students present adequate documentation and choose to disclose a disability they are entitled to accommodations and academic adjustments necessary to ensure equal access.

Accommodations and Support Services

The access needs of students with disabilities vary as much as the type and severity of disabilities. A universal description of a person with a disability does not exist, so institutions must provide accommodations on an individual basis. Section 504 of the Rehabilitation Act of 1973 states that accommodations may include academic adjustments, modification or alteration of course examinations, and the provision of auxiliary aids. These equal-access measures are required only after the student provides documentation that specifically states his or her level of functioning, the diagnosis, and the necessary accommodations (Jarrow, 1997).

Accommodations and services may vary from student to student and across institutions, however, common services are available to students through disability support offices (Shaw & Dukes, 2001). Typical services offered by support offices include regular meetings with a counselor or disability specialist, consultation and collaboration with members of the campus community who serve as support to students (e.g., tutors, advisers, counseling staff), time extensions on tests and assignments, academic adjustments and restructuring of class assignments, counseling and advocacy to assist a student as a self-advocate, extended time for test taking in a separate quiet location to reduce distractions, note takers in the classroom to supplement the student's notes, document conversion services (e.g., from print to Braille or electronic text), sign language interpreters, real-time captioning, adaptive technology, and instructional interventions. In addition, working collaboratively with an academic adviser has proven to increase student competence and confidence in achieving success (Hunter, McCalla-Wiggins, & White, 2007).

To determine eligibility for these types of services, many disability support programs require students to present documentation that not only verifies a disability but highlights functional limitations. Students are also responsible for providing recent documentation from an appropriate expert at their own expense (Colker & Milani, 2006). Although this process is consistent with ADA regulations, it may serve as another burden for the student and bring focus on the student's disability. Rather than focusing on the environment as disabling, this approach focuses on what is in the student that is disabling (Hahn, 1988). Szymanski and Trueba (1994) stated that "some of the theoretical classification systems and societal institutions that have been invented to assist minority individuals can also serve to oppress those individuals" (p. 16). Existing policies and procedures commonly require students to register with the disability services office and allow the professionals to assist them in advocating for equal access. The rationale for this process is that it supports professionals as the experts in verifying the legitimacy of disabilities for the institution and making recommendations for accommodations that are consistent and appropriate. This system, although set up to assist students, may actually dissuade them from becoming self-advocates and perpetuate dependence on professionals. It may also isolate students from their peers and fail to adhere to the tenets of student development theory (Szymanski & Trueba).

Historically, the onus has been on the student to disclose diagnoses and request accommodations to make the college campuses accessible. Today administrators of disability service programs are beginning to focus on how to change or modify the environment to make it more accessible to students with disabilities (Kroeger & Schuck, 1993a). For instance, the universal design movement encourages professionals on campus, including counselors, advisers, administrators, faculty, and student affairs professionals to design their programs in advance to accommodate the needs of all students. This is described in more detail in the Examples of Practices section on pp. 364–367.

Developmental Issues

Students and their parents need to recognize the differences between the ADA regulations governing higher education and the Individuals With Disabilities Education Act (IDEA, 2004), established for students in elementary and secondary schools. The IDEA was formerly known as the Education for All Handicapped Children Act but was established by Congress in 1975 as a federal law. This act guaranteed a free and appropriate education for all children with disabilities. After several amendments, the resulting IDEA stressed that students with disabilities must also be prepared for further education, employment, and independent living. IDEA provides students with an Educational Planning Team in the K through 12th grade educational process that prepares an educational plan with the appropriate supports based on students' needs.

In the higher education learning environment, different regulations apply. Accommodations are not initiated by an institution on behalf of students as in K–12. In postsecondary education, the responsibility lies with students to request each accommodation and to substantiate the need with documentation. Not all needs are automatically met at the college level, and this change in service delivery can present a challenge to students with disabilities entering postsecondary education. It is critical that students know their rights and responsibilities and their disability-related needs, and that they plan in advance for the accommodations necessary for them to be successful in their new learning environment. This requires students to be self-determined, independent, and employ self-advocacy skills. It is important that faculty, staff, and student affairs professionals play a critical role in promoting self-advocacy skills that will help students gain confidence in their abilities.

Another critical issue involves developing healthy self-identities. This process can take time and can mirror the coming out process that people in other cultural groups experience (Cass, 1979; Helms, 2003). The psychosocial impact of acquiring a disability later in life can be different from that of a person who is born with a disability. Although not absolute, being born with a disability can allow students to handle the adjustment and their identity throughout their lifetime. In the population of students with disabilities, evidence suggests that those with visual or hearing impairments and learning disabilities may differ in psychosocial development from others in the subpopulation because of disability-specific environmental responses to their disability (Ryan & McCarthy, 1994, p. 20).

Adaptation to disability is not a static concept; it is constantly changing and is often complicated by several different phases of development. Livneh and Sherwood (1991) present a summary of eight phases of adaptation to a traumatic disability:

1. Shock. The initial phase of disbelief when a sudden and severe impairment occurs;
2. Anxiety. A panic response to the initial understanding of the trauma of the event;
3. Denial. An attempt to mask the painful realization of the condition;
4. Depression. A full look at the loss of one's prior physical/sensory abilities;
5. Internalized anger. A reaction of resentment accompanied by guilt and self-blame;
6. Externalized hostility. A reaction which is other-directed as a way to retaliate against imposed limitations;
7. Acknowledgment. Cognitive recognition of the implications of the disability and gradual acceptance of its permanency and limitations;
8. Adjustment. Affective internalization of the disability along with behavioral adaptation to the newly perceived life situation. (p. 525)

The following example illustrates how these phases can affect a student who experiences a sudden change in his or her abilities because of a traumatic event.

During fall semester, Michael, a freshmen student at a large research institution, is driving home from college one evening and has a car accident on a major Interstate. As a result of his injuries, he has to withdraw from school during his first semester and spends 3 months in rehabilitation for severed nerves in his arm and wrist. His mother contacts the Office of Disability Services at his institution to see if Michael could receive accommodations once he returns to school. She was instructed to help her son fill out the appropriate paperwork and send documentation about his disability to disability services. Mike's mom did everything as instructed and brought in the completed paperwork. At that time, she said, "I'm not sure if Mike really understands how his life may have changed. He doesn't want to talk about anything and all he wants to do is get back and visit with his friends."

The professional in disability services assures her that this is normal and that her son will soon learn how to get the appropriate support when he returns to school. However, Mike wouldn't acknowledge that life had changed and when he returned the following semester, he spent most of his time with his old friends in his residence hall and never met with anyone in disability services. He was contacted several times by the Department of Disability Services professionals, however, he never met with his disability specialist to get note takers for his classes, and he would not try to find any type of support for accomplishing his academic work. His mom continued to talk with the disability services staff, but she was at a loss and couldn't force her son to get academic accommodations or other support services. As a result, he ended up failing all his classes during the semester following his accident. The realization of his limitations didn't hit him until he saw his grades and recognized that he did not face the fact that life had changed because of his injuries. Mike's denial of the realities of this accident caused him to spiral into depression and finally into anger toward himself for being so slow to catch on about his new disability status as a student. During the summer following his 1st year, he met with staff at disability services and talked about all he had learned by not facing the fact of his limitations. He admitted to his mother that he had not been ready to adjust to the changes, and he had ignored her pleas for him to seek academic support. Unfortunately, this story mirrors what many students may experience if they have a sudden life-altering injury or chronic health diagnosis. A disability that changes students' health status or their overall ability to accomplish their academic work as they did prior to the disability can be hard for an able-bodied college student to grasp and immediately recognize and accept.

When reviewing other stages of identity development for different underrepresented groups in society, it is helpful to look at some of the similar paths of acceptance a student with a disability may experience. In addition to undergoing traditional student development stages that apply to all college students, students with acquired disabilities go through their identity stages as they learn to accept their disability. A student, regardless of race, ethnicity, age, religion, or sexual orientation, may view the initial period of being disabled through an unquestioning acceptance of societal stereotypes and oppression. At this point, the student may be unaware of alternative, positive views of disability and may attribute problems to personal deficits. Some students will attempt to pass as nondisabled and distance themselves from others with disabilities and reject membership in this population. Eventually, a student will begin to develop an awareness of the reasons behind feelings of difference and begin to identify with the issues of oppression he or she has experienced. This may evoke feelings of anger and eventually lead to action in the form of activism or through legal challenges. If a student with a disability gains acceptance in an environment and feels valued through interactions with others, eventually he or she will achieve identity synthesis.

Discrimination and Oppression

It has been pointed out in federal legislation that historically society tended to isolate and segregate people with disabilities and that this type of discrimination creates a grave social problem. The findings and purpose section of the ADA (1990) states the following:

> Individuals with disabilities are a discrete and insular minority who have been faced with restrictions and limitations, subjected to a history of purposeful unequal treatment, and relegated to a position of political powerlessness in our society, based on characteristics that are beyond the control of such individuals and resulting from stereotypic assumptions not truly indicative of the individual ability of such individuals to participate in, and contribute to, society. (p. 4)

Congress recognized the existence of unfair and unnecessary discrimination and established federal legislation to support equal access for students with disabilities in higher education, but true inclusion for students with disabilities will only be advanced as the campus culture shifts from a medical approach to disability to a sociopolitical one. This sociopolitical approach does not focus on the disability in the individual mind or body but views disability as what Hahn (1988) refers to as "a product of interactions between individual and environment." Since college and university administrators are concerned about the campus environment and are seeking ways to promote learning for all students (Strange, 2000), this sociopolitical model warrants further exploration.

Language can be very powerful in reinforcing the dominant culture's view of disability. Terms such as *ableist* and *ableism* can be used to organize ideas about the centering and domination of the nondisabled experience. For some people with disabilities, this point of view defines discrimination or prejudice against people with disabilities. Like racism, sexism, and ageism, which are terms more commonly recognized than ableism, ableist attitudes refer to the construction of societal values, beliefs, norms, and even the infrastructure in a society that can systematically exclude disabled people. For example, a new student who uses a wheelchair wants to attend orientation, but the program is held in an inaccessible residence hall. If this first experience isolates the student from his or her peers, how does this set the stage for the rest of the college experience? Will the student feel included if he or she is not able to live in the same housing facility with his or her peers? Will the transportation provided for the entire group once again segregate the student from classmates? Although federal regulations allow the provision of equal access through separate programs, it truly is not the most welcoming and inclusive environment.

The student with a disability may have a heightened sense of not fully belonging in an ableist society. The student can experience a growing sense of personal isolation and lack of group identity. The student may acknowledge being a member of the disabled community but be hesitant or refuse to claim membership. Many times students who visit the disability services office on campus to discuss their eligibility for services based on a diagnosis of ADHD have stated that they always thought of the disability office as the place where the people who "ride the short bus come." This comment refers to what is observed during earlier years in K–12 when a school bus is designated to pick up individuals with disabilities. In most school systems, this bus is a smaller bus, and as a result of being separate and different, other students may assume it is not something they can relate to in their own diagnosis of having a disability. If students are encouraged to talk about their feelings and are educated about their rights as a person with a disability, they might begin to identify with others in the disability culture and may seek out support and avoid isolation. As students increase their identity in the campus community, connections can be made with other people with disabilities. Students may react by limiting their relationships and contacts to people with disabilities and reject or retreat from people from the ablest society. This level of involvement can lead to a separatist response. Finding a balance between being separate from an ableist society and being identified solely with a group with disabilities can help bridge attitudes about people with disabilities and lead a person to a stronger sense of pride. As an individual balances personal and community disability identity with past identities, memberships, and relationships, he or she has a renewed appreciation for diversity and multicultural society. Students with disabilities may be overlooked as a minority group that has been oppressed because of the medical model approach in gaining documentation and in part because of society's stereotypes about people with disabilities. Because a disabled student must show documentation from a health care provider, a staff member as well as some students and their parents may see the disability as a disease or illness instead of a unique quality of who the student is. In some cases, *disease, impairment,* or *disorder* is part of the diagnostic name of a specific disability, however, the student receives all the same opportunities as any other student. The label itself does not define him or her as a student or a person seeking to gain further education and employment. With appropriate academic supports, students with disabilities can achieve success in and beyond their college education. The disability support offices established to advance the rights of students with disabilities may also hinder their progress by adhering to a system that promotes dependence on others. In addition, Hall and Belch (2000) argue that

> although disability programs offer necessary accommodations and services that may offer a comfortable place for students to establish community, student affairs professionals need to consider if, as an unintended consequence, special programs and centers also relieve staff who are not located in those centers from acting on their responsibility to understand and address the diverse needs of underrepresented groups. (p. 13)

Discrimination can occur in a number of different ways. People with disabilities encounter discrimination that consists of outright acts of bias, intentional exclusion, communication barriers, inaccessible technology, transportation barriers, and segregation. The following case study describes how discrimination, although unintentional, can show its face on the college campus.

Case Study 1

A large university offers an orientation program for all new freshman and transfer students. Campus administrators believe that participation in orientation is critical to achieve a successful transition and the retention of new students. In addition to a variety of programs that introduce students to college life, a comprehensive tour of campus is provided to parents and students that highlight key features and services. A first-year student, Frank, is unable to get on the tour bus because he uses a wheelchair and the bus does not have a lift. Attempts are made to get a van with a lift so a tour can be provided for Frank and his parents. The orientation leader calls campus transit and secures the van to transport Frank and his parents on a personal tour of the campus with a personal tour guide.

In this case study the accommodation satisfies the law by providing what the ADA refers to as *program access* but does so with separate programming. Unfortunately, the accessible transportation excludes the student from interaction with his peers and brings unnecessary attention to Frank and the fact that he uses a wheelchair. In this case, a little advance planning could have provided access in a more inclusive manner. Most transportation services have at least one bus that is lift equipped. It should become standard procedure to request accessible transportation even if participants have not revealed the need for this. For example, many institutions of higher education provide a specialized computer center with assistive computer technologies, training, and technical support. Common assistive technology consists of magnification software, screen reader software, speech-to-text software, ergonomic workstations, chairs, and other peripherals such as alternative keyboards and mice (Knox, Higbee, Kalivoda, & Totty, 2000). Supplemental computer labs are beneficial but are not sufficient. The current challenge is to create a welcoming environment where students feel like they matter and belong, and to avoid discrimination by providing adequate services and accommodations in the most inclusive manner.

By introducing assistive technology and equipment into existing computer facilities on campus, participation from students with disabilities will increase. New technologies for students with visual and mobility impairments, but also for students with a wide range of disabilities, need to be introduced in all computer labs on campus. The ideal is to offer the same choices to all students in as many locations as possible.

Students with invisible disabilities (e.g., chronic health issues, ADHD, psychological impairments) may elect to participate in university-sponsored events and hesitate to reveal their disability for fear of being excluded. The following case study examines how students encounter communication barriers that impede students with disabilities from participating in campus programming.

Case Study 2

Margaret attends a college that has an excellent reputation for leadership programs. The student affairs staff is dedicated to meeting the mission of the institution in developing good citizens and leaders who will contribute to their home state after completing their college degrees. Administrators of the Department of Student Activities have developed a 4-year leadership series that guides students in learning about and gaining skills in specific developmental and theoretical areas, such as service leadership, communication, conflict management, grassroots organizing, community development, and career development planning. Margaret is a junior majoring in business. She is an excellent student maintaining a 3.6 grade point average while working part-time to pay for her college education. She applies for the leadership development program after reading about it in the student newspaper. The program is described as targeting juniors and seniors seeking to develop specific skills that would prepare them for their job search process. She also is pleased with the prospect of adding her involvement in this organization to her résumé. Although she has the credentials to qualify, she first has to participate in an interview that involves reading a passage of text and giving an oral summary to the committee. She has a visual processing disorder and obtains books and articles on tape or electronically. The computer program in her residence hall room reads the text to her with a voice-synthesized program. Although she uses this method of reading for her course work, she hesitates to reveal her disability and related accommodation needs to the leadership staff because of stereotypes about learning disabilities and a fear that the committee may not be flexible in its standard interview procedure. Margaret proceeds to read the document but does not readily comprehend the meaning. Nevertheless, she attempts to provide a summary of the key points. The committee members note her nervousness and lack of ability to adequately process and communicate information in a timely manner. They reject her application. Margaret never knew why she didn't get accepted, but she felt sure her ability to participate in that one evaluation activity was a significant deterrent to being objectively evaluated by the committee. She thought about going back to ask why she was not accepted, but she decided it was not worth the energy.

This case study illustrates a situation that unfortunately is all too common. The student had legitimate concerns about disclosing her disability because of her fear of being excluded or of appearing to be too different from other students applying for the program. The leadership program had a standard, uniform way of selecting applicants. Perhaps a statement on the application form indicating a desire to accommodate people with disabilities would have encouraged Margaret to request an accommodation. A general statement that asserts the desire to accommodate a diverse student body and different learning styles communicates a desire to accept and understand individual differences. Program administrators are not asked to lower standards for acceptance but to acknowledge the inequity inherent in setting standards based on the traditional student. Imagine if Margaret had gone back to receive feedback and learned that if they had known of her disability they would have been willing to evaluate her in another manner that fit her learning style. This would be optimal, but in most cases, students with disabilities do not want to continually have to expend energy to reveal their disabilities and request others to think or redo their current standards.

The following case study illustrates the issues encountered by students who use wheelchairs, scooters, or crutches.

Case Study 3

Thad is a graduate student in English literature at a campus that is old and has hilly terrain and facilities dating from the 19th century. The English department is located on the third floor in a building without an elevator, and Thad uses a wheelchair because of paralysis. The graduate offices, including the administrative offices, the mailroom, the computer lab, and offices for graduate assistants are located on the third floor, up two flights of stairs. The graduate students each have a designated cubicle in a large room on the third floor. Thad is given an office on the main floor with a computer. His peers tease him and state that if they had a disability maybe they could get a private office and personal computer too.

The department head, recognizing the need to make accommodations for Thad, delegates this responsibility to his secretary. She advertises in all departmental publications and announcements that programmatic access is provided for people with limited mobility. The access statement reads as follows: "Alternative access provided for people with mobility impairments. Call Debra two weeks before the event to provide ample time for reloca-tion." Her intention is to communicate to people with disabilities that they are welcome to participate in the English literature program and sponsored events and that they need to identify themselves as disabled with special needs.

Thad also is a teaching assistant and is routinely scheduled to teach in classes that are architecturally inaccessible. The secretary arranges with cam-pus administrators for these classes to be moved. On the first day of class a sign on the original classroom door states that the location has been changed to accommodate an instructor with a disability.

Thad is involved in a number of student activities. He is an active table tennis player and vice president of that club. He also expresses interest in attending the campus activity organization, Literature Chat, but the meet-ings are held in the graduate student lounge on the third floor of his aca-demic building. He approaches his peers about moving the meeting to the student union but they are hesitant because the student union charges room rental for student organizations. The group leaders state it is not the group's responsibility to shoulder the cost of reserving a room at a location that is accessible to Thad.

This case study illustrates the social stigmatization that can occur with an obvious and visible disability. On the one hand, a student like Thad is seen in a special light with an ideal office in a central location in the department. In addition he has a great parking space outside the building that his peers feel gives him another added benefit. The teasing is done to show their acceptance of him, but the underlining sentiment is not one of understanding or acknowledgment of the realities that Thad faces on a daily basis in accessing spaces and getting to and from classrooms and meeting spaces on campus. In this way, Thad may feel awkward about asking about being a member of the literary group, and he may not want to push for inclusion because he recognizes that he might cost the group money, cause hard feelings for inconveniencing others, and ultimately experience exclusion from his peers. The medical model approach requires Thad to identify his needs and advocate for access rather than requiring the institution as a whole to make the accommodation and respond in a way that communicates to everyone that the problem lies in the campus environment rather than with the individual with a disability.

Ultimately, administrators of programs or departments located on inaccessible floors are responsible for finding alternative methods of providing accessibility, but this needs to be accomplished without assigning blame, no matter how subtle, to people with disabilities. They did not cause the problem. We must recognize, as Weitz (1996) asserted, that when "the problem resides primarily in social attitudes and in the social and built environment, then we can solve the problem most efficiently by changing attitudes and environments, not by rehabilitating people with disabilities" (p. 156).

The issue of architectural barriers has received a great deal of attention on college campuses since the Rehabilitation Act of 1973 when many colleges first started to make modifications (Anderson & Coons, 1979). The passage of the ADA in 1990 added additional and renewed impetus to the effort to make campus environments accessible. The ADA required colleges and universities to develop a transition plan that addressed facilities targeted for improvement (Duston & Provan, 1995). Despite the legal requirements and the passage of time, barriers still exist today. This may be because of the cost associated with building modifications or structural problems that inhibit renovations. In addition, the ADA does not require all existing buildings to be barrier free. For instance, if the cost of providing an elevator is what the

ADA refers to as an *undue financial burden,* then it is not legally required (Kalivoda & Higbee, 1994).

Since access to older facilities may be limited to the main floor via an elevator or ramp, program and department staff located on inaccessible floors must find alternative methods of providing accessibility. The ADA requires that the same service be provided to people with disabilities even though it may be in a separate location. For instance, a program may be moved to an accessible location or its staff may send requested information (e.g., scholarship applications, student employment information) directly to the student. But is this really the same service, or is it the old, familiar separate but equal standard?

An increasing number of students are being diagnosed with chronic health illnesses and are faced with fatigue, flare-ups, regular medical treatments, and ongoing pain. It is difficult to recognize chronic health issues because a person may not appear to have a disability. Some people have spent many doctor visits trying to find out what was wrong and to finally be given an exact diagnosis can be a relief as well as a challenge.

Students need to have the support and accommodations necessary to allow them to complete assignments and accomplish academic requirements without being penalized for disability-related absences or missed deadlines as illustrated in the following case study.

Case Study 4

Anne is a sophomore majoring in psychology. She is from a rural area in the Northeast and attends a large university several hundred miles from home. In the middle of the fall semester she developed health problems and went to the university health service. After numerous consultations and tests the physician diagnosed Anne with multiple sclerosis (MS). Anne was overwhelmed with the diagnosis of a progressive and often debilitating health condition, especially at such an early age. Nevertheless, she chose to continue her college education.

Because of the fatigue associated with MS she missed numerous classes and had to take a reduced course load. Anne's instructors agreed to allow her to remain in their class despite her absences if the campus disability service office would corroborate her disability. This required that Anne register with disability services. On days when she was not feeling well, she parked in the designated wheelchair spot near the building then went to class. People would stare at her as if she didn't have a legitimate disability and she wondered if she needed to get a T-shirt stating "I have MS."

People with nonobvious disabilities have to decide if they are going to disclose information about their disability. They face a different kind of stigma than those with obvious disabilities and sometimes choose to act as if they did not have one. Since revealing a disability may have negative consequences, people may choose to act as if they did not have one (Goffman, 1963).

"Students with mental illness face the suspicion that they deceive others in order to secure accommodations with regard to coursework and other responsibilities" (McCune, 2001, p. 9). The stigma of a psychological disability may prevent many students from disclosing their disability. As a result, their symptoms may worsen and many may not get the appropriate treatment and assistance as they progress in college. In the following case, this student did communicate his past struggle with a psychological disability and the staff in his academic program sought to assist him so he could be successful.

Case Study 5

Mike did not ask for special treatment in his classroom, but his professors thought they had better provide it anyway. As a highly sought-after doctoral candidate for a very rigorous chemistry department, Mike told his major professor that prior to his arrival in graduate school, he was hospitalized for bipolar disorder. After being at the university for 3 months, he told his professor he was feeling stressed out. The professor also noticed that his schedule was overbooked during his manic phases, and during his depressive phases he would not wake up to teach his lab classes and he missed appointments. His professor accommodated Mike by developing a flexible schedule for the following semester that allowed him time off for therapy and helped him balance some of the demands of the graduate program and assistantship.

Many professors and student affairs professionals do not understand how to best support a student with a psychological disability. Through discussions with his brightest student, this professor displayed a level of understanding and support that helped Mike accomplish his work and get treatment. Instead of feeling like he was causing the department to go out of its way for him, he found that everyone respected his skills and valued his work and was willing to make accommodations because of his disability. This is ideal and not typical, but many faculty can and will help support students with psychological disabilities.

Examples of Practices

Student affairs professionals are challenged to embrace values of community, human dignity, and equality (Hall & Belch, 2000). The importance of creating a welcoming environment for all students is recognized, but what is the best way to successfully communicate to students with disabilities that they do matter and are important? Positive inclusive messages should not only be communicated orally and in writing but through behavior (Hall & Belch). Administrators of some institutions have recognized that students with disabilities want to participate along with their peers in sponsored events such as leadership activities, field trips, and recreational sports. Common practice has been for these institutions to issue a standard access statement that places the responsibility for revealing a disability and the needs associated with that disability on the student (Johnson, 2000). This can be an efficient and effective means of providing access to students but may also be a stigmatizing process.

Students report that the current system of accommodations and the negative attitudes of faculty in handling their specific needs still lead to frustration. The current process of identifying a disability and obtaining accommodations that appear to be separate and in some cases special treatment can lead to greater discrimination in the classroom by faculty and peers.

Cutting-edge programs like those at the University of Arizona and the University of Minnesota are setting best practices for the disability service community by embracing the ideals of universal design as the foundation for these programs. The University of Minnesota's Disability Services mission statement on its website reads, "Disability Services promotes access and equity for all students, faculty, staff and guests of the University of Minnesota through the exceptional design of innovative learning and working environments and the collaborative education and partnership with the University community" (http://ds.umn.edu/about/index.html).

One of the operating guidelines of the program is to provide leadership in implementing the principles of universal design and promoting the concept of a disability community and developing a sense of pride and empowerment for this group of people. Unlike traditional disability service programs that may actually oppress the students they seek to serve, Disability Services at the University of Minnesota strives to structure and deliver services in ways that promote individual growth, development, and self-determination (Szymanski & Trueba, 1994). Advancing these values and principles promote inclusion without singling out students or attributing certain characteristics or flaws to people with disabilities.

Universal Instructional Design

The University of Minnesota General College Curriculum Transformation and Disability Grant, funded by the U.S. Department of Education, provides a model for faculty education and training about universal instructional design (UID) in the classroom. UID involves multimodal teaching and multimodal assessment methods to enhance learning for all students. The goal of UID in the classroom is to meet the unique needs of the student body and reduce the need for special academic accommodations by being as inclusive as possible in the planning process (Silver, Bourke, & Strehorn, 1998). Student affairs professionals may find it helpful to adopt some of the same principles for programming and services that faculty have in the classroom. Programming with a universal design approach takes into consideration the individual differences and needs of all students in planning and implementing the program or services.

Minnesota's grant promotes UID by using faculty mentors to conduct outreach with faculty. Some of the universal design components faculty are encouraged to use include putting course material online; using group discussions and cooperative learning situations; providing a comprehensive syllabus; using a variety of instructional methods; providing illustrations, handouts, and auditory and visual aids; allowing students to tape-record lectures; and providing students with alternative means to demonstrate knowledge of the subject matter (Hodge & Preston-Sabin, 1997). Hodge and Preston-Sabin (1997) referred to these as good teaching practices in higher education and said that these practices will enhance learning for all students not just those with disabilities. In addition to helping the entire student body, these practices decrease the social stigmatization associated with requiring students to request special accommodations.

Staff at the University of Connecticut's Center on Postsecondary Education and Disability take the approach to teaching proactively through the use of instructional strategies that benefit a large range of learners, including individuals with cognitive disabilities (Scott, McGuire, & Embry, 2002). Faculty are challenged to create the kind of environment that fits all types of students instead of trying to create alternatives to their teaching plans after a student in their class requests a specific documented academic accommodation need. This is essentially the concept behind creating a universally designed space where the space and products can be used by the greatest number of people (Center for Universal Design, 1997).

Dialogues on Diversity

Another example of best practices in education is the University of Michigan's campuswide program Dialogues on Diversity. This theme-based semester program began as a way to open dialogue on campus to examine the many areas of diversity. When a student with a disability asked the coordinator of the program, "Are the disabled a part of diversity?" (McCune, 2001, p. 6), administrators of the program developed a video project designed to raise awareness about people with disabilities, specifically students at the university, and to generate discussion about the meaning and value of this group as a part of diversity. The completed video, *And You Can Quote Me on That: Students With Disabilities at U-M*, captures the words of students and presents specific themes on challenges, triumphs, and general experiences unique to this population of students (McCune). As a result of this film, students with disabilities have been included on the university's diversity agenda, and the film went far beyond educating just the campus; it has been requested throughout the United States from administrators of other universities and colleges seeking to use it as a way to create discussion. Because one student affairs professional listened to a student's question, it created a ripple effect and, subsequently, a large impact on behalf of students with disabilities on college campuses.

Leadership Making a Difference

Benchmark activities include support groups and other groups organized to educate the campus community about students with disabilities. Some of these are deaf clubs; ADHD chat groups; chronic health support groups for illnesses such as MS, lupus, chronic fatigue, arthritis, and so on; and psychological support groups for students with depression and other mental health disorders. Through these groups students can identify and connect with peers who have similar disabilities. This type of programming on campus can be done in conjunction with other offices, such as academic assistance, counseling centers, and housing. While the ADA (1990) does not require it, this type of program has assisted many campus administrators with connecting students so they gain strength and find outlets and resources to assist them in their academic progression.

Other examples of this type of program include bringing together groups of students with disabilities to serve as advocates, creating a speakers bureau, or establishing an educational outreach team. Students with disabilities are a large component of the diverse population at the University of Georgia. The school's Disability Resource Center organized a student group called Leadership, Education, and Advocacy for Disabilities (LEAD) to heighten disability awareness on campus and in the community, to represent students with disabilities, and to advance students' leadership and advocacy skills (University of Georgia, 2000). LEAD students, along with a staff adviser, represent the department on campus and in the state of Georgia. Members communicate with faculty, staff, other students, and community members about issues related to the needs of students with disabilities. Group members are encouraged to participate in campus functions, thereby enhancing their role as leaders at the university and in the community.

LEAD students serve as advisers for the Disability Resource Center, host speakers for personal leadership and communication skills development workshops, and participants in training programs to develop their own leadership skills. This group has experienced continued success as opportunities for faculty education have increased and student interest has grown among students with disabilities who want to join LEAD. When LEAD received an Outstanding New Organization award from the university's Leadership Program Office, being recognized in a ceremony for all campus student activity programs was a tremendous boost to LEAD members, and it added to their overall feeling of inclusion as a student group making a difference.

Goals for the group include seminars for high school students and their parents, the development of a handbook outlining methods for teaching students with a variety of learning abilities, and participation in regional and national conferences. One LEAD student member who is a junior majoring in studio art and has a hearing impairment, said, "I have often encountered people with preconceived notions about what a person with a disability can and cannot do. I thought LEAD would be a great way to educate people and reformulate their preconceived ideas." Nonobvious disabilities like ADHD, other learning disabilities, and psychological issues are more common on campus than visible disabilities like mobility and sensory impairments. Another member, a junior with ADHD majoring in psychology, said, "A little help is something I've always needed, but never asked for. . . . I'm here to help make sure other students don't make the same mistakes I did."

Conclusion

Life for students with disabilities on a college campus can present some difficult and complex challenges. No one student or one disability is exactly alike. Internalized oppression and separation and isolation from sources of support and strength are some of the main barriers to developing a positive identity for a student with a disability. A collective identity for this student subgroup is very hard to obtain and create when students are developing individually and in some cases are struggling to make ends meet. Practical problems associated with daily living include financial hardships brought on by disability-related treatments, physical issues related to obtaining transportation, or proximity issues because resources are located throughout the campus.

Campus administrators have recognized the barriers and have worked hard to eliminate outright intentional exclusion. Self-advocacy is a challenge for students with disabilities because they are typically functioning on their own to make change happen. This type of energy can be exhausting and can result in consequences for students. Many students have resorted to letting things ride and many have taken a more aggressive route by hiring lawyers to speak for them. Neither situation offers the type of solution that is appropriate and respectful of students trying to be understood, valued, and accommodated in all aspects of student life.

Disability service providers and other advocates on campus have begun to address these challenges. A partnership between the student with a disability and the administrator, faculty member, or fellow student can create new avenues for inclusion. The greatest benefit is the educational opportunity others gain by being connected to students with disabilities. It can be a valuable and positive learning experience.

References

Americans With Disabilities Act of 1990, 42 U.S.C. § 12101 (1990).

Anderson R. W., & Coons, M. (1979). Architectural accessibility: Matching places to people. In M. R. Rodden (Ed.), *Assuring access for the handicapped* (pp. 61–68). San Francisco: Jossey-Bass.

Cass, V. C. (1979). Homosexual identity formation: A theoretical model. *Journal of Homosexuality, 4*(3), 219–235.

Center for Universal Design. (1997). *The center for universal design: Environments and products for all people.* Retrieved March 28, 2008, from http://www.ncsu.edu/ncsu/design/cud/

Colker, R., & Milani, A. A. (2006). *Everyday law for individuals with disabilities.* Boulder, CO: Paradigm.

Duston, R. L., & Provan, R. (1995, June 2). The perils of ignoring the Disabilities Act. *Chronicle of Higher Education, 41*(38), B1–B2.

Getzel, E. E., & Wehman, P. (2005). *Going to college: Expanding opportunities for people with disabilities.* Baltimore: Brooks.

Goffman, E. (1963). *STIGMA: Notes on the management of spoiled identity.* Englewood Cliffs, NJ: Prentice-Hall.

Hahn, H. (1988). The politics of physical differences: Disability and discrimination. *Journal of Social Issues, 44*(1), 39–47.

Hall, L. M., & Belch, H. A. (2000). Setting the context: Reconsidering the principals of full participation and meaningful access for students with disabilities. In H. A. Belch & L. M. Hall (Eds.), *Serving students with disabilities* (pp. 5–17). San Francisco: Jossey-Bass.

Helms, J. E. (2003). Racial identity in the social environment. In P. B. Pedersen & J. C. Carey (Eds.), *Multicultural counseling in schools: A practical handbook* (pp. 44–58). Boston, MA: Allyn & Bacon.

Henderson, C. (1995). *College freshmen with disabilities: A statistical profile.* Washington, DC: American Council on Education.

Hodge, B. M., & Preston-Sabin, J. (1997). *Accommodations or just good teaching?* Westport, CT: Praeger.

Horn, L., & Nevill, S. (2006). *Profile of undergraduates in U.S. postsecondary education institutions: 2003–04.* Retrieved from http://nces.ed.gov/pubs2006/2006184_rev.pdf

Hunter, M. S., McCalla-Wiggins, B., & White, E. R. (Eds.). (2007). *Academic advising: New insights for teaching and learning in the first year* (Monograph No. 46 [National Resource Center]; Monograph No. 14 [National Academic Advising Association]). Columbia: University of South Carolina, National Resource Center for the First-Year Experience and Students in Transition.

Individuals With Disabilities Education Act of 2004, Pub. L. No. 108–446, 20 U.S.C. § 1400 et seq.

Ivory, S. (1986, September). Campuses expand services for disabled students. *Higher Education and National Affairs, 1,* 5.

Jarrow, J. E. (1997). *Higher education and the ADA: Issues and perspectives.* Columbus, OH: Disability Access Information & Support.

Johnson, D. (2000). Enhancing out-of-class opportunities for students with disabilities. In H. A. Belch & L. M. Hall (Eds.), *Serving students with disabilities* (pp. 41–53). San Francisco: Jossey-Bass.

Kalivoda, K. S., & Higbee, J. L. (1994). Implementing the Americans With Disabilities Act. *Journal of Humanistic Education and Development, 32*(3), 133–137.

Knox, D. K., Higbee, J. L., Kalivoda, K. S., & Totty, M. C. (2000). Serving the diverse needs of students with disabilities through technology. *Journal of College Reading and Learning, 30*(2), 144–157.

Kroeger, S., & Schuck, J. (Eds.). (1993a). *Responding to disability issues in student affairs.* San Francisco: Jossey-Bass.

Kroeger, S., & Schuck, J. (Eds.) (1993b). Moving ahead: Issues, recommendations, and conclusions. In S. Kroeger & J. Schuck (Eds.), *Responding to disability issues in student affairs* (pp. 103–110). San Francisco: Jossey-Bass.

Livneh, H., & Sherwood, A. (1991). Application of personality theories and counseling strategies to clients with physical disabilities. *Journal of Counseling & Development, 69*, 525–538.

McCune, P. (2001). What do disabilities have to do with diversity? *About Campus, 6*(2), 5–12.

Murphy v. United Parcel Service, 527 U.S. 516 (1999).

Non-discrimination on the Basis of Disability in State and Local Government Services Final Rule, 28 CFR § 35 (1991).

Rehabilitation Act of 1973, as amended, 29 U.S.C. § 794 (Section 504).

Ryan, D., & McCarthy, M. (Eds.). (1994). *A student affairs guide to the ADA & disability issues.* Washington, DC: National Association of Student Personnel Administrators.

Scott, S., McGuire, J., & Embry, P. (2002). *Universal design for instruction fact sheet.* Storrs: University of Connecticut, Center for Postsecondary Education and Disability.

Shapiro, J. P. (1993). *No pity: People with disabilities forging a new civil rights movement.* New York: Times Books.

Shaw, S. F., & Dukes, L. L. (2001). Program standards for disability services in higher education. *Journal of Postsecondary Education and Disability, 14*(2), 81–90.

Silver, P., Bourke, A., & Strehorn, K. C. (1998). Universal instructional design in higher education: An approach for inclusion. *Equity & Excellence in Education, 31*(1), 47–51.

Strange, C. (2000). Creating environments of ability. In H. A. Belch & L. M. Hall (Eds.), *Serving students with disabilities* (pp. 19–30). San Francisco: Jossey-Bass.

Sutton v. United Air Lines, 527 U.S. 471 (1999).

Szymanski, E., & Trueba, H. T. (1994). Castification of people with disabilities: Potential disempowering aspects of classification in disability services. *Journal of Rehabilitation, 12*, 12–20.

Toyota Motor MFG., KY. v. Williams, 534 U.S. (2002).

University of Georgia, Athens, Georgia. (2010). *LEAD Mission Statement.* Retrieved January 10, 2010, from http://www.uga.edu/lead

Weitz, R. (1996). *The sociology of health, illness, and health care: A critical approach.* New York: Wadsworth.

16

RELIGIOUS AND SPIRITUAL DIVERSITY AMONG COLLEGE STUDENTS

Laura A. Dean and Edward A. Grandpré

U.S. higher education has its roots in the Judeo-Christian tradition, yet the reality on campuses today is that religious diversity is increasing. From the early colleges that were founded to train clergy to the modern nonsectarian state universities accented by campus centers for multiple religions and denominations, faith and spirituality have always been present on campus in some capacity. While religious freedom has been guaranteed by the U.S. Constitution and any number of court cases, the campus climate for religious minorities is still different from that of the religious majority. The purpose of this chapter is to illustrate the issues of religious minority students and to provide an overview of issues of spirituality that affect all students. To clarify the role of religion in the modern system of higher education, this chapter looks at the history of religion at colleges, including religious diversity and religious conflict over higher education. A review of current research about the religious and spiritual leanings of U.S. college students includes a quantitative picture of religious diversity on campuses. An examination of the role of religion in the theoretical underpinnings of student development provides insight into the assumptions held by student affairs professionals. Finally, results from focus groups and surveys of students, paraprofessionals, professionals, faculty, and campus chaplains give voice to the religious minority experience on U.S. college campuses.

This chapter contains the results of several years of workshops for paraprofessional and professional student affairs staff, including those from majority and minority religions. While the illustrations are often drawn from groups that are usually seen as religious minorities, it must be noted that in the right setting, a member of any religious community could be in the minority, and in an overwhelmingly nonsectarian, secular environment, members of any religion may experience marginalization. Depending on the college, or the region, a student of one religion may be in the majority on one campus but in the minority on another. For example, a Catholic student at a Jesuit institution could easily be part of the religious majority. That same student at a public institution in the South could be in a small minority. Jewish and Islamic students, on the other hand, with few institutional exceptions, always experience higher education from the perspective of being a religious minority. The notion of religious majority or minority, then, like any form of diversity, can only be understood within a specific context. Similarly, the experience of a student will be shaped by the degree to which that student identifies with his or her religious affiliation. Just as students differ in their identity development related to issues of ethnicity or sexual orientation, they also differ in the extent to which their religion is an integral part of their identity or outlook.

History of Religious Diversity in U.S. Higher Education

Some level of religious diversity was present even at the beginning of U.S. higher education, but in the earlier years, diversity was represented only by Christian denominations. Some institutions were affiliated with specific denominations, while others were religiously pluralistic or secular. Religion on the college campus began with "the role of organized Christianity . . . [which was] important in the founding of eight of the nine pre-Revolutionary colleges. . . . the purpose of training students for the Christian ministry is specified in all colonial college charters, with the single exception . . . of the College of Philadelphia" (Brubacher & Rudy, 1997, p. 7). Later, even the College of Philadelphia came under religious control—the Anglican Church. The "desire of important religious denominations (such as the Anglican and the Calvinists) for a literate, college-trained clergy was probably the single most important factor in the founding of the colonial colleges" (p. 8). The clergy were instrumental in the founding of these colleges, in defining their missions, and in setting policies.

Sectarian Institutions

In their book *Religion in Contemporary Society*, Chalfant, Beckley, and Palmer (1994) said that the "most important source for the present forms of U.S. education was Puritan New England [and] its Calvinist commitment to the universal education of believers and potential believers" (p. 309). Religion was the primary subject, while reading was taught as a way to "improve the quality of Christian life" (p. 309). In contrast, in the primarily Anglican southern colonies, education was focused on training "the Anglican elite to govern the uneducated masses" (p. 309). Puritans, Congregationalists, and Baptists from New England gave life to Harvard, Yale, and Brown. Virginia's College of William and Mary was Anglican, and Scottish Presbyterians founded Princeton.

This proliferation of different schools, each affiliated in some way with a Christian denomination, shows the spread of denominational institutions and influence. If a denomination had a need to train its clergy, that denomination founded a college. This trend was also followed by many non-Protestant religious groups. For example, Georgetown College, a Catholic institution, was founded in 1789, and by 1860 "14 permanent Catholic colleges had already been established" (Brubacher & Rudy, 1997, p. 72). By 1930 there were 126 Catholic colleges, including 49 for women (Brubacher & Rudy). A number of these colleges were run by the Society of Jesus, or Jesuits.

Catholic institutions, expanding with increased immigration from countries with significant Catholic populations, had to contend with religious prejudice and antagonism. "American nationalism had long been identified with Protestantism, and a particularly bitter anti-Catholic agitation expressed itself in the nineteenth century" (Brubacher & Rudy, 1997, p. 72). For example, citing fears that the Catholic Church was trying to undermine the principle of the separation of church and state, the granting of a charter for Boston College was delayed until provisions were added that would protect non-Catholics from discrimination at the institution (Brubacher & Rudy). The practice of establishing other denominational or nondenominational religious institutions has continued into the 20th century, with institutions such as Oral Roberts University, an evangelical Christian university founded in 1963 by its namesake, and Regent University, founded in 1978 by evangelist Pat Robertson.

With an increasingly competitive market, colleges began early to stress interdenominational policies and practices in their public pronouncements.

For example, Quakers and Jews were "exempted from religious requirements at some of the colonial colleges" (Brubacher & Rudy, 1997, p. 9). The College of Rhode Island prohibited the establishment of any religious tests and "forbade the injection of religious bias into teaching" (p. 9). King's College forbade faculty or trustees to exclude any person of any religious denomination. At the College of New Jersey, people of every religious denomination were free to participate. It would be "not so much a seminary for Presbyterian divines as a school for statesmen" (Rudolph, 1990, p. 12). In the 1740s Princeton added New Jersey's governor and four others to its board of trustees, an action "taken as insurance against possible consequences of the religious controversies of the time" (p. 15). This trend toward accommodating other denominations was the beginning of religiously pluralistic institutions.

Some institutions, however, instituted maximum quotas on the enrollment of some religious minorities, most notably Jewish students. Freedman (2000) discussed the practice of quotas on Jewish enrollment and the hiring of Jewish faculty at Harvard, Yale, Dartmouth, and Columbia. Quotas were used at these institutions from the early 1900s to the middle of the century. Yale kept a 13% limit of Jewish and Catholic enrollment. Harvard seemed to keep minority religious enrollment at 10%. Columbia cut its Jewish enrollment from 40% in 1914 to 15% in the 1920s. By the 1930s, Dartmouth accepted only 10% of Jewish applicants, while at the same time admitting 75% of non-Jewish applicants.

Although enrollment at many schools was limited, minority religions were not as prolific in establishing colleges. Sporadic attempts were made by Jewish groups to establish colleges as early as 1821 (Brubacher & Rudy, 1997). However, lack of support and strong differences among Jewish religious groups within the small U.S. Jewish community resulted primarily in the establishment of rabbinical seminaries (Brubacher & Rudy). The Union of American Hebrew Congregations, the Reform Jewish organization, founded Hebrew Union College in 1875, and the Conservative Jewish movement founded the Jewish Theological Seminary of America in 1887. Founded in 1886, Yeshiva University is the oldest comprehensive educational institution under Jewish auspices in the United States. Some later attempts have also been successful. The University of Judaism, founded in 1947, has a conservative rabbinical seminary as well as undergraduate and graduate programs. Brandeis University, founded in 1948, is the "only nonsectarian Jewish-sponsored college or university in the country" (Brandeis, 2008). Brandeis has undergraduate and graduate programs in a variety of areas, including a variety of ethnic studies majors such as African American studies, Islamic and Middle Eastern Studies, and Latin American studies.

Other minority religions have established even fewer institutions. While Petersons' (2008) online search for colleges by denomination does not list any Islamic-affiliated institutions, Cordoba University, which includes the Graduate School of Islamic and Social Sciences and the Cordoba School of Professional Studies for continuing education, is located in Virginia and offers a master of arts in social studies in its Islamic studies program (Cordoba University, n.d.a.). It is also the first Muslim school to join a consortium of Christian seminaries, the Washington Theological Consortium, that offers a certificate in Muslim-Christian dialogue (Cordoba University, n.d.b). The existence of Cordoba, along with its decision to join the consortium, is an example of the expanding diversity of religious institutions.

State Institutions

Another important trend in the development of religiously pluralistic colleges and universities was the advent of state-controlled institutions. While the early colleges were mostly church sponsored, the earliest state universities of "North Carolina, Georgia, Vermont, Ohio, Tennessee, Maryland, and also South Carolina College and Transylvania University in Kentucky . . . were more nearly private than public" (Brubacher & Rudy, 1997, p. 145). The first public institutions founded after the Revolutionary War were chartered like private corporations, an interpretation that was successfully defended in court (Brubacher & Rudy). Although the University of Vermont was founded in 1791, it was not until 1810 when the Vermont legislature took over the selection of its trustees. Similarly, although the University of Georgia was chartered in 1789, the Georgia legislature did not take over the appointment of trustees until 1876. Further, direct appropriations to the university from the state only began in 1881 (Brubacher & Rudy). "In many of these states, the principle of regular tax support for university work did not become established until after the Civil War" (p. 146).

There was competition among Protestant denominations as they built colleges and fought for control of increasingly secular state institutions. At Indiana College, Methodists and Presbyterians fought for control, even insulting each other in debate at the state legislature (Rudolph, 1990). Additional battles were fought over colleges in Illinois and Kentucky. Competition within denominations also took a toll on some institutions. For example, "In the 1840's, Miami University became an object of desire for competing groups of Presbyterians" (p. 71). When Methodists gained control of Ohio University in the mid-1800s, the faculty was quickly replaced by Methodist ministers (Rudolph).

Perhaps the most influential state institution in terms of religious diversity is the University of Virginia. When it opened for classes in 1825 the University of Virginia was "by the express intent of its constitution a thoroughly public enterprise. . . . its early orientation was distinctly and purposely secular and non-denominational" (Brubacher & Rudy, 1997, p. 148). Thomas Jefferson insisted that religious groups not appoint the faculty but supported the idea that they could build student centers around the campus for students who were affiliated with them. However, this idea did not sit well with some denominations (Brubacher & Rudy). Jefferson believed that instead of controlling the institution, the various religious groups should "erect places of worship in areas adjacent to the university grounds" (p. 149). At the University of Virginia, one can easily see the roots of the modern state university surrounded by a Newman Center, a Hillel, a Baptist Student Center, an Islamic Society, a Wesleyan Foundation, and the campus chapels of any number of religious organizations.

State multidenominational institutions faced "jealousy [from] established private colleges and the suspicions and fears of denominational interests" (Brubacher & Rudy, 1997, p. 154) as they expanded. For example, religious groups in Illinois prevented the state from founding an institution for many years. In Ohio, the state institution elected presidents who were clergy, and "compulsory chapel continued to be required at such schools as late as the 1880s and 1890s" (p. 155). Battles over control of state institutions by denominations also took place in Indiana and Michigan. Still, the rise of the state university, with its multidenominational, nonsectarian atmosphere emerged as a great force in U.S. higher education.

Institutions struggle with the nature of religious practice and its focus on their campuses as demographics change, sometimes bringing large numbers of students from different faith traditions including religious minority students. The Wellesley College Religious and Spiritual Life Program, for example, is based on a philosophy of religious pluralism and spirituality and education; the Religious Life Team includes a Buddhist adviser, Catholic chaplain, Hillel director, Hindu adviser, Muslim adviser, Protestant Christian chaplain, and Unitarian Universalist chaplain, all working closely with the dean of religious and spiritual life (Kazanjian & Laurence, 2007). At Emory University, affiliated with the United Methodist Church, the dean of the chapel and religious life works with a group of 15 affiliated campus ministers, including those who minister to students who are Jewish, Muslim, Hindu, Zen Buddhist, Greek Orthodox, Unitarian Universalist, and Independent Christian (Emory University, n.d.). The wealth of religious diversity at some denominational institutions raises complex questions about the role of religion at church-affiliated colleges. As is true for the students they serve, institutions also vary greatly in the priority they place on their religious traditions.

Religious Centers and Organizations

Butler (1989) noted that by the 1850s and continuing with the Morrill Act of 1862, also called the Land Grant College Act, public education became more widely available and offered a broader range of disciplines. The increasing diversity of options and decreasing control by religious denominations led to major changes in the face of higher education. By the 1880s, as many colleges and universities became increasingly secular, various religious denominations began seeking new ways to reach out to students. The "appearance in sufficient numbers of Catholics and Jews at institutions that were nominally Protestant in tradition" led to student centers for individuals of those faiths (Rudolph, 1990, p. 459). The first undergraduate Catholic club appeared at the University of Wisconsin in 1880, a precursor of the Newman Centers that serve to meet the religious needs of Catholic students at many non-Catholic colleges and universities (Rudolph). As of 2008 the Catholic Campus Ministry Association (2008) listed 321 Newman Centers or Catholic Campus Ministry in the United States. The Hillel (2008) movement, founded by B'nai B'rith, a Jewish service organization, began at the University of Illinois in 1923, and in 2008 had over 500 student centers/organizations. The Muslim Students Association (n.d.) of the United States and Canada, which began in 1963 at a meeting of 10 schools at the University of Illinois-Urbana, claimed nearly 150 affiliated campus organizations in 2008.

With the increasing religious diversity in the United States and on campuses, it is not possible for every student, regardless of faith, to have the benefit of an organized campus religious center. At many institutions, local churches, mosques, and synagogues play an important support role for religious minority students when there is no campus-based program. Campus religious clubs, often advised by a faculty or staff member of the group's religion, also provide support. Some denominations prefer to integrate college students of their faith into the existing community religious establishment. For example, many of the historically African American churches, such as African Methodist Episcopal Zion (AME-Zion), Christian Methodist Episcopal (CME), or the historically African American Baptist churches, do not establish campus religious centers, instead bringing students of their denomination to local churches. On the other hand, Newman Centers, especially the larger ones, reach out to the entire campus Catholic community of students, faculty, staff, and even local residents.

Over time, other organizations have also contributed to a religious presence in higher education. The Young Men's Christian Association (YMCA) was a dominant presence in religious life at many institutions. In 1877 "an intercollegiate YMCA was formed, and the movement soon came to have great influence throughout the American academic world" (Brubacher & Rudy, 1997, p. 126). College fraternities and sororities also took on a role in religious life by including minority religious groups. Early in their histories, many fraternal organizations either denied membership to Jews or Catholics, or had such a strong Protestant bent to their purpose that non-Protestant students began to found their own organizations. According to *Baird's Manual of College Fraternities* (Anson & Marchesani, 1998), several Greek letter organizations were founded for religious minority students. In 1903 Zeta Beta Tau, the first fraternity for Jewish men, was founded at Cornell. Alpha Epsilon Phi, the first sorority for Jewish women, began in 1909 at Barnard College. Catholic men also founded their own fraternities. Phi Kappa Theta had its beginning in 1959 through the merger of two existing Catholic men's fraternities, Phi Kappa, founded in 1889 at Brown University, and Theta Kappa Phi, founded at Lehigh University in 1917. Today, these organizations and the other Greek letter societies founded for religious minorities welcome members of all faiths.

Interestingly, not all Greek letter organizations began as monocultural organizations. Alpha Phi Omega was founded in 1925 at Lafayette College in Pennsylvania as an organization for men of all religions. While it is more appropriately classified as a service fraternity rather than a social Greek fraternity, it is an example of an early Greek letter organization with broader foundations than others of the time. Alpha Phi Omega later also established chapters at historically African American institutions beginning at Howard University in 1948. In 1976 the fraternity became even more diverse by admitting women students as full members. For several years prior to that change, women students had been admitted as associate members (Anson & Marchesani, 1998).

The history of religious diversity on campus is complicated, filled with conflict, compromise, and change. Every campus is a unique picture of the religious experience and must be understood in that context; however, the student experience also occurs on an individual level, as well as in the larger societal context.

Student Development Theory and Religious Diversity

Religious diversity is rarely discussed in texts on student development theory, although the inclusion of material on spiritual development is becoming more common. Perry (1970) briefly discussed the difference between belief and faith, indicating that belief comes from parents and culture, while faith is a personal affirmation. The fifth position—Relativism Correlate, Competing, or Diffuse—in Perry's scheme of development represents the division between belief and faith in an individual's growth. Kohlberg (1984) also discussed how religious values change from those received from parents to those resulting from personal commitment. Kohlberg made the assumption that the process is the same, regardless of the particular religion. Chickering and Reisser (1993) discussed religion as part of two vectors, Developing Integrity and Developing Purpose, with specific examples of students dealing with Christianity. Fowler's (1981) work on the development of faith is a valuable resource for understanding how religious belief and faith change as the individual develops. Later work by Parks (1986, 2000) contributed even more to an understanding of how religious faith develops and changes. However, it is difficult to find literature specifically on the development of religious minority students and how it may differ from religious majority students.

In *What Matters in College*, Astin (1993) reported differences between Protestant, Catholic, and Jewish students on a wide range of variables such as Greek letter organization membership, alcohol use, degree completion, and career choice. His results present more of a snapshot of student behavior and choices in campus involvement. The information does not, however, provide any greater understanding on why these differences exist and how they might be understood.

A review of research in several journals yielded very little about religion and student development. For example, a search of the *Journal of College Student Development* (*JCSD*) from 1990 to 2003 yielded only eight articles on these topics. Low and Handal (1995) examined the relationship between religion and college adjustment. Strange and Alston (1998) involved 70 students in a program to explore human differences, including religious differences. Rogers and Dantley (2001) discussed how student affairs leadership should use spiritual intelligence in their work with students. Jones and McEwen (2000) presented a conceptual model of identity that included an emphasis on religion as an important aspect of identity. They further suggested that identity evolves and that the multiple aspects of an individual's identity change in salience over time. This inclusion of religion and spirituality as an aspect of multiple identity development is reflected in an increase in the number of relevant articles in the *JCSD* after 2003. Whereas the preceding 13 years included only 8 such articles, there were 12 in the 4-year period between 2004 and 2008, including several exploring religion or spirituality as a dimension of multiple identity development (e.g., Abes, Jones, & McEwen, 2007; Abes & Kasch, 2007; Love, Bock, Jannarone, & Richardson, 2005; Sanchez & Carter, 2005).

There is still a need for further theory and research on religion and student development. The theories that do exist seem to assume that students from different religions will develop their respective faiths through the same process; however, to date no attempt has been made to prove or disprove this idea. Research must not only include the religious preference and identity development of students, it must also make comparisons between denominations, or at least groups of denominations, to determine the generalizability of a theory across such groups. For example, how does the understanding of *authority* in Perry's (1970) scheme differ between Catholic students and other Christian students, or between Christian, Jewish, and Islamic students? Like the blind eye researchers turned to gender for so many years, there too often continues to be a blind eye turned toward religious diversity.

What seems clear, however, is that while students expect their colleges and universities will play a role in their spiritual development, nearly half of college juniors in one survey reported dissatisfaction with opportunities for religious or spiritual reflection available during their college experience (Lindholm, 2007). However, findings from this same 2004 survey of entering college students indicated that "roughly two-thirds feel that their spiritual beliefs have helped them develop their identity and that these beliefs give meaning and purpose to their lives" (Lindholm, p. 12). Research under the direction of Astin, Astin, and Lindholm has been focused on understanding how students' spirituality affects their self-concept and their connections with others (Lindholm). Preliminary results indicate that students who are highly spiritual have more positive outlooks, more engagement in charitable work, more ecumenical worldviews, and a stronger ethic of caring. Positive associations have also been reported between participation in religious organizations and social integration, emotional well-being, and spirituality (Bryant, 2007).

Similarly, analysis of results from the 2004 National Survey of Student Engagement indicated that students who frequently engage in spirituality-enhancing practices also participate more in other campus activities and are somewhat more satisfied with college than their peers (Kuh & Gonyea, 2006). In the same study, students from different racial and ethnic groups were found to vary in their frequency of engaging in spirituality-enhancing activities, with African American students engaging more often than White students. Tisdell (2003) said the development of a positive cultural identity is also a spiritual process for many; spirituality can also play an important role in dealing with internalized oppression. As educators committed to the development of the whole student, we must not ignore the important role of religion and spirituality in our students' lives and their identity development. Further, as Jones and McEwen (2000) pointed out, "Student affairs educators must not presume what is most central to individuals, but must instead listen for how a person sees herself" (p. 412).

While it is important to recognize differences between students of different religious backgrounds, it is also important to recognize the similarities. Astin et al. (2005) discovered clusters of similar religious preferences among students from very different religions and denominations, reinforcing the need to understand not only religions but the students who ascribe to them.

Distinguishing Spirituality and Religion

One concept that has begun to emerge more clearly in higher education literature is spirituality as distinct from religion. One way of distinguishing them is defining religion as "an affiliation with and practice of an established denominational tradition" and spirituality as involving "a highly personal search for ultimate meaning, purpose, and values wherever they may be found" (Stamm, 2006, p. 38). In other places, spirituality has other connotations. While no common definition of spirituality exists, Estanek (2006) conducted a qualitative analysis of sources on spirituality in higher education and identified five recurring patterns that characterize this new discourse: spirituality defined as spiritual development, used as critique, understood as an empty container for individual meaning, understood as common ground, and discussed as quasi religion. What this suggests is there is no broad, common understanding of religion and no broadly accepted common understanding of spirituality. Nonetheless, Estanek advocated for a developmental approach to spirituality that

> recognizes the diversity of spiritual and religious understandings. However, with this approach we ask of students what we ask of them in other areas of development: that they reflect upon their spirituality, however they understand it, in light of experience and integrate it into their emerging adult self. We ask them to learn more about their own faith tradition, if they have one, and those of others, not only in a religious sense but in the active sense of meaning-making. (p. 277)

This approach to understanding spirituality incorporates it into the framework of student development and so suggests that it can be a part of a holistic understanding of all students. Strange (2000) noted that education itself may be an inherently spiritual process and so compels us to rethink the ways we engage students in it.

Demographics of Religious Diversity on Campus

Public state institutions in many ways reflect the breadth of denominations of their constituent population. According to the Higher Education Research Institute (HERI) in a study of 40-year trends in U.S. freshmen, the number of students indicating no religious preference increased from 6.6% in 1966 to 19.1% in 2006 (Pryor, Hurtado, Saenz, Santos, & Korn, 2007); however, it remains true that over 80% of incoming college students do identify a religious preference. The percentage of students identifying as Protestant dropped from slightly more than half to 45%, while the number identifying as Catholic remained fairly constant at 27.7%. The number of those identifying as Jewish also decreased, moving from 4.9% to 2.6% (Pryor et al.).

As mentioned at the beginning of this chapter, defining a religious minority is dependent on context. For example, although the largest single denomination represented at a particular institution may be Catholic, seeing Catholic students as a majority flies in the face of the history of anti-Catholic sentiment and misunderstandings and the experience of many Catholic students.

Across campuses and religious preferences, students overall continue to exhibit strong connections to their faith. In a 2004 study conducted by

HERI, over 112,000 entering freshmen across the U.S. indicated a high level of interest and involvement in spirituality and religion (Astin et al., 2005). About 80% of those surveyed reported attending religious services in the last year; similar numbers discussed religion with others and reported belief in God. Religious preferences in this study were similar to those reflected in other HERI studies. In terms of religious affiliation, the highest percentage in this study was Roman Catholic (28%), followed by mainline Protestant faiths (17%), none (17%), Baptist (13%), and other Christian (11%). About one fourth (26%) said they consider themselves to be born-again Christians (Astin et al.). Jewish students made up 2% of the respondents, and Buddhist, Eastern Orthodox, Hindu, and Islamic students each constituted 1% of the total (Astin et al.). The challenge for many campus administrators is to respond to the needs and interests of all students while recognizing that their numbers and preferences vary greatly.

While the number of entering college students reporting no religious preference at all has doubled in the past 20 years, an even larger increase has been reported by those noting their religious preference as "other Christian (Protestant)," the percentage of which has more than tripled in the past two decades (Pryor et al., 2007). Included in the latter category are nondenominational Christian churches, many of which are conservative and evangelistic in nature. Affiliation with these groups was claimed by nearly 20% of entering students (Pryor et al.). While discussion of religious diversity is generally focused on the experiences of students in the religious minority, these statistics reflect the reality that such diversity increasingly includes those with no religious affiliation as well as those with ties outside the traditional denominational structures.

Culture of Religious Diversity

When students were asked if they had attended a religious service during the last year, 76.8% reported they had (Hurtado & Pryor, 2006). When asked to rate their level of spirituality as compared to the average for people their age, 36.7% rated themselves as above average or in the top 10%. In 2005, the most recent year reported for the question, 40.5% said they considered it to be "essential or very important" to integrate spirituality into their lives (Pryor et al., 2007).

Clearly, religious life and spirituality are an important part of students' lives. In the book *Religion on Campus*, Butler (1989) concluded that "religion is quantitatively and qualitatively more diverse and more present on campus than it has ever been" (p. 15). In a different book with the same title, Cherry, DeBerg, and Porterfield (2001) examined the religious culture of four different institutions that included public, Catholic, and Protestant colleges and universities. The authors interviewed students, faculty, staff, and campus chaplains. They examined religion in practice and in the academic offerings of departments of religion. They concluded "religion on the four campuses [to be] sufficiently vital and inviting. . . . It is possible that young people in American culture have never been more enthusiastically engaged in religious practice or with religious ideas" (pp. 294–295). While participation in formal religious activities often declines in college, interest in spirituality tends to increase (Lindholm, 2006; Stamm, 2006). There is evidence that religion and spirituality are alive and well in U.S. higher education.

For students from religious minorities, however, campus life can be a special challenge. These voices were heard by one of the authors through several years of training paraprofessionals; giving presentations at conferences (e.g., Granpré, 1995), first-year experience classes, first-year experience faculty workshops, and campus religious groups; and interviewing minority religion faculty, staff, and campus chaplains and ministers specifically for this chapter. This data was qualitatively reviewed using techniques suggested by Lincoln and Guba (1985). It is in no way a complete picture for every religious minority in every setting, but it does give some insight to the student experience. In addition, some incidents that received attention in the press are also included.

Taking America's Pulse III, a project sponsored by the National Conference for Community and Justice (formerly the National Council of Christians and Jews) indicated that while there has been some improvement in attitudes toward others in different groups, negative perceptions persist and views on intergroup relations vary widely (Smith, 2006). In presentations to paraprofessionals and to first-year experience classes, students were asked to name the faiths of people they knew at their institution. Once the list was written on a board, the students were asked about their stereotypes of that faith. Students were quickly able to compile stereotypes of Jews, Muslims, and Catholics. They were also able to compile stereotypes of some Protestant denominations, especially Mormons and Baptists. When discussing where the stereotypes came from, the students identified their parents and family, media, friends, and, interestingly, their own religion and religious leaders. When discussing non-Christian religious denominations, some Christian students said they had been taught it was their religious duty to convert non-Christians. One student explained that he "felt sorry" for his friends who were not Christian because they were, according to his religious upbringing, eternally damned.

Non-Christian and Catholic students in the presentations were not surprised to hear these stereotypes. Many stated they had grown up knowing the stereotypes other people held about them. In fact, some stated that their families and religious leaders had prepared them for such attitudes and had given them stereotypes of some Christian denominations and their attitudes. Family members seemed to be afraid the students would stop practicing their religion while away at college or convert to another religion. Some students said their parents were afraid they would marry outside their faith. Many of the minority religious students reported they had experienced the effects of stereotypes and prejudices in their daily campus life (Grandpré, 1995).

When discussing prejudices, minority religion students had numerous examples. For example, Jewish and Islamic students reported having evangelical pamphlets placed under their residence hall doors, having students invite them to meetings at various Christian denomination campus centers, and having relationships alter when new acquaintances discovered their religious faith. Jewish undergraduates reported being cut during fraternity and sorority rush by certain chapters and told later it was because of their religion.

Islamic students also noted increased hostility from some individuals after the September 11, 2001, attacks on the World Trade Center and Pentagon. Specifically, students mentioned experiencing racial slurs and insults and having notes put under their doors. However, the students also noted numerous attempts to include them in campus memorials and to offer support and protection (Grandpré, 1995). At the University of Michigan, for example, Jewish and Islamic students worked together on memorial vigils and to help each other deal with discrimination and backlashes from the attacks (Hoover, 2001).

When discussing the difficulties of being a religious minority on a college campus, students, faculty members, and college chaplains reported problems in practicing their specific faith. The traditional college calendar allows for the celebration of Christian holidays but not typically for holidays of other religions. Jewish students expressed numerous difficulties taking time away from classes and student activities. One student reported being told that if she did not attend band practice, she would lose her position when she returned. Students also discussed having to "justify" a holiday. For example, when an Orthodox student wanted to follow the strict observance of Jewish holidays as he was brought up to do, one faculty member refused to give approval to let him take an exam at another time because the faculty member had never heard of that holiday. The local Hillel director had to step in and explain the holiday and the specific Orthodox observances before the faculty member would concede permission for a makeup exam. Islamic students also experienced similar problems regarding daily prayer times, Jumma, and meal scheduling during Ramadan. In the article "For Many Muslims, College Is a Balancing Act" (McMurtie, 2001), Muslim students discuss the challenges of campus life, including fears about discrimination, differences in dating customs, and exposure to alcohol.

Another area of difficulty reported was in food. Islamic and Jewish laws ban the consumption of certain kinds of food. The most well known may be the ban on pork products and shellfish, and on the consumption of meat and milk at the same meal. For observant students, even avoiding such food in a cafeteria is not sufficient. Meat animals must be killed according to the kosher rules (for Jewish students) or halach (for Muslim students). Hindu students also avoid beef, and some try to be completely vegetarian. Some Buddhist students also prefer to be vegetarian as part of their faith. Some strictly observant Jewish and Muslim students reported simply going vegetarian while living on campus as a way to cope with limited options. Some Hillels, such as Ohio State's, offer kosher dining plans (Jacobson, 2001); the university has in some cases released students from their on-campus dining plan to participate in the Hillel plan. A few universities even offer kosher or halach dining plans on campus.

The most difficult issue reported by Catholic, Islamic, and Jewish students was confronting the Christian evangelical movements on their respective campuses. Students reported being invited to social events, only to find themselves at a prayer meeting. Others reported feeling targeted by another student for conversion. One Jewish student likened it to being stalked. On one campus, for example, people carrying large placards with Christian biblical quotes formed a line at a main stop on the campus bus route. Students had to run a gauntlet to get from the bus to the student center. Students mentioned having professors invite students in class to come to Bible studies. Others reported resident assistants holding Bible study groups in their room and inviting students at hall meetings to come and attend. While no one felt it was inappropriate for the professor or the resident assistant to attend Bible study groups, there was concern about the use of their positions to promote these activities. As one student put it, "No one on my campus would think about telling an African American student to act more white, or invite a female student to a program to teach her to act more like a man, but they [Christian evangelicals] will tell me that I have to change my ethnicity; it's a unique form of racism because they see it as their sacred duty to change who I am, to eliminate who I am."

Free speech has also been an issue in discussions on religious diversity. Some Christian students in discussion groups felt they could not express their views without being ridiculed or chastised. At the same time, religious minority students felt targeted and persecuted by members of other faiths. The University of Virginia lost a free speech case before the Supreme Court in 1995 in *Rosenberger v. Rector and Visitors of University of Virginia* when the university denied funding from student activity fees for the student-published journal *Wide Awake: A Christian Perspective at University of Virginia*. The university argued the publication could not be funded with student fees without violating the Establishment Clause of the First Amendment, while the student group argued that the actions of the university violated its free speech rights (White, 1995). While the long-term implications of the decision have yet to be determined, institutions must remain cognizant of the multiple issues surrounding the intersection of freedom of speech and freedom of religion.

Some students have objected to being required to live in mixed-gender housing. For Orthodox Jewish students, regular programs on sexual responsibility, preventing HIV transmission, and the sexual habits of people around them are seen as violations of traditional Jewish laws against premarital sex (Crissey, 1997). Some Islamic students have also had difficulties with these issues (McMurtie, 2001). A court case filed by a group of Orthodox Jewish students at Yale University (*Hack, et al. v. President and Fellows of Yale College*) claiming that requiring them to live in such an environment was discriminatory was decided in favor of the university (Biemiller & Reisberg, 1998). Subsequently, the Supreme Court declined to review the case (Bartlett, 2001). While this seems to indicate that a university can require participation in a program even if the students find it difficult because of their religion, it still leaves open the question of how institutions can best meet the needs of all students and create environments that are welcoming to them.

Examples of Practices in Religious and Spiritual Diversity

One way to frame engagement with religious diversity is to take the perspective of pluralism. Religious pluralists hold that people believing in different creeds and belonging to different communities need to learn to live together. It is therefore a sociological, not theological, pluralism. Religious pluralism is neither mere coexistence nor forced consensus. It is a form of proactive cooperation that affirms the identity of the constituent communities while emphasizing that the well-being of each and all depends on the health of the whole. It is the belief that the common good is best served when each community has a chance to make its unique contribution. (Patel, 2007, pp. 5–6)

As religious diversity on campuses has increased, institutions have begun to reflect a pluralistic approach, developing creative and inclusive approaches to meeting student needs.

Campus Support Agencies

Many campuses have a wealth of religious student organizations and campus clergy. Relationships between campuses and religious organizations range from benign neglect to enthusiastic acceptance. The Campus Ministry Association (CMA, n.d.) at the University of Georgia is one example of how a public institution can establish a working relationship with these groups. The CMA is an independent alliance of campus chaplains from the various denominational student centers, paradenominational organizations, and the university. The CMA has its own elected officers and admits members based on their involvement on the campus. Some are campus chaplains dedicated solely to the campus program, some are clergy working with a congregation from the university and the community, and some are working with student organizations that have no specific denominational affiliation but instead work from a general Christian or Protestant framework.

CMA publishes a directory of religious organizations on campus for students, parents, and faculty. This pamphlet is designed to offer a contact from each denomination for referrals, questions, and services. The university has allowed this material to be distributed on campus through a variety of sources. The vice president for student affairs has a liaison who works closely with CMA members to ensure access to the university when needed (CMA, n.d.). Staff in the vice president's office also send out notices to faculty reminding them of non-Christian religious holidays and that some students may be absent to participate in their faith observances. During emergencies, such as notifying a student about a family crisis, the liaison can call upon the appropriate college chaplain to assist.

Among private institutions, the University of Richmond (n.d.) is another good example of how to deal with religious diversity. Although the university was founded as a Baptist institution, it is now independent. The Cannon Memorial Chapel on the Richmond campus is a beautiful building with stained-glass windows that represent different academic disciplines. Attached to the building is a wing that houses the office of the university chaplain and includes small offices for the adviser or chaplain from every religious student organization on campus. The following text from the university's website describes the breadth of the program:

> 15 campus ministries serving 3 world religions and a commitment to serve those who adhere to a specific religious tradition or not, the Office of the Chaplaincy offers opportunities for students, faculty, and staff to explore their own convictions, faith, and spirituality within a welcoming inter-religious context. (University of Richmond, n.d.)

Behind the building is a small garden with a walking path and areas to meditate. Along the path, various plants are identified with small plaques that note not only the botanical name and information but also their religious significance. The college chapel is a physical reflection of religious pluralism that sends a clear message to the campus.

Creating a multidenominational space on campus is an emerging national trend. According to McMurtie (1999), private institutions like Mount Holyoke College, Johns Hopkins University, and the University of Southern California have been at the forefront in renovating chapels to make them multidenominational. Private institutions have an advantage over public ones because they are not affected by issues of church and state in the same way public entities are. Administrators of some public institutions, such as Pennsylvania State University, have dealt with the issue by raising private funds. McMurtie described another difficult issue for religious organizations:

> Secular colleges have always made some effort to carve out space for students to practice religion, but the results have often been lopsided. Christians end up with the prime real estate—perhaps a quaint campus chapel—while other religious groups make do with a room in the student center or the basement of a dormitory. (p. A48)

When creating a truly multidenominational area, some groups may feel empowered, but others may feel they are giving up campus space and a preferred role. Such campus changes must be carried out with care and sensitivity so that a decision designed to facilitate diversity does not breed resentment.

While working with campus chaplains can be an effective way to assist religious minority students, at some campuses a religious minority group may not have the resources of a campus center and a full-time professional religious leader. For example, at the University of Maryland, a search for religious student organizations yields a list of 62 groups (University of Maryland, n.d.b.), but the University's Memorial Chapel webpage lists just 14 recognized chaplaincies (University of Maryland, n.d.a.).

Some institutions have more than one campus ministers' organization. For example, the University of North Carolina at Chapel Hill (2010) has a Campus Minister's Association and an Evangelical Campus Ministries Association. The members of the Campus Minister's Association represent a wide range of faiths, majority and minority. Evangelical Campus Ministries is made up predominantly of representatives from nondenominational Christian organizations.

An unusually broad approach is taken at Georgetown University. Georgetown is a Jesuit institution with a wide-ranging campus ministry that includes Catholic, Orthodox, Jewish, Muslim, and Protestant chaplains and student organizations (Georgetown University, n.d.b.). In 1968 it became the first Catholic university to employ a full-time rabbi (Georgetown University, n.d.c.), and later became the first to appoint a full-time Muslim chaplain (Georgetown University, n.d.a.). The university also hosts a chair in Jewish Civilization. The Annual Interfaith Passover Seder, held for more than 30 years, brings together Jewish, Christian, and Muslim campus chaplains and their students for the ritual Passover meal and religious service about the struggles for freedom and an end to slavery.

Policies and Privilege

Spirituality is another framework used by some campus administrators to address this dimension of their students' lives. At Bowling Green State University, spiritual growth is one of the core values in the institution's statement of mission; the focus is not on any specific belief system but rather on the nature of spiritual questions in the lives and development of students (Strange, 2000). Such questions focus on self-definition and understanding, relationships with others, and purpose and direction. This emphasis on helping students to ask themselves the right questions and search for their own answers reflects the best of what we know about effective teaching and learning.

The Council for the Advancement of Standards' (2009) section on religious and spiritual programs is an excellent resource for exploring the issues of religion on campus for religious majority and minority students and staff. The standards are an excellent place to start a review of the role of campus chaplains, programs for students from various religious groups, and the role of religion and spirituality on campus.

This question of religious privilege on campus is one that has only lately been acknowledged. It is important to recognize the presence and effects of religious privilege; to address them administratively, in the classroom, and in the co-curriculum; and to assist students in their awareness and responses as well. As Fried (2007) pointed out, "Christian perspectives and practices are generally so embedded in institutional policies and practices that many people do not even pause to reflect on them, particularly if those policies and practices embody the beliefs of the dominant culture" (p. 3). Fried asserted that to have effective discussions of religious privilege, participants must commit to moving beyond dualistic ideas about religious truths to focus on understanding other perspectives without judging them. Further, faculty, academic administrators, and student affairs professionals alike must work, in and outside the classroom, to increase knowledge of differences and trust between groups so that authentic and productive dialogue can occur and the negative effects of privilege on religious minorities can be minimized. Jones and McEwen (2000) reminded us that student affairs educators, and others on campus,

> can encourage students who are members of groups whose identity is not examined to consider these aspects of their identity. Similarly, educators must exercise caution in making assumptions about the relative salience of particular identity dimensions for students in traditionally marginalized groups. (p. 413)

Conclusion

From the earliest days of U.S. higher education, religion has been an issue in and outside the classroom. The Bill of Rights provides for freedom of religion, and numerous court cases have helped to further define religious pluralism of U.S. society. The common thread through all the best practices described in this chapter is that at an institutional level they create space for religious variety and recognize the breadth of religious faith and spirituality that exists on the modern campus. Stamm (2006) reflected on changes in the country and our relationship to the world:

In the more than 35 years since enactment of the Civil Rights Act, great advances have occurred in establishing racial and ethnic diversity as basic to campus life. Too many students, however, remain ignorant about religious beliefs and practices other than their own. It is now time to give the same attention to creating a campus environment that encourages understanding of and appreciation for the religious diversity and pluralism of American life and peoples around the world. (p. 7)

Patel (2007) echoed this perspective, noting,

The American campus is a unique space. It gathers people from small towns and big cities, superpower nations and countries who can barely feed their own population; it manages to encourage both identity commitment and pluralist community; it values both individual freedom and contribution to the common good. Its experience with addressing the issue of race, while far from a perfect parallel, might well provide some clues, and some mistakes to avoid, regarding how to engage religious diversity in a way that impacts individual campuses, the broader system of higher education, the country we live in, and perhaps even the world. (p. 5)

We know that our students are concerned about matters of religious faith, spirituality, purpose, and meaning in their lives. As we work to create campuses that support their learning and development, we must also work to create campus communities that understand that religion and spirituality are to be embraced rather than shied away from, understood rather than feared, and discussed rather than ignored.

Questions for Reflection and Discussion

1. When discussions of diversity occur at your institution, is religion included? Do diversity awareness workshops for student affairs staff, professional and paraprofessional, include training on religious diversity? What about training programs for faculty and administrators? Do academic administrators make sure that non-Christian holidays are included on the official university calendar? Are religious observances of students ever discussed at faculty meetings? If not, how would you start these programs or discussions?
2. What are the religious demographics of your institution? How easy or difficult is it to find this information?

3. What is the relationship between the institution and various campus ministries and campus ministers' organizations? If a formal organization exists, what are the organization's criteria for membership? Are all campus ministers welcome, or is it denominationally specific? Is there more than one organization? What about students from denominations where there is no designated campus minister? Are religious student organizations that are advised by a layperson welcome?

4. For those at private sectarian institutions, what is the role of religion on your campus with respect to those who are not of your sponsoring denomination's faith? Is there a relationship with campus ministers from other faiths who work with students not of the institution's faith? How is the role of religion presented to prospective students and their families?

5. What do you know about the experiences of religious minority students on your campus? How do you know it?

6. Do you, or does your institution, intentionally address issues of spirituality and faith with students? Why or why not?

7. How can you contribute to the creation of an institution that is free of religious discrimination and harassment, and open to religious expression?

References

Abes, E. S., Jones, S. R., & McEwen, M. K. (2007). Reconceptualizing the model of multiple dimensions of identity: The role of meaning-making capacity in the construction of multiple identities. *Journal of College Student Development, 48,* 1–22.

Abes, E. S., & Kasch, D. (2007). Using queer theory to explore lesbian college students' multiple dimensions of identity. *Journal of College Student Development, 48,* 619–636.

Anson, J. L., & Marchesani, R. A. (Eds.) (1998). *Baird's manual of American college fraternities.* Indianapolis, IN: Baird's Manual Foundation.

Astin, A. W. (1993). *What matters in college? Four critical years revisited.* San Francisco: Jossey-Bass.

Astin, A. W., Astin, H. S., Lindholm, J. A, Bryant, A. N., Calderon, S., & Szelenyi, K. (2005). *The spiritual life of college students: A national study of college students' search for meaning and purpose.* Los Angeles: Higher Education Research Institute at UCLA.

Bartlett, T. (2001, October 19). Orthodox Jewish students lose fight with Yale. *The Chronicle of Higher Education,* A38.

Biemiller, L., & Reisberg, L. (1998, September 4). Judge dismisses suit by Orthodox Jewish students objecting to Yale's housing policy. *The Chronicle of Higher Education,* A69.

Brandeis University. (2008). *About Brandeis: Defining Brandeis.* Retrieved June 29, 2008, from http://www.brandeis.edu/about/defining.html

Brubacher, J. S., & Rudy, W. (1997). *Higher education in transition: A history of American colleges and universities* (4th ed.). New Brunswick, NJ: Transaction.

Bryant, A. N. (2007). The effects of involvement in campus religious communities on college student adjustment and development. *Journal of College and Character, 8*(3). Retrieved August 23, 2010, from http://journals.naspa.org/cgi/viewcontent .cgi?article = 1178&context = jcc

Butler, J. (1989). An overview of religion on campus. In J. Butler (Ed.), *Religion on campus* (pp. 3–16). San Francisco: Jossey-Bass.

Campus Ministry Association. (n.d.). *Campus Ministry Association at the University of Georgia.* Retrieved July 6, 2009, from http://www.uga.edu/cma/

Catholic Campus Ministry Association. (2008). *Links to Catholic campus ministry websites.* Retrieved March 5, 2008, from http://www.ccmanet.org/ccma.nsf/cam pussites?OpenPage

Chalfant, H. P., Beckley, R. E., & Palmer, C. E. (1994). *Religion in contemporary society.* Itasca, IL: F. E. Peacock.

Cherry, C., DeBerg, B. A., & Porterfield, A. (2001). *Religion on campus.* Chapel Hill: University of North Carolina Press.

Chickering, A. W., & Reisser, L. (1993). *Education and identity.* San Francisco: Jossey-Bass.

Cordoba University. (n.d.a.). *Introduction to the Graduate School of Islamic and Social Sciences.* Retrieved August 22, 2010, from http://www.cordobauniversity.org/ gsiss/introduction.asp

Cordoba University. (n.d.b.). *Welcome to Cordoba University.* Retrieved May 3, 2008, from http://www.cordobauniversity.org/welcome.asp

Council for the Advancement of Standards in Higher Education. (2009). *CAS professional standards for higher education* (7th ed.). Washington, DC: Author.

Crissey, M. (1997, September 12). Orthodox Jews protest Yale's rule on campus housing. *Chronicle of Higher Education,* A50.

Emory University. (n.d.). *Office of the Dean of the chapel and religious life: Campus ministry affiliates.* Retrieved May 5, 2008, from http://www.religiouslife.emory .edu/about/ministries.cfm

Estanek, S. M. (2006). Redefining spirituality: A new discourse. *College Student Journal, 40*(2), 270–281.

Fowler, J. W. (1981). *Stages of faith.* San Francisco: Harper & Row.

Freedman, J. O. (2000, December 1). Ghosts of the past: Anti-Semitism at elite colleges. *Chronicle of Higher Education,* B7.

Fried, J. (2007). Thinking skillfully and respecting difference: Understanding religious privilege on campus. *Journal of College and Character, 9*(1). Retrieved August 23, 2010, from http://journals.naspa.org/cgi/viewcontent.cgi?article=1103&context=jcc

Georgetown University. (n.d.a.). *Campus ministry: Religious traditions: Muslim.* Retrieved August 23, 2010, from http://campusministry.georgetown.edu/traditions/muslim/33836.html

Georgetown University. (n.d.b.). *Mission & ministry: The spirit of Georgetown.* Retrieved August 23, 2010, from http://missionandministry.georgetown.edu/spiritofgeorgetown.html

Georgetown University. (n.d.c.). *University news: Keeping the faith.* Retrieved August 23, 2010, from http://explore.georgetown.edu/news/?ID=36488

Grandpré, E. A. (1995). *Freedom of religion?* Paper presented at the meeting of the Southeastern Association of Housing Officers, Greenville, SC.

Hillel. (2008). *About Hillel.* Retrieved March 5, 2008, from http://www.hillel.org/about/default

Hoover, E. (2001, September 28). At a university proud of diversity, Jewish and Muslim students set aside differences—at least for now. *The Chronicle of Higher Education,* A15.

Hurtado, S., & Pryor, J. H. (2006). *The American freshman: National norms for 2005.* Los Angeles: Higher Education Research Institute at UCLA. Retrieved August 23, 2010, from http://www.heri.ucla.edu/PP/Norms05-Summary.ppt#. The American Freshman: National Norms for Fall 2005 Sylvia Hurtado & John H. Pryor January 26, 2006

Jacobson, J. (2001, April 27). The new Hillel: It's not just about praying anymore. *The Chronicle of Higher Education,* A49.

Jones, S. R., & McEwen, M. K. (2000). A conceptual model of multiple dimensions of identity. *Journal of College Student Development, 41*(4), 405–413.

Kazanjian, V., & Laurence, P. (2007). The journey toward multi-faith community on campus: The religious and spiritual life program at Wellesley College. *Journal of College and Character, 9*(2). Retrieved August 23, 2010, from http://journals.naspa.org/cgi/viewcontent.cgi?article=1123&context=jcc

Kohlberg, L. (1984). *The psychology of moral development.* San Francisco: Jossey-Bass.

Kuh, G. D., & Gonyea, R. M. (2006, winter). Spirituality, liberal learning, and college student engagement. *Liberal Education,* 40–47.

Lincoln, Y., & Guba, E. (1985). *Naturalistic inquiry.* Newbury Park, CA: Sage.

Lindholm, J. A. (2006). The "interior" lives of American college students: Preliminary findings from a national study. In J. L. Heft (Ed.), *Passing on the faith: Transforming traditions for the next generation of Jews, Christians, and Muslims* (pp. 75–102). New York: Fordham University Press.

Lindholm, J. A. (2007). Spirituality in the academy: Reintegrating our lives and the lives of our students. *About Campus, 12*(4), 10–17.

Love, P., Bock, M., Jannarone, A., Richardson, P. (2005). Identity interaction: Exploring the spiritual experiences of lesbian and gay college students. *Journal of College Student Development, 46,* 193–209.

Low, C. A., & Handal, P. J. (1995). The relationship between religion and adjustment to college. *Journal of College Student Development, 36*(5), 406–412.

McMurtie, B. (1999, December 3). Pluralism and prayer under one roof. *The Chronicle of Higher Education,* A48.

McMurtie, B. (2001, November 9). For many Muslims, college is a balancing act. *The Chronicle of Higher Education,* A55.

Muslim Students Association. (n.d.). *Muslim Students Association: Our history.* Retrieved August 23, 2010, from http://www.msanational.org/about

Parks, S. D. (1986). *The critical years: The young adult search for a faith to live by.* New York: Harper & Row.

Parks, S. D. (2000). *Big questions, worthy dreams: Mentoring young adults in their search for meaning, purpose, and faith.* San Francisco: Jossey-Bass.

Patel, E. (2007). Religious diversity and cooperation on campus. *Journal of College and Character, 9*(2). Retrieved August 23, 2010, from http://journals.naspa.org/cgi/viewcontent.cgi?article = 1120&context = jcc

Perry, W. G. (1970). *Forms of intellectual and ethical development in the college years.* New York: Holt, Rinehart and Winston.

Peterson's. (2008). *College search.* Retrieved May 3, 2008, from http://www.peter sons.com/ugchannel/code/searches/srchCrit2.asp?sponsor = 1

Pryor, J. H., Hurtado, S., Saenz, V. B., Santos, J. L., & Korn, W. S. (2007). *The American freshman: Forty year trends, 1966–2006.* Los Angeles: University of California, Los Angeles.

Rogers, J. L., & Dantley, M. E. (2001). Invoking the spiritual in campus life and leadership. *Journal of College Student Development, 42*(6), 589–603.

Rudolph, J. R. (1990). *The American college and university: A history.* Athens, GA: University of Georgia Press.

Sanchez, D., & Carter, R. T. (2005). Exploring the relationship between racial identity and religious orientation among African American college students. *Journal of College Student Development, 46,* 280–295.

Smith, T. W. (2006). *Taking America's pulse III: Intergroup relations in contemporary America.* New York: National Council for Community and Justice.

Stamm, L. (2003). Can we bring spirituality back to campus? Higher education's re-engagement with values and spirituality. *Journal of College and Character,* (4)5. Retrieved August 23, 2010, from http://journals.naspa.org/cgi/viewcontent.cgi?article = 1354&context = jcc

Stamm, L. (2006). The dynamics of spirituality and the religious experience. In A. W. Chickering, J. C. Dalton, & L. Stamm, (Eds.), *Encouraging authenticity and spirituality in higher education* (pp. 37–65). San Francisco: Jossey-Bass.

Strange, C. (2000). Spirituality at state: Private journeys and public visions. *Journal of College and Character, 1*(3), art. 1. Retrieved August 23, 2010, from http://jour nals.naspa.org/cgi/viewcontent.cgi?article = 1273&context = jcc

Strange, C., & Alston, L. (1998). Voicing differences: Encouraging multicultural learning. *Journal of College Student Development, 39*(1), 1–13.

Tisdell, E. J. (2003). *Exploring spirituality and culture in adult and higher education.* San Francisco: Jossey-Bass.

University of Maryland. (n.d.a.). *Memorial Chapel: Chaplains.* Retrieved August 23, 2010, from http://www.chapel.umd.edu/chaplains.php

University of Maryland. (n.d.b.). *STARS: Student activities reporting system.* Retrieved August 23, 2010, from http://www.stars.umd.edu/orgs/Default.aspx

University of North Carolina at Chapel Hill. (2010). *2010–2011 undergraduate bulle-tin: Religious activities.* Retrieved August 23, 2010, from http://www.unc.edu/ ugradbulletin/facilities.html#religious

University of Richmond. (n.d.). *Office of the chaplaincy: History of the chaplaincy.* Retrieved August 23, 2010, from http://chaplaincy.richmond.edu/about/history .html

White, L. (1995, July 14). The profound consequences of the "Rosenberger" ruling. *The Chronicle of Higher Education,* B1.

Appendix

Useful Web Resources

The following is a list of websites of national organizations for several minority religious groups' college programs, sites for researching religious issues, and sites for various national organizations for campus chaplains and ministers.

Association for Christians in Student Development: http://www.acsd home.org/

Beliefnet.com. Religious and spiritual e-community: http://www.belief net.com

Campus Ministry Association: http://www.ccmanet.org/ccma/index .html

Hillel. The Foundation for Jewish campus life: http://www.hillel.org

Hindu Students Council: http://hscnet.org

Jesuit Association of Student Personnel Administrators: http://jaspa .creighton.edu/

Muslim Students Association: http://msanational.org

National Association of College and University Chaplains: http://www
.nacuc.net/

National Campus Ministry Association: http://www.campusministry
.net/

The Pluralism Project at Harvard University: http://www.pluralism.org/
index.php

University of Wyoming, Religious Studies Program, Exploring Religions:
http://uwacadweb.uwyo.edu/religionet/er/DEFAULT.HTM

SECTION THREE

COMPONENTS OF CULTURAL COMPETENCE IN PRACTICE

17

ACHIEVING CULTURAL COMPETENCE AS A PRACTITIONER, STUDENT, OR FACULTY MEMBER

Theory to Practice

Diane L. Cooper, Mary F. Howard-Hamilton, and Michael J. Cuyjet

Teaching, reading, and learning about different racial, ethnic, and cultural groups can be a daunting task for everyone. Demographic data are constantly shifting, as is the landscape of our college campuses. When we began this project several years ago the predictions about the campus multicultural and multiethnic environment did not include the political, social, or economic changes that have taken place in the past few years. A melding of the political ideologies in this country because of the financial meltdown and dissatisfaction with continuous wars overseas have provided a common platform of thinking, particularly among the millennial generation, to move beyond differences and find common ground to change a system that is typically very slow to embrace change.

This book was written to create and continue the dialogue and action necessary for transformation and change in our higher education institutions and subsequently within our society (Freire, 2000). It addresses culture as more than racial or ethnic identity, even though racial or ethnic identity is a critical component of culture for many individuals. For that reason, the editors of this book have included discussions about the impacts of nationality, gender, sexual orientation, age, able-bodiedness, and religious affiliation on cultural identification, along with case studies, discussion questions, or exercises at the end of each chapter. Those exercises can be put into practice to develop the cultural competence of administrators, faculty, and students. In addition to providing a wide range of perspectives to help in understanding the many diverse peoples in our national cultural mosaic, the editors offer a list of supplemental texts, films and DVDs, and instructional materials on pp. 413–420 that may be useful when teaching sections of this book or presenting material to colleagues on diversity issues. As Howard-Hamilton and Hinton (2004) stated, "Using entertainment media allows individuals to step inside the shoes of another person or immerse themselves in another culture in a safe fashion without the high risk of failing" (p. 34). Using media and other creative teaching tools can aid the transformation of thought and the role we all play in making our society more empathetic toward others. Our recommendations include a brief description of the material and how it can be used as a teaching tool.

Theory to Practice for Student Affairs and Academic Administrators

Many administrators experience difficulty in translating theory into practice in their day-to-day activities. Moreover, delving into the complexities of diversity and multicultural identity development can be extremely challenging. Barcelo (2007) stresses the importance of grounding administrators' work in a wide variety of theoretical frameworks and sources of knowledge. Effective higher education leaders continuously ask members of their community the following questions (Barcelo):

> What do we aspire to be?
> What do we value?
> What do we want our students to know? How do we want them to act?
> What kind of climate do we want at our community and how do we get there?
> How should diversity efforts be organized to be both inclusive and effective? (p. 6)

Several methods exist to begin delivering the material in this book to administrators and faculty throughout your institution. A staff or faculty retreat during critical junctures of each academic year, for example, once or twice during fall and spring, can bring groups of institutional participants together for an opportunity to answer the questions posed by Barcelo (2007). The first review of diversity initiatives should be based on a multicultural organizational audit. Pope, Reynolds, and Mueller (2004) share several assessment instruments that could be used to evaluate the services provided by campus administrators. Specifically, if cultural competency is to be achieved, the multicultural organization development template (Pope et al.) points to the importance of reviewing the following concepts and functions: comprehensive definition of the term *multicultural,* the mission statement, leadership and advocacy, policy, recruitment and retention of a diverse staff and faculty, multicultural competency expectations and training, scholarly activities, departmental/divisional programs and services, physical environment, and assessment.

As change agents, student affairs staff and other institutional administrators who begin the arduous work of implementing a strategic diversity plan need to be aware of the importance of modeling the appropriate behaviors. Administrators and faculty should routinely evaluate their own level of multicultural competence, including attending diversity seminars and workshops annually. Every programmatic thrust should end with administrative leaders' posing the question "Did we include everyone?" By doing so, they will ensure each component is reviewed to maintain sensitivity to diversity and multicultural input. The modeling begins at the top and is measured by support and incentives provided by the institution's leaders. Outstanding programs can reap rewards depending on their content and creativity and their successful attempts at attracting a diverse audience of particpants.

Leaders can promote diversity initiatives by providing staff development workshops on diversity theories and current research in the field particularly for staff members who may not have degrees from graduate preparation programs or may not have studied some of the current multicultural research (see Appendix A for a model of a staff development program). Critical race theory (Delgado & Stefancic, 2001) discusses the importance of marginalized groups' ability to share stories about microaggressions that occur on and off campus. Making administrators and faculty aware of such stories will heighten their understanding of the emotional toll these aggressions take on college students and increase administrators' level of awareness and their ability to respond appropriately. The knowledge that their concerns are being heard could improve the retention of diverse students. The quality of administrators' training could have a positive effect on the university's reputation of being supportive of diversity issues.

Student affairs and academic administrators should use the guidelines of the Council for the Advancement of Standards in Higher Education (CAS; Dean, 2009) as a model for programs related to diversity. The standards can be used as an assessment tool as well as a creative programmatic guide for every functional area in student affairs. Using CAS guidelines will also help facilitate meaningful conversations with faculty regarding course structures and the inclusion of diversity material in their curricula and in graduate preparation course work.

Theory to Practice for Teaching Faculty

The most difficult courses to teach induce cognitive dissonance in students and prompt them to decipher the nature of and reasons for this discomfort over issues they may not have been conscious of in their day-to-day interactions or activities. Courses that require students to step outside their comfort zone also require faculty who are very comfortable with their racial/ethnic and cultural identities. Comfort with one's own cultural identity (and its various facets) is a prerequisite for a faculty member's acceptance of the nondeficient legitimacy of other cultures that he or she may be addressing in course content. That is why honest introspection about one's cultural identity is a prerequisite to success in teaching students about other cultures (Pope et al., 2004). Diversity courses in ethnic studies, women's studies, sociology, psychology, counseling, and higher education challenge everyone to become aware of oppressed and marginalized groups in our society and of the interrelations among people with diverse cultural identifications. hooks (1994) stated,

> Progressive professors working to transform the curriculum so that it does not reflect biases or reinforce systems of domination are most often the individuals willing to take the risks that engaged pedagogy requires and to make their teaching practices a site of resistance. (p. 21)

Implementing a teaching philosophy built upon the banking education model (Freire, 1968/2000) is an inappropriate method of instruction, thus faculty should find ways to open up dialogue in the classroom. The method of teaching must be congruent with the material shared to effectively enhance the student's knowledge of, awareness about, and abilities of multiple groups and their cultures.

Faculty who teach diversity courses should provide frequent opportunities for all students to relate their fears, anxieties, cultural experiences, classroom expectations, and epiphanies. (See Appendix B for sample syllabi.) Journal writing is one useful form for students to express how the course content has had an impact on them. The opportunity to express feelings after an intellectually challenging class is needed to engage students. The process of writing a journal (shared only with the instructor) allows the student's voice to be heard and enables the professor to gauge and sensitively respond to any shift in thinking or to any resistance from the student. By giving students the opportunity to tell their stories about how they learned about race, class, gender, and privilege, journals also enable faculty to pace their class to achieve an appropriate amount of challenge and support that is compatible with the students' level of development.

Placing information in the proper context is another important role for faculty when teaching students about new cultures. As described in chapters 3 and 4 of this book, culture is influenced by time and place. As explained in chapter 4 on shifting paradigms, when new information is added to existing knowledge on issues such as identity development, the common perspective shifts and perceptions are altered. A student who adopted a particular perspective on a culture earlier in life might discover that newer information can radically change that perception. It is the faculty member's job to challenge any such stereotypes students have that were formed earlier and without sufficient knowledge by being aware of new knowledge and by giving the students that new knowledge. Similarly, as described in chapter 3, the college environment can have a significant impact on culture and especially on interaction among different cultures. However, the faculty member must remind students that other environmental societal influences outside academe can affect other cultures differently and can influence a student's cultural identity development in significantly distinct ways.

The application of theory to the classroom, as detailed in chapter 2, also includes providing students with material that increases their knowledge about diverse populations. Traditional elementary and secondary school textbooks typically repeat uncritically the stories or history of the dominant group in this country and portray the stories of nondominant peoples through the viewpoint of the dominant group. The result is often a distorted or even untrue recounting of the history of nondominant people, and reinforces the implied belief that the history of oppressed groups is not important or relevant to the development of this country.

Empowering students to reach a critical transforming stage of development (Alschuler, 1986) also requires some type of action-oriented activity that provides them with a skill set that induces a shift in their racial identity development allowing them to be comfortable with dissonance and the struggles marginalized groups face on campus and in society. Providing students with an opportunity to create programs and projects that teach others about power, privilege, and oppression is liberating for the facilitator and the participant. Examples include diversity programs for student leaders, culturally sensitive advising programs for professional staff, international service-learning projects, and the creation of new programs specifically for diverse student populations.

Theory to Practice for Students in Preparation Programs

Undergraduate students have opportunities to enhance their multicultural competence on a daily basis. Whether they engage in those opportunities depends not only on what administrators and faculty do to facilitate learning, but also on the student's developmental level, personal values, and peer group norms. Graduate students in student affairs, however, are in a unique position to enhance their multicultural competence not only through their academic work but also through the various forms of supervised practice that are typically part of their degree program.

Creamer and Winston (2002) noted that

> applied knowledge in student affairs is acquired through extensive contact with students within an academic context while discharging one's responsibilities as an institutional agent. When this experience is combined with an understanding of the developmental processes experienced by students and theories of organization and management, the student affairs practitioner is able to contribute to students' academic and personal growth and to the institution's organizational effectiveness. (p. 7)

Hoberman and Mailick (1994) asserted that

> professional education is directed toward helping students acquire special competencies for diagnosing specific needs and for determining, recommending, and taking appropriate action. Professional education is also expected to socialize students in the "thought processes" of the profession

and to inculcate them with its customs, ethics, working relationships, and the behaviors expected from members of the profession. (pp. 3–4)

The curriculum is in place for students to not only gain theoretical knowledge but also to engage in supervised experiences in which they can put theory into practice. These experiences typically can be either paid work experiences (assistantships) and paid or nonpaid experiences tied directly to an academic course (often referred to as practica or internships).

Supervised Practice

A key process in internships and assistantships is the supervision of students from on-site professionals. Supervision is defined as "a method of training and teaching in which experienced professionals provide guidance, opportunities for skill development, crucial feedback, and general support in a field setting to graduate students who are enrolled in a professional preparation program" (Winston & Creamer, 2002, p. 69). Multicultural competencies students need to develop include "gaining knowledge of other cultures through study and direct experience, developing a greater awareness of . . . [one's] own cultural make-up, decreasing . . . [one's] ethnocentrism, and increasing . . . [one's] respect of other traditions" (Kiser, 2000, pp. 100–101).

Skill development related to multicultural issues should be part of every supervised practice opportunity and included in the learning goals for every student. This means the next generation of student affairs professionals and faculty will come into the field with knowledge, skills, and attitudes that embrace the need to create and maintain campuses where all students feel welcome, included, and supported.

Assessment

It is important to evaluate activities and interventions that enhance diversity and multicultural competence to determine success or progress. A recommended benchmark for the assessment of the acquisition of skills and knowledge by administrators, faculty, and students is the description of cultural competence developed by Pope, Reynolds, and Mueller (2004). Readers are urged to refer to chapter 1, pp. 12–14) and review the examples of awareness, knowledge, and ability in cultural competence and to incorporate such competencies as criteria for evaluating development in members of the campus community.

Supplemental Texts—Multicultural Knowledge

The following sections provide several examples of how texts, media, and supplemental materials can be used to increase the level of knowledge, awareness, and skills among staff and administrators, faculty, and students. These tools can be used in professional development programs, training seminars, diversity courses, and personal edification. The list, not intended to be exhaustive, is a sampling of material to begin the process.

Publications

Wise, T. (2007). *White like me: Reflections on race from a privileged son.* New York: Soft Skull Press.

Wise is an antiracist writer who has written numerous books and articles on the importance of recognizing privilege in a society that benefits Whites. His works can be used in multiple settings that could provide meaningful dialogue for everyone.

Delgado, R., & Stefancic, J. (2001). *Critical race theory: An introduction.* New York: New York University Press.

This text provides the history and framework for critical race theory. Students respond to the questions at the end of each chapter so they can process their reactions to the issues presented. At the end of the course students are asked to review what they had written at the beginning of the term and respond to any changes in how they processed the material.

Freire, P. (2000). *Pedagogy of the oppressed* (M. B. Ramos, Trans.). New York: Continuum. (Original work published 1968)

This text provides a thorough and in-depth discussion of who the oppressed and the oppressor are as well as what needs to take place for a society to transform itself and be more caring and loving.

Forney, D. S., & Cawthon, T. W. (2004). *Using entertainment media in student affairs teaching and practice.* San Francisco: Jossey-Bass.

This gives instructors examples of relevant media to supplement the literature. Chapters relate to race, gender, sexual orientation, leadership, and student development theory and how to find materials to enhance discussion and lectures.

Spring, J. (2010). *Deculturalization and the struggle for equality: A brief history of the education of dominated cultures in the United States* (6th ed.). New York: McGraw Hill.

The latest edition of this text provides an overview of our 21st-century racial/ethnic society and a thorough review of policies that have had an impact on marginalized groups in this country. The historical material enlightens students about how much information has been left out of the history books about dominated groups in the United States.

Suskind, R. (2005). *A hope in the unseen.* New York: Broadway.

According to critical race theory, the process of storytelling is a convincing method of sharing the plight of the oppressed in our society. This book is about an African American male, Cedric Jennings, who aspires to achieve a higher education despite the obstacles before him. A video clip on YouTube provides students with an updated story on Jennings, "A Hope in the Unseen, Interview with Cedric Jennings," Montgomery College Campus Conversations #51, part 1 of 4, http://www.youtube.com/watch?v=9Gj Px6Ewcp8

We show our class two segments of Cedric Jennings discussing how the book was written and what impact the production of the story has made on his life. It is best to show the vignettes when the students have finished reading the book so they can participate in a dialogue about what their image of Cedric was prior to observing the YouTube interview.

Supplemental Feature Films and DVDs—Story Telling

Hausman, M. (Producer), & Benton, R. (Writer and Director). (2001). *Places in the heart.* United States: Delphi II Productions.

After a series of catastrophic events in a small Texas town in the 1930s, people find a way to empower themselves even though the oppressive odds are against them. This film gives students an understanding of how events that have an impact on one person can indirectly affect several people. The film also contains numerous examples of how the oppressor(s) attempts to subjugate others, but the spirit of care, justice, love, and compassion can open hearts and minds. This can be used as a final class teaching product that connects with Freire (2000), critical race theory, heterosexism, ableism, socioeconomic status, and the ethic of care.

Weinstein, B. (Producer), Eisele, R. (Writer), & Washington, D. (Director). (2007). *The great debaters.* United States: Weinstein Company and Harpo Films.

Segments of this film can be used to help students understand the background of historically Black colleges, the politics of the separate but equal doctrine, and the importance of storytelling as a tool to enhance empathy between oppositional groups, which is portrayed in the final debate. The final scene can also be used in student development theory classes as an example of a dilemma discussion and moral reasoning.

Reimer, A. (Producer), & Haggis, P. (Writer and Director). (2005). *Crash*. United States: Lions Gate, Bob Yari Productions.

The film is an exploration of 12 people in Los Angeles who are racially and ethnically diverse and whose lives converge or crash by the end of the movie. The film can be used to discuss the concept of the threat of stereotyping, prejudice, and racism and can be connected to Freire (1968/2000), racial identity, and oppression.

What's race got to do with it: Social disparities and student succes. (2006). California Newsreel. http://newsreel.org/nav/title.asp?tc = CN0188

This documentary film produced at the University of California, Berkeley, chronicles the experiences of an undergraduate class studying issues related to race during one semester. This film can help students in student affairs graduate preparation programs understand the complexities of generational differences when millennial students have conversations about race in our society.

Mun Wah, L. (Producer and Director). (1994). *The color of fear*. United States: Stir-Fry Productions (http://www.stirfryseminars.com/store/store _ind.php)

This film is one of the best companion pieces to *Pedagogy of the oppressed* (Freire, 1968/2000) and *Critical race theory: An introduction* (Delgado & Stefancic, 2001) because of the different emotional and poignant conversations that occur among a group of racially diverse men in the movie. Several methods that could be used to help participants reflect on the film include journaling, examining/discussing each person's racial identity progression, and connecting the transformation process with Freire's description of praxis and transformational thought.

Pixar Short Films Collection (2007). Walt Disney Films *For the Birds* and *Boundin'*.

For the Birds gives us an example of what it's like for a bird to try to fit in with a group of birds of a different species. The birds from the same species are very hostile toward the different bird even though the outsider attempts to be open and caring. The end result is the marginalized bird has the last laugh in a lesson of the importance of doing unto others.

Boundin' is about a sheep that has a very high sense of self-esteem and is revered by the community. However, when the sheep is sheared, the community teases it, and the animal's self-esteem plummets. A supportive mentor comes along and helps the sheep lift its self-esteem and empowers it to embrace its differences. This film can be used to impart the importance of understanding differences and encouraging others to be the mentor who empowers and listens to anyone who has experienced a setback.

Supplemental YouTube Vignettes and Web Sites—Multicultural Awareness

Color me blind (http://www.youtube.com/watch?v = bALpBCwvHWM)

This 10-minute vignette was produced by a group of college students who created a scenario of what it would be like if everyone was color blind to the issues affecting others in our society. The vignette can be used in conjunction with a discussion on the color-blind philosophy in the critical race theory literature. The vignette also provides the viewer with the understanding that ignoring one's race or gender does not help society but limits communication because there is still one voice or mind-set that is dominant among those who have been ignored historically.

Teaching Tolerance (http://www.tolerance.org/teach/index.jsp)

Several teaching tools and DVDs are available free of charge from the Teaching Tolerance organization. The history material can be used to supplement Joel Spring's (2001) *Deculturalization and the Struggle for Equality*. The films brings life to the data and historical events Spring describes that were part of U.S. history but seldom discussed.

Supplemental Instructional Materials—Increase Knowledge

The Game of Oppression (http://bookstore.naspa.org/gameofoppression .aspx)

This educational tool provides students, administrators, and faculty with the opportunity to challenge individuals to tell their stories about oppression, privilege, and diversity issues in a safe and interactive environment. The game is a perfect companion piece to readings related to privilege, Freire (2000), and critical race theory. The game should be played within the first 2 to 4 weeks of the semester so the participants can understand the covert pervasiveness of oppression because it affects everyone regardless of race, class, or gender.

Council for the Advancement of Standards in Higher Education (CAS; http://www.cas.edu/index.htm)

Higher education administrators can use the CAS material to guide institutional services and programs. The standards provide specific evaluation tools to assess multicultural programming for various student affairs units.

Conclusion

We are at a unique time and place in our society, with a national political structure going through transition to include women and people of color in leadership positions in unprecedented ways. Three national milestones are the election of Barack Obama as the 44th president of the United States; the nomination and confirmation of Sonia Maria Sotomayor, the first Latina and third woman appointed associate justice of the U.S. Supreme Court; and the addition of Elena Kagan, the fourth woman on the U.S. Supreme Court. This is the first time three woman have sat on the U.S. Supreme Court at the same time. Our colleges and universities have more racially and culturally diverse administrators and faculty as well as White males who have a more enlightened perspective on their institutions and the diversity of the individuals who populate them. Diversity today is not an obsolete peripheral topic but has become more than simple wording in mission statements, strategic plans, position announcements, and at meetings with key stake-holders. Institutions are hiring chief diversity officers to educate the campus community and monitor the success of multicultural initiatives, programs, and activities on and off campus. Students often ask at the end of their course work on diversity and oppression if people are going to change and become more caring, empathetic, and humane toward others. The hopeful response is that it can and will happen if the students are willing to be open to dialogue and use their new-found knowledge to transform their environment.

West (2008) said that "you can't lead the people if you don't love the people. You can't save the people if you don't serve the people" (p. 151). Everyone must be involved if society is going to change and if this type of revolutionary action is to be continuous (Freire, 1968/2000). Moving beyond an oppressive society means there must be some form of sacrifice by every-one, and we must all be willing to give up some power, privilege, positions, and political favors for inclusion, shared empowerment, mutual critical con-sciousness, and multicultural enlightenment throughout our society.

References

Alschuler, A. S. (1986). Creating a world where it is easier to love: Counseling appli-cations to Paulo Freire's theory. *Journal of Counseling and Development, 64*, 492–496.

Barcelo, N. (2007). Transforming our institutions for the twenty-first century: The role of the chief diversity officer. *Diversity Digest: Advancing Diversity in Higher Education, 10*(2), 5–6.

Creamer, D. G., & Winston, R. B., Jr. (2002). Foundations of supervised practice experience: Definitions, context, and philosophy. In D. L. Cooper, S. A. Saunders, R. B. Winston Jr., & J. Hirt (Eds.), *Learning through supervised practice in student affairs.* New York: Brunner-Routledge.

Dean, L. A. (2009). *CAS standards and guidelines* (7th ed.). Washington, DC: Council for the Advancement of Standards.

Delgado, R., & Stefancic J. (2001). *Critical race theory: An introduction.* NY: New York Press.

Forney, D. S., & Cawthon, T. W. (2004). *Using entertainment media in student affairs teaching and practice.* San Francisco: Jossey-Bass.

Freire, P. (2000). *Pedagogy of the oppressed* (M. B. Ramos, Trans.). New York: Contiuum. (Original work published 1968)

Hoberman, S., & Mailick, S. (1994). Introduction. In S. Hoberman & S. Mailick (Eds.), *Professional education in the United States: Experiential learning, issues, and prospects* (pp. 3–6). Westport, CT: Praeger.

hooks, b. (1994). *Teaching to transgress: Education as the practice of freedom.* New York: Routledge.

Howard-Hamilton, M. F., & Hinton, K. G. (2004). Using entertainment media to inform student affairs teaching and practice about multiculturalism. In D. S. Forney & T. W. Cawthon (Eds.), *Using entertainment media in student affairs teaching and practice* (pp. 25–35). San Francisco: Jossey-Bass.

Kiser, P. M. (2000). *Getting the most from your human service internship: Learning from experience.* Belmont, CA: Brooks/Cole.

Pope, R. L., Reynolds, A. L., & Mueller, J. A. (2004). *Multicultural competence in student affairs.* San Francisco: Jossey-Bass.

Spring, J. (2010). *Deculturalization and the struggle for equality: A brief history of the education of dominated cultures in the United States* (6th ed.). New York: McGraw Hill.

Suskind, R. (2005). *A hope in the unseen.* New York: Broadway.

West, C. (2008). *Hope on a tightrope: Words and wisdom.* New York: Hays House.

Winston, R. B., Jr., & Creamer, D. G. (2002). Supervision: Relationships that support learning. In D. L. Cooper, S. A. Saunders, R. B. Winston, Jr., & J. Hirt (Eds.), *Learning through supervised practice in student affairs* (pp. 65–96). New York: Brunner-Routledge.

Wise, T. (2007). *White like me: Reflections on race from a privileged son. New York: Soft Skull Press.*

Appendix A

Professional Development Program

As noted on p. 402 in this chapter, modeling begins at the top The following proposed staff development program for student affairs professionals is only one way to start the process of change and inclusion for everyone on a campus. This model is not meant to be replicated in its exact form; it is an outline to be adjusted and developed to fit staff and campus needs. Although this is one program outline, it is important to note that this type of training should not have an ending point when making any transformations in the campus culture.

Target audience:

> Student affairs practitioners (Campus size will define levels to be involved. The goal is to reach all levels, but this may need to be done in phases.)

Key participants/leaders:

> Chief student affairs officer introduces the concepts and purpose of program for staff.
>
> Facilitator(s) to conduct the training (external or internal individuals)
>
> Recorders to document the activities, dialogue, and action steps defined

Suggested program length:

> Semester-long or year-long thematic intentional

Participant numbers:

> Ten to twenty, or a process for hosting more staff but using small groups for staff development activities

Materials needed:

> Space with moveable furniture
>
> Book or chapters from this book

Format:

1. Introductory statement (sent in advance with registration materials; book/chapters from this book and the theme should be introduced at this time also. Theme should underscore the importance of this activity.
2. Guidelines for group sharing such as confidentiality, "I" statements, discussion on how the group can achieve trust and how confrontation will be handled. Ask the participants to assist with creating

group norms for the culminating staff development event (see number 8).

3. If the program is spread out over a full semester or year, provide the group with an outline for a curriculum of activities (this entire book should be used as a guide in developing this schedule outline.

4. Journals may be handed out at the start of the program to offer participants a personal outlet for reflection and their reactions throughout the program activities (journals will not be shared with other participants).

5. Facilitators can use the questions and case studies in the book to guide discussion.

6. All sessions need an evaluation tool for feedback in strengthening the program. The more staff can be included in offering ideas, such as continued dialogue sessions, increased ways to infuse learning into the whole division, and better vehicles for reaching everyone, the more ownership and involvement may result.

7. If discussion items or any specific identifiable quotes or actions are attributed to a participant and posted publicly, permission is necessary prior to using the material.

8. Finally, a culminating event that marks the completion and success of the full staff development program is necessary. Since so much of professional development is process and dialogue, suggesting some next steps, such as inviting speakers on various diversity issues or having a shared-book activity, will keep growth and change moving forward.

Appendix B

Sample Course Syllabi

Sample Syllabus I: Seminar on Students in Higher Education

COURSE DESCRIPTION

As aspiring senior-level professionals in higher education, it is imperative to have an understanding of the theory and research associated with the main constituency of higher education students. The purpose of this course is to explore and review key student developmental theories that describe student patterns of growth and development during the college years. This course will also explore emerging theories and models that may be translated into practice for working with or understanding diverse cohorts of students enrolled in institutions of higher education. Specifically, this course will place emphasis on the study of changing demographics, patterns of growth and development, educational outcomes, and the experience of historically underrepresented and marginalized students.

RESPECT FOR DIVERSITY

It is my intention to conduct this course in such a manner that a clear respect for diversity is maintained throughout the course content, activities, and with materials used. This includes respect for the treatment of materials related to gender, sexual orientation, different abilities, age, socioeconomic status, ethnicity (race, nation, or culture), race (physical characteristics transmitted by genes, body of people united by a common history or nationality), and culture (beliefs, customs, arts, and institutions of a society). Feedback and suggestions are welcome.

TEXTS, READINGS, AND INSTRUCTIONAL RESOURCES

Howe, N., & Strauss, W. (2007). *Millennials go to college.* Great Falls, VA: LifeCourse Associates.

Kreuter, G. V. L. (1996). *Forgotten promise: Race and gender wars on a small college campus.* New York: Knopf.

Pascarella, E. T., & Terenzini, P. T. (2005). *How college affects students: A third decade of research* (2nd ed.). San Francisco: Jossey-Bass.

Torres, V., Howard-Hamilton, & Cooper, D. L. (2003). *Identity development of diverse populations: Implications for teaching and administration in higher education.* San Francisco: Jossey-Bass.

Other optional texts, depending on the class demographics and course content, to be emphasized:

Suskind, R. (1998). *A hope in the unseen: An American odyssey from the inner city to the Ivy League.* New York: Basic Books.

Navarrette, R. (1993). *A darker shade of crimson: Odyssey of a Harvard Chicano.* New York: Bantam.

ASSIGNMENTS, EVALUATION CRITERIA, AND EXPECTATIONS

1. Your Story of Psychosocial, Multicultural, and Cognitive Development: One of the best ways to understand student development theory is to connect it to our own experience. In order to use the narrative mode of knowing, we will write our own stories to "get inside" the particulars of student development. Then we will use the theoretical perspectives to reflect on our own stories, using the rational mode of knowing.

2. Group readings review, active participation, media sharing, and in-class "hear me exercise": On designated days, an assigned group will present a review of the assigned readings for the day.

   At the end of each class (last 15 minutes) we will engage in a "hear me exercise" in which one person will answer the following two questions: (1) Who am I and (2) What was I like in college. The class will listen, paraphrase, and then ask questions (if necessary). We will end the hear me exercise with an affirmation.

3. *Forgotten Promise*—Theory-Practice-Theory Analysis: Write a paper analyzing the developmental characteristics, leadership styles, and behaviors of three (3) individuals in *Forgotten Promise.*

4. Cultural Immersion Project: For this assignment, you are to find a group you want to learn about and immerse yourself in that group. It may involve going to a particular festival, religious gathering, or engaging a friend/neighbor in an intense and respectful dialogue regarding his or her culture. This experience must be a genuine one, and you must stretch yourself by going outside your comfort zone.

CLASS SCHEDULE

The format recommended for this course is as follows:

1. Read *Millennials Go to College* and discuss how the descriptions are compatible with the students' own experiences.

2. Read selected sections in Pascarella and Terenzini beginning with an overview of developmental theories and history of student affairs/ higher education. Continue reading selected sections that connect

with class readings (e.g., race and ethnicity section when reading Torres et al.)

3. Start students on writing their story the 1st week of class and continue to link their developmental journey with each theory studied in class.

4. Read *Forgotten Promise, A Hope in the Unseen*, or *A Darker Shade of Crimson: Odyssey of a Harvard Chicano*. Have students connect the theories studied to the developmental journey of the individual(s) in the true stories written about diversity issues on campus.

5. Read Torres et al. and study racial/ethnic identity development within the first 3–4 weeks of the semester.

Sample Syllabus 2: Critical Race Theory

PURPOSE

The educational practices and personal beliefs we embody shape and have an impact on the creation and design of our society. Therefore, it is important that we engage in self-reflection and personal introspection about our race, gender, class, and other deep-seeded identities continuously. Who we are shapes our beliefs and values. The purpose of this course is to help students develop an ability to be reflective about the relationship between the role of education and the larger society that education and educators help form.

DISCUSSION STARTER

Students will select a topic that will be covered in class and use the readings associated with that particular topic to lead the discussion.

CRITICAL RACE THEORY

Respond to the questions and comments at the end of chapters 1 through 7 in *Critical Race Theory: An Introduction*.

HOPE IN THE UNSEEN REFLECTION PAPER

Pick out three issues or themes (e.g., banking education, stereotype threat, microaggressions, counterspaces, counterstories, hybridity, deculturalization, etc.) we have discussed in class and connect them to Cedric's experiences as a person of color attempting to complete his high school diploma and college degree.

LIBERATING EDUCATIONAL EXPERIENCE

Using ideas from Delgado and Stefancic, Freire, Spring, and Taylor et al., design a liberating educational experience. This can be a college/university program or activity, a curriculum, an educational workshop, or you can design or redesign a particular class.

TEXTBOOKS

Delgado, R., & Stefancic, J. (2001). *Critical race theory: An Introduction.* New York: New York University Press.

Freire, P. (2000). *Pedagogy of the oppressed* (M. B. Ramos, Trans.). New York: Continuum. (Original work published 1968)

Spring, J. (2009). *Deculturalization and the struggle for equality* (6th ed.). Boston: McGraw Hill.

Suskind, R. (1998). *A hope in the unseen.* New York: Broadway Books.

Taylor, E., Gillborn, D., & Ladson-Billings, G. (2009). *Foundations of critical race theory in education.* New York: Routledge.

ARTICLES

Alschuler, A. S. (1986). Creating a world where it is easier to love: Counseling applications of Paulo Freire's theory. *Journal of Counseling and Development, 64,* 492–496.

Carbado, D. W. (2000). Men, feminism, and male heterosexual privilege. In R. Delgado & J. Stefancic (Eds.), *Critical race theory: The cutting edge* (2nd ed., pp. 525–531). Philadelphia: Temple University Press.

Grillo, T., & Wildman, S. M. (2000). Obscuring the importance of race: The implication of making comparisons between racism and sexism (or other-ism). In R. Delgado & J. Stefancic (Eds.), *Critical race theory: The cutting edge* (2nd ed., pp. 648–656). Philadelphia: Temple University Press.

Ladson-Billings, G. (2002). New directions in multicultural education: Complexities, boundaries, and critical race theory. In J. A. Banks & C. A. M. Banks (Eds.), *Handbook of research on multicultural education* (pp. 50–65). San Francisco: Jossey-Bass.

McIntosh, P. (1988). *White privilege and male privilege: A personal account of coming to see correspondence through work in women's studies.* Wellesley, MA: Center for Research on Women.

Patton, L. D., McEwen, M. L., Rendon, L., & Howard-Hamilton, M. F. (2007). Critical race perspectives on theory in student affairs. In S. R. Harper & L. D. Patton (Eds.), *Responding to the realities of race on campus* (pp. 39–54). San Francisco: Jossey-Bass.

Sleeter, C. E., & Bernal, D. D. (2002). Critical pedagogy, critical race theory, and antiracist education: Implications for multicultural education. In J. A. Banks & C. A. M. Banks (Eds.), *Handbook of research on multicultural education* (pp. 240–260). San Francisco: Jossey-Bass.

Solorzano, D., Ceja, M., & Yosso, T., (2000). Critical race theory, racial microagressions, and campus racial climate: The experiences of African American college students. *Journal of Negro Education, 69*(1–2), 60–73.

SCHEDULE OF ACTIVITIES/READINGS

1. After reading *Critical Race Theory*, have students answer the questions at the end of each chapter and share selected responses in class. Within the first two weeks of class the students should complete *Pedagogy of the Oppressed.*

2. After reading these books, the Game of Oppression can be facilitated and *Color of Fear* should be shown. These materials can be connected with the theories and information from *Critical Race Theory* and *Pedagogy of the Oppressed.*

3. Students should read *A Hope in the Unseen* and connect the theories from *Critical Race Theory* and *Pedagogy of the Oppressed* with the issues presented in *A Hope in the Unseen.*

4. Students should read each chapter of *Deculturalization and the Struggle for Equality*. The instructor should emphasize the importance of having a historical knowledge of underrepresented populations since most history courses do not review the struggles they have endured since their arrival to the United States or since the arrival of Europeans to this country. Each chapter can be supplemented with media documenting the information in Spring's book, for example, *Showing the Shadow of Hate: A History of Intolerance in America* (1995), which summarizes and provides pictoral documentation with Spring's content.

5. At the end of the semester students are asked to review the responses they wrote to the *Critical Race Theory* questions and discuss whether their opinions have changed after the presentation of other literature related to oppression, race, ethnicity, and diversity.

CONTRIBUTORS

Editors

Diane L. Cooper is a professor of college student affairs administration in the Department of Counseling and Human Development Services at the University of Georgia. She served for 8 years as a student affairs professional at the University of North Carolina at Greensboro before joining the faculty in student development at Appalachian State University from 1992 to 1995. Cooper served for 6 years as the editor of the *College Student Affairs Journal* and was on the editorial board for the *Journal of College Student Development.* She is coauthor of several books, including *Identity Development of Diverse Populations: Implications for Teaching and Practice in Higher Education* and *Learning Through Supervised Practice in Student Affairs.* Her research interests are in multiple identity development, program design and assessment, legal and ethical issues in student affairs practice, and professional issues related to underrepresented groups in higher education.

Michael J. Cuyjet is a professor in the College of Education and Human Development at the University of Louisville where he has been teaching and mentoring students in the College Student Personnel Program since 1993. Prior to that, he served more than 20 years as a student affairs professional at Northern Illinois University and at the University of Maryland-College Park. During his more than 17 years at the University of Louisville, he has served as associate dean of the graduate school and acting associate provost for Student Life and Development. His research areas include underrepresented college student populations and competencies of new student affairs professionals. He is the editor and one of the authors of *African American Men in College* and a coauthor of the 2002 book *How Minority Students Experience College.* He has edited two other books, including the 1997 publication *Helping African American Men Succeed in College,* published more than 20 other journal articles or book chapters, and has made more than 100 presentations at national and regional conferences.

Mary F. Howard-Hamilton is a professor of higher education at Indiana State University. She previously served as a higher education administrator for 15 years where her responsibilities included orientation, developmental education, judicial affairs, multicultural affairs, commuter life, and residence life. As a faculty member for 19 years, she taught courses in student affairs, higher education, and counseling at the University of Florida, Bowling Green State University, and Indiana University Bloomington where she was also associate dean for graduate studies in the School of Education. Her areas of expertise are multicultural issues in higher education, student development theories, feminist theory and therapy, and consultation. She has published over 80 articles and book chapters, and coauthored or coedited several books including *Standing on the Outside Looking In: Underrepresented Students' Experiences in Advance Degree Programs* and *Unleashing Suppressed Voices on College Campuses: Diversity Issues in Higher Education.* The Robert S. Shaffer Award for Excellence as a Graduate Faculty Member was presented to Howard-Hamilton in 2007 from the National Association of Student Personnel Administrators.

Contributors

LeManuel Lee Bitsói is director of Minority Training in Genomics in the Department of Genetics at Harvard Medical School. Prior to this appointment, he was a research fellow in the O'Neill Institute for National and Global Health Law and assistant professor in the Department of Human Science in the School of Nursing and Health Studies at Georgetown University. Bitsói also served as director of Minority Training in Bioinformatics and Genomics at Harvard University where he continues to be an associate in the Department of Molecular and Cellular Biology. Bitsói earned a bachelor of science degree from the University of New Mexico (1995), holds a master of education degree from Harvard University (1998), and received a doctorate from the University of Pennsylvania (2007). Bitsói has devoted his career to enhancing opportunities for underrepresented minority students to become scientists and science educators.

Tony W. Cawthon is a professor and department chair of leadership, counselor education, human and organizational development at Clemson University. Prior to this position, he served as coordinator of the Counselor Educations/Student Affairs Graduate Preparation Program at Clemson after beginning his faculty career in 1996. Prior to his positions at Clemson University, he worked as a student affairs administrator for over 15 years at Clemson, Mississippi State University, and the University of Tennessee Knoxville. His work as a student affairs professional was in university housing. He has written extensively in the areas of student affairs and higher education. He has presented nationally and internationally on numerous student and higher education issues. Specifically, his publications and presentations have been in the areas of career/professional development; new professional, student, and faculty issues; and student affairs administrative issues. He has published more than 30 journal articles and book chapters, and he has made more than 90 national and regional presentations. He is coeditor of *Using the Entertainment Media to Facilitate Student Learning: Movies, Music, Television, and Popular Press Books in Student Affairs Classrooms and Practice* that is part of the New Directions for Student Services series.

B. Afeni McNeely Cobham is assistant provost of student life at the University of Denver. She has served as a student affairs administrator for 19 years, working at eight institutions, where her responsibilities included assessment, residence life, student leadership and development, Greek life, crisis management, and multicultural affairs. She is also an affiliate faculty member teaching courses in gender and women's studies, in the Higher Education Program, and in the Department of African and African American Studies at Metropolitan State College of Denver. Her areas of expertise are race and ethnic identity development, access and equity in higher education, women in sports, and the history and evolution of the hip-hop culture. She has made over 100 presentations at local, regional, and national conferences, and was a contributing author of *Responding to the Realities of Race on Campus.*

Laura A. Dean is an assistant professor in the College Student Affairs Administration Program at the University of Georgia. Prior to joining the faculty, she worked at several small, religiously affiliated colleges, including serving for 10 years as senior student affairs officer. She is president elect of the Council for the Advancement of Standards in Higher Education (CAS) and serves as the CAS representative from the American College Counseling Association (ACCA), of which she is past president and has also been a member at large on the Executive Committee, and publications editor. She has served on editorial boards for the *College Student Affairs Journal* and the *Journal of College Counseling.* Dean's research interests include small college environments, the use of professional standards in student affairs, and college counseling issues.

Merrily S. Dunn is an associate professor in the College Student Affairs Administration Program at the University of Georgia. Prior to this she spent 8 years as a faculty member at Mississippi State University. In addition she has more than a decade of student affairs' experience in a variety of positions at Ohio State University, Marquette University, and Iowa State University. She has served her profession through a number of positions and roles in ACPA-College Student Educators International, the Council for the Advancement of Standards in Higher Education (CAS), the Southern Association for College Student Affairs (SACSA), and the Association for College and University Housing Officers-International (ACUHO-I). Her research centers on the professional preparation of student affairs educators, gender issues, and living learning environments.

Lamont A. Flowers is the Distinguished Professor of Educational Leadership in the Department of Leadership, Counselor Education, Human and Organizational Development and is executive director of the Charles H. Houston Center for the Study of the Black Experience in Education in the Eugene T. Moore School of Education at Clemson University. He has authored or coauthored several scholarly publications pertaining to the educational experiences and outcomes of African Americans from prekindergarten through college, diversity issues in education, as well as organizational and leadership issues in education.

Rosiline D. Floyd is a research associate for the African American Male Equity Project at Indiana University-Purdue University at Indianapolis, focusing on effective policies and programs for African American males and issues of equity in PK–16 education. As executive director of the Coalition of Equitable Organizations Floyd works with schools and communities to use antiracist and antibias activism to deconstruct the institutionalized practices that victimize historically marginalized populations. Her work seeks to eliminate the predictive nature of race, socioeconomics, and gender on student achievement As CEO of RDF Consultants, her work focuses on supporting schools and communities to increase high school and college graduation rates of African American students. Floyd recently received the Adams Student Research Dissertation of the Year Award for *Yes We Can: How Membership in Black Greek Letter Organizations Impacts the Experience* *of Black Women Students at 4-year Predominantly White Institutions.* Her research interests are in issues of equity in education, the role of race in academic achievement, and professional issues related to underrepresented groups in higher education.

Jane Fried is a professor in the Department of Counseling and Family Therapy at Central Connecticut State University where she chairs the master's degree program in student development in higher education. Fried's scholarship covers the areas of ethics, cultural diversity, spirituality, wisdom, and transformative approaches to student learning. She is one of the original authors of *Learning Reconsidered,* published by NASPA and ACPA in 2004 and is a contributing author of *Learning Reconsidered 2,* published in 2006. Her major works include *Shifting Paradigms in Student Affairs: Culture, Context, Teaching and Learning,* published by ACPA in 1995; *Understanding Diversity,* with Marsha and Barbara Okun, published by Brooks/Cole in 1999; and *Ethics for Today's Campus,* 1997. She has also authored numerous book chapters on ethics, spirituality, transformative learning, and diversity in student affairs. In 2010 she was named a Legacy of the Profession by NASPA and has also received the Professional Service and the Annuit Coeptis awards from ACPA.

Edward A. Grandpré, who passed away in March 2006, held a BS degree from High Point College, an MEd from Wake Forest University, and a PhD from Ohio State University. In a 25-year career focused primarily on working with and for students, he held a variety of positions in student and academic affairs at Mississippi State University, Florida State University, Ohio State University, and the University of Georgia. Grandpré's final position was as a faculty member in the Educational Leadership Program at Clemson University.

Victoria L. Guthrie is dean of students at St. Catharine College. Prior to assuming her current role in 2007, Guthrie served for 8 years as a faculty member in the College Student Personnel Programs at the University of Louisville and at Ohio University. She is coauthor of *Understanding and Applying Cognitive Development Theory* as well as several journal articles. Her previous administrative roles include assistant vice president for student affairs, Bellarmine University; assistant dean of students, University of Tennessee at Chattanooga; assistant director for residential development, Loyola

University in New Orleans; and associate dean of students, Lambuth University.

Susana Hernandez is a doctoral student at Iowa State University in the Educational Leadership and Policy Studies Program with a concentration in social justice. She earned a master's degree in counseling with an emphasis in student development in higher education at California State University, Long Beach, at the time the chapter was written. Prior to moving to Iowa, she held several student affairs positions in the Hispanic-Serving Institution Office at California State University, Long Beach, as well as in the Admissions and Student Outreach Office at the University of California, Irvine. Her current research interests include college access and equity, the experience of first-generation students, and the retention of students of color, particularly Latino/Latina students.

Kandace G. Hinton is an associate professor in the educational leadership, administration, and foundations department's Higher Education Leadership Program at Indiana State University. Hinton holds a master's and PhD in higher education administration from Indiana University and a bachelor of arts degree from Jackson State University. Her research interests are African American women in higher education, multicultural identity development, and institutional support of community-based programs. Hinton has created a theoretical model that describes African American women's professional development, and her teaching areas include the history of higher education, philosophy of education, academic leadership, ethics, and college student development and diversity. She is the coeditor of *Unleashing Suppressed Voices on College Campuses: Diversity Issues in Higher Education and Student Affairs*. Other publications include "Mentoring" in *Standing on the Outside: Exercising Power With Wisdom* (2006), *Using Entertainment Media in Student Affairs Teaching and Practice* (2004), and *Meeting the Needs of African American Women in Higher Education*, and numerous other book chapters. Hinton won the Reitzel Faculty Research Award in 2008 and the Holmstedt Dissertation of the Year Award in 2001.

Karen S. Kalivoda is director of the Disability Resource Center, director of University Testing Services, and adjunct faculty for the Department of Counseling and Human Development Services at the University of Georgia. As director of the Disability Resource Center since 1985, she has guided it to dramatic growth. As the primary university resource for disability-related concerns, Kalivoda's expertise has been instrumental in the university's response to the Americans With Disabilities Act. Kalivoda was also named director of University Testing Services in 2004, where she manages the administration of numerous examinations for the campus and wider communities. Her research interests include the implementation of universal instructional design in higher education and the theory of planned behavior as applied to faculty attitudes in accommodating students with disabilities. She is published in regional and national journals and presents at the local, state, and national level.

Fiona J. D. MacKinnon retired in 2008 as associate professor emeritus from the Department of Higher Education and Student Affairs and coordinator of the Adult Learner Focus Program at Bowling Green State University. At the time of her retirement, she was associate dean for Student and Academic Services for the College of Education and Human Development. At Bowling Green she served as chair of Educational Foundations and Inquiry, chair of the Faculty Senate, and provost associate. She was the editor of Rentz's *Student Services in Higher Education* (2004) and is the author of the Adult Persistence in Learning Model, the focus of her research. In 1997 she received a Fulbright Award as senior scholar at Beijing Normal University, People's Republic of China. MacKinnon's career in higher education spanned 45 years; she served in every area of student affairs and university administration at Bowling Green, Southern Illinois University at Carbondale, the University of Akron, Syracuse University, Ohio State University, and Denison University.

Anna M. Ortiz is professor and director of educational leadership at California State University, Long Beach. She teaches student development theory and qualitative research methods. She is coauthor of *Ethnicity in College*, editor of *Addressing the Unique Needs of Latino/a Students*, and author of numerous articles and book chapters in multicultural education, ethnic identity, Latino/Latina and Native American students, and career issues for student affairs professional and faculty members. She earned her bachelor of science at the University of California, Davis; her master of arts from Ohio State University; and her doctorate from the University of California, Los Angeles. She has served on the faculty of Michigan State University and is an active member of the many higher education professional associations where she has served on editorial boards and in leadership positions.

Leigh Ann Osborne is coordinator of International Student Services at the Florida State University Center for Global Engagement. Previously, she served as a study abroad adviser at the University of Florida International Center. She received a master of arts in education from the social foundations program at the University of Florida. Her thesis examined the history of international students at the University of Florida in the post–World War II era.

Kristen A. Renn is associate professor of higher, adult, and lifelong education at Michigan State University. Previously, she was a dean in the Office of Student Life at Brown University for 10 years and a policy analyst for the Massachusetts Board of Higher Education. Her research and teaching interests include college students and student development, particularly in the areas of mixed-race identities, lesbian/gay/bisexual/transgender issues, and student leaders in identity-based organizations. She conducts international research on women's colleges and universities with a focus on their roles and status. She is associate editor for international research and scholarship for the *Journal of College Student Development.* Renn has served on the editorial boards of the *NASPA Journal, Review of Higher Education, Journal of College Student Development,* and the *Journal of Higher Education.*

Bettina C. Shuford is an assistant vice president for student affairs at Bowling Green State University. Her other administrative positions at Bowling Green State include posts in academic affairs, multicultural affairs, and TRIO programs. She has supervised a wide range of areas in student affairs including student health, counseling, disability, career center, TRIO programs and multicultural affairs. Prior to coming to Bowling Green State, she held positions in residence life and served as an assistant dean of students and director of minority student affairs at the University of North Carolina at Greensboro. Her research interests, publications, and presentations have focused on student learning, functions in multicultural affairs offices, assessment of multicultural affairs programs, minority student development, retention of students of color, affirmative action, and African American women in student affairs.

Anneliese A. Singh is an assistant professor in the Department of Counseling and Human Development Services at the University of Georgia. She received her doctorate in counseling psychology from Georgia State University in 2007. Her clinical, research, and advocacy interests include Asian

American/Pacific Islander counseling, LGBTQQ youth, multicultural counseling and social justice training, qualitative methodology, and feminist empowerment interventions. Singh is a past president of the Association of Lesbian, Gay, Bisexual, and Transgender Issues in Counseling. She is a founder of the Georgia Safe Schools Coalition, an organization that works at the intersection of heterosexism, racism, sexism, and other oppressions to create safe school environments. She is the recipient of the 2007 Ramesh and Vijaya Bakshi Community Change Award and the 2008 O'Hana Award from Counselors for Social Justice of the American Counseling Association for her organizing work with Asian American/Pacific Islander individuals and other historically marginalized groups.

Sevan G. Terzian is an associate professor and associate director for graduate studies in the School of Teaching and Learning at the University of Florida where he teaches courses in the historical and philosophical foundations of education. He is also the recipient of a University of Florida Research Foundation Professorship (from 2009 to 2012). Terzian has authored various articles and book chapters on the history of students in American education. He is currently completing a book that traces the origins and proliferation of science clubs, fairs, and talent searches for American youth.

Vasti Torres is professor of higher education and student affairs administration in the School of Education at Indiana University. Prior to joining the faculty, she had 15 years of experience in administrative positions most recently serving as associate vice provost and dean for Enrollment and Student Services at Portland State University. Torres's research focuses on how the ethnic identity of Latino students influences their college experience. She has written many articles and book chapters on Latino college students, survey development and use, as well as on other diversity issues. She was the principle investigator for a multiyear grant on the choice to stay in college for Latino students and for a grant to investigate working students at urban institutions. She is active in several student affairs and higher education associations. During 2007–2008 she served as the first Latina president of a national student affairs association—the American College Personnel Association (ACPA). She received several honors from ACPA, the National Association of Student Personnel Administrators, the College of Education at the University of Georgia, and served as a program associate for the National Center for Policy in Higher Education. She received her BA from Stetson University and her MEd and PhD from the University of Georgia.

Martha E. Wisbey has worked for over 20 years in higher education. She currently serves as associate director for Disability Services in the Division of Community and Diversity at Emory University. She received her degrees from Miami University and the University of Georgia and has served as an administrator at several institutions in student affairs and as an adjunct professor teaching courses in multicultural education, student development, social work, and counseling. Her research interests are in disability studies, student development theory, women's identity development, and cultural diversity. She has published over 20 journal articles on disability, counseling, diversity awareness, women's identity, student development theory, residence hall community development, and Greek life peer development.

INDEX

community colleges
AAPI students and, 121
international students and, 240
Latino and Latina students and, 93–97,
99–100, 106, 107–108
nontraditional students and, 329–330, 339
complex organizational structure, 51–52
conformity stage of ethnic identity development, 124–125
consistency of campus population, 43–44,
45–46, 66
Consortium of Higher Education LGBT
Resource Professionals, 297
constructed environments, 55–61
context dimension of social oppression, 25
contextual identity, 66
Coordinated Interagency Partnership Regulating International Students (CIPRIS),
252
Council for the Advancement of Standards
in Higher Education, 390–391, 404, 412
counseling
AAPI students, 122, 131, 133–134
adult learners, 336
identity development models and, 69–71
international students, 241, 243–244, 253,
254, 256
on a multicultural campus, 51–52
students with disabilities, 350, 366
counterspaces, 27–29, 228
critical race theory, 27–29, 403
critical reforming response to oppression, 22
cross-categorical constructing, 73–74
cross-dressers, 294–295. See also lesbian, gay,
bisexual, and transgender (LGBT)
students
Cross's racial identity development model,
151–153, 279
Cuban students, 88, 89–90. See also Latino
and Latina students
cultural bias in testing, 96
cultural change, 67
cultural competencies
assessment of, 407
model staff development program for,
413–415

Pope on, 12–14, 403, 407
sample course syllabi for, 418–422
for student affairs and academic administrators, 402–404
for students, 406
for supervised practice, 407
for teaching faculty, 404–406
use of resource tools for developing,
408–412
cultural genocide, 12
cultural perspectives, 59–61
cultural pluralism, 67
culture shock, 243, 244

Daniels, Anthony "TD", 230
D'Augelli's model of sexual orientation
development, 308–309
Daughters of Bilitis, 295
decentered self, 68
deculturalization, 11–12, 21, 171, 172
Dialogues on Diversity (University of Michigan), 366
differentiation, 43–45
difficult dialogues, 227
Dine' College, 174
disability rights movement, 348. See also students with disabilities
discrimination
AAPI college students, 125
African American students, 143, 145, 153
international students, 244, 248, 250
Latino and Latina students, 92–93, 101
LGBT students, 295, 301, 314, 316
men, 272
religious denominations, 301, 373, 385–387
students with disabilities, 347, 355–357,
364
White identity and, 223, 225, 227
women, 224, 272
display of self, 42–43
dissonance stage of ethnic identity development, 125
Doctoral Scholars Program of the Southern
Regional Education Board, 109
dominant groups. See privileged groups